Study Guide

for **NAIRNE'S**

PSYCHOLOGY:

THE ADAPTIVE MIND

Second Edition

Janet D. Proctor
Purdue University

With a Language Enhancement Guide
by
Mary Beth Foster

Wadsworth
Thomson Learning

Australia • Canada • Denmark • Japan • Mexico • New Zealand • Philippines
Puerto Rico • Singapore • South Africa • Spain • United Kingdom • United States

ISBN 0-534-36774-7

For more information, contact
Wadsworth/Thomson Learning
10 Davis Drive
Belmont, CA 94002-3098
USA
www.wadsworth.com

International Headquarters
Thomson Learning
290 Harbor Drive, 2nd Floor
Stamford, CT 06902-7477
USA

UK/Europe/Middle East
Thomson Learning
Berkshire House
168-173 High Holborn
London WC1V 7AA
United Kingdom

Asia
Thomson Learning
60 Albert Complex
Singapore 189969

Canada
Nelson/Thomson Learning
1120 Birchmount Road
Scarborough, Ontario M1K 5G4
Canada

TABLE OF CONTENTS

INTRODUCTION TO THE STUDY GUIDE

Throughout your text you will find an emphasis on the *adaptive mind*, the fact that we use our brains in a purposive and strategic fashion to meet the challenges of a changing environment. Each chapter will address certain conceptual, adaptive or practical problems facing most organisms and will guide you to an understanding of how these adaptive and practical problems are resolved.

As a student in this introductory psychology class, you face certain adaptive and practical problems, also. Stated most broadly, you must learn the material presented in class and in the text, and you must demonstrate your knowledge on tests and other assignments. The purpose of this study guide is to help you solve these adaptive and practical problems.

USING THE STUDY GUIDE

Part of the challenge of introductory psychology is the sheer mass of material to be learned. There is a great deal of new vocabulary, in addition to many concepts and specific facts. The study guide's organization breaks down the material into more manageable units. Studying an entire chapter at one time is overwhelming to many students and can lead to very poor learning. Taking too big a bite of food can lead to choking; trying to tackle too much new material at one time can have a similar effect. Therefore, each chapter in this study guide is divided into smaller units that follow the major sections of the text material.

Exercises designed to help you learn the vocabulary, practice recalling specific facts, and evaluate your basic comprehension of the material are provided for each section of the chapter. You will not need to study the entire chapter before doing these early exercises in the study guide. You can study one topic, work with the material, and evaluate your comprehension before moving on to another topic in the chapter. Then, at the end of each chapter there are additional exercises that revisit the entire chapter and give you additional opportunity to practice working with the material and to evaluate your readiness for an exam. I hope this will encourage you to study for mastery on a daily basis, rather than trying to learn an entire chapter (or chapters, worse yet) in a single marathon study session a day or two before your exam.

Establishing Learning Objectives

Each study guide chapter begins with a set of learning objectives. These will provide a quick summary of what the text chapter is all about, and what you should be trying to accomplish. Review them before you read the text, and use them to test your comprehension of each section. If your instructor gives essay exams, use these objectives as more possible essay questions, and practice formulating a response to them. If your exams will include only multiple choice questions, use the objectives to evaluate your knowledge. If you can recite the relevant information for each objective, you probably have a good understanding of the material.

Mastering the Material

Mastering the Vocabulary. Each section of the chapter has a list of important terms. In most cases these terms are defined and printed in bold in your text, but I have added other terms in some cases. You might want to develop a set of note cards instead of writing the definitions in the study guide. Many students keep their note cards handy to pull out and review during short breaks between classes or other activities. You will be surprised how much progress you can make if you take advantage of those occasional spare minutes.

Mastering the Concepts. This fill-in-the-blanks exercise will give you practice recalling the vocabulary and basic conceptual material from a section of the text. When completed, this exercise will provide a reasonably detailed review you can use when doing your final work before an exam. If you have great difficulty with this section, you need to go back and work with the text again. An answer key is provided, but try to complete the exercise on your own before looking at the answer key, working with the text if necessary.

Evaluating Your Progress. Each section includes multiple choice questions to help you evaluate whether you have achieved at least a basic level of mastery of the facts and vocabulary. For the most part, these questions will require lower levels of comprehension than the questions in the pretests found at the end of each chapter. Many will emphasize definitions or will address general issues. Errors here indicate you have missed some basic information or do not know the important terms. Go back and fill in those gaps before you move on to new material. Note that the answer key includes both the correct answer and explanations about why the wrong answers are wrong. Use this feature to understand your mistakes and learn even more.

Making Final Preparations

You should work on this section after you feel you have achieved a basic mastery of the entire chapter. In fact, it is a good idea to wait a day or two before beginning this section. As you will learn in Chapter 8, the most significant forgetting occurs soon after the original learning period. You will overestimate your mastery if you complete these exercises right after studying the chapter.

Short Essay Questions. Each chapter includes several practice essay questions. Answering essay questions requires that you recall the information, rather than recognize it as in matching or multiple-choice questions. In general, essays require that you know the material well and that you understand the concepts thoroughly. Answering essay questions is excellent practice regardless of the format of your exams, but it is essential if your exams will include essay questions. Test performance is best if the material has been studied using the same processes that will be used in testing. Sample answers are provided, but write your own answers first.

Matching. This exercise provides practice with a matching format and requires that you be able to link terms with their definitions or their importance to the chapter. This is also the exercise that tests your recognition of the names of notable people. Some instructors require their students to know the names of major researchers or theorists; others do not. Find out your instructor's policy before your first exam.

Multiple Choice Pretests. Two pretests are provided to give you more practice answering multiple-choice questions and to help you evaluate your mastery of the text material prior to taking your exams. Pretest 1 tends to focus more on specific factual information than Pretest 2. However, some questions will require you to summarize the current view of a topic or to apply your knowledge. Pretest 2 emphasizes application and prediction. Can you recognize a concept in action? Can you take a theory or set of research data and make predictions about what will happen in a situation? Can you see the relationships between concepts? These questions require more complete conceptual understanding.

If you have no trouble with Pretest 1, but make many errors on Pretest 2, you probably know facts but do not really understand them or their significance. You might try discussing the material with a study partner or friend, or go to your instructor and ask for some help in reaching this level of comprehension. Also, be sure to look at the explanations for the incorrect alternatives given in the answer key. Knowing why something is wrong is often as informative as knowing that something is right.

Answers and Explanations

Use this feature to evaluate why you made a mistake and to help you understand difficult material. Each question is page-referenced to direct you to the relevant material in the text, and explanations of wrong answers are provided. Even if you answer a question correctly, review the explanations of incorrect answers and see if your reason for not choosing one of the incorrect answers was similar.

Language Enhancement Guide

Each chapter in the study guide includes a separate section intended to help students whose native language is not English or whose vocabulary is below the 12th grade level. Non-technical terms that might be unfamiliar to you are defined, and exercises to boost general language comprehension skills are included. The Introduction to the Language Enhancement Guide gives more details about using this feature.

STRATEGIES FOR MASTERING THE MATERIAL

Being a successful student requires more than a text and study guide. The best materials are worthless if the student approaches the course inappropriately or uses poor study strategies. This section will discuss some basic behaviors that are important for success in any class, not just introductory psychology.

Go to Class Regularly. This seems pretty obvious, right? Still, many students miss class frequently, especially in large lecture classes in which their absence is unlikely to be noticed. Going to class has many benefits. First, the lectures might be the only source of some of the information you are expected to learn. If you are not in class, you are missing that information. Second, the focus of the lectures can be a good guide as to what topics your instructor feels are important, and exams are likely to reflect this emphasis. Third, your instructor will present the material in a different "voice" or perhaps from a different orientation than your text. Material in the text that you have difficulty understanding might be easier to understand when presented in class. Also, the different style or form of presentation may help create more retrieval cues. The more ways and times information is presented, the more chances you have to remember it. Also, demonstrations, videos, and exercises that are included in class can provide wonderful memory cues for the related material.

Simply showing up for class is insufficient, however. To get the most benefit from your attendance you need to come prepared and you need to be an active participant. Try to survey the material that will be discussed. Look through the relevant material, paying attention to section headings, figures, and tables. Familiarize yourself with the topic and some of the vocabulary. If you go to class with a foundation, the lecture will be easier to understand, and you will be able to take notes more effectively.

Pay attention in class. If you are socializing rather than paying attention, you not only miss the information you supposedly came to class to learn, but you also interfere with your neighbors' ability to pay attention. Try to sit in the front of the class, especially in large lecture halls. You will be able to see and hear better, and there will be fewer distracting things between you and the instructor.

Get involved in the lecture. Think about what is being said; do not just listen passively. Active involvement in learning produces better memory for the material. Taking notes is one way to actively process the information. Do not try to write down every word, though. Be selective, and use your own words except in cases in which exact recall will be necessary. Have an organization to your notes. Indicate major topic headings and the supporting information, and include enough information to make your notes meaningful. Find a time fairly soon after class to review your notes. If something is unclear then, it certainly will be unclear later when you begin studying. Clarify those points as soon as possible.

Use Your Textbook. Failing to read your textbook is similar to cutting class: you are wasting an important source of information, not to mention the money you spent for the book. Why buy a book and then not use it?

Your textbook not only presents the information you will be expected to know, but also includes many features that will help make your studying easier and more effective. The important terms are highlighted and defined right in the chapter. Summary tables for concepts and theories are provided and make great study aids. You can use them to quickly review the concepts and easily compare the different theories. Figures and other illustrations provide a clear visual representation of information. Learning objectives and self-tests can help you organize your studying and evaluate your progress. Chapter summaries offer a chance to preview the material before you begin your reading and to review the material when you are preparing for an exam.

Ask Questions. Asking questions serves several purposes. Most obviously, if you do not understand something, asking questions can get you the needed information. If you are hesitant to ask for clarification on some point during class, talk with your instructor or TA before or after class or during their office hours. Don't be shy about asking for help understanding something. This is also true during exams. If you do not understand a question or a specific word, ask for help interpreting it. If you are generally struggling in class, ask your instructor or TA for help or go to your school's learning center for suggestions.

Asking questions is also a wonderful way to get involved in the material and to process it to a deeper level of understanding. As you study and as you listen in class, ask yourself what the information really means or what the objective of the discussion is. The more deeply you process the material, the more likely you will remember it.

Make a Plan. Once you have a syllabus for each of your classes, evaluate what each class will require and mark on your calendar important assignments. For most courses you should plan to study about two hours per week for every hour spent in class. Carve out a regular study time for each class and consider those work periods comparable to a job. You do not put off going to work; do not put off studying. Do not waste free time between classes. Use it to study, or make it part of your planned recreational time.

Each time you sit down to study, set objectives about how long you will study and what material you will cover. Be realistic about your objectives. Consider both the study time needed and your attention span. If you have trouble concentrating for more than 30 minutes, do not plan to study 3 hours. Plan shorter but more frequent study sessions, or plan brief breaks within a study session.

Study As You Go. This requires discipline, but it is essential for most students. For classes like introductory psychology that have a large amount of material, waiting until a few days before an exam to begin serious study is deadly and is a mistake that many students make.

As you will learn in Chapter 8, massed practice (cramming) produces poorer memory for material than distributed (day by day) practice. Study for mastery on a daily (or at least weekly) basis, studying a small amount of material as if you will have test the next day. By the time the actual exam approaches, you will have learned most of what you need to know, and you can spend the final study periods filling in details and expanding your comprehension to deeper levels. You will be less likely to end up with everything in a jumble in your mind than if you try to learn it all at the last minute.

Study Effectively When You Study. A popular study technique is the SQ3R method: *Survey, Question, Read, Recite, Review.* My recommendations do not conform to this plan exactly, but the emphasis is similar: To study effectively requires action and thought on the part of the student.

1. Know where you are headed when you begin to study. Have learning objectives. To formulate objectives, briefly survey the material and ask yourself what the general issues are. This is basically the S(urvey) and Q(uestion) steps in the SQ3R study method. Compare your objectives to those provided in this study guide.

2. Organize your studying and reading. Focus on a topic to be mastered. Integrate your class notes with the text material. The topic context will help you learn and remember the information. Further organize the material by developing outlines, or create tables that summarize and relate material. Make use of the Concept Summary tables in your text. They provide a clear summary and comparison of many of the concepts and theories you will need to know. Expand these tables with information from lectures.

3. Be an *active* reader and learner. Reading rather passively and hoping that the material will find its way into your memory automatically is not an adaptive strategy. You might understand everything you read, but understanding and remembering are two different things. You need to understand something to maximize the chance you will remember it, but remembering requires more. Simple repetition is better than nothing, but thinking deeply is the best way to ensure you will remember something. Look for relationships or critical differences between terms or concepts. Apply the concepts to your own experiences. Generate your own examples. Tell somebody what you have learned. Get involved.

4. Develop materials for later review. As mentioned before, some students find note cards with a term on one side, and a definition and other important material on the other side to be very useful. You might also develop outlines, or create summary tables similar to your text's Concept Summary tables mentioned above. Your active involvement will help you remember the information, and you will be creating study materials for use during final preparations for exams.

5. Periodically evaluate your progress. Use the learning objectives as cues for recall. Recite (the second R in SQ3R) the basic ideas and the important details. Answer the questions in the study guide to quiz yourself. If you do not understand or remember something, do not move on to new material until you do.

Be A Teacher. Teaching a concept to someone else is an excellent way to ensure you will remember that information for a long time. It also is one of the quickest ways to find out that you do not really understand something and that you need to do more work. Teaching a parent or friend will work, but taking turns teaching with a study partner is best. Encourage your "student" to ask questions to test your comprehension. The act of recalling, organizing, and presenting information develops additional retrieval cues and reviews the material at the same time.

Practice writing test questions. This will force you to think about the major points and to look for the details. Exchange questions with a study partner to get more practice answering questions. Active practice with information in the format you will face in the exam will improve your chances of remembering the information during the exam.

Practice, Practice, Practice. Review (the final R in SQ3R) material right after you finish reading and frequently during the following week. Do not consider it learned and then never think about it again. Make part of each study session a quick review of past material. Each time you review material you are strengthening the retrieval cues for that information.

Practice answering questions similar to those you will encounter on the exam. The study guide has questions in different formats. Ask your instructor if any old exams are available for students to use for practice. Sometimes dorms or campus organizations maintain test files. Don't assume that your exam will focus on the same material or be exactly the same difficulty. Use old tests simply for practice in using your knowledge, not to figure out what will be on your exam. You might also find a different study guide and use the questions in it for additional practice. Most introductory psychology texts overlap considerably in what they cover, so many of the exercises will be appropriate.

Adapt Your Strategies. Evaluate your study strategies periodically. If you do not perform well on the first exam, try to figure out why. Look over your exam, and ask your instructor or TA for suggestions. Modify your strategies to fit your particular learning style and the demands of your particular course.

STRATEGIES FOR TAKING TESTS

Although the level of comprehension of the material is certainly the most critical determinant of test performance, taking tests is somewhat of an acquired skill. Poor test-taking behaviors can undo much of the hard work done to prepare for the test. Here are some general suggestions concerning taking tests:

Come Prepared. As stated above, the critical requirement for doing well on an exam is to know the material. Being well prepared has another benefit, though. Feeling confident about your knowledge reduces the anxiety you will experience during the exam. Being a little nervous is a good thing, but in large doses it interferes with the ability to concentrate and think. No matter how well prepared you are, there likely will be a question or two that will require you to stop and think for a minute. If you are filled with anxiety, you will have difficulty figuring out the correct answer.

Come Alert and Well-Rested. Being tired increases the chance you will make careless mistakes and degrades your ability to reason through difficult questions. As you will discover in Chapter 6, sleeping several hours after studying can improve memory for the material, too.

Survey the Test Before You Begin. Make sure there are no missing pages. Review the format of the questions, and evaluate how to budget your time. If you are unsure what you are expected to do on some parts of the exam, ask for assistance.

Budget Your Time. Figure out approximately how long you can work on each question. For essay or other non-objective questions, the point value provides information about how complete an answer is expected and how much time you might need for a question. Do not spend half an hour on one 5-point question and 5 minutes on a 25-point question. If you encounter a question you cannot answer in your budgeted time, make your best guess (if multiple choice), mark it for reconsideration, and move to the next question. After finishing the rest of the questions, go back and spend any extra time on the ones needing more thought.

Be an Intelligent Test-Taker. Read the entire question before formulating an answer. Do not focus on one or two key terms and then assume you know what the question is asking. Be careful to notice critical words such as "not" or "except." On multiple choice questions, try to figure out the answer before you look at the alternatives. If your answer is there (make sure it really says what you think it says), chances are it is the right choice. Before leaving the question, however, read all the alternatives to be sure your choice is the best.

If you do not immediately know the answer to a question, do not panic. First, reread the question to make sure you know what it is asking. For multiple choice questions, reread the alternatives. Sometimes the alternatives will alert you to important details to consider. Then ask yourself what you *do* know about the topic. Use this information to reconsider the possibilities and to eliminate any answers that are clearly inappropriate. Finally, if all else fails, guess (unless your instructor is one of the very rare types who penalizes wrong answers more than answers left blank). For a multiple choice question, you have probably been able to eliminate one or two of the alternatives, increasing your odds of picking the correct answer. Non-objective questions provide a greater challenge, but if you know anything about the topic you have a chance of getting at least partial credit.

Don't be afraid to change an answer. Your first impression is not always right. Information you find later in the exam or a miraculous release from your blocked memory might show you an earlier answer needs to be reconsidered. If you can clearly explain why your first choice is wrong, change it.

Be Careful and Check Your Work. If you must record your answers on a scan sheet for computer scoring, be careful to record the answers correctly. Periodically check to make sure you are on the same number on your answer sheet as on your exam. Some students prefer to mark their answers directly on the test first, and then transfer them to the answer sheet. If time is a major factor, this approach can sometimes create problems. As you hurry to finish transferring answers, careless mistakes become more likely.

If you have extra time, go back through the exam and check your answers and make sure none have been left blank by mistake. Make sure your name, identification number, and any other information are correct.

Adapt Your Strategies to the Type of Test. Obviously, an essay exam requires a different strategy than a multiple choice exam. First, make sure you know what the essay question is asking. A wonderful answer to the wrong question is not worth much. Second, take a minute to plan your answer. Jot down the points you need to make, and think about how you should organize those points. An organized answer gives the impression that you really know the material and usually receives a higher grade. Poorly organized answers suggest that you are merely putting down everything you know about a topic without understanding the answer to the question. Also, your instructor is more likely to miss information you have included if it is in a jumble of unorganized facts. Third, be concise. Include adequate supporting details, but do not add irrelevant information to pad your answer. Get to the point, and stay there. Fourth, make sure that your answer says what you think it says. You know what you mean to say, but sometimes that is not what actually ends up on paper. Reread your answer, and make sure the information is there and accurately stated. Finally, write legibly and use reasonable grammar. What your instructor cannot read or understand will not earn points.

A FINAL WORD

I hope that this study guide helps make your experience in introductory psychology both enjoyable and successful. I welcome any comments about the study guide that you care to share with me. Let me know what worked well for you, what didn't, and what you think would be valuable to include in future editions.

Janet Proctor
Department of Psychological Sciences
Purdue University
1364 Psychological Sciences Building
West Lafayette, Indiana 47907-1364
psy120@psych.purdue.edu

INTRODUCTION TO THE LANGUAGE ENHANCEMENT GUIDE

As you read the textbook, you will probably come across some words (and groups of words) you've never read before. Or maybe they seem familiar, but you aren't sure what they mean when in a psychology textbook. That's what this guide is for: to help you with some of the difficult parts of the reading.

Here is what you will find at the end of each chapter in this study guide:

1. A section calling attention to some "**core terms**". These may or may not appear in the chapter, but you are very likely to hear them in lecture. They are words that college instructors sometimes use *without ever explaining them*. Understanding them should help you get more out of the lectures and the text. You might want to read this part before the lectures on a given chapter begin.

2. A list of some other important terms and **"idioms"** -- groups of words that have a special meaning (for example, "has its roots," "coined a term," or "great strides"). There are quite a few in the book, so I will choose only the ones that are more difficult to figure out from their context, and that you are likely to run across again. (See, there's another one -- "run across"!)

3. A short exercise with "**word parts**" that appear often in that chapter. Word parts are just what they sound like: little sets of letters that make up words. Most of them are based on Latin or Greek, and by putting them together you can make lots of longer words. These happen to be just the kind of words that college professors use often, so it's a good idea to get comfortable with them. I will show you how some words from the chapter are made up of word parts, and then I will let YOU work with some other words that can be made with those same word parts.

Here are some further suggestions for building your vocabulary while you learn psychology:

•   Make flash cards of the unfamiliar words and carry them around with you. Or write them down on a sheet of paper and look at them from time to time for a couple of days. Maybe even try to find chances to use the words as you talk with friends or write papers.

•   Whenever you find a word or string of words that you stumble over, slow down and read it through carefully. Look up any words you just can't get. Then, put it in your own words! For some people, this is a hard thing to make themselves do. If you have trouble doing it, promise yourself that you will look up ONLY 5 words per chapter. Or 10. Whatever. Just do a few. (By the way, we have a name for this technique in Psychology -- it's the "foot in the door" technique. More on that later in the psychology book.)

Mary Beth Foster

CHAPTER 1: INTRODUCTION TO PSYCHOLOGY

ESTABLISHING LEARNING OBJECTIVES

Use these learning objectives as a preview of the chapter, a guide for active reading, and to evaluate your mastery of the material. Review the relevant objectives as you begin and end your reading of each major section of the chapter of your text.

After studying this chapter of your text you should be able to:

I. Solve the conceptual problem of how to define and describe psychology.
   A. Give the modern definition of psychology.
      1. Explain what is meant by mind and behavior.
   B. Discuss the different ways to study the mind scientifically.
   C. Describe what psychologists do, distinguishing among clinical, applied, and research psychologists.
      1. Describe the primary focus and typical workplace of clinical, applied, and research psychologists.
      2. Distinguish between psychologists and psychiatrists.

II. Solve the conceptual problem of tracing the evolution of psychological thought.
   A. Explain what is meant by the mind-body problem.
      1. Describe Descartes' interactionist position.
      2. Describe the modern approach to the mind-body problem.
   B. Discuss differing viewpoints on the origins of knowledge.
      1. Define natural selection and explain how it relates to the debate about the origin of knowledge and behavior.
      2. Summarize the current view of the influence "nature" and "nurture" have on the mind and behavior.
   C. Trace the development of the first scientific "schools" of psychology: structuralism, functionalism, and behaviorism.
      1. Describe the guiding focus and methods of structuralism, functionalism, and behaviorism.
      2. Identify the major figures associated with each "school," and early women in psychology.
      3. Explain why these different approaches to the study of psychology developed.
   D. Discuss the early clinical contributions of Freud and the humanists.
      1. Identify and compare the central concepts and techniques of psychoanalysis and humanistic psychology.
      2. Identify the major figures associated with each approach.

III. Solve the conceptual problem of understanding the focus of modern psychology.
   A. Describe what is meant by an eclectic approach.
   B. Discuss the origins and meaning of the cognitive revolution.
   C. Describe recent developments in biology and how they have influenced modern psychology.
   D. Discuss why psychologists think cultural factors are important determinants of behavior and mind.

MASTERING THE MATERIAL

Preview & Defining and Describing Psychology   (pp. 4-10)

Mastering the Vocabulary.   Define or explain each of the following terms. To check your answers, consult the text pages listed.

1.   psychology (p. 4) *the scientific study of behaviour and mind.*

2.   mind (p. 7) *the contents and processes of subjective experience: sensations, thoughts and emotions*

3.   behavior (p. 7) *observable actions such as moving, talking, gesturing, and so on; behaviours can also refer to the activities of cells, as measured through physiological recording devices, and to thoughts and feelings, as measured through oral and written expression.*

4.   clinical psychologists (p. 9) *professional psychologists who specialize in the diagnosis and treatment of psychological problems.*

5.   applied psychologists (p. 9) *psychologists who try to extend the principles of scientific psychology to practical, everyday problems in the world.*

6.   research psychologists (p. 9) *psychologists who conduct experiments or collect observations designed to discover the basic principles of behaviour and mind.*

7   psychiatrists (p. 10) *are medical doctors who specialize in psychological problems.*

Mastering the Concepts. Fill in the blanks to create a summary of this section. Answers are on page 12.

Psychology is defined as the scientific study of __mind__ (1) and __behaviour__ (2). The __mind__ (3), the contents and processes of subjective experience, cannot be observed directly, so psychologists observe behavior, noting the __environmental__ (4) conditions accompanying the behavior, and make inferences about the mental processes involved. Behavior includes actions, expressed feelings, and cellular activity. __Clinical__ (5) psychologists treat psychological problems or counsel people about parenting or relationships. __Psychiatrists__ (6) are not psychologists; they are medical doctors trained in psychology who treat mental disorders. __Applied__ (7) psychologists, such as human factors or industrial/organizational psychologists, extend principles of psychology to industry. __Research__ (8) psychologists explore basic principles of psychology by conducting experiments, often in laboratories at universities.

Evaluating Your Progress. Select the best response. Answers are found on page 13. If you make any errors, reread the relevant material before proceeding.

1. Which of the items below would not be considered an example of behavior by most psychologists?
    a. the electrical activity of cells in the brain.
    b. marking an answer on a survey.
    c. reciting a list of words from memory.
    d. your subjective experience of the color red.

2. The mind cannot be studied directly because mental processes
    a. are very easily observed.
    b. are subjective.
    c. are too rapid to record.
    d. come from the pineal gland.

3. Which of the following people is most likely to be considered an applied psychologist?
    a. Jack, who advises parents about dealing with drug abuse in teenagers.
    b. Pat, who conducts experiments on the basic memory processes of children.
    c. Sara, who uses the principles of psychology to design control panels in new airplanes.
    d. Miko, who treats patients with serious mental disorders such as schizophrenia.

4. Which of the following types of psychologists is likely to work in an academic setting (e.g., a college)
    a. applied psychologist
    b. research psychologist
    c. clinical psychologist
    d. all of the above

5. Chris has a medical degree and specializes in treating mental disorders. Chris is
    a. a clinical psychologist.
    b. a counseling psychologist.
    c. an applied psychologist.
    d. a psychiatrist.

Tracing the Evolution of Psychological Thought (pp. 10-19)

Mastering the Vocabulary. Define or explain each of the following terms. To check your answers, consult the text pages listed.

1. empiricism (p. 11) *The idea that knowledge comes directly from experience.*

2. mind-body problem (p. 11)

3. nativism (p. 12) *The idea that certain kinds of knowledge and ideas are innate, or present at birth; innate ideas do not need to be learned!*

4. natural selection (p. 12)

5. structuralism (p. 14)

6. systematic introspection (p. 15)

7. functionalism (p. 15)

8. behaviorism (p. 16)

9. psychoanalysis (p. 18)

10. humanistic psychology (p. 19)

Mastering the Concepts. Fill in the blanks to create a summary of this section. Answers are on page 12.

The roots of psychology are in _____(9) and _____(10) and date back to ancient Greece. Psychology merges these, studying both the mind and the biological processes of mental activity. The question of how the mind relates to the body is known as the _____(11) question. Descartes, a philosopher, said that mind and body are _____(12), but the mind controls the body through the _____(13) gland. Psychologists now view the mind as a product of brain activity and inseparable from the body.

Another question concerns the origins of knowledge. The empiricist view of Aristotle states knowledge is obtained through _____(14), whereas the _____(15) view of Kant and others states some knowledge is innate. Darwin's concept of _____(16) predicts adaptive traits are likely to be passed on in the genes, making it possible that behavioral tendencies might be inherited. The _____(17) psychologists suggest perceptual organization is one of these innate abilities. Today, most psychologists agree both _____(18) (innate factors) and _____(19) (experience) are important.

In 1879 in Leipzig, Germany, _____(20) founded psychology by establishing the first psychology _____(21),, and psychology became a distinct scientific discipline. Since that time, psychologists have debated about the proper focus of psychology. _____(22), such as Wundt and Titchener, sought to study the mind by breaking experiences into basic components using systematic _____(23). Later, _____(24) emerged in America and emphasized studying the function and purpose of mental operations. In the 20th

4

century, the _____(25), including Watson, argued that the focus of scientific psychology should be observable _____(26) rather than the mind. Mary Calkins and Margaret Washburn are two of the women who contributed to early psychology, in spite of discrimination.

Clinical psychology also changed in the early 20th century with the publication of Freud's theory of mind and therapy called _____(27). Here, the emphasis was on _____(28) determinants of behavior, which could only be discovered through the symbolic analysis of such things as dreams, and the experiences and sexual urges of _____(29). Disliking Freud's negative view, the _____(30), such as Rogers and Maslow, proposed that humans possess the potential for positive growth and self-awareness.

Evaluating Your Progress. Select the best response. Answers are on page 13. If you miss any questions, reread the relevant material before proceeding.

1. Darwin suggested that certain traits are likely to persist through generations due to natural selection because they are
    a. subjective.
    b. adaptive.
    c. reflexive.
    d. empirical.

2. "Nature" in the nature-nurture issue refers to
    a. innate factors.
    b. the influence of experience.
    c. subjective experiences.
    d. empiricism.

3. Psychology emerged as a science in _____ when _____ established a psychology laboratory.
    a. 364 BC; Aristotle
    b. 1879; Wilhelm Wundt
    c. 1884; William James
    d. 1913; John Watson

4. Structuralists studied the mind by
    a. using systematic introspection.
    b. analyzing dreams and slips of the tongue.
    c. examining the adaptive function of behavior.
    d. studying the pineal gland.

5. You believe that psychology should strive to discover the elements of immediate experience and how they combine to produce meaningful wholes. Your view is most similar to
    a. structuralism.
    b. functionalism.
    c. behaviorism.
    d. psychoanalysis.

6. The early functionalist approach was most influenced by the work of
   a. Margaret Floy Washburn.
   b. Sigmund Freud.
   c. Carl Rogers.
   d. Charles Darwin.

7. Watson's behaviorism and Freud's psychoanalysis differ because
   a. behaviorism stresses the function of the mind, but psychoanalysis stresses the potential for growth.
   b. behaviorism stresses the potential for human growth, but psychoanalysis stresses unconscious urges.
   c. behaviorism stresses biological activity, but psychoanalysis stresses observable behavior.
   d. behaviorism stresses observable behavior, but psychoanalysis stresses unconscious conflicts or urges.

8. A capacity for self-awareness and personal growth are most associated with
   a. psychoanalysis.
   b. empiricism.
   c. humanistic psychology.
   d. cognitive psychology.

Understanding the Focus of Modern Psychology (pp. 20-26)

Mastering the Vocabulary.   Define or explain each of the following terms. To check your answers, consult the text pages listed.

1. eclectic approach (p. 20)

2. cognitive revolution (p. 21)

3. natural mapping (p. 22)

4. culture (p. 24)

Mastering the Concepts. Fill in the blanks to create a summary of this section. Answers are on page 12.

Modern psychology is best described as _____(31), not tied to one point of view, but two approaches are common: the emphasis of cognitive and _____(32) factors. The _____(33) revolution was a shift away from behaviorism and a return to an interest in mental processes. It was stimulated by new research techniques and the invention of the _____(34) and resulted in an appreciation of the influence of thoughts and perception on behavior. Psychologists help design new products to be easily used by considering the _____ (35) factor, the user, and the user's natural behavioral tendencies. New technology allows experimental study of biological aspects of behavior. Psychologists also consider the role that shared values, customs, and beliefs, or _____ (36), has in behavior.

Evaluating Your Progress. Select the best response. Answers are found on page 14. If you make any errors, reread the relevant material before proceeding.

1. Most modern psychologists use
    a. a strict structuralist approach.
    b. a strict functionalist approach.
    c. a strict behaviorist approach.
    d. a mixture of approaches.

2. In the mid-20th century, psychology moved away from a _____ to a _____ approach, which is popular today.
    a. cognitive; behaviorist
    b. behaviorist; cognitive
    c. structuralist; humanistic
    d. humanistic; structuralist

3. The cognitive approach represents a return to
    a. the study of the mind.
    b. the study of only observable behavior.
    c. the study of the brain.
    d. the study of the adaptive function of behaviors.

4. Both the cognitive and biological approaches were influenced by the development of
    a. new technology.
    b. better introspective techniques.
    c. dream analysis.
    d. Darwin's concept of natural selection.

5. Designers consider how a product will accomplish its task and the characteristics of the person who will use it. The user is the _____ in product design.
    a. buyer variable
    b. client content
    c. human factor
    d. people principle

6. If a behavior is influenced by the values or beliefs of the community, the behavior is influenced by
    a. innate factors.
    b. cultural factors.
    c. humanistic factors.
    d. natural selection factors.

MAKING FINAL PREPARATIONS

Complete these sections without consulting your book or notes. For a more accurate estimate of how well you know this material, wait at least a day or two after studying the chapter before working on the questions. Some of the material you "know" immediately after working with the chapter will be quickly forgotten. Immediate tests will overestimate what you know well.

Short Essay Questions. Write a brief answer to each question. Sample answers are on page 14.

1. Explain why scientifically studying the mind is not simple, and describe how it can be studied.

2. Compare the structuralist and behaviorist views about the proper focus and techniques of psychology.

3. Compare Freud's psychoanalytic approach with the humanistic approach of Rogers.

4. Describe the cognitive revolution, and discuss why it occurred.

Matching. Select the correct definition or description for each item. Answers are on page 15.

_____	1. systematic introspection	a.	proposed interactionist view of mind-body problem
_____	2. tabula rasa	b.	founded behaviorism
_____	3. Wundt	c.	treats less serious disorders or adjustment problems
_____	4. nature-nurture issue	d.	view that certain knowledge is innate
_____	5. Watson	e.	idea that knowledge comes from experience
_____	6. human factors	f.	the idea that at birth the mind is a "blank slate"
_____	7. empiricism	g.	issue of the role of innate & environmental factors
_____	8. Descartes	h.	major figure in functionalism
_____	9. nativism	i.	favorite technique of structuralists
_____	10. psychiatrist	j.	medical doctor who treats mental disorders
_____	11. natural mapping	k.	original structuralist
_____	12. developmental psychologist	l.	studies how behavior changes through the lifespan
_____	13. counseling psychologist	m.	behavioral tendencies that guide industrial design
_____	14. mind-body problem	n.	problem of the relationship between consciousness or the mind and the brain and body
_____	15. James	o.	a relationship that follows a person's tendencies of organization and categorization

Multiple Choice Pretest 1. Select the one best response. Answers are on page 15.

1. According to your text, psychology is currently defined as
   a. the scientific study of mind and behavior.
   b. the systematic study of mental processes.
   c. the systematic study of brain activity.
   d. the scientific study of mental illness.

2. The origins of psychology are in
   a. literature and philosophy.
   b. philosophy and physiology.
   c. education and literature.
   d. education and physiology.

3. Which view suggests that personality is determined by one's biological or genetic makeup?
   a. empiricist
   b. nativist
   c. functionalist
   d. behaviorist

4. Who is credited with establishing psychology as a science?
   a. William James
   b. Sigmund Freud
   c. John Watson
   d. Wilhelm Wundt

5. You are scheduled to take part in an experiment examining basic processes in memory and reasoning. The psychologist in charge is most likely
   a. an applied psychologist.
   b. a clinical psychologist.
   c. a research psychologist.
   d. a school psychologist.

6. Gestalt psychologists propose that _____ is (are) innate.
   a. perceptual organization
   b. cross cultural differences
   c. introspection
   d. empiricism

7. A young man is sitting in a lab giving a detailed account of his subjective experiences concerning the taste of lemonade in hopes of discovering the basic units of the mind and perception. This is most characteristic of the research of
   a. behaviorism.
   b. structuralism.
   c. functionalism.
   d. psychoanalysis.

8. "Yes, there are four basic tastes, but I'm interested in how this has helped us adapt and survive." What kind of psychologist is most likely to make such a statement?
   a. a psychoanalyst
   b. a structuralist
   c. a behaviorist
   d. a functionalist

9. Which statement most likely would be heard in a therapy session with a Freudian psychoanalytic psychologist?
   a. "There is a great person in there if you'll just let her out."
   b. "I don't want to hear about your dream. I'd rather talk about what you think is making you anxious."
   c. "I want you to tell me as completely as possible what you experience as you feel this satin cloth."
   d. "Your fear of dogs is really just a symptom of your real problem--a failure to resolve important sexual conflicts in childhood."

10. Calkins and Washburn are notable for
    a. establishing the first psychology laboratory.
    b. developing humanistic psychology.
    c. first studying cross-cultural differences in behavior.
    d. being among the first female psychologists.

11. Why did behaviorists think the structuralist approach to psychology was not truly scientific?
    a. Structuralists based their theories on a person's report of subjective events.
    b. Structuralists emphasized unconscious conflicts and sexual urges, rather than the person's potential.
    c. Structuralists studied animal behavior instead of human behavior.
    d. Structuralists took a too deterministic view of behavior.

12. Current explanations of behavior tend to refer to the person's memories or interpretation of events. This reflects the popularity of which approach to psychology?
    a. humanistic
    b. cognitive
    c. biological
    d. behaviorist

13. Utilizing a variety of theoretical approaches rather than a single approach is referred to as the
    a. eclectic approach.
    b. humanistic approach.
    c. nativist approach.
    d. behaviorist approach.

14. A steering wheel that must be turned right in order to turn the car to the right was designed to use
    a. attractive appearance.
    b. Gestalt principles.
    c. natural mappings.
    d. unnatural mappings.

Multiple Choice Pretest 2. Select the one best response. Answers are found on page 16.

1. The subject matter of psychology is studied today as a science, but it originally was studied by
   a. physicians.
   b. writers.
   c. philosophers.
   d. the religious community.

2. Mary is an M.D. who specializes in treating people with mental disorders. Mary is
   a. a clinical psychologist.
   b. a psychiatrist.
   c. an applied psychologist.
   d. a cognitive psychologist.

3. Personality psychologists, developmental psychologists, and social psychologists are categorized as
   a. clinical psychologists.
   b. research psychologists.
   c. applied psychologists.
   d. counseling psychologists.

4. Which person-item pair is incorrectly linked?
   a. Carl Rogers---unconscious mind
   b. John Watson---observable behavior
   c. Wilhelm Wundt---systematic introspection
   d. William James---adaptive function

5. You are in a time machine. If you want to visit the beginning of the science of psychology how should you set the time machine?
   a. Greece, 350 BC
   b. Leipzig, Germany, 1879
   c. Vienna, Austria, 1900
   d. Johns Hopkins University, Baltimore, Maryland, 1929

6. "How can you think that our consciousness is simply the result of activity of our brain cells? Do you really believe that our ability to love, to remember our past, and to plan for the future is just biochemical activity?" your classmate argued. "I know if the brain is damaged there can be changes in consciousness and mental abilities, but surely the mind is something apart from blood and tissue." Your classmate is considering the
   a. mind-body problem.
   b. structuralist-functionalist debate.
   c. nature-nurture problem.
   d. cognitive revolution.

7. A pigeon pecks a key and is then given food. A psychologist records each response and notes the environmental conditions that influence pecking. To what "school" does this psychologist belong?
   a. structuralist
   b. functionalist
   c. behaviorist
   d. cognitive

8. With which of the following are you most likely to agree if you fall on the "nurture" side of an issue?
   a. Preschool programs like Head Start are unlikely to improve school performance because intelligence is a matter of genes, not experience.
   b. Aristotle and the British Empiricists were wrong to believe that the mind is a "tabula rasa" at birth.
   c. The personality characteristics of an individual are determined by biological factors prior to birth.
   d. Watching violence on TV is responsible for much of the increase in violent behavior in children.

9. Dr. Hart is interested in the differences in dating behavior found in communities with different religious, ethnic, and socioeconomic characteristics. Dr. Hart's research is an example of
   a. humanistic research.
   b. psychoanalytic research.
   c. cognitive research.
   d. cross-cultural research.

10. Psychologists studying smoking and nicotine addiction emphasize the examination of the smoker's physiology, their attitudes and perceptions about smoking, and the behaviors and environmental conditions that are associated with smoking and addiction. What best describes this approach?
    a. behaviorism
    b. cognitive
    c. psychoanalytic
    d. eclectic

11. The cognitive revolution refers to
    a. the shift away from behaviorism's emphasis on behavior and to a renewed interest in the mind.
    b. the development of computers by using information about the organization and processes of the mind.
    c. the rapid shift in thinking that accompanied each shift in approach to studying psychology.
    d. the furor created by Freud's theory of sexual urges during childhood.

12. Americans, who drive on the right side of the road, are likely to have difficulty driving in England, where people drive on the left side of the road. A psychologist might describe this as an example of
    a. eclectic orientation.
    b. natural selection.
    c. an unnatural mapping.
    d. a natural mapping.

ANSWERS AND EXPLANATIONS

Mastering the Concepts

1. mind (p. 4)	10. physiology (p. 11)	19. nurture (p. 13)	28. unconscious (p. 18)
2. behavior (p. 4)	11. mind-body (p. 11)	20. Wundt (p.14)	29. childhood (p. 18)
3. mind (p. 7)	12. separate (p. 11)	21. laboratory (p. 14)	30. humanists (p. 19)
4. environmental (p. 8)	13. pineal (p. 11)	22. Structuralists (p. 14)	31. eclectic (p. 20)
5. Clinical (p. 9)	14. experience (p. 12)	23. introspection (p. 15)	32. biological (p. 21)
6. Psychiatrists (p. 10)	15. nativist/nativism (p.12)	24. functionalism (p. 15)	33. cognitive (p.21)
7. Applied (p. 9)	16. natural selection (p.12)	25. behaviorists (p. 16)	34. computer (p. 21)
8. Research (p. 9)	17. Gestalt (p. 13)	26. behavior (p. 16)	35. human (p. 22)
9. philosophy (p. 11)	18. nature (p. 13)	27. psychoanalysis (p. 18)	36. culture (p. 24)

Evaluating Your Progress

Defining and Describing Psychology

1. **d**   a. Wrong.   Electrical activity can be measured (observed), so it is a behavior.
    (p. 7)   b. Wrong.   Marking an answer is an overt action, and therefore, a behavior.
                c. Wrong.   Speaking is an overt action, and therefore, a behavior.

2. **b**   a. Wrong.   Mental processes cannot be observed directly.
    (p. 7)   c. Wrong.   The brain activity accompanying mental activity can be recorded.
                d. Wrong.   Descartes thought the mind involved the pineal gland, but modern psychology does not.

3. **c**   a. Wrong.   Jack is a clinical or counseling psychologist.
    (p. 9)   b. Wrong.   Pat is a research psychologist studying basic principles of behavior and mind.
                d. Wrong.   Miko is a clinical psychologist or psychiatrist.

4. **d**   a, b, & c.   Wrong.   Applied, research, and clinical psychologists all work in academic settings.
    (p. 9)

5. **d**   a. Wrong.   Clinical psychologists have a Master's degree or a Ph.D., not a medical degree.
    (p. 10)   b. Wrong.   Counseling psychologists have a Master's degree or a Ph.D., not a medical degree.
                c. Wrong.   An applied psychologist doesn't treat mental disorders and doesn't have a medical degree.

Tracing the Evolution of Psychological Thought

1. **b**   a. Wrong.   Subjective means relative to one's personal mental experience.
    (p. 12)   c. Wrong.   A reflex is an automatic response to environmental events.
                d. Wrong.   Empirical refers to observations or learning.

2. **a**   b. Wrong.   Nurture refers to experience, not innate factors.
    (p. 13)   c. Wrong.   Subjective experience is personal experience, not part of the nature-nurture issue.
                d. Wrong.   Empiricism is the view that knowledge is developed from experience and is not innate.

3. **b**   a. Wrong.   Aristotle wrote about topics related to psychology from a philosopher's approach.
    (p. 14)   c. Wrong.   William James was an important figure in functionalism, a later development.
                d. Wrong.   John Watson was an important figure in behaviorism, a later development.

4. **a**   b. Wrong.   Freud used these techniques in psychoanalysis, which is not part of structuralism.
    (p. 15)   c. Wrong.   The functionalists were concerned with the adaptive function of behavior.
                d. Wrong.   Structuralists didn't study brain structures. Descartes was interested in the pineal gland.

5. **a**   b. Wrong.   Functionalism stressed discovering the function of an experience, not the contents.
    (p. 14)   c. Wrong.   Behaviorism stresses studying only observable behaviors, not consciousness.
                d. Wrong.   Psychoanalysis stresses the discovery of hidden conflicts that affect behavior.

6. d   a. Wrong.   Wasburn, a structuralist, was the first woman to receive a Ph.D. in psychology.
    (p. 16)   b. Wrong.   Freud founded the psychoanalytic approach, but did not influence functionalism.
                c. Wrong.   Carl Rogers, a humanistic psychologist, is more contemporary than early functionalism.

7. **d**   a. Wrong.   This is functionalism and humanism.
    (pp. 16,18) b. Wrong.   This is humanism and psychoanalysis.
                c. Wrong.   This is the biological approach and behaviorism.

8. **c**   a. Wrong.   Psychoanalysis stresses the unconscious and determinism.
    (p. 19)   b. Wrong.   Empiricism is the idea that knowledge results from experience.
                 d. Wrong.   Cognitive psychology stresses information processing.

Understanding the Focus of Modern Psychology

1. **d**   a, b, & c.   Wrong.   Most are eclectic, not tied to one approach.
    (p. 20)

2. **b**   a. Wrong.   The order is reversed here.
    (p. 21)   c. Wrong.   Structuralism was replaced by functionalism, not the humanistic approach, much earlier.
                 d. Wrong.   The humanistic view was developed more recently than structuralism.

3. **a**   b. Wrong.   This describes behaviorism.
    (p. 21)   c. Wrong.   This describes the physiological approach.
                 d. Wrong.   This describes functionalism.

4. **a**   b. Wrong.   Introspection is not widely used in either approach.
    (pp. 21-23) c. Wrong.   Dream analysis is a psychoanalytic technique.
                 d. Wrong.   Natural selection does not directly relate to these approaches.

5. **c**   a, b, & d.   Wrong.   These are just distracters and have no place in human factors design.
    (p. 22)

6. **b**   a. Wrong   Innate factors are present at birth and are not due to environmental influences.
    (p. 24)   c. Wrong   Humanistic psychology involves environmental influences, but not really those given.
                 d. Wrong   Natural selection is a process by which traits either persist or die out through evolution.

MAKING FINAL PREPARATIONS

Short Essay Questions

1. The mind is the contents and processes of subjective experience, perception, and feelings. Because it is subjective, it cannot be observed directly. Without directly observable activities, it is difficult to study scientifically. Three approaches are possible: (1) a person can report subjective experiences using systematic introspection to provide information about the mind; (2) the structure and function of the brain can be studied; and (3) a person's behavior can be observed under different conditions and regularities and relationships in behavior can be noted. Because of limitations of the first two, modern research utilizes method three. (pp. 7-8)

2. The structuralists focused on immediate conscious experience and attempted to determine the basic elements of the mind and how they combine into meaningful wholes. They sought to understand the structure of the mind. To do so, they employed the research technique of systematic introspection, in which trained observers gave detailed accounts of their subjective experiences. Behaviorists, on the other hand, argued that to be a science, psychology should not attempt to study the mind or consciousness because its subjective nature made direct observation impossible and placed it outside of science. Instead, they proposed studying only overt behavior and how changes in environmental events affect behavior. (pp. 14, 16)

3. Freud's psychoanalytic approach emphasized the role of unconscious influences. He felt that people had little insight into these unconscious, animalistic urges, conflicts, and memories. Mental problems would be solved only by insight through an analysis of the symbolic content of dreams, slips of the tongue, etc. His view was a very pessimistic, deterministic view of people. Humanists such as Rogers had a more optimistic view. They proposed that people had great abilities to achieve growth, self-awareness, and self-determination. The therapist's role is to nurture these strengths to allow the person to develop to their potential. (pp. 17-19)

4.   The cognitive revolution was a turn away from the behaviorist approach of studying only overt behavior, back to an interest in studying the mind and cognitive processes (perception, memory, reasoning, etc.). The cognitive revolution was possible because: (1) advances in research techniques in which measurements of behavior (reaction time, etc.) could be used to infer the characteristics of mental processes; and (2) computers were developed and provided a convenient model for mental processes (information processing systems). (pp. 21)

Matching

1. **i** (p. 15)	4. **g** (p. 13)	7. **e** (p. 11)	10. **j** (p. 10)	13. **c** (p. 9)
2. **f** (p. 11)	5. **b** (p. 16)	8. **a** (p. 11)	11. **o** (p. 22)	14. **n** (p. 11)
3. **k** (p. 14)	6. **m** (p. 22)	9. **d** (p. 12)	12. **l** (p. 10)	15. **h** (p. 15)

Multiple Choice Pretest 1

1. **a**   b. Wrong.   Psychology is a science and it studies more than mental processes.
(p. 4)   c. Wrong.   Psychology is a science and studies more than just brain activity.
          d. Wrong.   Psychology studies more than just mental illness.

2. **b**   a, c, & d.   Wrong.   Psychology did not originate in literature or education.
(p. 6, 14)

3. **b**   a. Wrong.   Empiricists stress learning and experience.
(p. 12)   c. Wrong.   Functionalists stress the function of a behavior or characteristic.
          d. Wrong.   Behaviorists stress experience and environmental influences.

4. **d**   a. Wrong.   James founded functionalism after psychology had become a science.
(p. 14)   b. Wrong.   Freud is important in the development of clinical, but not scientific, psychology.
          c. Wrong.   John Watson founded behaviorism after psychology had become a science.

5. **c**   a. Wrong.   Applied psychologists apply psychology to practical settings, not basic research.
(p. 9)   b. Wrong.   Clinical psychologist research and treat mental disorders or problems with adjustment.
          d. Wrong.   School psychologists counsel students concerning basic adjustment, career choice, etc.

6. **a**   b. Wrong.   Cross cultural differences are environmental, not innate, in origin.
(p. 13)   c. Wrong.   Introspection is a self-report technique used by the Structuralists, not an innate process.
          d. Wrong.   Empiricism is the idea that knowledge comes from experience, not innate processes.

7. **b**   a. Wrong.   Behaviorism didn't use introspection and studied only observable behavior, not the mind.
(p. 15)   c. Wrong.   Functionalism was concerned with the function of the mind, not its basic units.
          d. Wrong.   Psychoanalysis, Freud's approach to therapy, did not use systematic introspection.

8. **d**   a. Wrong.   A psychoanalyst was interested in unconscious determinants of behavior, not adaptation.
(p. 15)   b. Wrong.   A structuralist was interested in the structure of mind, rather than its adaptive value.
          c. Wrong.   A behaviorist was interested in environmental determinants of behavior, not function.

9. **d**   a. Wrong.   Psychoanalysis is more negative. This is probably from a humanistic therapist.
(p. 18)   b. Wrong.   A psychoanalyst would analyze dreams. This is probably from a humanistic therapist.
          c. Wrong.   This describes systematic introspection, not a therapy.

10. **d**   a. Wrong.   Wilhelm Wundt established the first psychology lab.
(p. 17)   b. Wrong.   Carl Rogers developed humanistic psychology.
          c. Wrong.   Wasburn studied consciousness, and Calkins studied learning, not cultural differences.

11.	**a**	b.	Wrong.	This is the point of disagreement between psychoanalysis and humanism.
	(p. 16)	c.	Wrong.	This is not true, and behaviorists used animals in much of their research.
		d.	Wrong.	This is not true of structuralism, and behaviorists were equally deterministic.

12.	**b**	a.	Wrong.	The humanistic approach stresses personal choice and potential.
	(p. 21)	c.	Wrong.	The biological approach stresses the biochemical and cellular activity of the brain.
		d.	Wrong.	The behaviorist approach stresses the influence of experience and the environment.

13.	**a**	b.	Wrong.	The humanistic approach utilizes a single philosophy, centered on personal growth.
	(p. 20)	c.	Wrong.	The nativist approach emphasizes the influence of innate tendencies.
		d.	Wrong.	The behaviorist approach utilizes a single philosophy, centered on experience.

14.	**c**	a.	Wrong.	Although appearance may be a factor in a product's success, it is not important here.
	(p. 22)	b.	Wrong.	Gestalt principles relate to perceptual organization, not functional relations.
		d.	Wrong.	Unnatural mappings make use more difficult and are avoided in human factors design.

Multiple Choice Pretest 2

| 1. | **c** | a, b, & d. | Wrong. | The origin of psychology was in philosophy. |
| | (pp. 6, 14) | | | |

2.	**b**	a.	Wrong.	A clinical psychologist is a Ph.D., not an M.D. (medical doctor).
	(p. 10)	c.	Wrong.	Applied psychologists work with practical environmental problems, not mental problems.
		d.	Wrong.	Cognitive psychologists study primarily normal thought processes, not mental problems.

3.	**b**	a.	Wrong.	Clinical psychologists include clinical and counseling psychologists.
	(p. 10)	c.	Wrong.	Applied psychologists are school, industrial/organizational, & human factors psychologists.
		d.	Wrong.	Counseling psychologists fall within the category of clinical psychology.

4.	**a**	b.	Wrong.	Watson, a behaviorist, stressed studying observable behavior.
	(p. 19)	c.	Wrong.	Wundt, a structuralist, used systematic introspection.
		d.	Wrong.	James, a functionalist, was interested in the adaptive function of the mind and behavior.

5.	**b**	a.	Wrong.	The philosophical, not scientific, roots of psychology began in Greece at about this time.
	(p. 14)	c.	Wrong.	Freud's psychoanalysis originated in Vienna at about this time.
		d.	Wrong.	Psychology did not originate in America; this is the origin of early behaviorism.

| 6. | **a** | b. | Wrong. | Your friend's view is fairly similar to the interactionist theory. |
| | (p. 11) | c & d. | Wrong. | The nature-nurture problem involves the origin of knowledge, not mind-body relations. |

7.	**c**	a.	Wrong.	Structuralism was more concerned with the mind than stimulus-response relations.
	(p. 17)	b.	Wrong.	Functionalism was more concerned with the adaptive function of behavior.
		d.	Wrong.	Cognitive psychologists are more concerned with mental processes behind behavior.

8.	**d**	a.	Wrong.	This view would put you on the "nature" (genes, biology) side.
	(p. 12)	b.	Wrong.	*Tabula rasa* emphasizes experience, or the "nurture" factor.
		c.	Wrong.	This view would put you on the "nature" (genes, biology) side.

9.	**d**	a.	Wrong.	Humanism stresses the potential for personal growth, not cultural variables.
	(p. 24)	b.	Wrong.	Psychoanalysis emphasizes unconscious influences, not cultural differences.
		c.	Wrong.	Cognitive research involved memory and thinking, not differences in dating behavior.

10.	**d**	a.	Wrong.	Behaviorist aspects are present, but the variety of emphases describes an eclectic approach.
(p. 20)		b.	Wrong.	Cognitive aspects are present, but the variety of emphases describes and eclectic approach.
		c.	Wrong.	Nothing was said about unconscious components or other aspects of psychoanalytic theory.

11.	**a**	b.	Wrong.	Computers provided a model of the mind and promoted the cognitive revolution.
(p. 21)		c.	Wrong.	Cognitive revolution only refers to the shift from behaviorism to a cognitive view.
		d.	Wrong.	Freud's theory did raise a furor, but not the cognitive revolution.

12.	**c**	a.	Wrong.	An eclectic orientation is an orientation that uses many different ideas.
(p. 22)		b.	Wrong.	Natural selection is Darwin's view of how traits become common due to evolution.
		d.	Wrong.	Natural mappings match common patterns of behavior; the pattern is violated here.

LANGUAGE ENHANCEMENT GUIDE

CORE TERMS

You might hear the word *discipline* or *school* in a discussion of psychology. Psychology, sociology, anthropology, history, and so on., are all disciplines -- branches of knowledge -- that study behavior, but each has its own unique focus and methods of study. Even within a discipline there may be different *schools* of thought -- different ideas about the best way to study or explain something. Sometimes, as Dr. Nairne puts it, these different ideas can lead to "vigorous arguments."

Psychology is considered a *social science*, which means that it uses the principles of scientific investigation to study individual people and groups. As in sciences like chemistry and biology, psychology has *theories* -- detailed explanations -- that are tested through experiments. *Empirical research*, including experiments, involves the systematic observation of an event or behavior. Similarly, the philosophical view of *empiricism* that is discussed in your text suggests that knowledge comes from a person's own observations (experience).

IDIOMS

4	receive tangible benefits	get good things that are real and useful
4	method of inquiry	a way of thinking and questioning
4	think critically	to ask questions and actively think about a topic
10	determinants of	things which cause
10	fall outside the domain of	are not the kinds of thing that this science studies
12	principle vehicle for the transmission and expression of an inherited predisposition	the main way that a trait is passed along and then shown in an organism's offspring

13	appeal to	look to; look for help toward
21	to infer	to guess or predict based upon what you already know
21	conceive of	think of in a new way, develop a way of thinking about
24	an integral part	an important, necessary part; essential
26	gains cohesion	hangs together better

WORD PARTS

Here are some words that are made up of word parts, and that you can find in this chapter. After you've looked at these, you can look for others in the chapter that use the same word parts (they are there, but YOU have to find them!)

WORD	WORD PART IT USES	MEANING
exclusively	ex = out of clud, clus = to shut, close	only, keeping out all others
influential	in = in, into, within flu, flux = to flow	exerting power over others, affecting the direction of events
intact	in = in, into, within tact, tang = touch	whole, not broken
predictors	pre = before dict = speak, say, tell	things which foretell
reconstruction	re = again con = together struct = build	to put back together, rebuild; that which has been rebuilt

Knowing the word parts listed above, you can also create the following words. You can get an idea of their meanings from the word parts they use. You fill in the blanks!

conclusive	con + clus	finally, to come together in a final way
confluence	con + flu	_____
influx	_____ + _____	a flowing in
reflux	re + flux	_____

contact   con + tact   _____

intangible   in + tang   _____

(That last one was a tricky one! In some cases, "in" can mean "not", as in incorrect or inadequate. How do you know when it means "in" and when it means "not"? You just have to figure it out from context, or else look the word up!)

CHAPTER 2: THE TACTICS OF PSYCHOLOGICAL RESEARCH

ESTABLISHING LEARNING OBJECTIVES

Use these learning objectives as a preview of the chapter, a guide for active reading, and to evaluate your mastery of the material. Review the relevant objectives as you begin and end your reading of each major section of the chapter.

After studying this chapter you should be able to:

I.   Describe the role of the scientific method in psychology.
    A. Describe the scientific method, and identify the roles of observation and operational definitions.

II.   Solve the practical problem of how best to observe and describe behavior.
    A. Describe the goals and pitfalls of descriptive research.
    B. Explain how psychologists conduct naturalistic research.
        1. Discuss possible solutions to the practical problem of making truly unobtrusive observations.
        2. Evaluate the strengths and limitations of naturalistic observation as a method to study behavior.
    C. Discuss the gains and costs of case studies and surveys.
        1. Discuss the problem of external validity in relation to surveys and case studies.
        2. Explain how and why representative samples are obtained.
    D. Explain how statistics can summarize and help interpret data.
        1. Discuss why both measures of central tendency and variability are needed, and identify them.
        2. Compare descriptive and inferential statistics.

III. Solve the practical problem of how to predict behavior.
    A. Define correlation and explain how correlations can be used to predict behavior.
        1. Compare positive and negative correlations, and give examples of each.
        2. Characterize the relationship between two variables based on the correlation coefficient.
    B. Explain why correlations cannot normally be used to determine the cause of behavior.

IV.   Solve the practical problem of determining why a behavior occurs.
    A. Define experimental research and explain why experiments are conducted.
    B. Discuss the differences between independent and dependent variables.
    C. Explain what is meant by experimental control and how it allows for the determination of causality.
        1. Discuss the problem of confounded variables and how they can be avoided.
        2. Describe random assignment, and explain why it is used.
    D. Describe the problems caused by expectancies and biases and how these problems are solved.

V.   Solve the practical problem of how to ensure research participants are treated ethically.
    A. Explain the principle of informed consent.
    B. Discuss the roles of debriefing and confidentiality in research.
    C. Discuss the ethical issues involved in animal research.

MASTERING THE MATERIAL

Preview & Observing and Describing Behavior: Descriptive Research (pp. 34-46)

Mastering the Vocabulary. Define or explain each of the following terms. To check your answers, consult the text pages listed.

1. scientific method (p. 34)

2. operational definition (p. 35)

3. descriptive research (p. 36)

4. reactivity (p. 36)

5. external validity (p. 37)

6. naturalistic observation (p. 37)

7. case study (p. 39)

8. survey (p. 39)

9. random sampling (p. 41)

10. mean (p. 42)

11. mode (p. 43)

12. median (p. 43)

13. variability (p. 43)

14. range (p. 44)

15. standard deviation (p. 44)

16. descriptive statistics (p. 44)

17. inferential statistics (p. 44)

18. law of large numbers (p. 45)

Mastering the Concepts. Fill in the blanks to create a summary of this section. Answers are on page 34..

Psychology uses the _____(1) method to examine the mind and behavior. This approach involves four steps: _____(2) of a behavior, detection of _____(3) in the data, the generation of a _____(4), and additional observations to check the _____(5) of the hypothesis. To ensure that psychological terms or concepts can be observed, _____ (6) definitions, which are based on how the concepts are measured, are used.

This chapter examines four conceptual and practical problems: how to observe and describe behavior; how to _____(7) behavior; how to determine what _____(8) a behavior; and how to ensure research participants are treated ethically.

_____(9) research involves observing and describing behavior. One possible problem is that the observer's presence can cause _____(10), a change in behavior caused by being observed. As a result, observations will not _____(11) to other situations and will lack _____(12) validity. This problem can be reduced by using unobtrusive techniques such as _____(13) observation, in which behavior is observed in its natural environment without interference by the experimenter. In a related method, _____(14) observation, the experimenter becomes a participant in the activities of interest. _____(15) observation, examining the aftereffects of a behavior, is also useful for avoiding reactivity.

A _____(16) involves detailed observations of a single person. The detailed information helps develop hypotheses, but because only one person is observed, _____(17) validity may be poor, and verifying the accuracy of the information is difficult. _____(18) relationships cannot be determined.

Another approach, using _____(19), gathers less detailed information from many individuals. To get representative data and to avoid bias, _____(20) sampling must be used. Every member of a population must have an equal chance of participation. Limitations of surveys include a lack of in-depth information and poor _____(21) of the information, so surveys often are combined with other techniques.

Psychological testing can be used to measure _____(22) differences. Achievement tests measure current level of knowledge, while _____(23) tests measure potential ability.

_____(24) are used to summarize and interpret the results of observations. Measures of central tendency describe the point at which scores tend to cluster and include the _____(25) or average, the _____(26) or most frequent score, and the _____(27) or middle score. Measures of _____(28) describe how far apart the scores are spread and include the _____ (29) and the standard deviation.

_____(30) statistics are used to decide whether the data are representative and to evaluate the probability that observed differences are due to chance. If the probability of being due to chance is 5% or less, the difference is statistically _____(31).

Without a statistical education, people often draw general conclusions based on only a few observations. This violates the law of _____ (32) which states larger samples are more likely than smaller samples to accurately represent the entire population.

Evaluating Your Progress. Select the one best response. Answers are on page 34. If you make any errors, reread the relevant material before proceeding.

1. The scientific method begins and ends with
    a. observation.
    b. operational definitions.
    c. data analysis.
    d. detecting regularities in behavior.

2. An operational definition defines a concept in terms of
    a. the most current hypothesis concerning the concept.
    b. how the concept can be measured.
    c. knowledge based on authority.
    d. the most general and abstract characteristics of the concept.

3. If you study one person in great detail, you are using
    a. a survey.
    b. inferential statistics.
    c. a case study.
    d. naturalistic observation.

4. People's behavior sometimes changes simply because they are being observed. This effect is known as
    a. external validity.
    b. standard deviation.
    c. reactivity.
    d   experimental control.

23

5. What statistic should be computed to describe how scores differ from one another (the spread of the distribution)?
   a. mean
   b. median
   c. mode
   d. range

6. What technique is used to obtain a representative sample of a population?
   a. naturalistic observation
   b. participant observation
   c. random selection
   d. voluntary, self-selection by participants

7. What statistic identifies a typical score in your data or the value around which the scores cluster?
   a. the standard deviation statistic
   b. a measure of external validity
   c. a measure of variability
   d. a measure of central tendency

8. What is the law of large numbers?
   a. The larger the sample size, the more likely the observations will accurately represent the population.
   b. The larger the number of possible outcomes, the more likely the conclusion will be wrong.
   c. The more people surveyed, the less agreement there will be in the responses.
   d. The larger the number of observations, the more chances there will be careless errors.

Predicting Behavior: Correlational Research (pp. 46-51)

Mastering the Vocabulary. Define or explain each of the following terms. To check your answers, consult the text pages listed.

1. correlation (p. 46)

2. positive correlation (p. 47)

3. negative correlation (p. 47)

Mastering the Concepts. Fill in the blanks to create a summary of this section. Answers are on page 34.

Another purpose of research is to predict behavior. _____(33) research looks for relationships between behaviors. A correlation (or correlation coefficient) reflects the way and degree to which two measures of behavior vary systematically together. _____(34) correlations indicate that the measures vary in the same direction; _____(35) correlations indicate that the measures vary in opposite directions. The strength of the correlation, determined by how close the coefficient is to 1.0 (or -1.0), reflects the variability of the relationship. Zero correlations indicate no relationship. Correlations describe relationships, but they do not prove _____(36) and effect, mainly because of the problem of possible _____ (37) variables. Events might appear to involve a predictable relationship if only part of the _____ (38) plot is examined, because events can occurs together by chance.

Evaluating Your Progress. Select the one best response. Answers are found on page 35. If you make any errors, reread the relevant material before proceeding.

1. Which is false concerning correlational research?
   a. Measures of two variables are obtained from each person in the group.
   b. Correlational research can be used to predict behavior.
   c. Correlational research can establish the cause of a behavior.
   d. Correlational research determines whether there is a relationship between two variables.

2. Suppose the correlation between behaviors X and Y is +0.90. This means that
   a. as Behavior X increases, Behavior Y would be expected to increase.
   b. as Behavior X increases, Behavior Y would be expected to decrease.
   c. as Behavior X decreases, Behavior Y would be expected to increase.
   d. there is no predictable relationship between Behavior X and Behavior Y.

3. Which of the following correlation coefficients represents the strongest (most reliable) relationship?
   a. +0.50
   b. +0.20
   c. -0.10
   d. -0.60

Determining Why Behavior Occurs: Experimental Research (pp. 51-59)

Mastering the Vocabulary. Define or explain each of the following terms. To check your answers, consult the text pages listed.

1. experimental research (p. 51)

2. independent variable (p. 52)

3. dependent variable (p. 53)

4. confounding variable (p. 54)

5. internal validity (p. 54)

6. random assignment (pp. 55-56)

7. placebo (p. 57)

8. single-blind study (p. 57)

9. double-blind study (p. 57)

Mastering the Concepts. Fill in the blanks to create a summary of this section. Answers are on page 34.

Experiments can evaluate the cause of behavior because _____(39) is possible. Experiments differ from correlational studies because the experimenter directly _____(40) some environmental condition thought to influence the behavior being studied. The condition that is varied is the _____(41) variable. The experimenter observes behavior and examines whether it changes when environmental conditions change. The behavior observed and measured is called the _____(42) variable.

To make cause-effect statements, the only systematic changes in the experimental conditions that can occur are those of the independent variable. For this reason, two groups are used: an _____ (43) group, which receives the independent variable manipulation, and a _____(44) group, which does not. If a _____(45) variable, an uncontrolled variable that varies systematically with the independent variable, is present, differences between groups might be due to this variable rather than the independent variable, and the experiment will have poor _____(46) validity. Experimenters control as many variables as possible and use _____(47) assignment of subjects to reduce other differences between groups.

The expectations of the subjects and the experimenter can influence their behavior and the research outcome. This is controlled by using placebos or misleading information to equate people's expectations or by restricting the available information. _____(48) studies keep the experimental condition secret from the subject to avoid subject expectancy effects. _____(49) studies keep group membership secret from subjects and experimenter to avoid both subject and experiment expectancy effects.

Laboratory research often generalizes to natural environments, but experimenters consider the possibility that the control needed to prove cause-effect relationships can lead to behavior that would not occur in less artificial environments. Principles established in the lab are sometimes later verified in natural environments.

Evaluating Your Progress. Select the one best response. Answers are on page 35. If you make any errors, reread the relevant material before proceeding.

1. In an experiment, the researcher
   a. makes observations of naturally occurring behavior and does not interfere in any way.
   b. changes some aspect of the environment and observes the effect of that change.
   c. takes measurements of two variables for every person in the group being observed.
   d. examines one person in great detail.

2. What is the independent variable of experiments?
   a. the behavior that is being measured
   b. a characteristic that is not under experimental control
   c. an environmental condition that is manipulated by the experimenter
   d. a group of participants that is not given the experimental treatment (e.g., gets no drug)

3. A confounding variable in an experiment is an uncontrolled variable that
   a. varies systematically with the independent variable.
   b. increases the internal validity of the experiment.
   c. reduces the problem of expectancy effects.
   d. produces confusing data that do not match the results of previous research.

4. How would members of the control group be treated in a study on the effect of caffeine on heart rate?
   a. They would drink coffee with caffeine.
   b. They would drink coffee with no caffeine.
   c. They would not have their heart rate measured.
   d. They would be tested before the experimental group.

5. If random assignment is used, researchers assume that differences in group performance are not due to
   a. experimenter expectancies about the experiment.
   b. subject expectancies about the experiment.
   c. differences in the personal characteristics of subjects in each group.
   d. the environmental conditions that are intentionally manipulated in the experiment.

6. Single-blind and double-blind procedures are used to
   a. reduce expectancy effects.
   b. avoid the need for a control group.
   c. fulfill the requirements for ethical research.
   d. increase the likelihood of confounding variables.

7. If all possible confounding variables are controlled, the experiment
   a. has only one independent variable.
   b. has only one dependent variable.
   c. has internal validity.
   d. has external validity.

Treating Research Participants Ethically: Human and Animal Guidelines (pp. 60-64)

Mastering the Vocabulary.   Define or explain each of the following terms. To check your answers, consult the text pages listed.

1.   informed consent (p. 61)

2.   debriefing (p. 62)

3.   confidentiality (p. 63)

Mastering the Concepts. Fill in the blanks to create a summary of this section. Answers are on page 34.

Researchers follow ethical guidelines to protect the rights of research participants. One requirement is

_____(50) consent, consent given after information about the risks and procedures of the research have

been provided. Deception is allowed if it does not involve potential harm and would not affect the person's

willingness to participate. Researchers also _____(51) participants by explaining the research, and

must protect their privacy by maintaining the _____(52) of personal information.

Ethical requirements have been established that require animals be treated humanely and given proper

care. Animal research is important because of the greater ability to _____(53) the environment, to

complete studies rapidly, and to deal with simpler systems. In spite of criticisms that conclusions from animal

research are invalid for humans, many findings do generalize.

Evaluating Your Progress. Select the one best response. Answers are on page 36. If you make any errors, reread the relevant material before proceeding.

1.   Telling potential participants in research the nature and possible risks of the research prior to their participation is part of the ethical requirement of
    a.   debriefing.
    b.   informed consent.
    c.   confidentiality.
    d.   compensation.

2.   Keeping personal information about research participants private is part of the ethical requirement of
    a.   debriefing.
    b.   informed consent.
    c.   confidentiality.
    d.   compensation.

3. Which of the following is not an advantage of using animals in research?
    a. There are no ethical requirements to be followed with animals.
    b. The environment and experiences of the animals can be tightly controlled.
    c. Some animals have simpler systems than humans, which makes research simpler.
    d. Animals often have short lifespans, allowing developmental research to be conducted more quickly.

MAKING FINAL PREPARATIONS

Complete these sections without consulting your book or notes. For a more accurate estimate of how well you know this material, wait at least a day or two after studying the chapter before working on the questions. Some of the material you "know" immediately after working with the chapter will be quickly forgotten. Immediate tests will overestimate what you know well.

Short Essay Questions. Write a brief answer to each question. Sample answers are on page 36.

1. Briefly outline the four steps of the scientific method.

2. Compare measures of central tendency and measures of variability. Why are both needed?

3. Explain what a correlation describes, and give examples of positive and negative correlations.

4. Compare reactivity and expectancy effects, and explain how they can be reduced in research.

5. Why can experiments establish cause-effect relationships but correlational research cannot?

6. What is random assignment, and why is it used in experiments?

7. Identify and briefly explain the three major ethical requirements for research with human participants.

Matching. Select the correct definition or description for each item. Answers are on page 37.

_____	1. positive correlation	**a.**	ability of data to generalize to other situations
_____	2. standard deviation	**b.**	a change in behavior because of being observed
_____	3. case study	**c.**	mathematical techniques used to describe data
_____	4. external validity	**d.**	detailed description of a single person
_____	5. reactivity	**e.**	subjects do not know their group assignment
_____	6. inferential statistics	**f.**	observing while taking part in the observed activity
_____	7. dependent variable	**g.**	measure of how much a score differs from the mean
_____	8. median	**h.**	mathematical techniques for evaluating data and estimating whether differences are due to chance
_____	9. negative correlation		
_____	10. participant observation	**i.**	behavior that is measured in an experiment
_____	11. internal validity	**j.**	two variables related such that a change in one is accompanied by an opposite change in the other
_____	12. independent variable		
_____	13. descriptive statistics	**k.**	condition manipulated by the experimenter
_____	14. single-blind study	**l.**	the middle point or score in a set of scores
		m.	two variables related such that a change in one is accompanied by similar changes in the other
		n.	amount of control over confounding variables

Multiple Choice Pretest 1. Select the one best response. Answers are on page 37.

1. Which describes the components of the scientific method in the correct order?
   a. hypothesis formation, observation, evaluation of hypothesis accuracy, observation.
   b. hypothesis formation, observation, search for regularities in data, revision of hypothesis if needed.
   c. observation, search for regularities in data, hypothesis formation, observation to check hypothesis.
   d. observation, hypothesis formation, observation, search for regularities in data.

2. Naturalistic observation, case studies, and surveys are all examples of
   a. descriptive research.
   b. experimental research.
   c. double-blind research designs.
   d. single-blind research designs.

3. Survey results will be more likely to accurately represent the opinions of the entire population if
   a. a control group is used.
   b. random sampling is used.
   c. a double-blind design is used.
   d. a single-blind design is used.

4. To study sex differences in aggression, researchers sat in a park and watched children at play. What research approach did they use?
   a. a case study
   b. an experiment
   c. a survey
   d. naturalistic observation

5. You obtained the following data (2, 2, 3, 5, 8). The mean, median, and mode of these data are
   a. 2, 3, 6
   b. 3, 3, 2
   c. 4, 3, 2
   d. 3, 3, 3

6. Hal's class' average on the final was 75 and your class' average was 70. What type of statistic would help you interpret these data and decide whether the difference was due to class differences or to chance?
   a. a measure of central tendency
   b. a measure of variability
   c. a descriptive statistic
   d. an inferential statistic

7. Which represents a positive correlation?
   a. Older drivers tend to have fewer accidents than younger drivers.
   b. People with less education tend to have lower salaries than people with more education.
   c. People with few social contacts have higher depression rates than people with more social contacts.
   d. People who exercise a lot have lower cholesterol levels than people who exercise little.

8. You read that there is a statistically significant difference in the rate of depression among men and women. This means that the difference is not likely to be due to
   a. reactivity.
   b. chance.
   c. a confounded variable.
   d. an expectancy effect.

9. To determine the cause of a behavior researchers use
   a. a descriptive research method.
   b. a correlational research method.
   c. an experimental research method.
   d. all of the above

10. To examine whether sleep deprivation reduces problem solving ability, researchers woke groups of 10 subjects after 2, 4, 6, or 8 hours of sleep and had them try to solve 5 difficult math problems. They found that subjects allowed 2 or 4 hours of sleep answered fewer problems correctly than subjects who had had 6 or 8 hours of sleep. The dependent variable in this experiment is
    a. the amount of sleep allowed.
    b. the number of math problems answered correctly.
    c. the number of subjects in each group (10).
    d. the personal backgrounds of the students who participated.

11. Neither the subjects nor the experimenter recording the data knows which subject belongs to a particular group. This is an example of
    a. a confounding variable.
    b. random assignment.
    c. a single-blind experiment.
    d. a double-blind experiment.

12. After Chris finished the experiment, she was given a sheet explaining the purpose of the research and the name of a person to contact for any further information. This was part of the ethical requirement of
    a. humane treatment.
    b. informed consent.
    c. debriefing.
    d. confidentiality.

13. The law of large numbers suggests conclusions should not be based on limited observations because of
    a. the variability of behavior.
    b. the chance for negative correlations.
    c. the possibility of reactivity.
    d. the likelihood of expectancy effects.

Multiple Choice Pretest 2. Select the one best response. Answers are on page 38.

1. A good operational definition of aggression might be
    a. "the number of times someone hits, kicks, or yells at a person or an object within a 1 hour period."
    b. "behavior intended to harm someone or something."
    c. "a violent response most often accompanying frustration or anger directed toward someone."
    d. "a personality characteristic in which the individual tends to solve problems with violence."

2. An advice columnist asked her readers to write and tell her whether they prefer being cuddled or having sex. Most responses were in favor of cuddling. Why should we hesitate to accept these data?
    a. There is too much opportunity for reactivity to influence the data.
    b. Random selection of participants was not used in the survey.
    c. A placebo was not used in the survey.
    d. Surveys can't determine cause-effect relationships.

3. Production at the factory was low, so management ordered a study to discover why. Observers went to the factory and filmed the workers at their jobs. The films showed everyone working at top speed, and production was the highest in a year. A likely explanation for the change in the workers' behavior is
    a. external validity.
    b. placebo effect.
    c. reactivity.
    d. random assignment.

4. More accurate data about the factory (question #3) might have been obtained if an observer had secretly made the observations while posing as a new employee. That technique is known as
    a. a case study.
    b. introspection.
    c. participant observation.
    d. naturalistic observation.

5. Seat location and course grades are correlated. The closer to the front students sit, the higher their grades. Motivation might actually cause both good grades and a preference for sitting near the front. In other words, there might be the problem of
   a. reactivity.
   b. a third variable.
   c. an unrepresentative sample.
   d. an expectancy effect.

6. The primary advantage of experimental research over correlational research is that experiments
   a. are easier to conduct than correlational studies.
   b. use descriptive statistics rather than inferential statistics.
   c. involve more natural behavior than correlational studies.
   d. can determine cause-effect relationships.

7. Researchers found a moderate correlation between the length of a customer's driveway and the size of the tips the customer gave pizza delivery people. The longer the driveway, the smaller the tip the delivery person received. Which correlation coefficient most likely represents this relationship?
   a. +0.90
   b. +0.45
   c. -0.45
   d. -0.90

8. To discover whether highlighted terms in texts help students learn, researchers had one group of students read a biology chapter with highlighted terms and had another group read the same chapter without highlighted terms. Both groups then took the same 10-item test over the material, and their test scores were recorded. The independent variable in this experiment was
   a. the format of the chapter (highlighted terms or no highlighting).
   b. the students' test performance (the test score).
   c. the content of the chapter (the factual material).
   d. the personal backgrounds of the students who participated (intelligence, age).

9. A researcher noticed that all 50 of the subjects given the "good mood" manipulation happened to be tested at 8:00 p.m., whereas all 50 of the subjects given the "bad mood" manipulation happened to be tested at 8:00 a.m. She found a statistically significant difference in the memory scores for the two groups. She is not sure she should conclude that mood affects memory. What is the likely cause of her uncertainty?
   a. Her research is not an experiment.
   b. The memory scores for the two conditions were significantly different.
   c. The time the subjects were tested is a confounding variable.
   d. She had the same number of subjects (50) in both groups.

10. A research assistant was talking to a friend outside the lab, "I just tested Kim, the girl in Art 105, and boy, she is screwed up! She scored high on the paranoid scale." This violates the ethical requirement of
    a. humane treatment.
    b. informed consent.
    c. debriefing.
    d. confidentiality.

11. Teachers in a small town are protesting because their pay raises are based on teaching evaluations of one class period each year. They claim that such limited sampling of their teaching is likely to produce inaccurate evaluations, and they want at least five observations. What concept supports their argument?
    a. operational definition
    b. random assignment
    c. placebo effect
    d. law of large numbers

12. All of the following are used to reduce the problem of expectancy effects or bias in research except
    a. control groups.
    b. double-blind experiments.
    c. placebos.
    d. deception.

ANSWERS AND EXPLANATIONS

Mastering the Concepts

1. scientific (p. 34)	15. Indirect (p. 38)	29. range (p. 44)	43. experimental (p. 54)
2. observation (p. 34)	16. case study (p. 39)	30. Inferential (p. 44)	44. control (p. 54)
3. regularities (p. 34)	17. external (p. 39)	31. significant (p. 46)	45. confounding (p. 54)
4. hypothesis (p. 35)	18. Cause-effect (p. 39)	32. large numbers (p. 45)	46. internal (p. 54)
5. accuracy (p. 35)	19. surveys (p. 39)	33. Correlational (p. 46)	47. random (p. 56)
6. operational (p. 35)	20. random (p. 41)	34. Positive (p. 47)	48. Single-blind (p. 57)
7. predict (p. 36)	21. accuracy (p. 41)	35. negative (p. 47)	49. Double-blind (p. 57)
8. causes (p. 36)	22. individual (p. 41)	36. cause (p. 49)	50. informed (p. 61)
9. Descriptive (p. 36)	23. aptitude (p. 41)	37. third (p. 50)	51. debrief (p. 62)
10. reactivity (p. 36)	24. Statistics (p. 42)	38. scatter (p. 49)	52. confidentiality (p. 62)
11. generalize (p. 37)	25. mean (p. 42)	39. control (p. 51)	53. control (p. 62)
12. external (p. 37)	26. mode (p. 43)	40. manipulates (p. 51)	
13. naturalistic (p. 37)	27. median (p. 43)	41. independent (p. 52)	
14. participant (p. 37)	28. variability (p. 43)	42. dependent (p. 53)	

Evaluating Your Progress

Preview & Observing and Describing Behavior

1. **a**	b. Wrong.	Operational definitions are used early in the process, but not at the end.
(p. 34)	c. Wrong.	Data analysis is done late in the process, but not at the beginning.
	d. Wrong.	Detecting regularities in the data is done after observation.

2. **b**	a. Wrong.	Measurement, not hypotheses, are the basis of operational definitions.
(p. 35)	c. Wrong.	How the concept can be measured, not the source of knowledge, is important.
	d. Wrong.	Operational definitions are in terms of specific, objective measurements of the concept.

3. **c**	a. Wrong.	Surveys involve many people, not just one.
(p. 39)	b. Wrong.	Inferential statistics are not standard with single participant research.
	d. Wrong.	Although naturalistic observation can involve a single person, this term would not be used to describe single participant studies in general.

4.   **c**   a. Wrong.   External validity is the generalizablity of observations or conclusions to other situations.

(p. 36)   b. Wrong.   Standard deviation is a descriptive statistic reflecting the variability of the data.

             d. Wrong.   Experimental control involves controlling or equating variables in an experiment.

5.   **d**   a, b, & c.   Wrong.   These are all measures of central tendency, not variability.

(p. 44)

6.   **c**   a & b.   Wrong.   These are observation techniques, not ways to select research participants.

(p. 41)   d.   Wrong.   Self-selection causes bias. Some people are more likely to volunteer than others.

7.   **d**   a. Wrong.   Standard deviation is a measure of variability (spread) of the scores, not central tendency.

(p. 42)   b. Wrong.   External validity refers to the extent to which data will generalize to other situations.

             c. Wrong.   The question implies central tendency, not variability (spread).

8.   **a**   b, c, & d.   Wrong.   The law of large numbers emphasizes the benefits of repeated observations.

(p. 45)

Predicting Behavior: Correlational Research Methods

1.   **c**   a, b, & d.   Wrong.   These statements are all true, but correlations can't prove cause-effect.

(pp. 48-51)

2.   **a**   b. Wrong.   +0.90 is a positive correlation, so increases in X are linked to increases in Y.

(p. 47)   c. Wrong.   +0.90 is a positive correlation, so decreases in X are linked to decreases in Y.

             d. Wrong.   +0.90 is a strong positive correlation. A 0.00 correlation indicates no relationship.

3.   **d**   a, b, & c.   Wrong.   The sign (+) indicates the type, not strength, of a relationship. Strength is

(p. 48)   indicated by the absolute value of the coefficient. That is, ignore the + or - .

Determining Why Behavior Occurs: Experimental Research Methods

1.   **b**   a. Wrong.   This describes naturalistic observation, not necessarily an experiment.

(p. 51)   c. Wrong.   This describes the correlational research method, not an experiment.

             d. Wrong.   This describes the case study method, not an experiment.

2.   **c**   a. Wrong.   This describes the dependent variable.

(p. 52)   b. Wrong.   This is similar to a confounding variable.

             d. Wrong.   This describes a control group.

3.   **a**   b. Wrong.   Confounding variables reduce internal validity.

(p. 54)   c. Wrong.   Confounding variables are not related to expectancy effects.

             d. Wrong.   The cause-effect relationship is thrown into confusion, not the data.

4.   **b**   a. Wrong.   The experimental group would drink the caffeinated coffee.

(p. 54)   c. Wrong.   Control groups do not get the environmental manipulation, but they are tested.

             d. Wrong.   This would create a confounding variable and could make the control group useless.

5.   **c**   a. Wrong.   Experimenter expectancy effects are not eliminated by random assignment.

(p. 56)   b. Wrong.   Subject expectancy effects are not eliminated by random assignment.

             d. Wrong.   Differences are *more* likely to be due to the experimental manipulation.

6. **a**   b. Wrong.   Control groups provide a source of comparison, not a reduction of expectancy effects.
   (p. 57)   c. Wrong.   Ethical requirements are not related to these designs.
                  d. Wrong.   Confounding variables (expectancy differences) are reduced by these designs.

7. **c**   a. Wrong.   Controlling confounding variables doesn't limit the factors manipulated in an experiment.
   (p. 54)   b. Wrong.   Controlling confounding variables doesn't limit the factors measured in an experiment.
                  d. Wrong.   Confounding variables don't relate to an experiment's generalizability (external validity).

Treating Research Participants Ethically

1. **b**   a. Wrong.   Debriefing is disclosing the purpose of the research at its conclusion.
   (p. 61)   c. Wrong.   Confidentiality involves keeping personal information private.
                  d. Wrong.   There is no requirement that participants be compensated, but some are.

2. **c**   a. Wrong.   Debriefing is discussing the purpose of the research after someone participates.
   (p. 62)   b. Wrong.   Informed consent involves getting the person's consent to participate after providing
                              information about the risks and nature of the research.
                  d. Wrong.   There is no requirement that participants be compensated, but some are.

3. **a**   b, c, & d.   Wrong.   These are major advantages of using animals, but there are ethical requirements
   (p. 62)   for animal research.

MAKING FINAL PREPARATIONS

Short Essay Questions

1. The four steps of the scientific method are: (1) Observations of a behavior are made. (2) The data are examined for systematic regularities. (3) An hypothesis is formulated. (4) More observations are made to evaluate the accuracy of the hypothesis. (pp. 34-35)

2. Measures of central tendency describe the point around which most data clusters. They describe a typical score. Measures of variability describe how the distribution of scores is spread out. To have the full description of the score distribution necessary to accurately interpret the data requires both types of measures. (pp. 42-44)

3. A correlation describes a relationship between two variables. In a positive correlation, both variables change in the same direction (e.g., height and shoe size: Taller people tend to have bigger feet than shorter people). In a negative correlation the variables change in opposite directions (e.g., class absences and grades: Students with many absences tend to have lower grades than those with few absences). (pp. 46-48)

4. Reactivity and expectancy effects are biases that can occur. Reactivity, a change in a subject's behavior caused by being observed, can lead to inaccurate conclusions. Expectancy effects, changes in subjects' (or experimenter's) behavior caused by their expectations about the research, also lead to errors. A solution is to restrict the subject's knowledge about the research. Naturalistic observation or other unobtrusive observation techniques can reduce reactivity. "Blind" designs, in which subjects (and experimenter) do not know the group assignments, reduce expectancy effects. Deception also can be used. (pp. 36-38; 56-57)

5. Correlational research lacks the experimental control that is possible in experiments. By controlling for the influence of other variables, behavior changes can be attributed to the variables under study. (pp. 48-51; 51-52)

6. In random assignment, participants have an equal chance to be assigned to any group in the experiment. This reduces group differences in uncontrolled variables and equates the characteristics of the groups. (pp. 55-56)

7. (1) Informed consent: Participants must be informed of the nature of the research and any possible effects of their participation and must give their consent prior to participating. (2) Debriefing: Participant must be informed about the purpose of the experiment and any deception after their participation. (3) Confidentiality: Personal information about participants must not be disclosed to other people. (pp. 61-62)

Matching

1. **m** (p. 47)	4. **a** (p. 37)	7. **i** (p. 53	10. **f** (p. 37)	13. **c** (p. 44)
2. **g** (p. 44)	5. **b** (p. 36)	8. **l** (p. 43)	11. **n** (p. 54)	14. **e** (p. 57)
3. **d** (p. 39)	6. **h** (p. 44)	9. **j** (p. 47)	12. **k** (p. 52)	

Multiple Choice Pretest 1

1. **c**   a & b.   Wrong.   Observation comes first and is the basis of later hypothesis formation.
(pp. 34-35) d.   Wrong.   Regularities in data from observations is the basis for hypothesis formation.

2. **a**   b.   Wrong.   Experiments involve manipulation of conditions; case studies, etc., don't.
(pp. 36-41) c & d.   Wrong.   "Blind" designs restrict information about group assignment, not relevant to surveys.

3. **b**   a. Wrong.   Surveys can't include control groups; there is no variable being manipulated.
(p. 41)   c. Wrong.   Double-blind designs can't be used in surveys; subjects aren't assigned to groups.
         d. Wrong.   Single-blind designs can't be used in surveys; subjects aren't assigned to groups.

4. **d**   a. Wrong.   A case study is a detailed study of one person; here, many children were observed.
(p. 37)   b. Wrong.   They didn't manipulate any condition, so it wasn't an experiment.
         c. Wrong.   Surveys are interviews or paper-and-pencil questionnaires.

5. **c**   a, b, & d.   Wrong.   The mean (average) = (sum of scores / number of scores) = 20/5 = 4. The median
(pp. 42-43)   is the middle score (3). The mode is the most common score (2)

6. **d**   a & b.   Wrong.   You need inferential statistics for statistical significance; these are descriptive
(p. 44)   statistics.
         c.   Wrong.   You need an inferential statistic.

7. **b**   a, c, & d.   Wrong.   Opposite changes equal negative correlation.
(p. 47)

8. **b**   a, c, & d.   Wrong.   Statistical significance only indicates a result is unlikely to be due to chance. It
(p. 46)   does not address whether or not the data are accurate or unbiased.

9. **c**   a, b, & d.   Wrong.   Only experiments determine cause-effect relationships.
(p. 51)

10. **b**   a.   Wrong.   This is the independent variable.
(p. 53)   c & d.   Wrong.   The dependent variable is the behavior that is measured.

11. **d**   a. Wrong.   Confounding variables are uncontrolled variables that vary systematically with the
(p. 57)   independent variable.
         b. Wrong.   Random assignment doesn't involve keeping group membership secret.
         c. Wrong.   A single-blind design keeps group membership secret from only the subject.

12. **c**   a. Wrong.   Humane treatment is proper care (usually referring to animals).
(p. 62)   b. Wrong.   Informed consent is obtained before a person participates.
         d. Wrong.   Confidentiality is the right to have personal information kept private.

13. **a**   b. Wrong.   Negative correlations aren't a problem, and don't relate to the law of large numbers.
(p. 45)   c. Wrong.   Reactivity is not eliminated by multiple observations.
             d. Wrong.   Expectancy effects are not found only when limited sampling is done.

Multiple Choice Pretest 2

1. **a**   b, c, & d.   Wrong.   These aren't based on how the concept can be measured directly.
(p. 35)

2. **b**   a. Wrong.   Nobody was observed, so reactivity doesn't apply.
(p. 41)   c. Wrong.   A placebo is an inert substance used to prevent expectancy effects in drug studies.
             d. Wrong.   Surveys don't give cause-effect, but this question deals with description, not cause-effect.

3. **c**   a. Wrong.   External validity refers to the extent to which data will generalize to other situations.
(p. 36)   b. Wrong.   There's no reason here for an expectancy effect. Being observed was the key factor.
             d. Wrong.   Workers were not assigned to groups, so random assignment is not relevant.

4. **c**   a. Wrong.   A case study is a detailed description of an individual.
(p. 37)   b. Wrong.   The observations would involve external events, not personal, subjective experiences.
             d. Wrong.   In naturalistic observation the observer doesn't participate in the activities being studied.

5. **b**   a. Wrong.   An unobserved, additional variable is key, not changes in behavior due to being observed.
(p. 50)   c. Wrong.   An unobserved, additional variable is key, not how participants were selected.
             d. Wrong.   An unobserved, additional variable is key, not bias.

6. **d**   a. Wrong.   Experiments are usually more complicated than correlational studies.
(p. 51)   b. Wrong.   The data from experiments are analyzed using inferential statistics.
             c. Wrong.   Experiments are sometimes criticized for their artificial behaviors and settings.

7. **c**   a. Wrong.   +0.90 is a strong positive correlation, not a moderate negative correlation.
(p. 47)   b. Wrong.   +0.45 is a positive correlation, not a negative correlation.
             d. Wrong.   -0.90 is a strong negative correlation, not a moderate one.

8. **a**   b. Wrong.   This is the dependent variable.
(p. 52)   c. Wrong.   This was held constant; independent variables are manipulated by the experimenter.
             d. Wrong.   This was not manipulated by the experimenter, so it isn't the independent variable.

9. **c**   a. Wrong.   This is an experiment, so cause-effect conclusions are possible.
(p. 54)   b. Wrong.   Significant differences are necessary for concluding mood affects memory.
             d. Wrong.   This is an example of experimental control and is necessary in a good experiment.

10. **d**   a. Wrong.   He disclosed private information, violating confidentiality, not humane treatment.
(p. 63)   b. Wrong.   In informed consent a person agrees to participate after being told about the research.
             c. Wrong.   Debriefing is telling the person about the purpose of the experiment after it is over.

11. **d**   a. Wrong.   There's no argument over defining good teaching, just the accuracy of single samples.
(p. 45)   b. Wrong.   Randomly assigning subject to groups is not involved here.
             c. Wrong.   A placebo effect, subject expectancies influencing behavior, is not an issue here.

12. **a**   b. Wrong.   Double-blind designs reduce expectancy effects by keeping group identity secret.
(p. 57)   c. Wrong.   Placebos are inactive substances that keep secret whether a subject is getting a drug.
             d. Wrong.   Deception to keep secret the true purpose of the study reduces expectancy effects.

LANGUAGE ENHANCEMENT GUIDE

CORE TERMS

When you signed up for this course, you probably thought that a certain amount of what you would study would be "common sense." But it's the job of psychologists to question common sense, and to want to test it. Instead of "common sense," psychologists would use the term *intuitive* -- that is, coming from your intuition. You can't build a science on intuition or common sense; a science requires that before a fact is accepted as a fact it must be tested empirically. That means that psychologists have to set up some experiments to check whether things really work the way they seem to work.

Your instructor might use the term *classic* study or *seminal* study when describing an experiment. This is research that is very important because it proved some major fact to be true or because it changed the way people viewed a topic. *Seminal experiments* usually lead to a new theory and inspire many new experiments. When discussing a classic study, your professor might say something like, "This study clearly establishes *causality* between a lack of dopamine and Parkinson's disease." That means that the experiment is important because it showed that one thing (the amount of dopamine) causes another thing (Parkinson's disease). Remember, though, that some "classic" studies are discussed because of their impact in the past, not their current value. For example, because of problems with confirming it's accuracy, Freud's theory of personality is not the most popular theory, but it is discussed because of its past and current influence on psychology.

You might also hear other unfamiliar terms. The first is *methodology*, the specific procedures used in research. Your instructor might describe a study as having *rigorous* methodology, which means that the procedures used were very good and very carefully planned. In many cases, this will mean proper *controls* were used. The term *control* has several uses. The experimenter *controls* (has the power to determine or influence) the conditions in an experiment, such as controlling whether a room is cool or hot. The experimenter *controls for* (takes steps to avoid) differences in conditions that are not intended. A *control group* is an "untreated" group in an experiment, a neutral condition. Also, when your professor says an experiment must be *replicated*, the experiment must be repeated to show that the same results can be obtained again.

IDIOMS

35	meet this criterion	to have the necessary characteristics; to meet one necessary requirement. (A criterion is one requirement; criteria are several.)
35	conspire to produce the remarkable diversity	work together to cause so many differences between people
38	content and quality of the litter	exactly what kind of trash
38	a poor vehicle for determining causality	not a very good way to tell whether one thing causes another
38	phenomenon	an event; something that happens (plural is phenomena)

38	establish the generality of	to show that something is common; to show that it is usually what happens
39	place all their (theoretical) eggs in one basket	to unwisely depend upon just one thing to support you; for example, to build a whole theory on one example
41	a broadly based research effort	an approach to research that uses several different kinds of studies (surveys AND experiments, for example)
41	to characterize a person's tendencies to act in consistent ways	to describe the ways that a person usually acts
44	attributed to chance	"blamed on" random factors; caused by chance
49	a social outcry for the monitoring of televised violence	lots of people saying that they want violence on TV to be monitored by the government
54	if sales of the product subsequently differs between the two groups	if later one group buys more of the product than another
54	interpretation of the results will be hopelessly compromised	making sense of the results will be impossible
56	the problem of intrinsic subject differences	the problem that everybody is different in many ways from everyone else
59	a devastating critique	criticism that will make something useless
62	does sufficient justification exist for the invasive procedures	do we have enough good reasons for using methods that invade (and might permanently hurt)
62	advocated the complete elimination	spoke out for completely stopping
64	can result in censure or termination of membership by the governing body of the association	can mean that you are formally "scolded" by the organization, or that you are no longer allowed to belong to it

WORD PARTS

Here are some words that are made up of word parts, and that you can find in this chapter. After you've looked at these, you can look for others in the chapter that use the same word parts (they are there, but YOU have to find them!)

WORD	WORD PART IT USES	MEANING
advocated	ad = to, toward voc = voice, speak	to speak for

dependent	de = away, from, down pend = to hang	to hang upon, to require
incredibly	in = not cred = to believe	not believably
perspective	per = around spect = to look	a different view, a viewing angle
produce	pro = forward duc = to lead	to create, to make
submit	sub = under mit = to send	to give up, surrender

Knowing the word parts listed above, you can also create the following words. You can get an idea of their meanings from the word parts they use. You fill in the blanks!

independent	in + de + pend	_____
conduct	_____ + _____	to lead together, bring together
reduce	re + duc	_____
inspect	_____ + _____	to look into, to look at closely
impending	_____ + _____	to hang in the balance; about to happen
deduce	de + duc	_____

CHAPTER 3: BIOLOGICAL PROCESSES

ESTABLISHING LEARNING OBJECTIVES

Use these learning objectives as a preview of the chapter, a guide for active reading, and to evaluate your mastery of the material. Review the relevant objectives as you begin and end your reading of each major section of the chapter.

I. Solve the adaptive problem of how the nervous system communicates internally, linking world and brain.
    A. Describe the structure and function of neurons.
        1. Identify three types of neurons, and explain their functions.
        2. Describe how a reflex operates, and explain why reflexes are important.
        3. Identify the component parts of a neuron, and explain their functions.
    B. Explain how neurons transmit information.
        1. Define resting potential, and explain its adaptive role in neural transmission.
        2. Explain how action potentials are generated and travel down the axon and factors that effect this.
        3. Explain the role of neurotransmitters in neural transmission.
            a. Identify three common neurotransmitters and the behaviors with which they are associated.
        4. Explain how drugs effect the nervous system to alter behavior.
    C. Discuss how the neurons work together in communication networks.
        1. Explain how information is represented and communicated by neurons.
        2. Describe how computerized "neural" networks can simulate brain activities.

II. Solve the adaptive problem of how the nervous system initiates and coordinates behavior efficiently.
    A. Describe the organization of the nervous system.
    B. Explain the techniques that researchers use to study the brain.
        1. Identify the techniques that determine structure and those that determine activity or function.
    C. Describe the major structures of the brain and the functions associated with each structure.
        1. Identify the structures of the hindbrain, midbrain, and forebrain and the functions they control.
        2. Describe the organizational structure of the cortex, and identify the higher mental functions associated with each area.
    D. Describe how the two hemispheres of the brain divide and coordinate brain functions.
        1. Describe what happens when the two hemispheres are surgically "split."
        2. Describe non-surgical studies of lateralization and the conclusions reached with these methods.
        3. Summarize the current view concerning lateralization of hemispheric functions.

III. Solve the adaptive problem of how to regulate growth and internal functions.
    A. Explain how the endocrine system controls long-term and widespread communication needs.
    B. Note the differences between communication via the endocrine system and communication in the nervous system.
    C. Discuss the role that hormones play in establishing sexual identity and gender-specific behaviors.

IV. Solve the adaptive problem of how to store and transmit the genetic code.
    A. Describe the basic principles of the genetic transmission.
    B. Explain how psychologists study genetic influences on behavior.

MASTERING THE MATERIAL

Preview & Communicating Internally: Connecting World and Brain (pp. 72-85)

Mastering the Vocabulary. Define or explain each of the following terms. To check your answers, consult the text pages listed.

1. neuroscience (p. 72)

2. central nervous system (p. 73)

3. peripheral nervous system (p. 73)

4. neuron (p. 74)

5. sensory neuron (p. 74)

6. interneuron (p. 74)

7. motor neuron (p. 74)

8. myelin sheath (p. 74)

9. glial cell (p. 74)

10. reflex (p. 74)

11. dendrites (p. 74)

12. soma (p. 75)

13. axon (p. 75)

14. terminal buttons (p. 75)

15. synapse (p. 75)

16. resting potential (p. 76)

17. action potential (p. 77)

18. depolarization (p. 77)

19. hyperpolarization (p. 77)

20. neurotransmitters (p. 78)

21. acetylcholine (p. 79)

22. dopamine (p. 80)

23. serotonin (p. 80)

24. GABA (p. 80)

25. endorphins (p. 81)

26. refractory period (p. 83)

27. neural networks (p. 83)

Mastering the Concepts. Fill in the blanks to create a summary of this section. Answers are on page 60.

All behavior originates in the _____(1). Brain cells interact to form a communication network and to control behavior. The _____(2) and _____(3) make up the central nervous system. The _____(4) nervous system, the remaining nerves, serves as a link between the central nervous system and the body.

This chapter addresses four adaptive problems: How does internal communication occur to allow adaptation to the environment? How does the brain initiate and _____(5) behavior? How are _____(6) and internal functions regulated? How is the _____(7) code stored and transmitted?

_____(8) are cells of the nervous system and come in three major types. _____(9) neurons are in contact with the environment and carry messages to the spinal cord and brain. _____(10) serve as links between neurons. _____(11) neurons carry information from the brain and spinal cord to muscles and glands. The nervous system also contains _____(12) that perform "housekeeping" functions and form the _____(13) sheath, a kind of insulation on some neurons. Not all behavior is controlled by the brain. The spinal _____(14), in which responses are initiated in the spinal cord, allows a speedier response than one initiated in the brain.

Neurons are composed of four major parts. _____(15) are branches that receive and transfer input to the _____(16), the main body of the cell. The _____(17) transmits input (in the form of an action potential) toward another cell. Axons branch at the end, and in the tips are _____(18) that contain chemicals used to communicate with the next cell. Neurons are separated by a space, the _____(19).

Activity begins in the dendrites, and if strong enough, it is passed to the axon from the soma. It travels down the axon, causing the release of chemicals into the synapse, and thus, the stimulation of the next cell. When inactive, neurons have a _____(20), or imbalance of ions inside and outside the cell. Stimulation of the neuron causes ion movement and either _____(21) or _____(22), depending on whether the simulation is excitatory or inhibitory. If stimulation is strong enough, depolarization occurs, and an _____(23) is generated. Action potentials are _____(24); they either occur or not. They have a constant speed and intensity, but neuron size and shape affects this speed. The nodes of Ranvier are _____(25) in the myelin sheath and help speed neural transmission.

Neurotransmitters flow into the synapse and contact the next cell, stimulating or inhibiting generation of another action potential. Neurotransmitters include acetylcholine, serotonin, GABA and _____(26). Imbalances cause physical and mental disorders. Some drugs act as _____(27) and mimic neurotransmitters, or as _____(28) and block neurotransmitter action. _____(29), natural painkillers in the body, are neuromodulators that influence neurotransmitter levels.

Information is represented by the _____(30) of activation across many neurons and by changes in the neuron's _____(31). A _____(32) period in which neurons cannot fire again limits their firing rate. Neural _____(33) are computer programs that simulate the activity of neuron systems and behave in brain-like ways. Units corresponding to neurons are activated by input. The input is represented by the _____(34) activity of many units. Units are connected, and activity in one unit creates activity in others.

Evaluating Your Progress. Select the one best response. Answers are on page 60. If you make any errors, reread the relevant material before proceeding.

1. The type of neuron that is the communication link between the world and the spinal cord or brain is the
    a. motor neuron.
    b. sensory neuron.
    c. glial neuron.
    d. interneuron.

2. The neuron's branching fibers that receive input from a sensory organ or another neuron are called
    a. cell bodies.
    b. axons.
    c. terminal buttons.
    d. dendrites.

3. The pathway information travels in a spinal reflex is
    a. sensory neuron, interneuron, motor neuron.
    b. motor neuron, interneuron, sensory neuron.
    c. sensory neuron, brain, motor neuron.
    d. motor neuron, brain, sensory neuron.

4. The resting potential is caused by
    a. an uneven distribution of charged ions inside and outside the neuron.
    b. neurotransmitters being released by the terminal buttons of the neuron.
    c. a change in the axon cell membrane that allows depolarization of the neuron.
    d. strong input from another neuron stimulating the dendrites of the cell.

5. Action potentials
    a. are larger if the stimulus is intense rather than weak.
    b. travel faster if the stimulus is intense rather than weak.
    c. are generated along the axon.
    d. all of the above

6. The fluid-filled space between neurons is
    a. the interneuron.
    b. the soma.
    c. the synapse.
    d. the glial area.

7. The neural impulse is transferred to the next neuron via
    a. interneurons in the synapse.
    b. the myelin sheath.
    c. the sodium-potassium pump.
    d. neurotransmitters.

8. Parkinson's disease and schizophrenia both involve imbalances of the neurotransmitter
    a. acetylcholine.
    b. endorphin.
    c. dopamine.
    d. serotonin.

9. Stimulus characteristics are represented in the nervous system by the pattern of activation and the
   a. specific neurotransmitter involved in neural transmission.
   b. firing rates of the neurons.
   c. refractory period of the neurons.
   d. speed of neural transmission.

10. The term used to describe the representation of a concept by groups of activated units (rather than one active unit) in neural networks is
   a. connected representation.
   b. reproduceable representation.
   c. distributed representation.
   d. weighted representation.

Initiating and Coordinating Behavior: A Division of Labor (pp. 86-104)

Mastering the Vocabulary. Define or explain each of the following terms. To check your answers, consult the text pages listed.

1. nerves (p. 86)

2. somatic system (p. 86)

3. autonomic system (p. 86)

4. Wenicke's area (p. 87)

5. Broca's Area (p. 87)

6. electroencephalograph (EEG) (p. 90)

7. computerized tomography scan (CT scan) (p. 90)

8. positron emission tomography (PET) (p. 90)

9. magnetic resonance imaging (MRI) (p. 91)

10. hindbrain (p. 92)

28. somatosensory cortex (p. 97)

29. temporal lobe (p. 98)

30. occipital lobe (p. 98)

31. corpus callosum (p. 100)

32. concurrent activities paradigm. (p. 102)

Mastering the Concepts. Fill in the blanks to create a summary of this section. Answers are on page 60.

The two divisions of the nervous system are the _____(35) nervous system and the _____(36) nervous system. Messages are sent to the brain via _____(37) (sensory) pathways and out from the brain via _____(38) (motor) pathways. The peripheral nervous system contains the _____(39) nervous system, which serves the sensory and motor systems, and the _____(40) nervous system, which controls basic bodily functions and adjusts the body to meet emergency situations.

Brain function is studied by recording brain activity, stimulating the brain, and examining the effects of _____(41). Changes in behavior associated with stimulation or lesioning help link a function to an area of the brain. EEG, PET, and functional MRI record brain activity, and MRI and CT reveal brain structures.

The brain is organized into three major regions: the _____(42), midbrain, and _____(43). The hindbrain contains the _____(44) and pons, which control life-support systems, the reticular formation, which controls arousal, and the _____(45), which is important for smooth, coordinated movements. The midbrain contains the tectum, which includes areas used in relaying sensory information, and the substantia nigra, an area that produces dopamine. Damage to the substantia nigra reduces dopamine and causes _____(46) disease. The forebrain includes the _____(47) and subcortical structures, including the thalamus, hypothalamus, and limbic system. The thalamus processes and relays _____(48) input. The _____(49) is involved in eating, drinking, body temperature, sexual behavior and the control of the pituitary. The _____(50) includes the amygdala, which is involved in emotion and motivation, and the hippocampus, which is important for forming _____(51), and several other structures.

The cerebral cortex is divided into two halves, or hemispheres, each with four lobes. The _____(52) lobes contain Broca's speech area, the motor cortex, and areas important for planning and thought. The

_____(53) lobes contain the somatosensory area for touch. The motor and somatosensory cortex are arranged topographically (areas close on the body are handled in areas close in the brain) and the size of a body part's brain area is related to the sensitivity or level of control of the body part. Auditory and speech centers are in the _____(54) lobe, with speech typically in the left hemisphere. The occipital lobe processes visual input. Functions are localized, but there is much overlap.

Processing also is lateralized (divided between hemispheres), with each hemisphere handling certain tasks. The right hemisphere controls the _____(55) side of the body and receives sensory input from the left visual field; the left hemisphere controls and receives input from the right. Input is available to both hemispheres due to eye movements and because a bridge of tissue, the _____(56), allows information from one side to transfer to the other. Operations for epilepsy cut this bridge, splitting the hemispheres. Split-brain patients behave normally except in special situations that restrict both how information is received and how responses are made.

The hemispheres are specialized for certain tasks. The right hemisphere is important for _____(57) tasks; the left hemisphere is important for verbal tasks. According to the _____(58) activities paradigm for hemispheric specialization, if a second task interferes more with a right hemisphere task than with a left hemisphere task, the right hemisphere is specialized for the second task. However, the hemispheres usually work together, and ideas about "right-brained" or "left-brained" general styles have little scientific support.

Evaluating Your Progress. Select the one best response. Answers are on page 61. If you make any errors, reread the relevant material before proceeding.

1. The central nervous system is composed of
   a. the parasympathetic and sympathetic divisions.
   b. the autonomic and somatic divisions.
   c. the brain and spinal cord.
   d. all the nerves outside the brain and spinal cord.

2. The nerves that transmit information to the muscles are part of the
   a. autonomic nervous system.
   b. somatic nervous system.
   c. parasympathetic nervous system.
   d. sympathetic nervous system.

3. To identify the function of an area of the brain you might use all of the following techniques except
   a. damaging the area of interest.
   b. stimulating the area of interest.
   c. doing positron emission tomography (PET).
   d. doing standard magnetic resonance imaging (MRI).

4. Basic life-support systems are controlled by the
   a. forebrain.
   b. midbrain.
   c. hindbrain.
   d. cerebral cortex.

5. The cerebral cortex, limbic system, and hypothalamus are part of the
   a. hindbrain.
   b. midbrain.
   c. forebrain.
   d. tectum.

6. Parkinson's disease patients lack an adequate amount of dopamine due to malfunction of the
   a. substantia nigra of the midbrain.
   b. medulla and pons of the hindbrain.
   c. hypothalamus of the forebrain.
   d. cerebral cortex of the forebrain.

7. Aggression and other motivational and emotional behaviors are controlled by the
   a. thalamus.
   b. reticular formation.
   c. cerebellum.
   d. limbic system.

8. Based on the case of Phineas Gage and other cases of brain damage, we might reasonably conclude that the sense of self or personality is associated with activity in the
   a. frontal lobe.
   b. occipital lobe.
   c. parietal lobe.
   d. temporal lobe.

9. Which statement is true concerning the motor cortex and somatosensory cortex?
   a. The size of a brain area reflects the relative size of the body part controlled by that brain area.
   b. Areas that are near each other on the body are associated with brain areas that are near each other.
   c. The motor cortex is in the parietal lobe, and the somatosensory cortex is in the frontal lobe.
   d. The body's left side is associated with the motor and somatosensory cortex in the left hemisphere.

10. If a picture of a dog is flashed on the far right and a picture of a cat is flashed on the far left, a person whose corpus callosum has been destroyed will
    a. say a cat was presented if asked to respond verbally.
    b. indicate a dog was presented if asked to point to a matching picture with the right hand.
    c. report that a half-dog, half-cat creature was presented if asked to draw the figure with either hand.
    d. be unable to remember what was presented, regardless of the type of response.

11. The concurrent activities paradigm for studying lateralization of brain function is based on the idea that
    a. performance is poorer if tasks are processed in the same hemisphere than in different hemispheres.
    b. response times will be slower if input crosses to another hemisphere for processing.
    c. people are either "right-brained" or "left-brained" in their approach to the world.
    d. split-brain patients provide a unique opportunity to study hemispheric lateralization of function.

12. Most psychologists would agree that
    a. the idea of localization or lateralization of brain function has little scientific support.
    b. localization occurs for functions handled by subcortical structures, but not for cortical functions.
    c. almost all functions are highly localized or lateralized; each brain area works almost independently.
    d. even highly localized or lateralized tasks involve much cooperation between different brain areas.

Regulating Growth and Internal Functions: Extended Communication (pp. 105-108)

Mastering the Vocabulary. Define or explain each of the following terms. To check your answers, consult the text pages listed.

1. endocrine system (p. 105)

2. hormones (p. 105)

3. pituitary gland (p. 105)

Mastering the Concepts. Fill in the blanks to create a summary of this section. Answers are on page 60.

The _____(59) system uses hormones to regulate growth and the internal biological systems. Its activity is more widespread and of longer duration than neural activity. The brain, notably the hypothalamus, controls the "master" endocrine gland, the _____(60), which controls other endocrine glands, including those important for sexual and "fight or flight" behavior. Prenatal sex hormones may affect the brain, and thus, later gender behavior. Adult hormone levels might determine gender differences in some mental tasks.

Evaluating Your Progress. Select the one best response. Answers are found on page 62. If you make any errors, reread the relevant material before proceeding.

1. The "master gland" of the body is the
    a. pituitary gland.
    b. adrenal gland.
    c. ovary or testes.
    d. pineal gland.

2. Actually, the nervous system controls the endocrine system, because the "master gland" is controlled by
    a. the cerebellum.
    b. the hippocampus.
    c. the hypothalamus.
    d. the medulla.

3. The communication system provided by the endocrine system complements that of the nervous system because the actions of the endocrine system are
    a. more localized and more short-term.
    b. more localized and more long-term.
    c. more widespread and more short-term.
    d. more widespread and more long-term.

4. Research on gender differences in behavior has found that high verbal ability is correlated with
    a. high levels of testosterone at the time of testing.
    b. high levels of estrogen at the time of testing.
    c. high levels of epinephrine during the prenatal period of development.
    d. high levels of norepinephrine during the prenatal period of development.

5. In the flight-or-fight response, which adapts the body in threatening situations, epinephrine is released by
    a. the pituitary gland.
    b. the hypothalamus.
    c. the adrenal glands.
    d. ovaries or testes.

Storing and Transmitting the Genetic Code: Influences on Behavior (pp. 108-110)

Mastering the Vocabulary. Define or explain each of the following terms. To check your answers, consult the text pages listed.

1. genes (p. 109)

2. dominant gene (p. 109)

3. recessive gene (p. 109)

4. genotype (p. 109)

5. phenotype (p. 109)

6. family studies (p. 110)

7. twin studies (p. 110)

Mastering the Concepts. Fill in the blanks to create a summary of this section. Answers are on page 60.

The genetic code has two adaptive functions: providing a flexible blueprint for development, and providing for specific, often adaptive, traits to be transmitted to future generations. Humans have 23 pairs of chromosomes which contain the _____ (61) that determine personal traits. _____ (62) genes cause the expression of a trait even if the two genes for the trait differ. A matching pair of genes is needed for the expression of a _____ (63) trait. Most physical traits and behaviors are influenced by a complex interaction of many genes and environmental conditions. _____ (64) studies look for similarities in behavior among blood relatives. Comparisons of traits in identical and fraternal twins raised in same or different environments provide even better data about the genetic component of a trait.

Evaluating Your Progress. Select the one best response. Answers are on page 62. If you make any errors, reread the relevant material before proceeding.

1. A segment of chromosome that contains instructions for the development of a hereditary trait is called
   a. a phenotype.
   b. an efferent.
   c. an afferent.
   d. a gene.

2. To differentiate the genetic and environmental components of schizophrenia, researchers might use
   a. twin studies.
   b. CT scan studies.
   c. concurrent activities studies.
   d. EEG studies.

3. A person's phenotype concerning a genetic trait describes
   a. how many gene pairs determine the trait.
   b. whether the trait is dominant or recessive.
   c. the person's observable characteristics regarding a trait.
   d. the person's specific genetic pattern (AA, Aa, aa) regarding a trait.

4. A trait that is expressed even if the person has only one gene for that trait is called a
   a. dominant trait.
   b. recessive trait.
   c. sex-linked trait.
   d. homozygous trait.

MAKING FINAL PREPARATIONS

Complete these sections without consulting your book or notes. For a more accurate estimate of how well you know this material, wait at least a day or two after studying the chapter before working on the questions. Some of the material you "know" immediately after working with the chapter will be quickly forgotten. Immediate tests will overestimate what you know well.

Short Essay Questions. Write a brief answer to each question. Sample answers are on page 63.

1. Explain how drugs work in the nervous system to cause changes in behavior.

2. Movement can be initiated either by the usual neural pathway or by a spinal reflex. Compare these pathways for removing your hand from a sharp object. Explain a spinal reflex's adaptive value.

3. Describe three general approaches a psychologist might use to study brain functions. Explain how each approach is used to determine structure-function relationships.

4. Imagine your left hemisphere has been removed. Describe and explain at least two effects of this loss.

5. Explain how both long-term and short-term internal communication needs are met.

6. Explain the adaptive nature of the genetic code.

Matching. Select the correct function for each structure. Answers are on page 63.

_____ 1. cerebellum	**a.** allows transfer of information between hemispheres
_____ 2. amygdala	**b.** releases neurotransmitters
_____ 3. hippocampus	**c.** processes touch and temperature input
_____ 4. glial cell	**d.** aids formation of memories
_____ 5. medulla	**e.** regulates basic functions (heart rate, respiration)
_____ 6. axon	**f.** coordinates smooth movements
_____ 7. substantia nigra	**g.** relays sensory information to the cortex
_____ 8. terminal button	**h.** controls cellular metabolism of neuron
_____ 9. reticular formation	**i.** controls other endocrine glands
_____ 10. soma	**j.** receives neural input from a sense organ or neuron
_____ 11. corpus callosum	**k.** controls eating, drinking and sexual behaviors
_____ 12. hypothalamus	**l.** generates and transmits the action potential
_____ 13. thalamus	**m.** produces dopamine
_____ 14. dendrite	**n.** insulates and assists in function of neuron
_____ 15. somatosensory cortex	**o.** controls aggression and motivational behaviors
_____ 16. pituitary	**p.** controls general arousal and consciousness

Multiple Choice Pretest 1. Select the one best response. Answers are on page 64.

1. You just moved your finger. The command to activate the muscles involved came via
    a. motor neurons.
    b. sensory neurons.
    c. glial cells.
    d. hormones.

2. The correct sequence describing the pathway neural information travels is
    a. axon, soma, dendrite, terminal button.
    b. terminal button, axon, soma, dendrite.
    c. dendrite, soma, axon, terminal button.
    d. soma, dendrite, axon, terminal button.

3. The term most closely related to "depolarization" is
    a. inhibition.
    b. refractory period.
    c. resting potential.
    d. action potential.

4. The function of the terminal buttons is
    a. to receive incoming stimulation from another neuron.
    b. to store and release neurotransmitters.
    c. to insulate the neuron to assist transmission.
    d. to move sodium back out of the neuron after firing.

5. If an inhibitory message is passed to a neuron, the neuron will
    a. be hyperpolarized.
    b. be depolarized.
    c. release its neurotransmitters.
    d. stop the sodium-potassium pump.

6. Neurotransmitters affect the permeability of the
    a. axon.
    b. synapse.
    c. myelin sheath.
    d. postsynaptic membrane.

7. Uncle Joe has Alzheimer's disease. The neurotransmitter that has been linked to this disease is
    a. acetylcholine.
    b. serotonin.
    c. dopamine.
    d. endorphin.

8. The medulla, pons, and cerebellum are part of the
    a. hindbrain.
    b. midbrain.
    c. forebrain.
    d. cerebral cortex.

9. Cleo has a disorder of the autonomic nervous system. She is likely to have problems with
    a. controlling movements such as walking.
    b. one or more sensory systems such as vision.
    c. regulating heart rate, digestion, or other internal functions.
    d. thinking or problem solving.

10. Grandpa had a stroke and now has difficulty seeing. His stroke probably damaged the
    a. limbic system.
    b. reticular activating system.
    c. frontal lobe.
    d. occipital lobe.

11. A rat is receiving brain stimulation in the hypothalamus. The least likely thing to be observed is
    a. sexual behavior.
    b. changes in learning or memory.
    c. eating behavior.
    d. hormonal changes.

12. In a "split-brain" operation, the surgeon destroys the
    a. midbrain.
    b. corpus callosum.
    c. cerebral cortex.
    d. reticular formation.

13. A split-brain patient is allowed to examine a key with her left hand but not to see it. The patient will
    a. be able to name the object and to point to it with either hand.
    b. be able to name the object and to point to it with the left hand only.
    c. be unable to name the object but will be able to point to it with either hand.
    d. be unable to name the object but will be able to point to it with the left hand only.

14. A researcher using the concurrent activities paradigm would say hemispheric specialization is adaptive
    a. because it reduces the competition for brain resources when several tasks must be performed.
    b. because it allows input to be processed in the hemisphere it enters first, resulting in faster responses.
    c. because it reduces the chance that brain damage will result in the loss of important functions.
    d. because it allows the person to develop both a creative and an analytical perspective.

15. Coming off the battlefield, the soldiers hearts were racing, and their muscles were tense. This was due to
    a. estrogen.
    b. testosterone.
    c. endorphins.
    d. epinephrine.

16. The trait of red hair is recessive. If you have red hair, you can conclude that you must have
    a. no red hair genes.
    b. only one red hair gene.
    c. at least one (maybe two, but not necessarily) red hair genes.
    d. two red hair genes.

Multiple Choice Pretest 2. Select the one best response. Answers are on page 65.

1. Myelin is associated with
   a. inhibitory neurotransmitters.
   b. excitatory neurotransmitters.
   c. rapid neural transmission.
   d. the dendrites.

2. When sodium ions flow into the neuron
   a. hyperpolarization occurs.
   b. depolarization occurs.
   c. a resting potential is established.
   d. the refractory period ends.

3. The adaptive value of the resting potential is that it
   a. allows quick response to stimulation.
   b. protects the cell from over-stimulation.
   c. slows neurotransmitter loss.
   d. inhibits nearby neurons.

4. The midbrain and thalamus are both important for
   a. regulating basic body functions such as heart rate.
   b. relaying and processing sensory input.
   c. controlling sexual behavior.
   d. controlling hormone production in the pituitary.

5. Parkinson's disease symptoms are reduced by a drug that increases the level of
   a. acetylcholine.
   b. epinephrine.
   c. serotonin.
   d. dopamine.

6. Alzheimer's disease involves serious memory disorders. This suggests that Alzheimer's disease affects
   a. the medulla and pons.
   b. the tectum.
   c. the hippocampus.
   d. the cerebellum.

7. Tia's smooth, coordinated gymnastic movements are primarily the result of her well-functioning
   a. temporal lobe.
   b. cerebellum.
   c. limbic system.
   d. tectum.

8. To reduce the aggressive behavior of a wolverine, which limbic system structure should be lesioned?
   a. the hippocampus.
   b. the superior colliculus.
   c. the substantia nigra.
   d. the amygdala.

9. Damage to the reticular formation will most directly affect
   a. eating behavior.
   b. speech and language.
   c. thought and reason.
   d. consciousness and arousal.

10. Grandma's stroke damaged Wernicke's area of the left temporal lobe. She is most likely to experience
    a. problems moving the left half of her body.
    b. major personality changes.
    c. a reduce sense of touch.
    d. difficulty understanding spoken language.

11. Dr. Sperry stimulated the patient's brain and her mouth moved. Based on the topographic organization of the brain, if she is stimulated slightly to one side of the first spot, we should expect her to
    a. say something.
    b. report seeing a spot of light.
    c. twitch her cheek.
    d. report tasting something.

12. When Dr. Sperry caused the patient's mouth to move, he probably was stimulating cells in the
    a. temporal lobe.
    b. occipital lobe.
    c. parietal lobe.
    d. frontal lobe.

13. When the parasympathetic nervous system is activated
    a. sensory neurons increase their firing rate.
    b. most activity occurs in the form of spinal reflexes.
    c. heart rate and blood pressure are reduced.
    d. the body is readying itself for action.

14. Some data links "tomboy" behavior (rough and tumble play) in girls to
    a. prenatal exposure to testosterone.
    b. prenatal exposure to estrogen.
    c. early childhood (age 6) exposure to epinephrine.
    d. early childhood (age 6) exposure to pituitary growth hormone.

15. Curly hair is a dominant trait controlled by a single gene pair. If Tom has curly hair we know that
    a. both of Tom's parents have curly hair.
    b. at least one of Tom's parents has curly hair.
    c. it is possible that neither of Tom's parents have curly hair.
    d. None of the above. No conclusions are possible based on the information given.

16. If identical twins differ significantly in some trait, researchers would conclude the trait is determined by
    a. the environment.
    b. a dominant gene.
    c. a recessive gene.
    d. more than one pair of genes.

17. Studies of brain activity show that stimulus characteristics are coded in the nervous system in terms of the pattern of activity across many neurons rather than the activity profile of just one. In neural network computer programs this principle is called
    a. connectedness.
    b. robustness.
    c. distributed representation.
    d. generalization.

ANSWERS AND EXPLANATIONS

Mastering the Concepts

1. brain (p. 72)	17. axon (p. 75)	33. networks (p. 83)	49. hypothalamus (p. 94)
2. brain (p. 73)	18. terminal buttons (p. 75)	34. distributed (p. 84)	50. limbic system (p. 95)
3. spinal cord (p. 73)	19. synapse (p. 75)	35. central (p. 86)	51. memories (p. 95)
4. peripheral (p. 73)	20. resting potential (p. 76)	36. peripheral (p. 86)	52. frontal (p. 97)
5. coordinate (p. 73)	21. depolarization (p. 77)	37. afferent (p. 86)	53. parietal (p. 97)
6. growth (p. 73)	22. hyperpolarization (p. 77)	38. efferent (p. 86)	54. temporal (p. 98)
7. genetic (p. 73)	23. action potential (p. 77)	39. somatic (p. 86)	55. left (p. 99)
8. Neurons (p. 74)	24. all or none (p. 78)	40. autonomic (p. 86)	56. corpus callosum (p. 100)
9. Sensory (p. 74)	25. breaks (p. 74)	41. brain damage (p. 87)	57. spatial (p. 101)
10. Interneurons (p. 74)	26. dopamine (p. 80)	42. hindbrain (p. 92)	58. concurrent (p. 102)
11. Motor (p. 74)	27. agonists (p. 80)	43. forebrain (p. 94)	59. endocrine (p. 105)
12. glial cells (p. 74)	28. antagonists (p. 81)	44. medulla (p. 93)	60. pituitary (p. 105)
13. myelin (p. 74)	29. Endorphins (p. 81)	45. cerebellum (p. 93)	61. genes (p. 109)
14. reflex (p. 74)	30. pattern (p. 83)	46. Parkinson's (p. 94)	62. Dominant (p. 109)
15. Dendrites (p. 74)	31. firing rate (p. 83)	47. cerebral cortex (p. 94)	63. recessive (p. 109)
16. soma (p. 75)	32. refractory (p. 83)	48. sensory (p. 94)	64. Family (p. 110)

Evaluating Your Progress

Preview & Communicating Internally: Connecting World and Brain

1. **b** (p. 74)	a. Wrong.	Motor neurons link the brain or spinal cord with the muscles and glands.
	c. Wrong.	Glial cells (aren't neurons!) fill space and perform "housekeeping" duties for neurons.
	d. Wrong.	Interneurons link other neurons only and have no contact with the world.

2. **d** (p. 74)	a. Wrong.	The cell body receives input from the dendrites and contains the cell's nucleus.
	b. Wrong.	Axons transmit the impulse from the cell body to the next neuron or body organ.
	c. Wrong.	Terminal buttons are located at the end of the axons and contain neurotransmitters.

3. **a** (p. 75)	b. Wrong.	This is the opposite order. Sensory neurons receive input from the environment.
	c. Wrong.	The brain is not involved in a spinal reflex.
	d. Wrong.	Motor neurons are last, and the brain is not involved in a spinal reflex.

4. **a** (p. 76)	b. Wrong.	Neurotransmitters are released when the cell is active, not resting.
	c. Wrong.	Depolarization creates the action potential, not resting potential.
	d. Wrong.	The resting potential is present when the neuron is inactive and not being stimulated.

5. **c**   a. Wrong.   For a given neuron, the action potential is the same magnitude for all stimuli.
(p. 78)   b. Wrong.   For a given neuron, the action potential has the same speed for all stimuli.
             d. Wrong.   Only one is correct.

6. **c**   a. Wrong.   Interneurons are cells, not spaces.
(p. 75)   b. Wrong.   The soma is the part of the neuron that contains the cell nucleus.
             d. Wrong.   Glial cells (not glial area) are cells, not spaces.

7. **d**   a. Wrong.   Interneurons are a type of neuron, not a structure in the synapse.
(p. 78)   b. Wrong.   The myelin sheath is an insulating wrap on the axon.
             c. Wrong.   The sodium-potassium pump maintains the ion distribution in the neuron.

8. **c**   a. Wrong.   A shortage of acetylcholine is associated with memory loss in Alzheimer's disease.
(p. 80)   b. Wrong.   Endorphins are substances produced by the brain that mimic the action of morphine.
             d. Wrong.   Serotonin is associated with sleep, depression, and other mental disorders.

9. **b**   a. Wrong.   Neurotransmitters are specific to a neuron, not to a stimulus characteristic.
(p. 83)   c. Wrong.   A refractory period is a time in which neurons can't fire, not a code for a stimulus.
             d. Wrong.   Neural transmission speed is determined by the neuron, not the stimulus.

10. **c**   a. Wrong.   Connectedness links different units so that activating one affects others' activation.
(p. 84)   b. Wrong.   Reproducibility is the ability to recognize the concept even if the input changes.
             d. Wrong.   Weighted refers to the strengths of the connections in the network.

Initiating and Coordinating Behavior: A Division of Labor

1. **c**   a. Wrong.   The parasympathetic and sympathetic systems are in the peripheral nervous system.
(p. 86)   b. Wrong.   The autonomic and somatic systems are in the peripheral nervous system.
             d. Wrong.   The peripheral nervous system contains the nerves outside the brain and spinal cord.

2. **b**   a. Wrong.   The autonomic nervous system controls basic bodily functions, not movements.
(p. 86)   c. Wrong.   The parasympathetic nervous system returns the body to normal after emergencies.
             d. Wrong.   The sympathetic nervous system activates the body to deal with emergencies.

3. **d**   a. Wrong.   Looking for changes in behavior after brain damage is used to identify an area's function.
(pp. 90-91) b. Wrong.   Observing behavior during brain stimulation is used to identify an area's function.
             c. Wrong.   PET indicates brain activity and is used to identify an area's function.

4. **c**   a. Wrong.   The forebrain controls movement, motivation, emotion, and aspects of thought.
(p. 92)   b. Wrong.   The midbrain contains neural relay stations, particularly for sensory information.
             d. Wrong.   The cerebral cortex is part of the forebrain and controls higher mental processes.

5. **c**   a. Wrong.   The hindbrain contains the medulla, pons, and cerebellum.
(p. 94)   b. Wrong.   The midbrain contains the tectum structures and substantia nigra.
             d. Wrong.   The tectum is part of the midbrain and contains sensory structures.

6. **a**   b. Wrong.   The medulla and pons control breathing, respiration, and other life support systems.
(p. 94)   c. Wrong.   The hypothalamus is involved in eating, drinking, temperature, and sexual behavior.
             d. Wrong.   The cerebral cortex in involved in higher mental processes.

7. **d**   a. Wrong.   The thalamus is a major sensory center.
(p. 95)   b. Wrong.   The reticular formation controls general arousal and consciousness.
             c. Wrong.   The cerebellum is responsible for smooth, coordinated movements.

8. **a**   b. Wrong. The occipital lobe is responsible for visual processing.
(p. 97) c. Wrong. The parietal lobe is responsible for the skin senses and higher visual processes.
        d. Wrong. The temporal lobe is responsible for auditory processing and aspects of language.

9. **b**   a. Wrong. A body part's sensitivity or control, not its size, predicts the size of the related brain area.
(p. 97) c. Wrong. The motor cortex is in the frontal lobe, and the somatosensory cortex is in the parietal lobe.
        d. Wrong. The body's left side is associated with the cortex in the right hemisphere.

10. **b**   a. Wrong. Items on the left go to the right hemisphere, which cannot respond verbally.
(pp. 99-100) c. Wrong. Depending on the hand used, a dog or a cat would be drawn; information doesn't merge.
        d. Wrong. Memory is not damaged by cutting the corpus callosum.

11. **a**   b. Wrong. Concurrent activities paradigm stresses competition for resources, not transfer time.
(p. 102) c. Wrong. This is a popular (and probably mistaken) idea, but it doesn't relate to the concurrent
                 activities paradigm's assumption about resource competition.
        d. Wrong. Concurrent activities paradigm is a technique used with intact, not split, brains.

12. **d**   a. Wrong. Data support localization / lateralization of function (not "right-brained/"left-brained"
(pp. 101-104)   style.)
        b. Wrong. Cortical functions are at least as lateralized or localized as sub-cortical functions.
        c. Wrong. Data support cooperative processes in addition to some localization of function.

Regulating Growth and Internal Functions: Extended Communication

1. **a**   b. Wrong. Adrenal hormones energize the body for action, but don't control other glands.
(p. 105) c. Wrong. The ovaries and testes produce sex hormones, but don't control other glands.
        d. Wrong. The pineal gland in involved with biological cycles, but doesn't control other glands.

2. **c**   a. Wrong. The cerebellum is involved in coordination of movement, not endocrine control.
(p. 105) b. Wrong. The hippocampus is responsible for memory functions, not endocrine control.
        d. Wrong. The medulla controls life-support functions like hear rate, not the endocrine system.

3. **d**   a. Wrong. Endocrine system effects are more widespread and longer-term.
(p. 105) b. Wrong. Endocrine system effects are more widespread, not localized.
        c. Wrong. Endocrine system effects are longer-term,

4. **b**   a. Wrong. Testosterone (male hormone) has been linked to spatial skill, in which men excel.
(p. 106) c. Wrong. Prenatal sex hormones, not epinephrine, may be linked to behavioral gender effects.
        d. Wrong. Prenatal sex hormones, not norepinephrine, may be linked to gender effects.

5. **c**   a. Wrong. The pituitary doesn't secrete epinephrine; it stimulates the adrenal glands to do so.
(p. 106) b. Wrong. The hypothalamus doesn't secrete epinephrine; it stimulates the pituitary, which stimulates
                 the adrenal glands to do so.
        d. Wrong. The ovaries and testes secrete sex hormones (estrogen, testosterone), not epinephrine.

Storing and Transmitting the Genetic Code: Genetic Influences on Behavior

1. **d**   a. Wrong. A phenotype is a person's observable characteristic, such as eye color.
(p. 109) b. Wrong. Efferent refers to a neural pathway carrying information away from the brain.
        c. Wrong. Afferent refers to a neural pathway carrying information to the brain.

2. **a**   b. Wrong. CT scans would examine brain structure, not genetic or environmental determinants.
(p. 110) c. Wrong. Concurrent activities studies examine lateralization, not genetic vs. environmental factors.
        d. Wrong. EEGs represent brain activity, but cannot differentiate genetic and environmental factors.

3. **c**   a. Wrong.   Phenotypes describe the observable characteristics of a trait, not the number of genes.
  (p. 109)   b. Wrong.   Phenotypes describe the observable characteristics of a trait, not dominant/recessive.
             d. Wrong.   The specific genetic pattern is described by the genotype.

4. **a**   b. Wrong.   Recessive traits are expressed only if both genes are recessive.
  (p. 109)   c. Wrong.   Sex-linked traits are on the X sex chromosome and require 2 genes if the person is female.
             d. Wrong.   Homozygous refers to a genotype, not how a trait is transmitted.

MAKING FINAL PREPARATIONS

Short Essay Questions

1. Drugs act like natural neurotransmitters (agonists), by increasing the effectiveness of natural neurotransmitters (neuromodulators), or by blocking neurotransmitter activity (antagonists). The behavioral effects will depend on the specific combinations of inhibition and excitation of the nervous system. (pp. 78-80)

2. In the usual pathway, sensory input about the object is carried via sensory neurons to the spinal cord and then to the brain. The brain initiates commands to move which are carried via motor neurons to the spinal cord and the muscles. In a spinal reflex the sensory input is carried by sensory neurons to the spinal cord. Commands to move are initiated in the spinal cord (without involving the brain) and carried to the muscles by motor neurons. The spinal reflex allows more rapid responses because input does not have to travel all the way to and from the brain. This is advantageous in dangerous situations. (p. 74)

3. Brain functions are studied by damaging, recording, or stimulating the brain. The function of a brain area is inferred based on changes in behavior after brain damage, or based on changes in that area's level of activity during a particular behavior, or when a change in behavior occurs when that area is stimulated. (pp. 87-91)

4. Because the left hemisphere controls language in most people, I would lose the ability to use and comprehend speech. Sensory input from the right side of the body and right visual field is handled in the left hemisphere, so I would lose sight, touch, temperature, and pain information from the right. The left hemisphere controls movement on the right side of the body, so I'd be paralyzed in my right arm and leg. (pp. 100-102)

5. The nervous system allows short-term communication needs through neural transmission. Neural transmission is rapid, localized, and brief in duration. It allows communication of detail. Longer term and less localized communication is provided by the endocrine system, under the direction of the nervous system. Here, hormones circulate in the bloodstream, producing widespread and longer lasting effects. The endocrine system handles communication that is not immediate and involves more extended periods of time. (p. 105)

6. The genetic code is adaptive because it provides a way to transmit traits to future generations. Traits that increase the likelihood of survival tend to remain in the genetic code due to natural selection, so future generations will tend to accumulate adaptive traits. Also, the random selection of the genes during formation of eggs and sperm produces diversity and ensures that some members of the species will have traits necessary for survival. (p. 109)

Matching

1. **f** (p. 93)	4. **n** (p. 74)	7. **m** (p. 93)	10. **h** (p. 75)	13. **g** (p. 94)	16. **i** (p. 105)
2. **o** (p. 95)	5. **e** (p. 93)	8. **b** (p. 75)	11. **a** (p. 100)	14. **j** (p. 74)	
3. **d** (p. 95)	6. **l** (p. 75)	9. **p** (p. 93)	12. **k** (p. 94)	15. **c** (p. 97)	

Multiple Choice Pretest 1

1. **a**
   (p. 74)
   - b. Wrong. Sensory neurons carry input from the sensory organs to the brain.
   - c. Wrong. Glial cells do not transmit impulses. They provide support services to neurons.
   - d. Wrong. Hormones do not transmit movement commands to the muscles.

2. **c**
   (p. 75)
   - a. Wrong. The axon is not the first structure. Dendrite--soma--axon--terminal button.
   - b. Wrong. The terminal button is the last structure. Dendrite--soma--axon--terminal button.
   - d. Wrong. The soma is not the first structure. Dendrite--soma--axon--terminal button.

3. **d**
   (p. 77)
   - a. Wrong. Inhibition would be related to hyperpolarization.
   - b. Wrong. The refractory period is the time after a neural impulse when the cell can't fire again.
   - c. Wrong. The resting potential is the charge present in the neuron when at rest, not when firing.

4. **b**
   (p. 75)
   - a. Wrong. The dendrite receives incoming stimulation, not the terminal buttons.
   - c. Wrong. The myelin insulates some neurons.
   - d. Wrong. The sodium-potassium pump moves sodium out of the cell.

5. **a**
   (p. 77)
   - b. Wrong. Excitatory activity causes depolarization.
   - c. Wrong. Hyperpolarization prevents neural firing, so no neurotransmitters are released.
   - d. Wrong. The Na-K pump does not vary in speed.

6. **d**
   (p. 79)
   - a. Wrong. Neurotransmitter generally contact the dendrites, not the axon.
   - b. Wrong. The synapse is a fluid-filled space between neurons. There is no membrane.
   - c. Wrong. The myelin sheath insulates the axon and is not influenced by neurotransmitters.

7. **a**
   (p. 80)
   - b. Wrong. Serotonin is important in sleep and some psychological disorders, but not Alzheimer's.
   - c. Wrong. Dopamine is associated with schizophrenia and Parkinson's disease, not Alzheimer's.
   - d. Wrong. Endorphins are morphine-like substances, not a factor in Alzheimer's.

8. **a**
   (p. 93)
   - b. Wrong. The midbrain contains the structures of the tectum and the substantia nigra.
   - c. Wrong. The forebrain contains the cerebral cortex, hypothalamus and limbic system.
   - d. Wrong. The cerebral cortex is part of the forebrain. The medulla, etc. are in the hindbrain.

9. **c**
   (p. 86)
   - a. Wrong. Movement is controlled by the somatic and central nervous systems.
   - b. Wrong. Sensation is controlled by the somatic and central nervous systems.
   - d. Wrong. Thinking or problem solving is controlled by the central nervous system.

10. **d**
    (p. 98)
    - a. Wrong. The limbic system is involved with motivational and emotional behaviors.
    - b. Wrong. The reticular activating system controls arousal and consciousness.
    - c. Wrong. Frontal lobe damage would involve personality, movement, or thinking, more likely.

11. **b**
    (p. 94)
    - a. Wrong. The hypothalamus is important for sexual behavior.
    - c. Wrong. The hypothalamus is important for eating and hunger.
    - d. Wrong. The hypothalamus controls the pituitary, the "master gland."

12. **b**
    (p. 100)
    - a. Wrong. The midbrain doesn't connect the hemispheres, the corpus callosum does.
    - c. Wrong. The cortex is not destroyed, only the corpus callosum that links the hemispheres.
    - d. Wrong. The reticular formation doesn't connect the hemispheres, the corpus callosum does.

13. **d**
    (p. 100)
    - a. Wrong. Input will go to the right hemisphere, with no speech or control of right hand.
    - b. Wrong. Input will go to the right hemisphere, with no speech.
    - c. Wrong. Input will go to the right hemisphere, which doesn't control the right hand.

14. **a**   b. Wrong.   Input for a left (or right) hemisphere task can't always originate on that side, transfer is very
   (p. 102)   rapid, and the concurrent activities paradigm stresses competition for resources.
         c. Wrong.   If hemispheric specialization of a task is strong damage to that hemisphere will increase the
                     loss of function. Plus, the concurrent activities paradigm stresses resource competition.
         d. Wrong.   Specialization is not necessary for this, and the concurrent activities paradigm stresses
                     resource competition.

15. **d**   a. Wrong.   Estrogen is a female sex hormone, not a fight-or-flight adrenal hormone.
   (p. 106) b. Wrong.   Testosterone is a male sex hormone, not a fight-or-flight adrenal hormone.
         c. Wrong.   Endorphins cause reduced pain, not a fight-or-flight response.

16. **d**   a. Wrong.   Two dominant (non-red hair) genes produce the dominant trait (non-red hair).
   (p. 109) b. Wrong.   Recessive traits appear only if both genes are the recessive (red hair) type.
         c. Wrong.   One recessive (red hair) gene will not produce the recessive trait. It takes two.

Multiple Choice Pretest 2

1. **c**   a, b, & d.   Wrong.   Myelin is an insulating substance on the axon that helps speed neural
   (p. 78)   transmission.

2. **b**   a. Wrong.   Hyperpolarization occurs if more sodium is pushed out or chloride comes in.
   (p. 77) c. Wrong.   Sodium flowing in causes an action potential, not a resting potential.
         d. Wrong.   The refractory period ends when a period of time passes since the last impulse.

3. **a**   b. Wrong.   The resting potential is the charge of the neuron at rest, and unrelated to protection.
   (p. 77) c. Wrong.   The resting potential is the charge of the neuron at rest, not a neurotransmitter issue.
         d. Wrong.   Activity inhibits other neurons, not the charge of the neuron at rest (resting potential).

4. **b**   a. Wrong.   The medulla and pons control basic functions like heart rate.
   (pp. 93-94) c Wrong.   The hypothalamus or other limbic system structures control sexual behavior.
         d. Wrong.   The hypothalamus control the pituitary.

5. **d**   a, b, & c.   Wrong.   Parkinson's disease is due to a deficiency of dopamine.
   (p. 80)

6. **c**   a. Wrong.   The medulla and pons control basic functions like breathing and blood pressure.
   (p. 95) b. Wrong.   The tectum of the midbrain is important for sensory pathways.
         d. Wrong.   The cerebellum controls coordination of movements.

7. **b**   a. Wrong.   The temporal lobe is important for auditory functions. Coordination is cerebellar.
   (p. 93) c. Wrong.   The limbic system is involved with motivation and emotion, not coordination.
         d. Wrong.   The tectum contains sensory centers important for responding to sensory events.

8. **d**   a. Wrong.   The hippocampus is involved with memory, not aggression.
   (p. 95) b. Wrong.   The superior colliculus is a sensory area in the midbrain.
         c. Wrong.   The substantia nigra is the midbrain area responsible for dopamine production.

9. **d**   a. Wrong.   The reticular formation controls general arousal; the hypothalamus is linked to eating.
   (p. 93) b. Wrong.   The reticular formation controls general arousal; the cortex controls language.
         c. Wrong.   The reticular formation controls general arousal; the cortex controls thought.

10.	**d**	a.	Wrong.	Wernicke's area doesn't control movement, and the left hemisphere controls the *right* side.
	(p. 87)	b.	Wrong.	Personality changes are associated with frontal lobe damage.
		c.	Wrong.	Touch sensations are processed in the somatosensory cortex of the parietal lobe.

11.	**c**	a.	Wrong.	Speech and movement aren't as closely linked in the brain as movements of nearby areas.
	(p. 97)	b.	Wrong.	Visual functions are not near motor functions in the brain.
		d.	Wrong.	Body part and related functions are not necessarily nearby in the brain.

| 12. | **d** | a, b, & c. | Wrong. | Movement is controlled by the motor cortex of the frontal lobe. |
| | (p. 97) | | | |

13.	**c**	a.	Wrong.	Sensory neurons are not part of, nor affected by, the parasympathetic system.
	(p. 86)	b.	Wrong.	Spinal reflexes are "hardwired" systems that are not affected by autonomic nervous system.
		d.	Wrong.	Activation of the *sympathetic* nervous system produces the "fight or flight" reaction.

14.	**a**	b.	Wrong.	Estrogen is a female hormone and would facilitate normal "female" development.
	(p. 107)	c.	Wrong.	Epinephrine is an adrenal hormone with general activation, not sexual, effects.
		d.	Wrong.	Pituitary growth hormone controls bone growth and is normally present in childhood.

15.	**b**	a.	Wrong.	With a dominant trait, only one dominant gene (from one parent) is needed.
	(p. 109)	c.	Wrong.	If neither have straight hair, neither have a straight hair gene to pass on to Tom.
		d.	Wrong.	Dominant traits appear any time the dominant gene is present, so we know at least one parent has the gene and straight hair because Tom has straight hair, and thus, the gene.

| 16. | **a** | b, c, & d. | Wrong. | Identical twins have the same genes, so if traits differ, they are not caused by genes. |
| | (p. 110) | | | |

17.	**c**	a.	Wrong.	Connectedness is the activation of other units by activation of one.
	(p. 84)	b.	Wrong.	Robustness is the ability to function even if somewhat damaged.
		d.	Wrong.	Generalization is the ability to function if input is only similar to the original input.

LANGUAGE ENHANCEMENT GUIDE

CORE TERMS

In the lectures on this chapter, there are a few terms you are almost certain to hear. The first is *physiology*, the study of how a part of the body works. There are two ways to study body parts: you can look at their *structure* (their cells or how they are put together) or their *function* (what the parts do). Your instructor will probably cover both structure and function for each of the *anatomical features* (brain parts) discussed. The discussion will range all the way from the *grossest* structures (meaning the largest) to the *finest* (smallest), from whole sections of the brain to the inner workings of individual brain cells. To help keep things straight and make learning easier, you might use the Concept Summary Table on page 96 as a framework and add other information about the structure and function of the brain that you get from lectures. A similar table could be created for the cortex by itself, because there is a lot of material on that part alone.

You may be surprised by the number of ways psychologists have found to describe the brain, some of which seem to be in conflict with the others. The nervous system is a *hierarchy*, a strictly organized system with definite divisions and subdivisions, but organizing its functions is not that simple. The discussion of the functions of each *hemisphere* (half) of the brain will probably include the terms *lateralized* (found in only one of the halves) and *localized* (found in one specific area). Some functions seem to be controlled by a specific brain region. At the same time, other functions may be described as *diffuse* (spread among several locations). You also need to keep in mind the *malleability* and *plasticity* of the brain. Both of these terms mean that the brain is somewhat flexible in how it works, and can change some aspects of its functioning if necessary.

IDIOMS

72	"designer" drugs	illegal drugs made in home labs, especially drugs that are somewhat different from more common "street drugs"
79	dozens	many; several groups of 12 (a dozen is an old English word for 12)
80	maintain posture	stand upright steadily
80	a mimicking of	behaving just like; seeming just like
80	modulating	controlling the effects of; keeping an effect from being too extreme
82	rudimentary	basic, simple, elementary
82	by no means clearly established	not yet made clear; still being investigated
83	tapped briefly into	gotten a quick look into
86	via	by way of
88	capitalizing on	making use of
90	gross electrical activity	a general picture of the electrical activity throughout the brain
90	global	overall, throughout the whole thing
90	pictorial blueprint	a picture that maps out the parts in great detail
98	fine motor control	ability to move very small muscles in precise ways (such as facial or hand muscles)
101	personal anecdotes anecdotal reports	stories told by individuals of unusual experiences; reports of events that scientists have not heard from many people
103	holistic rather than analytic	tending to experience something as a whole, rather than analyzing the individual parts of the experience
111	try to disentangle the relative contributions of	try to figure out which of two or more elements have contributed more

WORD PARTS

Here are some words that are made up of word parts, and that you can find in this chapter. After you've looked at these, you can look for others in the chapter that use the same word parts (they are there, but YOU have to find them!)

WORD	WORD PART IT USES	MEANING
transmission	trans = across mit, mis = to send	sending something across
peripheral	peri = around	around the edges
hemispheric	hemi, demi, semi = half sphere = ball-shaped	having to do with half of a spherical object
receptor	re = again cept, cieve = to take	that which receives or takes back
ingest	in = in, into, within gest = to take in, to hold inside	to eat or otherwise take in
degenerate	de = down, from, away gen = birth, race, kind	to become worse than when it began
depolarize	de = down, from, away polar = opposite ends	to reduce the differences between opposite ends

Knowing the word parts listed above, you can also create the following words. You can get an idea of their meanings from the word parts they use. You fill in the blanks!

genetic	gen	_____
hyperpolarize	_____ + _____	to increase the differences between two opposites (hint - hyper means overly or excessive)
remit	re + mit	_____
gestate	_____	to incubate, to grow inside something
repolarize	re + polar	_____
genius	_____	one who creates a new idea
reception	re + cept	_____

CHAPTER 4: HUMAN DEVELOPMENT

ESTABLISHING LEARNING OBJECTIVES

Use these learning objectives as a preview of the chapter, a guide for active reading, and to evaluate your mastery of the material. Review the relevant objectives as you begin and end your reading of each major section of the chapter.

I.   Solve the adaptive problem of how the individual develops physically from a fertilized egg to an adult.
    A. Describe the physical changes that occur during prenatal development.
        1. Discuss the factors that influence or disrupt prenatal development.
    B   Describe growth during infancy and childhood.
        1. Discuss the influence of "nature" and "nurture" on the development of motor skills.
    C. Describe the physical changes that occur during adolescence.
    D. Describe the essential characteristics of the aging body and brain.
        1. Describe the physical and mental changes associated with menopause.
        2. Describe the neural changes in the brain and how they relate to behavioral changes.

II.   Solve the adaptive problem of how individuals develop the intellectual skills needed to deal effectively with the constantly changing circumstances encountered throughout life.
    A. Describe the tools that are used to study infant perception and memory.
    B. Discuss the perceptual capabilities of an infant.
    C. Describe the characteristics of memory loss in the elderly.
    D. Describe and evaluate Piaget's theory of cognitive development.
        1. Discuss the characteristics of each stage of cognitive development and the mechanisms of change.
        2. Discuss the recent criticism of Piaget's theory of cognitive development.
    E. Describe and evaluate Kohlberg's theory of moral development.
        1. Describe the reasoning found in the preconventional, conventional, and postconventional stages.
        2. Evaluate Kohlberg's theory in terms of its general approach and its applicability to all cultures.

III. Solve the adaptive problem of how individuals form the social relationships and a personal identity.
    A. Discuss the short-term characteristics and long-term consequences of early attachments.
        1. Describe the artificial mother research and how it relates to humans.
        2. Identify three types of attachment, and describe their long-terms consequences.
        3. Describe specific cross-cultural differences in children's behavior, and explain their causes.
        4. Discuss the impact of child care on social and intellectual development.
    B. Describe Erik Erikson's theory of personal identity development.
        1. Describe the personal crises characteristic of each stage, and explain their importance.
        2. Evaluate Erikson's theory.
    C. Discuss gender role development and the role of the family in adult development.
    D. Discuss the social and psychological factors faced by the elderly and the psychological issues connected with death and dying.
        1. Discuss ageism.
        2. Describe Kubler-Ross' stages of confronting death.

MASTERING THE MATERIAL

Preview & Developing Physically (pp. 118-128)

Mastering the Vocabulary. Define or explain each of the following terms. To check your answers, consult the text pages listed.

1. development (p. 118)

2. zygote (p. 120)

3. germinal period (p. 120)

4. embryonic period (p. 120)

5. fetal period (p. 120)

6. teratogen (p. 122)

7. puberty (p. 126)

8. menopause (p. 127)

9. dementia (p. 128)

Mastering the Concepts. Fill in the blanks to create a summary of this section. Answers are on page 87.

_____(1) is the age-related change in behavior and physical features that occurs over time. Developmental psychologists consider development to be due to the _____(2) of biological and environmental factors. Development is adaptive; it solves practical problems and allows for the _____(3) necessary to deal with a changing environment. This chapter involves three adaptive problems: How does the individual adapt _____(4), _____(5), and socially or personally?

Physical development begins with the formation of the single-cell _____(6) at conception. Not all survive the two-week _____(7) period and implant in the uterus. During the six-week _____(8) period the cells develop into a more recognizable structure and sexual differentiation occurs. From the eighth week until birth, the _____(9) period, development continues. Development can be disrupted if the mother exposes the developing child to _____(10), environmental agents that harm development. Alcohol use can lead to _____(11) syndrome. Structures have critical periods of susceptibility to teratogens, but exposure at any time can be dangerous.

Although only 25% of its adult weight at birth, brain growth involves development of branches and interconnections, not increased numbers of neurons. _____(12) allows the brain to respond to environmental influences. Development of the nervous system occurs in a _____(13) fashion and produces a predictable sequence of motor development whose timing may be modified by the environment. Growth slows during early childhood, and increases again at _____(14) when the release of estrogen or androgen initiates a growth spurt accompanied by _____(15) development. Age at puberty varies with sex and environment.

After age 20, a gradual _____(16) in physical condition begins. Women reach _____(17) at about age 50, and men may lose some reproductive capacity. The brain loses cells, and by age 80, Alzheimer's disease or other types of _____(18), may appear. However, cell loss might be offset by adaptation of other cells to compensate and maintain function.

Evaluating Your Progress. Select the one best response. Answers are on page 87. If you make any errors, reread the relevant material before proceeding.

1. The fertilized egg is called the
    a. embryo.
    b. fetus.
    c. zygote.
    d. teratogen.

2. Sexual differentiation, the development of the sexual reproductive system, occurs during the
    a. early germinal period.
    b. middle of the germinal period.
    c. late embryonic period.
    d. late fetal period.

3. The structures that are most likely to be affected by a teratogen are those that
    a. develop first (nervous system and heart).
    b. are undergoing initial development when the teratogen is present.
    c. have just completed their initial development when the teratogen is present.
    d. would be affected by the teratogen in adulthood (alcohol--liver).

4. The brain grows dramatically in size from birth to age 2 due to
   a. a rapid increase in the number of neurons present.
   b. a rapid growth of blood vessels within the brain.
   c. the development of the ventricles, fluid filled spaces found in the normal adult brain.
   d. the increase in the number of glial cells and the complexity of the neurons.

5. Prenatal development sets down basic neural circuitry, but environmental factors influence final circuitry. This describes the principle of
   a. schemata.
   b. habituation.
   c. critical periods.
   d. plasticity.

6. Neural development and thus, motor development, progresses
   a. in a top-down sequence.
   b. in a bottom-up sequence.
   c. in an outside-in sequence.
   d. in no predictable direction.

7. The developmental period during which individuals mature sexually is called
   a. menarche.
   b. puberty.
   c. the climacteric.
   d. menopause.

8. The age of the onset of puberty has decreased 3-4 years in the last century, probably due to
   a. changes in the genetic makeup of people today.
   b. poor diets that are high in junk foods.
   c. the emphasis on strenuous daily exercise and sports.
   d. improved medical care and living conditions.

9. Research on the speed of processing and reaction time in cognitive tasks suggests that processing
   a. slows from about age 20 to age 80.
   b. slows from about age 20 to age 40, then stays about the same until age 80.
   c. speeds up from about age 20 to age 80.
   d. speeds up from abut age 20 to age 40, then stays about the same until age 80.

Developing Intellectually (pp. 129-145)

Mastering the Vocabulary. Define or explain each of the following terms. To check your answers, consult the text pages listed.

1. preference technique (p. 130)

2. habituation (p. 130)

3. cross sectional design (p. 133)

4. longitudinal design (p. 133)

5. schemata (p. 135)

6. assimilation (p. 135)

7. accommodation (p. 135)

8. sensorimotor period (p. 136)

9. object permanence (p. 137)

10. preoperational period (p. 137)

11. conservation (p.137)

12. centration (p. 138)

13. egocentrism (p. 138)

14. concrete operational period (p. 138)

15. formal operational period (p. 140)

16. relativistic thinking (p. 142)

17. morality (p. 143)

18. preconventional level (p. 143)

19. conventional level (p. 144)

20. postconventional level (p. 144)

Mastering the Concepts. Fill in the blanks to create a summary of this section. Answers are on page 87.

Infants' limited ability to respond makes infant perception research difficult, but three characteristics of infants are useful: they show _____(19); they notice _____(20); and they can _____(21) to make a simple response. In the _____(22) technique, looking at one stimulus longer than another suggests that the infant can tell the two stimuli are different. Another method for testing an infant's ability to remember or discriminate stimuli is to use the _____(23) technique, repeating a stimulus until the infant quits responding (habituates), then changing to a new stimulus and noting whether the infant responds to it. Also, by rewarding a simple response such as sucking or kicking, those responses can be used in research.

The infant's perceptual system is immature, but it functions well. All senses are operational. Adaptive capabilities, such as recognizing the mother by _____(24), are particularly sophisticated. Their acuity is poor, but "visual cliff" experiments show infants perceive _____(25). In general, their perceptual systems need to be fine-tuned by maturation and experience.

Loss of _____ (26) skills is common in older adults, but finding problems depends on the way memory is tested. _____(27) is most likely to be affected.

Piaget proposed people develop _____(28), mental models of the world, that influence their interpretation of their experiences. Reasoning errors provide evidence about schemata development. Piaget proposed development proceeds in _____(29) characterized by different schemata. The _____(30) of development is variable, but the _____(31) is the same for all children. Cognitive development involves both assimilation and accommodation. _____(32) occurs when the child fits new experiences into existing schemata. In _____(33), schemata are modified to fit the new experiences.

Behavior in Piaget's first stage, the _____(34) period, includes survival reflexes such as the _____(35) and the sucking reflex. Children move from reflexive to deliberate interaction with the world. They develop _____(36), the ability to symbolically represent object not in view. From age 2 to 7, children are in the _____(37) period. Here, the child lacks an understanding of _____(38). Due to _____(39), or focusing on one dimension, and difficulty with reversibility, children think that changing shape causes a change in amount. Preoperational children also have difficulty putting themselves in others' positions, a trait called _____ (40). Children between 7 and 11 are in the _____(41) period, in which thinking in the abstract is greatly limited. The ability to deal with the abstract and hypothetical and to systematically solve problems is characteristic of the _____(42) period.

Piaget's theory has been criticized for underestimating what children know, for proposing sudden shifts from stage to stage, and for failing to explain the processes of change and the role of _____(43), the key to cognitive development according to Vygotsky. Postformal thinking might be needed to explain differences in adolescent and adult thought. Adults tend to use more _____(44) thinking and systems of ideas.

According to Kohlberg's theory, moral reasoning develops through 3 stages: the _____(45), _____(46), and _____(47) stages. Kohlberg assessed moral reasoning by evaluating the reasons given for answers to moral dilemmas. Preconventional reasoning is based on the _____(48) results of an action (e.g., punishment). Conventional reasoning is based on how an action affects the _____(49). Postconventional reasoning is based on _____(50) principles that can conflict with accepted norms.

Research supports the idea of a sequence of development and the link to cognitive skills. Criticisms of Kohlberg's theory include that it does not generalize across sexes or cultures. Actually, sex differences are minor, but cultural differences do present problems.

Evaluating Your Progress. Select the one best response. Answers are on page 88. If you make any errors, reread the relevant material before proceeding.

1. Two stimuli are presented simultaneously, and the time spent looking at one versus the other is noted in
    a. the habituation method.
    b. the reward method.
    c. the preference method.
    d. the cross-sectional method.

2. Research has shown that infants just a few days old can do all of the following except
    a. recognize their mother's voice.
    b. recognize their mother's smell.
    c. see clearly.
    d. taste sour, sweet, and salty substances.

3. Research that follows a group of people of the same age over an extended period of time, retesting them periodically and comparing their performance at different ages uses a
    a. cross-sectional design.
    b. longitudinal design.
    c. linked design.
    d. continuous design.

4. The process of fitting new information into existing schemata is called
    a. generalization.
    b. centration.
    c. accommodation.
    d. assimilation.

5. Piaget's stages, in order from first to last, are
   a. preoperational, sensorimotor, concrete operational, formal operational.
   b. concrete operational, formal operational, sensorimotor, preoperational.
   c. sensorimotor, preoperational, concrete operational, formal operational.
   d. preoperational, formal operational, concrete operational, sensorimotor.

6. The stage characterized initially by reflexive behavior that eventually broadens to voluntary behavior is
   a. the sensorimotor period.
   b. the formal operational period.
   c. the preoperational period.
   d. the concrete operational period.

7. Object permanence is the knowledge that
   a. the basic properties of an object don't change if superficial changes are made.
   b. if one operation causes a change, another operation can reverse that change.
   c. an object can still exist even if it is not currently in view or other sensory contact.
   d. changes is one dimension can be offset by changes in another dimension.

8. The rooting reflex is the tendency to
   a. consider only one dimension, the root, of an object or situation.
   b. consider the an action in relation to others.
   c. suck on anything that comes in contact with the mouth.
   d. turn the head toward the side of the cheek that was touched.

9. The conservation concept develops by the end of Piaget's
   a. preoperational period.
   b. formal operational period.
   c. sensorimotor period.
   d. concrete operational period.

10. Systematically solving problems and working with abstract concepts are characteristic of Piaget's
    a. preoperational period.
    b. concrete operational period.
    c. formal operational period.
    d. sensorimotor period.

11. Children in the concrete operational period are usually
    a. 3-6 years old.
    b. 7-11 years old.
    c. 12-17 years old.
    d. 18 years old or older.

12. All of the following are criticisms of Piaget's theory of cognitive development EXCEPT
    a. Research shows that children's schemata are not the same as adults'.
    b. Children know more, sooner, than Piaget gives them credit for.
    c. Piaget doesn't address the role social context plays in cognitive development.
    d. Children do not make sudden transitions from one stage to another as Piaget proposes.

13. Kohlberg's theory of moral reasoning proposes
    a. moral reasoning develops differently in different countries.
    b. children's moral reasoning is developed fully by the time they are 6.
    c. development proceeds through a series of orderly stages.
    d. the "yes" or "no" decision about a moral dilemma determines the level of moral reasoning.

14. Postconventional moral reasoning is based on
    a. whether the action disrupts or maintains the social order.
    b. the personal consequences of the action.
    c. abstract moral principles.
    d. the standards of morality defined by an authority figure.

15. Research on Kohlberg's theory of moral development has found that
    a. moral reasoning in India is quite different from moral reasoning in Western cultures.
    b. the moral reasoning of men and women is very different in most circumstances.
    c. the orderly progression of moral reasoning is found only in Western cultures, not elsewhere.
    d. it is more applicable to children between the ages of 6 and 10 than to adolescents and adults.

Developing Socially and Personally (pp. 146-161)

Mastering the Vocabulary. Define or explain each of the following terms. To check your answers, consult the text pages listed.

1. attachments (p. 146)

2. temperament (p. 148)

3. strange-situation test (p. 148)

4. personal identity (p. 153)

5. gender schemas (p. 157)

6. gender roles (p. 157)

7. family life cycle (p. 158)

8. ageism (p. 159)

Mastering the Concepts. Fill in the blanks to create a summary of this section. Answers are on page 87.

_____(51), the emotional ties to another individual, may be controlled by biological predispositions in both parent and child. Harlow's research with monkeys suggests contact _____(52), the warmth of physical contact is more important for attachment than being a source of food. Parental responsiveness is also important and is influenced by the child's _____ (53), which can be easy or difficult, uninhibited or inhibited. Attachment is evaluated using the _____(54) situation test. About 70% of children have secure attachment, 10% have _____(55) attachment, and 20% have insecure attachment. Secure attachment is associated with social and intellectual benefits. Assessments are not always stable, attachment can vary across parents, the data is correlational, and later experiences are important. Friendship attachment is also beneficial. Child-rearing approaches differ cross-culturally, can produce differences. Differences arise from parental beliefs, cultural customs and attitudes, and _____ (56). Research on the effects of day care indicates it has little effect on attachment and may have benefits.

Erikson states that personal identity is shaped by a series of personal _____(57) everyone confronts in life and which shape the personal identity. They extend from the trust vs. mistrust crisis of infancy to the integrity vs. despair crisis of _____(58). The ideas of life-long development and the importance of _____(59) interactions are valid contributions. Criticisms of the theory include the problem of distinct stages, the lack of an explanation as to how progress occurs, and its testability.

Basic gender identity seems to be present by age _____(60). By school age, gender identity is seen as permanent and behavior follows gender _____(61), behavior fitting society's concept of male or female behavior. In _____(62) theory, gender roles develop as the result of being rewarded for certain behaviors. Gender roles lead to gender schemas, beliefs about men and women, that guide later behavior.

The family _____(63) concept focuses on changes related to family life. Physical concerns and _____ (64) prejudices can be problems for the elderly, and the end of life must be faced. Kubler-Ross proposed a theory of dying: denial, anger, bargaining, depression, and acceptance. Her theory has been criticized for its stage format. Death trajectories provide an alternative without implying a "right" way to die.

Evaluating Your Progress. Select the one best response. Answers are on page 89. If you make any errors, reread the relevant material before proceeding.

1. The strong emotional bond between individuals is known as
    a. personal identity.
    b. attachment.
    c. contact comfort.
    d. dependency.

2. Harlow's research found that most monkeys raised with artificial mothers formed attachments if
   a. the "mother" had a warm, fuzzy cover.
   b. the "mother" provided the infant monkey's food.
   c. the "mother" was made out of wire mesh with no cover.
   d. all of the above conditions led to attachment in most monkeys.

3. Attachment is sometimes evaluated by placing a child in a new and stressful situation and observing how the child interacts with the mother. This is called the
   a. contact comfort test.
   b. stress reaction test.
   c. strange situation test.
   d. social stressor test.

4. Which of the below is not a classification of attachment?
   a. resistant attachment.
   b. avoidant attachment.
   c. antagonistic attachment.
   d. secure attachment.

5. Tina is described as an "easy" child who is not upset easily. This is a description of
   a. temperament.
   b. moral development.
   c. attachment.
   d. cognitive development.

6. Cross-cultural research has found that mothers in the United States
   a. hold their babies less than Gusii mothers in Kenya.
   b. talk with their babies less than Gusii mothers in Kenya.
   c. were less likely to leave their children unattended than Gusii mothers in Kenya.
   d. make less eye contact with their children than Gusii mothers in Kenya.

7. Recent studies of day care suggest that
   a. essentially all day care harms the development of attachment.
   b. even quality day care is associated with poor social development.
   c. quality day care is associated with improved cognitive skills for almost all children.
   d. general conclusions are difficult because of the many factors that interact.

8. According to Erikson, the first psychosocial crisis is that of
   a. autonomy vs. shame and doubt.
   b. trust vs. mistrust.
   c. integrity vs. despair.
   d. intimacy vs. isolation.

9. The psychosocial crisis most characteristic of adolescence is
   a. trust vs. mistrust.
   b. identity versus role confusion.
   c. autonomy vs. shame or doubt.
   d. generativity vs. stagnation.

10. The social learning theory of gender role development states that gender roles develop because
    a. children are rewarded for certain "masculine" or "feminine" behavior.
    b. children have few models for gender-appropriate behavior.
    c. children quickly determine that their genitals are different from others'.
    d. children are innately programmed to behave in stereotypically "masculine" or "feminine" ways.

11. Kubler-Ross' stages of death and dying are, in order,
    a. denial, depression, anger, bargaining, acceptance.
    b. denial, anger, bargaining, depression, acceptance.
    c. denial, bargaining, depression, anger, acceptance.
    d. denial, bargaining, anger, depression, acceptance.

MAKING FINAL PREPARATIONS

Complete these sections without consulting your book or notes. For a more accurate estimate of how well you know this material, wait at least a day or two after studying the chapter before working on the questions. Some of the material you "know" immediately after working with the chapter will be quickly forgotten. Immediate tests will overestimate what you know well.

Short Essay Questions. Write a brief answer to each question. Sample answers are on page 90.

1. Discuss why exposure to a teratogen during the first three months produces different effects than exposure during the last three months of pregnancy.

2. Generally describe a newborn infant's perceptual capabilities and how and why they change with time.

3. Describe the preference technique and explain what it tells us about an infant's perceptual capabilities.

4. Give an example of preconventional, conventional, and postconventional moral reasoning for the druggist moral dilemma and explain why each exemplifies the relevant level.

5. Identify three types of attachment and describe how each is reflected in the strange situation test.

6. Explain the identity vs. role confusion crisis and how it is resolved.

7. Compare the gender identities of a 3-year-old and a 7-year-old.

Matching. Select the correct definition or description for each item. Answers are on page 90.

_____	1. schemata	**a.**	first two weeks of prenatal period
_____	2. Harlow	**b.**	set of beliefs about men and women
_____	3. fetal period	**c.**	loss of mental function due to physical causes
_____	4. Erikson	**d.**	morality based on external consequences of action
_____	5. concrete operational period	**e.**	time of final development of physical systems
_____	6. menopause	**f.**	proposed theory of personal identity development
_____	7. sensorimotor period	**g.**	time of initial development of physical systems
_____	8. gender schema	**h.**	proposed theory of moral development
_____	9. embryonic period	**i.**	found importance of contact comfort in attachment
_____	10. Piaget	**j.**	mental models of the world
_____	11. preconventional level	**k.**	proposed classification system for attachment
_____	12. germinal period	**l.**	proposed theory of cognitive development
_____	13. conventional level	**m.**	morality based on maintaining social order
_____	14. dementia	**n.**	period when woman's menstrual cycles cease
_____	15. Kohlberg	**o.**	reflexive behaviors and no object permanence
_____	16. Ainsworth	**p.**	can't deal with abstract or hypothetical situations

Multiple Choice Pretest 1. Select the one best response. Answers are found on page 90.

1. During the third through eighth weeks of development, the organism is called a(n)
    a. fetus.
    b. embryo.
    c. zygote.
    d. menarche.

2. The number of neurons present at birth is
    a. the same number present at maturity.
    b. 25% of the number present at maturity.
    c. 50% of the number present at maturity.
    d. 75% of the number present at maturity.

3. The sequential development of motor skills is most dependent on
    a. the sequential development of muscle strength.
    b. the sequential development of bone strength.
    c. the sequential development of neural connections.
    d. a series of specific environmental experiences.

4. Lou, age 70, and Sara, age 20, participated in a memory experiment. What were the likely results?
    a. Lou did better on all tests of memory skills due to his extensive life experiences.
    b. Lou did worse than Sara on recall tests, but did as well as Sara on recognition tests.
    c. Lou did as well as Sara on all tests of memory skills.
    d. Lou did worse than Sara on all tests of memory skills.

5. As a class project on the development of hand-eye coordination, you tested a group of 3-year-olds, a group of 6-year-olds, and a group of 9-year-olds and compared their performance on the test. You used a
   a. cross-sectional design.
   b. latitudinal design.
   c. pieced design.
   d. longitudinal design.

6. Which is false?
   a. Infants perceive depth at least by the time they are 6 months old.
   b. Infants have at least basic color vision at birth.
   c. Infants prefer pictures of normal faces more than "scrambled" faces.
   d. At birth, infants hearing is equal to adults' hearing.

7. The process of changing existing schemata to fit new information is called
   a. accommodation.
   b. conservation.
   c. assimilation.
   d. relativistic thinking.

8. Not being able to understand conservation is partly due to centration. Centration is
   a. the tendency to consider only one dimension at a time.
   b. the inability to symbolically represent information.
   c. the inability to systematically explore problem solutions.
   d. thinking in terms of systems rather than isolated cases.

9. Kiri acts as if her toy doesn't exist when it rolls under the sofa. Kiri is probably in Piaget's
   a. formal operational period.
   b. concrete operational period.
   c. preoperational period.
   d. sensorimotor period.

10. Knowing that spreading out a pile of pennies doesn't change the number of pennies requires
    a. centration.
    b. relativistic thinking.
    c. object permanence.
    d. the conservation concept.

11. Dee understands conservation, but she can't handle questions that deal with the abstract. She is in
    a. the sensorimotor period.
    b. the formal operational period.
    c. the preoperational period.
    d. the concrete operational period.

12. Object permanence research has suggested that
    a. even 1-4 month-olds show surprise when an object does not reappear when a screen is removed.
    b. Piaget's estimate of good object permanence by about age 1 is reasonably accurate.
    c. children do not develop object permanence until they are close to age 3, rather than by age 1.
    d. children have object permanence for living things at birth, but not for nonliving things.

13. Some researchers argue for the addition of a post-formal stage of cognitive development characterized by
    a. centration.
    b. autonomy.
    c. seriation.
    d. relativistic thinking.

14. Fred said that stealing the drug would be wrong because if caught, the man would go to jail. This is an example of Kohlberg's
    a. preconventional reasoning.
    b. postconventional reasoning.
    c. conventional reasoning.
    d. concrete operational reasoning.

15. Attachment is influenced by all of the following except
    a. a biological predisposition for attachment behavior in the infant.
    b. a biological predisposition for attachment behavior in the parent.
    c. contact comfort.
    d. providing a source of food.

16. Mandy seems unconcerned when strangers appear or her mother leaves, and she shows little interest when her mother returns. She would most likely be classified as having
    a. secure attachment.
    b. avoidant attachment.
    c. antagonistic attachment.
    d. resistant attachment.

17. Patterns of behavior consistent with society's definition of how males and females should act are
    a. gender schemas.
    b. gender identities.
    c. gender theories.
    d. gender roles.

18. Viewing adult personal development in terms of transitions such as divorce, having children, or the beginning of school is characteristic of
    a. Kolhberg's theory of moral reasoning.
    b. Erikson's personal identity theory.
    c. the family life cycle approach.
    d. the relativistic thinking approach.

19. Jesse has quit denying he's dying of lung cancer. If Kubler-Ross is correct, Jesse will now experience
    a. acceptance.
    b. anger.
    c. bargaining.
    d. depression.

20. The least important reason for cultural differences in child care probably is
    a. the beliefs of the parents.
    b. the cultural customs.
    c. education about the right way to treat children.
    d. environmental or survival factors.

Multiple Choice Pretest 2. Select the one best response. Answers are found on page 92.

1. The critical factor that causes a female reproductive system to develop is
   a. testosterone release in the 7th-8th week of development.
   b. estrogen release in the 7th-8th week of development.
   c. having no testosterone released in the 7th-8th week of development.
   d. having a Y sex chromosome.

2. Although avoiding drugs, alcohol, smoking, and other toxins throughout pregnancy is best, generally the most important time to avoid them in order to prevent abnormalities is
   a. the first 2 weeks of the prenatal period.
   b. the first three months of the prenatal period.
   c. the middle three months of the prenatal period.
   d. the last three months of the prenatal period.

3. The adaptive value of the plasticity of the brain is
   a. the stability provided by having neural circuits firmly established and operating in a set way.
   b. the capability of adjusting to a particular environment and compensating for cell loss.
   c. the ability to transfer information for processing by a different hemisphere to avoid overload.
   d. the advantage of being able to grow new neurons to replace neurons lost through damage or aging.

4. Tom was given little opportunity to move around during the first 9 months of life. He probably will
   a. show life-long problems in motor development, especially walking.
   b. begin to walk at least 1 year later than children given free movement.
   c. begin to walk at least 6 months later than children given free movement.
   d. begin to walk at about the same time as children given free movement.

5. To study changes in processing speed with age, you might test a group of people when they were 20, 30, and 40 years old and compare their performance across tests. This is an example of a
   a. horizontal design.
   b. vertical design.
   c. cross-sectional design.
   d. longitudinal design.

6. Joey, age 1, normally drinks his juice from a baby bottle, but he had no trouble drinking it out of a juice box with a straw. This was possible because moving from a baby bottle to a straw only involves
   a. conservation of mass.
   b. object permanence.
   c. assimilation.
   d. accommodation.

7. To stop Rudy's fussing for an attractive (but dangerous) object, Rudy's mother put it in her pocket. "Out of sight, out of mind," she said, and it worked. Rudy's mother made use of his lack of
   a. conservation.
   b. object permanence.
   c. rooting reflex.
   d. assimilation.

8. Although she saw both pieces taken out of their cans, Amy now thinks that she has less clay than her brother because his has been squashed flat into a big circle. This behavior is characteristic of Piaget's
   a. formal operational period.
   b. preoperational period.
   c. postformal period.
   d. concrete operational period.

9. Lee doesn't understand why his friend doesn't like the same things he does. Lee's inability to consider the perspective of another person represents
   a. reversibility.
   b. accommodation.
   c. habituation.
   d. egocentrism.

10. Kim decided that stealing a drug would be wrong because it is against the law, and laws shouldn't be broken. Kim is reasoning at Kohlberg's
    a. postconventional level.
    b. conventional level.
    c. preconventional level.
    d. preoperational level.

11. Clarence is battling a sense of meaninglessness and the feeling that he is contributing nothing to the world. Clarence is probably _____ and confronting the crisis of _____.
    a. middle-aged; generativity vs. stagnation
    b. an adolescent; trust vs. mistrust
    c. a young adult; integrity vs. despair
    d. elderly; intimacy vs. isolation

12. Who is most likely to have reached puberty?
    a. Jack, age 12, an avid computer hacker from Los Angeles.
    b. Tom, age 12, who lives in a war-torn, primitive environment.
    c. Yolanda, age 12, whose hobby is horseback riding.
    d. Maria, age 12, whose diet is seriously deficient.

13. Which of the following is true?
    a. Menopause usually involves a sustained period of depression or crankiness.
    b. Perhaps 20% of individuals at age 65 have dementia of some form.
    c. After about age 20, most physical systems begin a general deterioration.
    d. All of the above are true.

14. The same tone was presented repeatedly until the infant quit responding, then a new, slightly higher pitch tone was presented, and the infant responded again. This is an example of the
    a. longitudinal technique.
    b. habituation technique.
    c. preference technique.
    d. use of reward.

15. In general, the role of experience in perceptual development is
    a. to establish all the basic neural circuits used in perception.
    b. to establish the basic neural circuits used for taste and touch, but not for the other senses.
    c. to make adjustments to the basic neural circuits already established at birth.
    d. very minimal; the neural circuits present at birth allow perception like that in adulthood.

16. Pat is struggling with Erikson's intimacy vs. isolation crisis. Pat is probably
    a. elementary school age.
    b. a teenager.
    c. a young adult.
    d. middle-aged.

17. Perhaps the most valid criticism of Kohlberg's theory of moral development is that
    a. men and women reason very differently about morality.
    b. people do not seem to go through orderly stages of moral reasoning.
    c. moral development has no relationship to cognitive development.
    d. cross-cultural differences in moral reasoning are not handled well by his theory.

18. Based on Harlow's artificial mother research, hospitals might best promote parent-child attachment if
    a. parents are encouraged to cuddle their newborn often.
    b. parents are encouraged to give their baby its bottle right from the start.
    c. parents are encouraged to wait a few minutes before seeing to the baby's needs.
    d. parents are encouraged to change the baby's diaper right from the start.

19. Evaluations of attachment indicate that about 70% of children have
    a. resistant attachment.
    b. antagonistic attachment.
    c. secure attachment.
    d. avoidant attachment.

20. A strength of Erikson's psychosocial theory of the development of personal identity is
    a. its proposal that personal identity development is a lifelong process.
    b. its clear and precise description of the psychological mechanisms that allow resolution of the crises.
    c. its scientific rigor (ability to be tested scientifically).
    d. all of the above

21. To avoid the problems of a stage approach, psychologists discuss death in terms of
    a. death watches.
    b. death schemata.
    c. death trajectories.
    d. death cascades.

ANSWERS AND EXPLANATIONS

Mastering the Concepts

1. Development (p. 118)
2. interaction (p. 118)
3. plasticity (p. 118)
4. physically (p. 118)
5. intellectually (p. 119)
6. zygote (p. 120)
7. germinal (p. 120)
8. embryonic (p. 120)
9. fetal (p. 120)
10. teratogens (p. 122)
11. fetal alcohol (p. 122)
12. Plasticity (p. 124)
13. down and out (p. 125)
14. puberty (p. 126)
15. sexual (p. 126)
16. decline (p. 127)
17. menopause (p. 127)
18. dementia (p. 128)
19. preferences (p. 129)
20. novelty (p. 129)
21. learn (p. 129)
22. preference (p. 130)
23. habituation (p. 130)
24. smell (p. 132)
25. depth (p. 132)
26. memory (p. 133)
27. recall (p. 134)
28. schemata (p. 135)
29. stages (p. 136)
30. timing (p. 136)
31. sequence (p. 136)
32. Assimilation (p. 135)
33. accommodation (p. 135)
34. sensorimotor (p. 136)
35. rooting (p. 136)
36. object permanence (p. 137)
37. preoperational (p. 137)
38. conservation (p. 137)
39. centration (p. 138)
40. egocentrism (p. 138)
41. concrete operations (p. 138)
42. formal operations (p. 140)
43. social context (p. 141)
44. relativistic (p. 142)
45. preconventional (p. 143)
46. conventional (p. 144)
47. postconventional (p. 144)
48. external (p. 143)
49. social order (p. 144)
50. abstract (p. 144)
51. Attachment (p. 146)
52. comfort (p. 147)
53. temperament (p. 148)
54. strange (p. 148)
55. resistant (p. 149)
56. environmental (p. 151)
57. crises (p. 153)
58. old age (p. 155)
59. social (p. 156)
60. two (p. 156)
61. roles (p. 157)
62. social learning (p. 157)
63. life cycle (p. 158)
64. ageism (p. 159)

Evaluating Your Progress

Preview & Developing Physically

1. **c**
   (p. 120)
   a. Wrong. The fertilized egg, or zygote, develops into an embryo after two weeks.
   b. Wrong. The developing child isn't called a fetus after the eighth week of development.
   d. Wrong. A teratogen is an environmental agent that causes prenatal damage.

2. **c**
   (p. 120)
   a, b, & d. Wrong. Differentiation occurs at 7-8 weeks, which is the late embryonic period.

3. **b**
   (p. 122)
   a. Wrong. Order is not important; whatever is in early stages of development is affected most.
   c. Wrong. Once initial development is over, the threat is greatly reduced.
   d. Wrong. The adult effect is not relevant; the structure in early development is at most risk.

4. **d**
   (p. 123)
   a. Wrong. All neurons are present at birth.
   b. Wrong. Blood vessel growth is minimal compared to that of neural branches and glial cells.
   c. Wrong. Ventricle enlargement is minimal compared to that of neuron size and complexity.

5. **d**
   (p. 124)
   a. Wrong. Schemata refers to mental models of the world, not the plasticity of neural circuitry.
   b. Wrong. Habituation is the reduction in responsiveness to repeated stimuli.
   c. Wrong. Critical periods are times that are particularly important to aspects of development.

6. **a**
   (p. 125)
   b, c, & d. Wrong. Development is generally top-down.

7. **b**
   (p. 126)
   a. Wrong. Menarche is the onset of menstruation, which occurs during puberty but doesn't define it.
   c. Wrong. The climacteric is the loss of reproductive ability in older men.
   d. Wrong. Menopause is the cessation of menstruation in older women.

8.   **d**   a. Wrong.   Age of puberty seems linked to environmental factors, not genetics.
     (p. 127)   b. Wrong.   Unhealthy lifestyles are associated with later puberty onset.
                c. Wrong.   Too much strenuous exercise tends to delay puberty.

9.   **a**   b, c, & d.   Wrong.   Processing gradually slows throughout the years from age 20 to 80.
     (p. 128)

Developing Intellectually

1.   **c**   a. Wrong.   The habituation method looks for a renewed response if a new stimulus replaces an old one.
     (p. 130)   b. Wrong.   The reward method teaches the infant to make a simple response in order to get a reward.
                d. Wrong.   The cross-sectional method looks at groups of different ages to study changes in behavior.

2.   **c**   a, b, & d.   Wrong.   These are all possible, but the infant has poor visual acuity.
     (p. 132)

3.   **b**   a.   Wrong.   A cross-sectional design would test groups of people of different ages all at once.
     (p. 133)   c & d.   Wrong.   There is no such thing as a linked design or continuous design

4.   **d**   a. Wrong.   Generalization is the application of a concept or response to new, similar situations.
     (p. 135)   b. Wrong.   Centration is the tendency to take into account only one dimension.
                c. Wrong.   Accommodation involves changing schemata to accommodate new information.

5.   **c**   a, b, & d.   Wrong.   These are all misordered. The sensorimotor period is first.
     (p. 136)

6.   **a**   b. Wrong.   The formal operational period is characterized by adult-like thought, not reflexes.
     (p. 136)   c. Wrong.   The preoperational period involves primarily voluntary behavior, but thought is limited
                d. Wrong.   The concrete operational period involves mental operations mostly limited to the concrete.

7.   **c**   a. Wrong.   This describes conservation.
     (p. 137)   b. Wrong.   This describes reversibility.
                d. Wrong.   This describes the ability to avoid centration.

8.   **d**   a. Wrong.   This describes centration.
     (p. 136)   b. Wrong.   This describes relativistic thinking.
                c. Wrong.   This describes the sucking reflex.

9.   **a**   b, c, & d.   Wrong.   Conservation develops during the preoperational period.
     (p. 137)

10. **c**   a, b, & d.   Wrong.   Systematic and abstract thought are not characteristic of these period.
     (p. 140)

11. **b**   a. Wrong.   This is the age range for preoperational children.
     (p. 138)   c. Wrong.   This is the lower portion of the age range for the formal operational period.
                d. Wrong.   This is the likely age range for the proposed postformal period.

12. **a**   b. Wrong.   Research shows earlier object permanence, for example, than Piaget proposed.
     (p. 140)   c. Wrong.   Vygotsky suggests that social context is a critical factor in cognitive development.
                d. Wrong.   Different types of conservation are acquired at different times, producing an indistinct
                            transition to the concrete operational period.

13. **c**   a. Wrong.   His theory is supposedly applicable world-wide (but critics say it isn't).
  (p. 143)   b. Wrong.   He proposes development continues into adulthood.
             d. Wrong.   He examines the justification for the "yes" or "no," not the "yes" or "no."

14. **c**   a. Wrong.   This is conventional reasoning.
  (p. 144)   b. Wrong.   This is preconventional reasoning.
             d. Wrong.   This is conventional reasoning.

15. **a**   b. Wrong.   Research finds minimal sex differences in moral reasoning.
  (p. 145)   c. Wrong.   Cross-cultural research confirms an orderly progression of reasoning.
             d. Wrong.   Kohlberg's theory applies to adolescents and adults.

Developing Socially and Personally

1. **b**   a. Wrong.   Personal identity is one's sense of self.
  (p. 146)   c. Wrong.   Contact comfort is important for forming attachments, but is not attachment.
             d. Wrong.   Dependency is a reliance on, or need for, another person or thing.

2. **a**   b. Wrong.   Attachment was not based on being provided food.
  (p. 147)   c. Wrong.   Monkeys did not become attached to wire mothers.
             d. Wrong.   b & c did not produce attachment.

3. **c**   a, b, & d.   Wrong.   This is the strange situation test.
  (p. 148)

4. **c**   a, b, & d.   Wrong.   These are all types of attachment.
  (p. 149)

5. **a**   b, c , & d.   Wrong.   Easy vs. difficult, and uninhibited vs. inhibited are dimensions of temperament.
  (p. 148)

6. **a**   b, c, & d.   Wrong.   These relationships are just the opposite of that found in the research.
  (p. 150)

7. **d**   a. Wrong.   Early studies showed this, but recent ones show little, if any, negative effect.
  (p. 152)   b. Wrong.   Quality care is associated with improved social development.
             c. Wrong.   Cognitive benefits are found only if the child's home environment is deficient.

8. **b**   a. Wrong.   Autonomy vs. shame or doubt is the second crisis.
  (p. 153)   c. Wrong.   Integrity vs. despair is the last crisis.
             d. Wrong.   Intimacy vs. isolation is the 7th crisis.

9. **b**   a. Wrong.   Trust vs. mistrust occurs in early infancy.
  (p. 154)   c. Wrong.   Autonomy vs. shame or doubt occurs during the preschool years.
             d. Wrong.   Generativity vs. stagnation occurs in middle adulthood.

10. **a**   b. Wrong.   Many models are available through other people, television, etc.
  (p. 157)   c. Wrong.   Genitals influence gender identity but don't relate to social learning theory.
             d. Wrong.   The learning in social learning refers to the impact of experience, not innate factors.

11. **b**   a, c, & d.   Wrong.   These are not in the correct order.
  (p. 160)

MAKING FINAL PREPARATIONS

Short Essay Questions

1. Teratogens usually affect whatever is undergoing initial development. Most organs undergo most of their development in the first three months of pregnancy, so teratogens during that period are likely to cause damage. The specific damage depends on the exact timing of the teratogen. Teratogens during the last three months are less likely to have an effect, because most development is complete except for the central nervous system. Thus, the nervous system is the likely site of damage from late teratogens. (pp. 122-123)

2. All of the newborn's senses are operational, but they do not have the capabilities of an older child. In general, the senses lack the precision and perhaps the sensitivity of more mature systems. Changes occur due to maturation of the nervous system, and to some extent, experience. (pp. 131-133)

3. In the preference technique, two stimuli are presented and the amount of time spent looking at each is recorded. If the infant looks at one more than the other (controlling for position, etc.) the infant must be able to discriminate one from the other. Thus, this technique can evaluate color vision, pattern perception, pattern recognition variables, etc. (pp. 129-131)

4. Preconventional (focus on external consequences): He shouldn't steal the drug because he will get caught and sent to jail. Conventional (focus on maintaining social order): He shouldn't steal the drug because stealing is against the law. If everyone stole what they needed, it would be chaos. Postconventional (focus on abstract principles): He shouldn't steal the drug because it is not right to take someone else's property. (pp. 143-144)

5. Secure attachment: Child is upset by mother's absence or stranger, but is calmed by mother's return. Resistant attachment: Child is upset by mother's absence or stranger, but is not calmed by mother's return. Avoidant attachment: Child is not upset by mother's absence or stranger. Mother's return receives little attention. (pp. 148-149)

6. This crisis is typical of adolescence. Teenager are faced with determining who they are and integrating their various attributes into a unified sense of self. Some develop their identity by using information from others (e.g., basing their identity on their parents' attitudes), others perform a personal evaluation, and others just don't define themselves at all. (p. 154)

7. A basic gender identity (I'm a girl) is present at age 3, but it is not stable. The 3-year-old will likely say that a boy can change into a girl if he grows his hair long or wears a dress. By age 7, the gender identity is stable (dresses don't make a boy a girl), and the child will be operating within well developed gender roles (behavior consistent with society's view of appropriate male or female behavior). (pp. 156-158)

Matching

1. j (p. 135)	4. f (p. 153)	7. o (p. 136)	10. l (p. 135)	13. m (p. 144)	16. k (p. 149)
2. i (p. 146)	5. p (p. 138)	8. b (p. 157)	11. d (p. 143)	14. c (p. 128)	
3. e (p. 120)	6. n (p. 127)	9. g (p. 120)	12. a (p. 120)	15. h (p. 143)	

Multiple Choice Pretest 1

1. **b**   a. Wrong.   The term fetus is used after the 8th week. During weeks 3-8, embryo is used.
    (p. 120)   c. Wrong.   The term zygote is used in the 1st-2nd week. In weeks 3-8, embryo is used.
               d. Wrong.   The term menarche refers to the onset of menstruation in females.

2. **a**   b.   Wrong.   At birth the brain is 25% of its final *weight*, but has all the neurons it will have.
(p. 123)   c & d.   Wrong.   At birth all the neurons are present. Weight increases, not neurons.

3. **c**   a. Wrong.   Without neural development, muscle strength is a minor factor.
(p. 125)   b. Wrong.   Without neural development, bone strength is a minor factor.
          d. Wrong.   Experience affects the rate of development, but neural development controls the sequence.

4. **b**   a & c.   Wrong.   Memory deficits are common in the elderly.
(p. 134)   d.   Wrong.   No differences are found for recognition memory.

5. **a**   b & c.   Wrong. These are not actual designs.
(p. 133)   d.   Wrong. Longitudinal designs test the same people at different points in time (at different ages).

6. **d**   a, b, & c.   Wrong.   Infants do all these things, but they cannot hear sounds as well as adults.
(p. 132)

7. **a**   b. Wrong.   Conservation is the idea that superficial changes don't change the basic properties.
(p. 135)   c. Wrong.   Assimilation involves fitting new information into old schemata.
          d. Wrong.   Relativistic thinking involves considering the relative nature of things.

8. **a**   b. Wrong.   This describes a component of the lack of object permanence.
(p. 138)   c. Wrong.   This describes a component of concrete operational thought.
          d. Wrong.   This describes postformal thought.

9. **d**   a, b, & c.   Wrong.   Kiri is showing a lack of object permanence, a sensorimotor period trait.
(p. 136)

10. **d**   a. Wrong.   Centration, considering only one dimension, would lead to thinking the number changed.
(p. 137)   b. Wrong.   Relativistic thinking involves considering the situation relative to others.
          c. Wrong.   Object permanence is the ability to know an object still exists if it is out of sight.

11. **d**   a. Wrong.   Neither conservation nor the abstract are understood during the sensorimotor period.
(p. 139)   b. Wrong.   Both conservation and the abstract are understood during the formal operational period.
          c. Wrong.   Neither conservation nor the abstract are understood during the preoperational period.

12. **a**   b & c.   Wrong.   Research shows object permanence develops earlier than Piaget's estimate.
(p. 140)   d.   Wrong.   A living-nonliving distinction has not been made, especially for an innate ability.

13. **d**   a. Wrong.   Centration is characteristic of childhood.
(p. 142)   b. Wrong.   Autonomy is one of Erikson's personal identity crises.
          c. Wrong.   Seriation is a skill of childhood.

14. **a**   b. Wrong.   Postconventional reasoning is based on abstract principles, not personal consequences.
(p. 143)   c. Wrong.   Conventional reasoning is based on maintaining the social order, not personal consequences
          d. Wrong.   This is not one of Kohlberg's levels of moral reasoning.

15. **d**   a & b.   Wrong.   Both infant and child seem to be predisposed to for attachments.
(p. 146)   c.   Wrong.   Contact comfort is an important influence, probably for both monkeys and humans.

16. **b**   a. Wrong.   A securely attached child is stressed, but the mother's presence is calming.
(p. 149)   c. Wrong.   This is not a type of attachment.
          d. Wrong.   A child with resistant attachment is stressed, but gains no relief from the mother.

17. **d** a. Wrong. Gender schemas are organized sets of beliefs held about men and women.
   (p. 157) b. Wrong. Gender identities are the gender people assign themselves.
             c. Wrong. Gender theories is a fabricated term.

18. **c** a. Wrong. Piaget's theory does not deal with adulthood events.
   (p. 158) b. Wrong. Although Erikson's theory includes adulthood, it does not focus on these events.
             d. Wrong. Relativistic thinking concerns cognitive development, not personal development.

19. **b** a. Wrong. Acceptance is the final stage. Jesse is just entering the second.
   (p. 160) c. Wrong. Bargaining is the third stage. Jesse is just entering the second.
             d. Wrong. Depression is the fourth stage. Jesse is just entering the second.

20. **c** a. Wrong. Parental beliefs (can infants understand language?) is very important.
   (p. 150) b. Wrong. Cultural customs (sleeping with infant) are very important.
             d. Wrong. Environmental factors (predators, economics) are very important.

Multiple Choice Pretest 2.

1. **c** a. Wrong. Testosterone produces a male system; the lack of testosterone produces a female system.
   (p. 120) b. Wrong. The lack of testosterone, not the presence of estrogen, produces a female system.
             d. Wrong. A Y would cause testosterone release, which would cause a male genital pattern to develop.

2. **b** a.   Wrong. Little differentiation occurs during the first two weeks, so susceptibility is limited.
   (p. 123) c & d. Wrong. Susceptibility is greatest when systems are undergoing initial development. Initial
                            development occurs between the 3rd and 12th weeks (first 3 months).

3. **b** a. Wrong. Plasticity involve changeable circuits, not set ones.
   (pp. 124, c. Wrong. Lateralization is not part of plasticity, the ability of the brain to adapt.
      128) d. Wrong. Plasticity is not this great; lost neurons cannot be replaced with new ones.

4. **d** a, b, & c. Wrong. Children learn to walk at about the same time as long as some opportunity to
   (p. 125)   move around is available prior to the normal age of walking (12 months).

5. **d** a & b. Wrong. These are not actual designs.
   (p. 133) c.   Wrong. A cross-sectional design tests groups of different ages at about the same time.

6. **c** a. Wrong. The conservation of mass is the idea that changes in shape don't change the mass of objects.
   (p. 135) b. Wrong. Object permanence is the ability to know an object still exists even if it is out of sight.
             d. Wrong. Accommodation involves changing schemata to fit new experiences. Here, drinking still
                       equals sucking, so no accommodation is required.

7. **b** a. Wrong. Conservation is knowledge that objects' basic properties don't change with surface changes.
   (p. 137) c. Wrong. The rooting reflex is turning the head to the side toward the cheek that was touched.
             d. Wrong. Assimilation is the fitting of new experiences into existing schemata.

8. **b** a, c, & d. Wrong. Amy is showing a lack of conservation, a characteristic of preoperational thought.
   (p. 137)

9. **d** a. Wrong. Reversibility is the ability to understand that actions can be reversed.
   (p. 138) b. Wrong. Accommodation occurs when schemata are changed to fit new information.
             c. Wrong. Habituation is the reduction of a response to repeated stimulation.

10. **b**   a. Wrong.   Postconventional reasoning uses abstract principles, not protecting the social order.
(p. 144)   c. Wrong.   Preconventional reasoning is based on the personal consequences of an action.
            d. Wrong.   The preoperational level is one of Piaget's levels, not Kohlberg's.

11. **a**   b. Wrong.   Trust vs. mistrust involves feelings about people's dependability and occurs in infancy.
(p. 155)   c. Wrong.   Integrity vs. despair involves an attempt to accept the past and occurs in old age.
            d. Wrong.   Intimacy vs. isolation involves relationships with others and occurs in early adulthood.

12. **c**   a. Wrong.   Average onset of puberty for boys is age 13-14, but for girls it is age 12-13.
(p. 127)   b. Wrong.   Boys enter puberty at age 13-14, girls at 12-13, and stressful, poor conditions delays onset.
            d. Wrong.   Maria's poor diet is likely to delay onset of puberty.

13. **c**   a. Wrong.   Sustained depression or crankiness is not common in menopause.
(p. 127)   b. Wrong.   Only 1% have dementia at age 65.
            d. Wrong.   Answers a and b are false.

14. **b**   a. Wrong.   The longitudinal technique tests people at different ages to examine development.
(p. 130)   c. Wrong.   The preference technique measures gaze time to stimuli presented simultaneously.
            d. Wrong.   Reward is used to teach an infant a response.

15. **c**   a. Wrong.   Infants have relatively good perception at birth; the basic neural circuits are in place.
(p. 133)   b. Wrong.   The basic circuitry for taste and touch is present at birth, along with that for other senses.
            d. Wrong.   Experience influences perceptual development significantly.

16. **c**   a. Wrong.   Industry vs. inferiority is the crisis of elementary school age.
(p. 155)   b. Wrong.   Identity vs. role confusion is the crisis of adolescence.
            d. Wrong.   Generativity vs. stagnation is the crisis of middle age.

17. **d**   a. Wrong.   Research indicates that sex differences are minimal.
(p. 144)   b. Wrong.   Research supports an orderly progression in moral reasoning.
            c. Wrong.   The link between cognitive development and moral reasoning is well accepted.

18. **a**   b. Wrong.   Being the food supplier, especially in a bottle, is not a major factor in attachment.
(p. 146)   c. Wrong.   Attachment is more likely if parents react promptly to the infant's needs.
            d. Wrong.   Providing basic physical needs is not the most important factor in attachment.

19. **c**   a. Wrong.   10% have resistant attachment.
(p. 149)   b. Wrong.   This is not a type of attachment.
            d. Wrong.   20% have avoidant attachment.

20. **a**   b. Wrong.   It does not clearly describe the psychological mechanisms of crisis resolution.
(p. 155)   c. Wrong.   It is not scientifically rigorous; it's concepts are vague and difficult to test.
            d. Wrong.   Both b and c are inaccurate.

21. **c**   a, b, & d.   Wrong.   These are not valid terms.
(p. 160)

LANGUAGE ENCHANCEMENT GUIDE

CORE TERMS

In this chapter, you can expect the terms *quantitative* and *qualitative* to come up. They mean pretty much what they would seem to. Your instructor may say something like, "the differences between children's cognitive development are not merely quantitative, but qualitative." What they are saying is that children don't think LESS than adults do, but DIFFERENTLY than adults do. The form, or quality, of their thinking is different.

Another pair of terms you might here are *abstract* and *concrete*. Something that is concrete can be touched, seen, and so on. Something that is abstract cannot. For example, a math problem using real beads or coins is concrete; a math problem using just numbers is abstract.

Some other terms have to do with the models of development. Most of these models present development as a *continuum* or *spectrum,* straight lines with different points along the way. You might imagine a number-line or time-line as a continuum, and the colors of a rainbow as a spectrum. Your instructor may talk about someone moving *sequentially* -- that is, step by step in one direction -- through the stages of development. But another pattern of movement is *recursive* -- that is, moving forward a bit, and then stepping back, and then moving forward.

IDIOMS

119	milestones	important points along a path
120	fraught with difficulties	filled with problems
122	susceptibility	vulnerability, openness to disease or damage
122	Russian Roulette	a game of chance in which, if you lose, you die
129	devise a way to infer perceptual capabilities	figure out a way to determine what someone can perceive with their senses
129	immobile, essentially uncommunicative infants	babies who can't move around or say much
130	switching their relative positions from trial to trial	switching them around each time before showing them to the subject
131	operating at peak efficiency	working at the best possible level
131	their biological equipment	their senses, brains and bodies
132	reasonably sophisticated perceptual processing	fairly complex ways of understanding what they are seeing, hearing, etc.

133	attend selectively to pertinent information	pay attention only to the things that are important right now
133	help us interpret ambiguous stimuli	help us figure out things that aren't straightforward and clear
136	attaining adequate nourishment	getting enough food
139	initial stirrings	first signs of; first movements
139	hypothetical outcomes	thinking through an imaginary situation to see what would happen next in it
142	the hallmark of	a main feature of; a good way of recognizing
142	tolerant of ambiguity	able to put up with situations where it isn't clear what is going on
144	the resident authority figures	the people in charge
144	society's dictum	society's rule
151	well-adjusted	mentally happy and healthy
152	detrimental effects	damaging effects
152	multifaceted concept	an idea with many different possible perspective
156	rudimentary foundations	basic building-blocks
159	at an economic disadvantage	be poor
160	sensitized legions of surgeons	made a great many surgeons aware of
162	couldn't care less	wasn't at all concerned; didn't get upset

WORD PARTS

Here are some words that are made up of word parts, and that you can find in this chapter. After you've looked at these, you can look for others in the chapter that use the same word parts (they are there, but YOU have to find them!)

WORD	WORD PART IT USES	MEANING
prenatal	pre = before natal = birth	before birth
germinal	germ = seed	from the earliest stage of development

conception	con = together cept = to receive	a beginning, a coming together
deform	de = down, from, away form = shape	to be or cause something to be misshapen
quadruple	quad = four	to multiply by four
reproduce	re = again pro = forward duce = to carry	to make another copy
supervise	super = over vise = to look	to watch over, to direct behavior

Knowing the word parts listed above, you can also create the following words. You can get an idea of their meanings from the word parts they use. You fill in the blanks!

misconception	mis (bad) + _____ + _____	a bad idea; an idea that was mistaken from the beginning
deception	_____ + _____	to lead someone away from the true idea
progeny	pro + gen (birth, race, kind)	_____
native	natal	_____
deduce	_____ + _____	to bring together ideas to form a new one; to come to a conclusion
devise	de + vis	_____

CHAPTER 5: SENSATION AND PERCEPTION

ESTABLISHING LEARNING OBJECTIVES

Use these learning objectives as a preview of the chapter, a guide for active reading, and to evaluate your mastery of the material. Review the relevant objectives as you begin and end your reading of each major section of the chapter.

After studying this chapter you should be able to:

I.   Describe the adaptive problem of creating an internal representation of the external world.
   A. Distinguish between sensation and perception.

II. Solve the adaptive problem of creating an effective perception of visual information.
   A. Explain how light energy is translated into the electrochemical language of the brain.
      1. Describe the path light travels through the eye, and explain the function of each part of the eye.
      2. Describe the process of dark adaptation.
   B. Describe how essential features of the visual message, such as color, are extracted by the brain.
      1. Trace the neural pathway from eye to brain, and describe the processing that occurs at each level.
      2. Explain how color information is extracted and different colors perceived.
   C. Describe how a stable interpretation of visual information is created, and why the interpretation process sometimes leads to visual illusions.
      1. Compare bottom-up and top-down processing, and discuss the roles of expectancy and context.
      2. Discuss how information is organized into groups or forms and then recognized.
      3. List and describe types of information used to create a perception of depth.
      4. Discuss perceptual constancy, and explain its relationship to depth perception and illusions.

III. Solve the adaptive problem of creating an effective perception of auditory information.
   A. Explain how the physical message, sound, is translated into the electrochemical language of the brain.
      1. Describe the path sound travels through the ear, and explain the function of each part of the ear.
   B. Discuss how pitch information is pulled out of the auditory message.
      1. Describe the place and frequency theories of pitch, and indicate their strengths and limitations.
   C. Explain how the auditory message is interpreted and how sound is localized.

IV. Solve the adaptive problem of creating an effective perception of information from skin and body senses.
   A. Explain how sensory messages delivered to the skin - touch and temperature - are translated and interpreted within the brain.
   B. Describe how we perceive and interpret pain.
   C. Discuss the operation and function of the body senses: movement and balance.

V.   Solve the adaptive problem of creating an effective perception of information from the chemical senses.
   A. Describe how chemical stimuli lead to neural activity that is interpreted as different smells and tastes.

VI. Solve the practical problem of quantifying the relationship of the physical and the psychological event.
   A. Explain the psychology of stimulus detection, including the technique of signal detection.
   B. Define difference threshold, and explain Weber's Law.
   C. Describe stimulus adaptation and its adaptive value.

MASTERING THE MATERIAL

Preview & Vision: *Building a World of Color and Form* (pp. 170-193)

Mastering the Vocabulary. Define or explain each of the following terms. To check your answers, consult the text pages listed.

1. sensation (p. 170)

2. perception (p. 170)

3. transduction (p. 171)

4. light (p. 172)

5. hue (p. 172)

6. brightness (p. 172)

7. cornea (p. 173)

8. lens (p. 173)

9. pupil (p. 173)

10. iris (p. 173)

11. accommodation (p. 173)

12. dark adaptation (p. 175)

13. retina (p. 175)

14. rods (p. 175)

32. phi phenomenon (p. 189)

33. perceptual constancy (p. 190)

34. perceptual illusions (p. 191)

Mastering the Concepts. Fill in the blanks to create a summary of this section. Answers are on page 116.

This chapter explores the adaptive problems of translating the external message into neural information, extracting the message components for analysis, and producing stable interpretations of changing stimulation. The basic components of an experience, _____(1), are processed to produce an interpretation or _____(2) of the stimulus. Light coming directly from a source or reflected by an object enters the eye, is _____(3) into neural energy, and is processed in the brain to create a perception of form and color. The cornea and lens of the eye _____(4) light on the retina, where it stimulates the visual receptors, cones and _____(5). Rods work in low light, whereas cones work in normal light and provide good _____(6), the ability to see detail, and color vision. _____(7) adaptation is needed for rods to work at top efficiency.

Receptor activity causes a neural response in the bipolar and ganglion cells. The message is carried to the visual cortex along two paths, the P-channel, which processes _____(8) and texture, and the M-channel, which processes movement. _____(9) detectors, single cells that respond to specific stimuli (e.g., 45 degree lines), are found in the visual cortex in a very organized arrangement. Other cortical areas are involved in higher-order visual processing.

Color vision is made possible by three types of cones, maximally responsive to short, medium, or long _____(10). _____(11) theory states color is perceived based on the relative activity in three cone types. Color _____(12) occurs when one of the types of cones is missing. _____(13) theory proposes complementary colors are paired, and activity of one member inhibits the other. Both theories are used today: trichromatic processes in the retina, and opponent process coding at higher levels.

Form perception involves bottom-up, or sensory, analysis and top-down, context or _____(14) based, processes. The _____(15) psychologists proposed principles of perceptual organization, including proximity, similarity, closure, good continuation, and common fate. Recognition by components theory states complex forms are recognized from _____(16), their simpler components.

Cues for depth, such as linear perspective, shading, convergence and _____(17) disparity, allow a 3-dimensional perception. Motion perception provides information about object shape, location, and figure-ground relationships. Retinal image movement is an inadequate cue for motion, and the _____ (18) phenomenon proves that no real movement is required to perceive motion. Although sensory input is variable, we are able to maintain an unchanging perception, or perceptual _____(19). Depth cues serve as cues for constancy, but if misapplied, _____(20) occur.

Evaluating Your Progress. Select the one best response. Answers are found on page 116. If you make any errors, reread the relevant material before proceeding.

1. The wavelength of a light generally corresponds to its perceived
    a. hue.
    b. acuity.
    c. brightness.
    d. accommodation.

2. Without her glasses, Leah sees everything out of focus. She probably has a defective
    a. retina.
    b. lens.
    c. pupil.
    d. iris.

3. Which is not a characteristic of the rods?
    a. located in the periphery (sides)
    b. give color vision
    c. work well in low light conditions
    d. long and thin in shape

4. Sensitivity to light increases during dark adaptation because
    a. photopigments are replenished.
    b. the receptive fields get larger.
    c. the brain "fills in" missing information.
    d. the vitreous humor becomes thinner.

5. Which part of the visual system dark adapts most quickly?
    a. the rods
    b. the cones
    c. the lens
    d. the cornea

6. Several receptor cells send input to a single ganglion cell. These receptors define the ganglion cell's
    a. blind spot.
    b. optic chiasm.
    c. receptive field.
    d. fovea.

7. Single cells in the cortex that respond best to lines at a specific angle are called
   a. akinetopsias.
   b. photoreceptors.
   c. feature detectors.
   d. bipolar cells.

8. The relative activity levels of three types of cones is used to perceive color according to the
   a. opponent process theory.
   b. recognition by components theory.
   c. place theory.
   d. trichromatic theory.

9. Each eye has a slightly different image than the other. This is the cue for depth known as
   a. linear perspective.
   b. convergence.
   c. retinal disparity.
   d. shading.

10. All of the following contribute to our perception of motion EXCEPT
    a. changes in the position of our eyes.
    b. changes in the size of the pupil.
    c. changes in the relative positions of objects in a scene.
    d. changes in the location of an object's image on the retina.

11. A distant car casts a smaller image than a nearby car, but we perceive them to be the same size due to
    a. bottom-up processing.
    b. feature detectors.
    c. good acuity.
    d. perceptual constancy.

Hearing: Identifying and Localizing Sounds (pp. 194-200)

Mastering the Vocabulary. Define or explain each of the following terms. To check your answers, consult the text pages listed.

1. sound (p. 195)

2. pitch (p. 195)

3. pinna (p. 195)

4. tympanic membrane (p. 195)

5. middle ear (p. 196)

6. cochlea (p. 196)

7. basilar membrane (p. 196)

8. place theory (p. 197)

9. frequency theory (p. 197)

10. sound localization (p. 200)

Mastering the Concepts. Fill in the blanks to create a summary of this section. Answers are on page 116.

Sound is mechanical energy from the movement of molecules within a physical medium such as air. The rate of these vibrations, measured in hertz (Hz), produce the _____(21) of the sound, and their amplitude (energy) produces the _____(22), which is measured in units called decibels (dB).

Sound is captured by the _____(23), travels down the ear canal to the _____(24) membrane, which vibrates. In the middle ear, three tiny bones behind the eardrum transfer the vibration to the oval window of the _____(25) in the inner ear. This vibration creates motion in the cochlear fluid, causing the _____(26) membrane to move. The movement bends _____(27) cells, the auditory receptors, generating a neural impulse that travels via the auditory nerve to the brain. Input from each ear is processed primarily by the _____(28) hemisphere. Neurons respond most to specific frequencies and less to others. Auditory cortex cells respond selectively to particular sequences of tones.

Different sound frequencies produce different patterns of movement along the basilar membrane, and thus, stimulate different hair cells. Low frequencies cause movement near the _____(29) end of the coiled basilar membrane; high frequencies peak near the _____(30). This location information is used to discriminate pitch, according to the _____(31) theory. The brain interprets activity in neurons from a specific location as reflecting a particular pitch (frequency). This is compatible with patterns of deafness, but it is limited by a lack of independence in hair cell activity. The _____(32) principle of pitch suggests the rate, or frequency, of neural firing signals pitch. That is, high frequency impulses reflect a high frequency (high pitch). The firing rate across groups of neurons, or _____(33), extends frequency information. Simple and complex auditory feature detectors are found in the cortex.

Ambiguity in auditory input limits identification based on physical characteristics. Auditory figure-ground is organized on the basis of _____(34), timing, and top-down factors such as knowledge and _____(35). Location is determined by input intensity and timing differences at the two ears.

Evaluating Your Progress. Select the one best response. Answers are found on page 117. If you make any errors, reread the relevant material before proceeding.

1. The frequency of a sound stimulus corresponds to its
   a. intensity.
   b. pitch.
   c. location.
   d. purity.

2. The structure that contains the hair cells, the auditory receptors, is the
   a. semicircular canal.
   b. tympanic membrane.
   c. cochlea.
   d. pinna.

3. A neural impulse is generated by the hair cells when
   a. neurotransmitters are released by the tympanic membrane.
   b. the malleus, incus, and stapes push against them.
   c. they are bent during movement of the basilar membrane.
   d. a chemical change occurs in the fluid of the cochlea.

4. The place theory states that pitch is perceived based on
   a. the frequency of the neural impulses generated in the cochlea.
   b. the strength of the neural impulses generated in the cochlea.
   c. the number of neurons activated by the sound.
   d. which specific neurons are firing the most during a sound.

5. A tone is presented to your left ear a fraction of a second before an identical tone is presented to your right ear. You are most likely to perceive
   a. two tones, with the one in your left ear slightly higher frequency than the one in your right.
   b. two tones, with the one in your left ear slightly louder than the one in your right.
   c. a single tone located to the right of center.
   d. a single tone located to the left of center.

6. The primary key to good auditory localization is
   a. having good pitch discrimination.
   b. knowing the content of the message.
   c. having two ears.
   d. having good frequency detectors in the auditory cortex.

The Skin and Body Senses: From Touch to Movement (pp. 201-203)

Mastering the Vocabulary. Define or explain each of the following terms. To check your answers, consult the text pages listed.

1. somatosensory cortex (p. 202)

2. cold fibers (p. 202)

3. warm fibers (p. 202)

4. pain (p. 203)

5. gate control theory (p. 203)

6 kinesthesia (p. 204)

7 semicircular canals (p. 204)

8 vestibular sacs (p. 204)

Mastering the Concepts. Fill in the blanks to create a summary of this section. Answers are on page 116.

The skin senses are touch, _____(36), and pain. Different types of pressure-sensitive receptor cells respond to different aspects of touch stimuli. Touch input goes to the _____(37) cortex. _____(38) and warm fibers react to changes in skin temperature. The change is critical, not the temperature of the object.

_____(39), the response to injury-causing stimuli, involves both stimulus and psychological factors. The _____(40) theory states pain signals can be blocked by closing a "gate" in the _____(41). Physical and cognitive factors close the gate. Pain can be reduced by release of _____(42) in the brain.

Kinesthesia is the ability to sense the _____(43) and position of body parts. Receptors are in the skin, tendons, muscles, and _____(44). Input goes to the somatosensory cortex. The _____(45) sense responds to movement, acceleration, and posture changes. Receptors in the _____(46) canals and vestibular sacs send input to the somatosensory cortex. Disturbances cause dizziness or nausea.

Evaluating Your Progress. Select the one best response. Answers are found on page 117. If you make any errors, reread the relevant material before proceeding.

1. The skin senses include all of the following except
   a. temperature.
   b. touch.
   c. kinesthesia.
   d. pain.

2. Neural responses for touch are generated when touch receptors are stimulated by
   a. mechanical energy.
   b. electromagnetic energy.
   c. changes in air density.
   d. chemical energy.

3. The gate control theory suggests cognitive factors influence pain by opening or closing a "gate" in
   a. the free nerve endings.
   b. the tympanic membrane.
   c. the spinal cord.
   d. the somatosensory cortex.

4. Receptors for the kinesthetic sense are located in the
   a. cortex.
   b. muscles, joints, tendons, and skin.
   c. semicircular canals of the inner ear.
   d. cochlea.

5. If you have a lot of activity coming from the semicircular canals, you probably
   a. are moving.
   b. are touching something.
   c. are listening to something.
   d. are smelling something.

6. The semicircular canals are in the
   a. inner ear.
   b. spine.
   c. muscles of the eyes, neck, and head.
   d. sinuses.

The Chemical Senses: Smell and Taste (pp. 205-207)

Mastering the Vocabulary. Define or explain each of the following terms. To check your answers, consult the text pages listed.

1. chemoreceptors (p. 205)

2.   olfaction (p. 205)

3.   gustation (p. 207)

4.   flavor (p. 207)

5.   taste buds (p. 207)

Mastering the Concepts. Fill in the blanks to create a summary of this section. Answers are on page 116.

The receptors for smell and taste are called _____(47). Olfactory receptors are found in the roof of the nasal cavity bind with molecules, and a neural impulse is generated and transmitted to the _____(48) and to the limbic system. Some odors, _____(49), are related to sexual behavior.

Taste, or _____(50), relies on receptors found in taste buds in the papillae of the tongue. Input is sent to the somatosensory cortex. Although there are four basic tastes, receptors are not finely tuned to only one. The pattern across many receptors is critical. Some tastes are dependent on olfaction.

Evaluating Your Progress. Select the one best response. Answers are found on page 118. If you make any errors, reread the relevant material before proceeding

1.   The receptors for smell and taste are called
     a.   vestibular sacs.
     b.   free nerve endings.
     c.   chemoreceptors.
     d.   mechanoreceptors.

2.   Some animals produce chemicals that produce very predictable, specific responses (often sexual) by other members of the species. These chemicals are known as
     a.   perfumes.
     b.   pheromones.
     c.   papillae.
     d.   endorphins.

3.   There are _____ basic tastes.
     a.   4
     b.   6
     c.   12
     d.   over 1000.

From the Physical to the Psychophysical (pp. 208-211)

Mastering the Vocabulary. Define or explain each of the following terms. To check your answers, consult the text pages listed.

1. psychophysics (p. 208)

2. absolute threshold (p. 208)

3. signal detection (p. 209)

4. difference threshold (p. 210)

5. Weber's law (p. 210)

6. sensory adaptation (p. 211)

Mastering the Concepts. Fill in the blanks to create a summary of this section. Answers are on page 116.

Psychophysics studies the relationship between the physical stimulus and the psychological event. The _____(51) threshold is the intensity at which a stimulus is detected 50% of the time. Responses are influenced by both sensitivity and bias. The _____(52) technique is used to find the impact of bias by comparing rates of hits and _____(53). Difference thresholds are the smallest detectable change, the just noticeable difference. Weber's Law states that the difference threshold is a constant _____(54) of the standard stimulus. With continuous stimulation, sensory _____(55) occurs, reducing sensitivity

Evaluating Your Progress. Select the one best response. Answers are found on page 118. If you make any errors, reread the relevant material before proceeding.

1. The absolute threshold is
   a. the stimulus energy that can be detected 50% of the time.
   b. the amount of change in stimulus energy that can be detected 50% of the time.
   c. the stimulus energy that results in pain sensations.
   d. the stimulus energy at which increases in intensity do not produce changes in perception.

2. To determine whether a person's apparent detection ability is due to true sensory sensitivity or due to strategy bias, researchers are most likely to use
    a. Weber's Law.
    b. sensory adaptation.
    c. the signal detection technique.
    d. transduction.

3. We don't notice the smell of our own perfume after a period of time. This is best explained by
    a. Weber's Law.
    b. signal detection theory.
    c. sensory adaptation.
    d. "direct" perception theory.

4. The field of psychophysics studies
    a. the relationship between the physical stimulus and the psychological experience.
    b. the way in which the stimulus stimulates the receptor organs.
    c. the neural pathway sensory information travels to the brain.
    d. the role of expectancy in perception.

MAKING FINAL PREPARATIONS

Complete these sections without consulting your book or notes. For a more accurate estimate of how well you know this material, wait at least a day or two after studying the chapter before working on the questions. Some of the material you "know" immediately after working with the chapter will be quickly forgotten. Immediate tests will overestimate what you know well.

Short Essay Questions. Write a brief answer to each question. Sample answers are on page 118.

1. Describe and explain the time course of dark adaptation.

2. Compare the characteristics and functions of the rods and cones.

3. Explain why expectancy is important and how it influences perception.

4. Define perceptual constancy and explain why it is adaptive.

5. Explain the relationship between depth perception and size perception.

6. Describe the place theory and frequency principle of pitch perception, and explain why both are needed to account for pitch discrimination.

7. Explain why you will have difficulty telling the direction from which an emergency vehicle is approaching if you drive with only your left windows open.

8. Explain why rubbing an injury often reduces the pain.

Matching. Select the correct definition or description for each item. Answers are on page 119.

_____	1. sensation	**a.**	visual center of the retina, containing only cones
_____	2. optic chiasm	**b.**	point in the retina where the optic nerve exits
_____	3. pheromones	**c.**	layer of tissue containing photoreceptors
_____	4. lateral geniculate nucleus	**d.**	brain structure that receives olfactory input
_____	5. P-channel	**e.**	the basic components of an experience
_____	6. top-down processing	**f.**	correctly detecting the presence of a stimulus
_____	7. fovea	**g.**	area of the thalamus that receives visual input
_____	8. acuity	**h.**	neurons that are activated by cooling of the skin
_____	9. cold fibers	**i.**	inner ear structures that signal motion and posture
_____	10. olfactory bulb	**j.**	crossover point for visual system neurons
_____	11. M-channel	**k.**	the ability to perceive fine detail
_____	12. vestibular sacs	**l.**	uses knowledge and expectancy to identify stimuli
_____	13. blind spot	**m.**	neural pathway involved in motion and depth
_____	14. iris	**n.**	scents that produce a specific response
_____	15. hit	**o.**	colored tissue surrounding the pupil
_____	16. retina	**p.**	neural pathway involved in color and detail

Multiple Choice Pretest 1. Select the one best response. Answers are found on page 119.

1. The first structure light encounters when it reaches the eye is the
    a. retina.
    b. lens.
    c. iris.
    d. cornea.

2. Most people need reading glasses when they get older because they lose accommodation power due to
    a. the shrinkage of the eyeball.
    b. a reduction in the amount of photopigment.
    c. reduced flexibility of the lens.
    d. an increase in the pressure in the eyeball.

3. Which is not a characteristic of the cones?
    a. contain any of three photopigments
    b. work best in bright light
    c. concentrated in the periphery (sides) of the retina
    d. give color vision

4. To be fully dark-adapted, you must remain in the dark about
   a. 5 minutes.
   b. 10 minutes.
   c. 15 minutes.
   d. 20 minutes.

5. Cells have been found in the lateral geniculate nucleus that increase their firing rate to red and decrease their firing rate to green. This data best supports
   a. opponent process theory.
   b. trichromatic theory.
   c. frequency theory.
   d. top-down processing theory.

6. Biederman's recognition by components theory states that objects are recognized on the basis of
   a. the activity in single-cell feature detectors.
   b. top-down processing more than bottom-up processing.
   c. simple component forms called geons.
   d. binocular disparity information.

7. Linear perspective, shading, and retinal disparity are all
   a. Gestalt principles of perceptual organization.
   b. cues for depth.
   c. types of perceptual constancy.
   d. types of geons.

8. Size perception is inaccurate in the Ames room, the Mueller-Lyer illusion and the Ponzo illusion because
   a. figure-ground relationships are not clear.
   b. stimulus distance is misjudged.
   c. binocular disparity is reversed.
   d. top-down processing is not possible.

9. Stationary, flashing lights make a wheel in a neon sign appear to move. This is an example of
   a. convergence.
   b. sensory adaptation.
   c. the volley principle.
   d. the phi phenomenon.

10. Humans are most sensitive to sounds with frequencies of
    a. 20 - 20,000 Hz.
    b. 20 - 500 Hz.
    c. 1,000 - 5,000 Hz.
    d. 10,000 - 12,000 Hz.

11. Sound travels through the ear canal and strikes the
    a. oval window.
    b. cochlea.
    c. semicircular canals.
    d. tympanic membrane.

12. A cochlear neuron is firing very rapidly. According to the frequency principle, the sound is probably
    a. loud.
    b. located very close by.
    c. high pitch.
    d. composed of several frequencies.

13. We perceive cold only when
    a. the temperature of our skin is reduced.
    b. cold fibers fire at a specific rate.
    c. the stimulus is below 50 degrees.
    d. the papilla are stimulated intensely.

14. Awareness of where your arms and legs are located is the product of the
    a. olfactory sense.
    b. vestibular sense.
    c. gustatory sense.
    d. kinesthetic sense.

15. Sensing movement and balance is the function of
    a. the semicircular canals and vestibular sacs.
    b. the cochlea and basilar membrane.
    c. the tympanic membrane and pinna.
    d. the lateral geniculate nucleus and superior colliculus.

16. Endorphins are
    a. the "gate" in gate control theory.
    b. "large" fibers in the pain system.
    c. located in the spinal cord.
    d. naturally occurring pain-killers.

17. Which is false?
    a. Loss of the olfactory system would affect the flavor of food.
    b. The receptors for gustation are located in the taste buds.
    c. Olfactory stimuli bind with the receptor cell cilia to generate a neural impulse.
    d. There are four specific types of olfactory receptors, corresponding to 4 basic smells.

18. Papillae are
    a. hair-like structures in the taste bud.
    b. bumps on the tongue that contain the taste buds.
    c. the actual receptor cells for taste.
    d. neurons that are linked with the taste receptors.

19. The dark adaptation curve is really a plot of _____ for vision as a function of time in the dark.
    a. Weber's Law
    b. false alarms
    c. absolute threshold
    d. difference threshold

20. In the signal detection technique a hit is recorded when the observer reports
    a. feeling a touch when he was touched.
    b. feeling a touch when he was not touched.
    c. feeling no touch when he was touched.
    d. feeling no touch when he was not touched.

Multiple Choice Pretest 2. Select the one best response. Answers are found on page 121.

1. Hubel and Wiesel found that if they moved the electrode just to the side of a cell that responded only to lines at a 30-degree angle they usually found cells that responded to
    a. lines at a 20 degree angle.
    b. depth.
    c. movement.
    d. faces.

2. A moving object high in the sky was seen as an enemy aircraft by the soldier on guard, but as a bird by the birdwatcher doing a bird count. This is explained best by
    a. recognition by components theory.
    b. top-down processing.
    c. Gestalt principles of perceptual organization.
    d. transduction.

3. While drifting among with the debris in the river current, the fugitive was undetected. However, as soon as he started swimming across the current, he was spotted. This is an example of the Gestalt law of
    a. closure.
    b. good continuation.
    c. common fate.
    d. proximity.

4. The adaptive value of accommodation is that it
    a. allows the lens to focus light from objects located at different distances.
    b. allows the rods to regenerate their photopigment in order to provide better vision in the dark.
    c. allows the organization of the stimulus input into different objects.
    d. allows the brain to "fill in" the blind spot.

5. Michael was born with no rods. We should expect that he
    a. cannot see well in low light conditions.
    b. cannot see color.
    c. has poor acuity.
    d. is essentially blind in the fovea.

6. The "break" at about 8 minutes in the dark adaptation curve represents the point at which
    a. rods have completed their adaptation, but the cones continue to increase in sensitivity.
    b. cones have completed their adaptation, but the rods continue to increase in sensitivity.
    c. photopigments are fully replenished, but the ganglion cells continue to increase in responsiveness.
    d. ganglion cells are at peak responsiveness, but the photopigments are continuing to be replenished.

7. All of the following data supports the trichromatic theory of color vision except
    a. the patterns of color blindness.
    b. the fact that all colors can be created by mixing the three primary colors.
    c. the fact different cones are maximally responsive to short, medium, or long wavelengths.
    d. the fact that staring at a green light results in a red afterimage.

8. The current view of the trichromatic theory and opponent-process theory of color is that
    a. the trichromatic theory is valid in the retina, and the opponent process theory is valid at higher levels.
    b. the opponent process theory is valid in the retina, and the trichromatic theory is valid at higher levels.
    c. the trichromatic theory is valid for primary colors, and opponent process theory is valid for others.
    d. the opponent process theory is valid for primary colors, and trichromatic theory is valid for others.

9. Ed lost one eye in an accident. His depth perception has been reduced because he no longer can use the depth cue of
    a. shading.
    b. accommodation.
    c. linear perspective.
    d. retinal disparity.

10. Depth cues make one square look farther away than another identical square. The "distant" square will be perceived as _____ than the other.
    a. more square
    b. less square
    c. larger
    d. smaller

11. The firing rate of neurons is limited by their refractory period to a maximum of about 500 impulses per second. This creates a problem for
    a. the frequency theory.
    b. the place theory.
    c. the opponent process theory.
    d. the gate control theory.

12. You're trying to hear an important news bulletin on the radio, but everyone around you is talking excitedly. You will be able to separate the bulletin from the other sounds most easily if
    a. you are male and the bulletin announcer is male, rather than female.
    b. the people talking around you are male and the bulletin announcer is male, rather than female.
    c. everyone is clustered around the radio.
    d. you know something about the expected content of the bulletin.

13. Auditory stimuli that occur close together in time are grouped together. This is a temporal (time) version of the visual, spatially based Gestalt principle of
    a. proximity.
    b. similarity.
    c. closure.
    d. common fate.

14. Which of the following is **false** concerning the skin senses?
    a. The amount of cortex that processes input from the skin is proportional to the size of the body part.
    b. People are very good at identifying common articles by touch.
    c. "Warm" or "cold" is determined by changes in skin temperature, not the object's actual temperature.
    d. Endorphins decrease the perception of pain.

15. During a battle for his life, the soldier did not notice the cuts he received from the rocks, but when you fell while rollerblading and received similar injuries, you felt significant pain. This is best explained by
    a. gate control theory.
    b. bottom-up processing.
    c. frequency theory.
    d. assuming you produced more endorphins.

16. You have a virus that has caused a disturbance in your vestibular system. This is most likely causing
    a. pain.
    b. a feeling of warmth.
    c. a loss of awareness of the position of your arms or legs.
    d. dizziness or nausea.

17. The apparent role of olfaction in sexual behavior, feeding, and emotion is not surprising given that the olfactory neural path includes links to
    a. the olfactory bulb.
    b. the amygdala, hippocampus, and hypothalamus.
    c. the somatosensory cortex.
    d. the thalamus.

18. To increase profits, the cereal company wants to reduce the amount of raisins in each cup of cereal, but they don't want consumers to notice the change. To know how many raisins they can remove they first need to obtain an estimate of the
    a. absolute threshold for raisins in a cup of cereal.
    b. difference threshold for raisins in a cup of cereal.
    c. signal detection threshold for raisins in a cup of cereal.
    d. hit rate for raisin detection in a cup of cereal.

19. The neural code for a specific taste is probably based on
    a. whether or not a specific receptor cell is active.
    b. how many papillae are stimulated.
    c. the relative amount of activity in 4 areas of the tongue.
    d. the pattern of activity across large groups of taste fibers.

20. Tom, 140 lb., Dick, 190 lb., and Harry, 240 lb., are going on a diet to lose weight. According to Weber's Law (and assuming they all lose the same number of pounds per week) we should expect that
    a. Tom's weight loss will be noticeable first.
    b. Dick's weight loss will be noticeable first.
    c. Harry's weight loss will be noticeable first.
    d. a noticeable reduction in weight will occur at the same time for the three.

ANSWERS AND EXPLANATIONS

Mastering the Concepts

1. sensations (p. 170)	15. Gestalt (p. 185)	29. far (p. 197)	43. movement (p. 204)
2. perception (p. 170)	16. geons (p. 187)	30. oval window (p. 197)	44. joints (p. 204)
3. transduced (p. 171)	17. retinal (p. 188)	31. place (p. 197)	45. vestibular (p. 204)
4. focuses (p. 173)	18. phi (p. 189)	32. frequency (p. 197)	46. semicircular (p. 204)
5. rods (p. 175)	19. constancy (p. 190)	33. volleys (p. 198)	47. chemoreceptors (p. 205)
6. acuity (p. 175)	20. illusions (p. 191)	34. similarity (p. 199)	48. olfactory bulb (p. 206)
7. Dark (p. 174)	21. pitch (p. 195)	35. expectations (p. 199)	49. pheromones (p. 206)
8. color (p. 177)	22. loudness (p. 195)	36. temperature (p. 201)	50. gustation (p. 207)
9. Feature (p. 178)	23. pinna (p. 195)	37. somatosensory (p. 202)	51. absolute (p. 208)
10. wavelengths (p. 181)	24. tympanic (p. 195)	38. Cold fibers (p. 202)	52. signal detection (p. 209)
11. Trichromatic (p. 181)	25. cochlea (p. 196)	39. Pain (p. 203)	53. false alarms (p. 209)
12. blindness (p. 183)	26. basilar (p. 196)	40. gate control (p. 203)	54. proportion (p. 210)
13. Opponent process (p. 183)	27. hair (p. 196)	41. spinal cord (p. 203)	55. adaptation (p. 211)
14. knowledge (p. 185)	28. opposite (p. 197)	42. endorphins (p. 203)	

Evaluating Your Progress

Preview & Vision: Building a World of Color and Form

1. **a**
(p. 172)
   - b. Wrong. Acuity is the ability to resolve fine details of a visual stimulus.
   - c. Wrong. Brightness is associated with the intensity of a visual stimulus.
   - d. Wrong. Accommodation is the adjustment of the lens to properly focus light on the retina.

2. **b**
(p. 173)
   - a. Wrong. The retina contains the receptor cells and is not involved with focusing the light.
   - c. Wrong. The pupil is the opening through which light passes and is not involved in focusing.
   - d. Wrong. The iris is the colored part of the eye and is not involved in focusing.

3. **b**
(p. 175)
   - a, c, & d. Wrong. These are all true attributes of rods.

4. **a**
(p. 174)
   - b. Wrong. Receptive fields size depends on the number of receptors linked to the ganglion cell.
   - c. Wrong. The brain fills in information in the blind spot, but this doesn't relate to adaptation.
   - d. Wrong. The vitreous humor is the "filler" in the eyeball and does not influence dark adaptation.

5. **b**
(p. 174)
   - a. Wrong. Rods require about 20 minutes, cones only 8.
   - c & d. Wrong. The lens and cornea are not involved in dark adaptation.

6. **c**
(p. 176)
   - a. Wrong. The blind spot is the place where the optic nerve exits the retina and there are no receptors.
   - b. Wrong. The optic chiasm is the crossover point in the visual pathway to the brain.
   - d. Wrong. The fovea, the center of vision, is not determined by receptor-ganglion linkage.

7. **c**
(p. 178)
   - a. Wrong. This is not a cell, it's a rare disorder in which only unmoving objects can be seen.
   - b. Wrong. The photoreceptors are not in the cortex, and they are selective only to wavelength.
   - d. Wrong. Bipolar cells in the retina are not selective to specific stimuli.

8. **d**
(p. 181)
   - a. Wrong. Opponent process theory states that pairs of colors are linked in an inhibitory manner.
   - b. Wrong. Recognition by components theory is an object recognition, not color, theory.
   - c. Wrong. Place theory is a theory of pitch perception.

9. c   a. Wrong.   Linear perspective involves converging lines as a cue for depth.
(p. 188)   b. Wrong.   Convergence is the degree to which the eyes turn inward to focus on near vs. far objects.
            d. Wrong.   Texture gradient involves the differences in texture visible in near vs. far objects.

10. b   a, c, & d. Wrong.   These ar all cues for motion. Changes in pupil size are not related to motion,
(p. 189)

11. d   a. Wrong.   Bottom-up processing analyzes image features. Changing features changes perceptions.
(p. 190)   b. Wrong.   Feature detectors would provide information about the image, not maintain constancy.
            c. Wrong.   Key here is the unchanging perception. Acuity is not related to maintaining constancy.

Hearing: Identifying and Localizing Sounds

1. b   a. Wrong.   Amplitude relates to intensity; frequency relates to pitch.
(p. 195)   c. Wrong.   Location is signaled by inter-ear differences in the input; frequency relates to pitch.
            d. Wrong.   A sound's purity is reflected in its waveform, not its frequency. Frequency relates to pitch.

2. c   a. Wrong.   The semicircular canals contain vestibular receptors, not auditory receptors.
(p. 196)   b. Wrong.   The tympanic membrane is the eardrum. It transmits sound but has no receptors.
            d. Wrong.   The pinna is the external ear "flap." It captures sound, but contains no receptors.

3. c   a. Wrong.   The impulse is generated in the cochlea, not the eardrum (which has no neurotransmitters).
(p. 196)   b. Wrong.   The bones of the middle ear don't touch the hair cells, which are inside the cochlea.
            d. Wrong.   The fluid movement, not any chemical reaction, is involved with generating the impulse.

4. d   a. Wrong.   This corresponds to the frequency theory of pitch perception.
(p. 197)   b. Wrong.   Impulses are all or none, remember? They vary in number, but not strength.
            c. Wrong.   The place theory uses location, not number. Number might relate to intensity.

5. d   a. Wrong.   Inter-ear timing differences produce perceptions of spatial location, not pitch changes.
(p. 200)   b. Wrong.   Inter-ear timing differences produce perceptions of spatial location, not intensity
                        differences.
            c. Wrong.   A tone to the right would arrive at the right ear first, not the left.

6. c   a & d.   Wrong.   Pitch (frequency) helps in auditory organization, but not in localization.
(p. 200)   b.   Wrong.   Top-down processing is not a factor in auditory localization.

The Skin and Body Senses: From Touch to Movement

1. c   a, b, & d.   Wrong.   These are all skin senses. Kinesthesia is a body sense, not a skin sense.
(p. 201)

2. a   b. Wrong.   Electromagnetic energy is the stimulus for vision.
(p. 201)   c. Wrong.   Changes in air density is the stimulus for audition (hearing).
            d. Wrong.   Chemical changes are the stimuli for the chemical senses of taste and smell.

3. c   a. Wrong.   The free nerve endings often carry pain input, but they are not the location of the gate.
(p. 203)   b. Wrong.   The basilar membrane is part of the auditory system, not the pain system.
            d. Wrong.   Skin sense input is processed in the somatosensory cortex, but it is not the gate's location.

4. b   a. Wrong.   No receptors are located in the cortex. The cortex does not contact the environment.
(p. 204)   c. Wrong.   The semicircular canals have the receptors for the vestibular, not kinesthetic, system.
            d. Wrong.   The cochlea contains the receptors for audition, not kinesthesia.

5. **a**   b, c, & d.   Wrong.   The semicircular canals have receptors for the vestibular sense (motion, posture).
    (p. 204)

6. **a**   b, c, & d.   Wrong.   The semicircular canals are in the inner ear and associated with the cochlea.
    (p. 204)

The Chemical Senses: Smell and Taste

1. **c**   a. Wrong.   Vestibular sacs are part of the vestibular system for motion and posture sensation.
    (p. 205)   b. Wrong.   Free nerve endings are usually associated with pain perception.
                d. Wrong.   Mechanoreceptors respond to the mechanical stimuli for touch.

2. **b**   a. Wrong.   Perfumes do not necessarily have a predictable, specific effect on an organism.
    (p. 206)   c. Wrong.   Papillae are the bumps on the tongue that contain the taste buds.
                d. Wrong.   Endorphins are brain chemicals that function as natural pain killers.

3. **a**   b, c, & d.   Wrong.   There are 4 basic tastes: sweet, salty, sour, and bitter.
    (p. 207)

From the Physical to the Psychophysical

1. **a**   b. Wrong.   This is a definition of the difference threshold.
    (p. 208)   c. Wrong.   This is usually referred to as the pain threshold and is a very intense stimulus.
                d. Wrong.   The absolute threshold defines the minimal detectable energy, not a maximum level.

2. **c**   a. Wrong.   Weber's Law predicts just noticeable differences, not sensitivity vs. bias.
    (p. 209)   b. Wrong.   Adaptation is reduced sensitivity due to constant stimulation. This wouldn't address bias.
                d. Wrong.   Transduction deals with production of neural activity, not psychophysical measurement.

3. **c**   a. Wrong.   Weber's Law involves difference thresholds, not changes in perceived intensity over time.
    (p. 211)   b. Wrong.   Signal detection theory considers sensitivity and bias in detection responses. It would not
                               predict the loss of sensitivity over time here.
                d. Wrong.   Perceptual constancy produces a constant perception, not a reduction.

4. **a**   b & c. Wrong.   Psychophysics relates the physical with the psychological; it doesn't involve
    (p. 208)   physiology.
                d.   Wrong.   Psychophysics relates the physical with the psychological. Expectancy has little role.

MAKING FINAL PREPARATIONS

Short Essay Questions

1. Full dark adaptation requires approximately 20-25 minutes and involves regeneration of photopigments in the rods and cones. Cones adapt quickly, reaching their potential within 3-4 minutes. Adaptation does not increase further until eight minutes into the period when the sensitivity of rods equals and surpasses that of cones. This creates the "break" in the adaptation curve. Rods continue to adapt until 20-25 minutes into the adaptation period. (p. 174)

2. Rods are long, slender visual receptors that are located outside the fovea. They are very sensitive to light but provide poor acuity and no color vision. Cones are short, thick, and pointed and are located in the fovea, and with less concentration in the periphery. They allow good acuity and color perception, but require a relatively high level of light to operate. (p. 175)

3. Expectancy influences interpretation of the stimulus, especially in cases of incomplete or ambiguous sensory information. It provides a guide for organizing ambiguous input, as in the case of much auditory stimulation, or for identification of other ambiguous stimuli. (pp. 185; 198-200)

4. Perceptual constancy is the unchanging perception of a stimulus even though the physical characteristics of the stimulus change. As an object moves away, its image shrinks. Instead of perceiving the object as shrinking, it is seen as a constant size due to the utilization of other information concerning size and distance. Constancy is adaptive. It prevents a constantly shifting world composed of unstable objects and relationships. (p. 190)

5. The perception of size depends in part on depth perception. Image size, one cue to object size, changes depending on the distance of the object. Thus, in perceiving size, the image is evaluated in relation to the object's depth. If depth is misjudged, size perception is often inaccurate. (pp. 191-193)

6. Place theory states that different pitches stimulate neurons at different places. The frequency principle states that a high pitch causes neurons to fire very rapidly, whereas a low pitch produces a lower firing rate. Both are used because place information is not as specific as necessary, and the frequency principle is limited by the neural refractory period, creating problems for high frequency perception. (pp. 197-198)

7. Auditory localization relies on inter-ear differences in stimulus intensity and arrival time. If only the left widows are open the sound will reach the left ear first and at greater intensity than the right because the sound will come in primarily through the left window, even if the source is to the right. This will result in localization of the sound source to the left in most cases. (p. 200)

8. According to the gate control theory of pain, a gate in the spinal cord controls the transmission of pain signals to the brain. Rubbing an injury simulates the "large" fibers in the body senses' neural path, which closes the gate and reduces the flow of pain signals to the brain. (p. 203)

Matching

1. e (p. 170)	4. g (p. 177)	7. a (p. 175)	10. d (p. 206)	13. b (p. 176)	16. c (p. 175)
2. j (p. 177)	5. p (p. 177)	8. k (p. 175)	11. m (p. 177)	14. o (p. 173)	
3. n (p. 206)	6. l (p. 185)	9. h (p. 202)	12. i (p. 204)	15. f (p. 209)	

Multiple Choice Pretest 1

1. **d** (p. 173)
   a. Wrong. The retina is at the very back of the eye. It's the last structure encountered.
   b. Wrong. The lens is an internal structure, not the first to be reached.
   c. Wrong. The iris is the second structure to be encountered.

2. **c** (p. 173)
   a. Wrong. This is not a common problem and would not significantly affect accommodation.
   b. Wrong. The photopigment only affects the likelihood of neural response, not focusing ability.
   d. Wrong. Increased pressure will damage the retina but will not affect accommodation.

3. **c** (p. 175)
   a, b, & d. Wrong. These are all attributes of cones.

4. **d** (p. 174)
   a, b, & c. Wrong. Dark adaptation continues for 20-25 minutes.

5. **a** (p.184)
   b. Wrong. Trichromatic theory centers on relative activity in three cones types, not opposite responses.
   c. Wrong. Frequency theory is a pitch perception theory, not a color theory.
   d. Wrong. Top-down processing refers to the use of knowledge or context for interpretation.

6. **c**   a. Wrong.   Biederman's theory is based on simple component structures, not feature detectors.
    (p. 187)   b. Wrong.   Biederman's theory is based on simple component structures, not context or knowledge.
                 d. Wrong.   Biederman's theory is based on simple component structures, not depth cues.

7. **b**   a. Wrong.   Gestalt laws are continuation, common fate, proximity, similarity, and closure.
    (p. 188)   c. Wrong.   Shape, size, brightness, and color constancy are perceptual constancies.
                 d. Wrong.   Geons are simple geometrical shapes objects of which objects are composed.

8. **b**   a. Wrong.   These illusions depth perception errors, not figure-ground ambiguity.
    (p. 192)   c. Wrong.   Binocular disparity is either unavailable (peephole view) or normal, not reversed.
                 d. Wrong.   Top-down processing contributes to the illusions (e.g., expect rectangular room).

9. **d**   a. Wrong.   Convergence is the angle of the eyes. Key here is motion from stationary flashing lights.
    (p. 189)   b. Wrong.   Sensory adaptation is reduced sensitivity to repeated stimulation, not a cue for motion.
                 c. Wrong.   The volley principle is related to pitch perception, not motion perception.

10. **c**   a. Wrong.   This is the entire range of hearing. Maximum sensitivity is in the 1000-5000 Hz range.
    (p. 195)   b. Wrong.   These are very low frequencies where sensitivity is poor. Sensitivity is best at 1000-5000 Hz.
                 d. Wrong.   These are beyond the most sensitive range of 1000-5000 Hz.

11. **d**   a. Wrong.   The oval window is in the cochlea in the inner ear.
    (p. 195)   b. Wrong.   The cochlea is not at the end of the auditory canal. It is in the inner ear.
                 c. Wrong.   The semicircular canals are in the inner ear and are not part of the auditory system.

12. **c**   a. Wrong.   In the frequency principle, neural firing rate relates to the stimulus' pitch, not its amplitude.
    (p. 197)   b. Wrong.   In the frequency principle for pitch, neural firing rate corresponds to pitch, not its location.
                 d. Wrong.   Frequency principle refers to pitch. Firing rate does not relate to the components of a sound.

13. **a**   b. Wrong.   There is no specific firing rate for cold.
    (p. 202)   c. Wrong.   The key is changing skin temperature, not stimulus temperature.
                 d. Wrong.   Papillae are part of the taste system.

14. **d**   a. Wrong.   The olfactory sense is the sense of smell.
    (p. 204)   b. Wrong.   The vestibular sense is the sense of movement and balance.
                 c. Wrong.   The gustatory sense is the sense of taste.

15. **a**   b & c. Wrong.   These are auditory structures.
    (p. 204)   d.   Wrong.   These are visual system brain areas.

16. **d**   a & b. Wrong.   These are structures. Endorphins are brain chemicals that reduce pain.
    (p. 203)   c.   Wrong.   Endorphins are brain chemicals that reduce pain.

17. **d**   a, b, & c.   Wrong.   These are true, but there are over 1000 kinds of olfactory receptors, not 4.
    (pp. 205-206)

18. **b**   a. Wrong.   Papillae contain taste buds, but taste buds do not have cilia, hair-like structures.
    (p. 207)   c. Wrong.   Papillae are not receptors. They are structures that contain the taste buds and receptors.
                 d. Wrong.   Papillae are not neurons. They are bumps on the tongue that contain the taste buds.

19. **c**   a. Wrong.   Weber's Law predicts difference thresholds based on original stimulus intensity.
(pp. 174,   b. Wrong.   False alarms in signal detection theory represent cases in which a stimulus is
208)   "detected" even though no stimulus was presented.
            d. Wrong.   The difference threshold is the minimum change in energy that can be detected.

20. **a**   b. Wrong.   This is a false alarm. A hit is reporting a touch that did occur.
(p. 209)   c. Wrong.   This is a miss. A hit is reporting a touch that did occur.
            d. Wrong.   This is a correct rejection. A hit is reporting a touch that did occur.

Multiple Choice Pretest 2

1. **a**   b, c, & d.   Wrong.   Although there are feature detectors for these characteristics, they are not side by
(p. 179)   side with the line detectors. Line detectors vary in terms of preferred orientation.

2. **b**   a. Wrong.   The key is the different expectations. Recognition by components doesn't address that.
(p. 185)   c. Wrong.   The key is the different expectations, which is not part of the Gestalt principles.
            d. Wrong.   The key is the different expectations, not the translation of the stimulus to neural energy.

3. **c**   a. Wrong.   Closure involves filling in gaps. Key here was the man moving differently than the river.
(p. 187)   b. Wrong.   Good continuation involves keeping intersected objects intact. Key here was the man
                        moving differently than the river.
            d. Wrong.   Proximity involves grouping objects that are close to each other. Key here was the man
                        moving differently than the river.

4. **a**   b. Wrong.   Accommodation is a change in lens thickness. Answer b describes dark adaptation.
(p. 173)   c. Wrong.   Accommodation is a change in lens thickness. Answer c describes Gestalt laws.
            d. Wrong.   Accommodation is a change in lens thickness. This has nothing to do with the blind spot.

5. **a**   b. Wrong.   Rods do not contribute to color vision.
(p. 175)   c. Wrong.   Cones have the best acuity, and Michael still has cones.
            d. Wrong.   The fovea doesn't contain rods, only cones, so his vision there will be fine.

6. **b**   a. Wrong.   The rods continue to adapt longer than cones.
(p. 174)   c. Wrong.   Only cone photopigments are replenished, and ganglion cells are not really involved.
            d. Wrong.   Ganglion cells have little to do with dark adaptation, and nothing to do with the break.

7. **d**   a, b, & c.   Wrong.   These all fit the trichromatic theory.
(pp. 181-183)

8. **a**   b.   Wrong.   This is the opposite relationship.
(p. 184)   c & d. Wrong.   Primary colors and other colors are processed and perceived in the same way.

9. **d**   a , b, & c.   Wrong.   Only binocular cues would be lost. These are monocular.
(p. 188)

10. **c**   a & b.   Wrong.   Shape constancy is not involved (both are square). This involves size constancy.
(p. 192)   d.   Wrong.   A distant object must be larger than a near object in order to cast the same size image.

11. **a**   b. Wrong.   Place theory uses neuron location, not firing rate, so coding high frequencies is no problem.
(p. 197)   c. Wrong.   Opponent process (color) theory doesn't require high frequencies, so this is not a problem.
            d. Wrong.   Gate control is a pain theory and doesn't need a high frequency code, so this isn't a problem.

12. **d** a. Wrong. The listener's sex provides nothing to help separate the bulletin from the rest of the noise.
(p. 199) b. Wrong. Good grouping requires the announcer and crowd to have different sex (frequency) voices.
  c. Wrong. If everyone is around the radio, spatial location would not be a cue to help group the bulletin.

13. **a** b. Wrong. Auditory similarity is based on frequency. Close in time or space = proximity.
(p. 186) c. Wrong. Auditory closure fills in missing input. Close in time or space = proximity.
  d. Wrong. Auditory common fate groups across input gaps. Close in time or space = proximity.

14. **a** b, c, & d. Wrong. These are all true statements. However, the size of the cortical area that processes
(pp. 202-3) input from the skin is proportional to the sensitivity of the body part, not its size

15. **a** b. Wrong. Bottom-up processing emphases stimulus characteristics, so his pain should equal yours.
(p. 203) c. Wrong. Frequency theory is a theory of pitch perception, not pain perception.
  d. Wrong. More endorphins would reduce pain more. The key here is cognitive or context factors.

16. **d** a. Wrong. The vestibular system is involved in sensing motion or posture, not pain.
(p. 204) b. Wrong. The vestibular system is involved in sensing motion or posture, not temperature.
  c. Wrong. The vestibular system is involved in sensing motion or posture, not limb position.

17. **b** a. Wrong. The olfactory bulb processes olfactory input, but does not control emotion or motivation.
(p. 206) c. Wrong. The somatosensory cortex is not involved in these motivational or emotional behaviors.
  d. Wrong. Olfaction is the only sense that does not include the thalamus in its neural path.

18. **b** a. Wrong. The absolute threshold would indicate the number of raisins detectable in cereal, not whether a change is detectable.
(p. 210)
  c. Wrong. Signal detection theory does not use thresholds.
  d. Wrong. This just relates to the detection of raisins, not the detection of differences in raisin number.

19. **d** a. Wrong. Papillae are not receptors. They contain the receptors.
(p. 207) b. Wrong. There are no known opponent process cells in taste. Maybe you were thinking of vision?
  c. Wrong. Areas of the tongue differ in sensitivity to certain tastes, but this is not the neural code.

20. **a** b, c, & d. Wrong. Weber's law states that the just noticeable difference is a constant proportion of
(p. 210) the magnitude of the original (standard) stimulus. That is, the greater the stimulus, the larger the absolute change required for detection. Tom weighs least, so he can lose fewer pounds than the others and the change will be noticed.

LANGUAGE ENHANCEMENT GUIDE

CORE TERMS

In the discussion of this chapter you are very likely to hear two expressions quite frequently: *to distinguish between, to differentiate* and *to discriminate*. The last one is likely to be confusing the first time you hear it, since it has such a particular meaning in most people's minds (something close to 'prejudice'). Actually, the terms all mean very nearly the same thing -- to tell the difference between. And of course, the ability to tell the difference between things is important when we are talking about the senses.

Beyond that, you will need to be comfortable with several Latin- and Greek-based words having to do with the senses:

vis or *vid,* to see, becomes vision or video

aud and *acous*, to hear, becomes auditory or acoustic (The word part *son* means sound)

tact or *tang*, to touch, becomes tactile or tangible

kinet, to move, becomes kinesthetic

olfac, to smell, becomes olfactory

gust, to taste, becomes gustatory

Vestibular, as it turns out, is an exception to the rule. A 'vestibule' is a sort of small entrance area, like a lobby -- or, in anatomical terms, a chamber or channel that leads into another chamber or channel. To figure out why this sense is named as it is, you'll need to pay attention to where this sense is located in the body.

IDIOMS

170	bolt upright	to suddenly sit up straight
170	beckon your interpretation	invite you to figure them out
171	cut across all	work in all cases; be relevant in all
172	tackle the topic	address the subject; talk about
179	orientation specificity	exact orientation or angle
179	physically adjacent	right next to
179	parses	breaks down into its parts
180	metabolically active	busy in terms of blood flow, chemical processes, etc.
180	upper- or lowercase	capital or small letters
188	three-dimensional	having height, length and depth
188	plastered on	laid flat onto
188	of comparable height	about as tall as one another
199	use the intricacies of	use the details and complexities of
199	cardiovascular system	the heart and blood vessels
202	adjacent cortical cells	the cells of the cortex that are right next to
202	perceptual enigma	confusing experience of the senses
203	locus of such effects	the main area where the effects come from or are focused

203	analgesic	pain-relieving
203	acupuncture	a medical procedure from the orient that involves the insertion of special needles into body parts
209	strategic bias	a desire or way to achieve a certain goal
211	a pervasive force	a force that reaches throughout

WORD PARTS

Here are some words that are made up of word parts, and that you can find in this chapter. After you've looked at these, you can look for others in the chapter that use the same word parts (they are there, but YOU have to find them!)

WORD	WORD PART IT USES	MEANING
subsequent	sub = under, next sequ = a group, a series	the next in order
recognize	re = again gno = to think, understand, know	to know again, to find familiar
ambiguous	ambi = both	having two or more interpretations; confusing
extract	ex = out of tract = to pull	to pull out of
translate	trans = across lat = line	to cross over, to change from one to another
receptive	re = again cept = to get, take	to be willing to take back again
regenerate	re = again gen = birth, race, kind	to start over again
transduce	trans = across duc = to carry	to carry across
periphery	per, peri = around	around the edges
dichromats	di = two chrom = color	those who can only see two colors

Knowing the word parts listed above, you can also create the following words. You can get an idea of their meanings from the word parts they use. You fill in the blanks!

except   ex + cept   _____

resequence   _____ + _____   to put back in order

perceptive   _____ + _____   to see what is around; to understand a
                                         situation

intractable   in (not) + tract   _____

retract   _____ + _____   to pull back

CHAPTER 6: CONSCIOUSNESS

ESTABLISHING LEARNING OBJECTIVES

Use these learning objectives as a preview of the chapter, a guide for active reading, and to evaluate your mastery of the material. Review the relevant objectives as you begin and end your reading of each major section of the chapter.

After studying this chapter you should be able to:

I.   Solve the adaptive problem of how to establish priorities for mental functioning.
    A.   Define attention and discuss its adaptive value.
    B.   Discuss how experiments on "dichotic listening" can be used to study attention.
    C.   Describe automaticity and its effects on awareness.
       1. Define subliminal, and discuss whether subliminal messages affect behavior.
    D.   Discuss disorders of attention such as visual neglect and attention deficit disorder.

II. Understand the characteristics of sleep and sleep's adaptive function.
    A.   Discuss biological rhythms and how they are controlled.
    B.   Describe the various stages and characteristics of sleep.
    C.   Discuss the function and adaptive significance of sleep.
       1. Describe the consequences of sleep deprivation.
    D.   Discuss current theories of dreaming and its function.
       1. Describe Freud's wish fulfillment theory of dreams.
       2. Describe the activation-synthesis hypothesis of dreams.
       3. Describe the problem solving view of dreams.
    E.   Describe the various disorders of sleep.
       1. Differentiate dyssomnias and parasomnias and give an example of each.

III. Solve the adaptive problem of how consciousness can be altered biochemically.
    A.   Compare neurotransmitters with psychoactive drugs.
    B.   Discuss the different categories of psychoactive drugs and provide examples from each.
       1. Describe the effects of each drug, and identify the method of action.
    C.   Discuss the psychological factors that influence the effects of psychoactive drugs.

IV. Solve the adaptive problem of how consciousness can be altered without drugs.
    A.   Describe the physiological and behavioral effects of hypnosis.
    B.   Discuss whether hypnosis can be used effectively as a memory aid.
    C.   Describe the dissociation and role-playing accounts of hypnosis.
    D.   Discuss the physical, behavioral, and psychological effects of meditation.

MASTERING THE MATERIAL

Preview & Setting Priorities for Mental Functioning: Attention (pp. 220-229)

Mastering the Vocabulary. Define or explain each of the following terms. To check your answers, consult the text pages listed.

1. consciousness (p. 220)

2. attention (p. 222)

3. dichotic listening (p. 223)

4. cocktail party effect (p. 224)

5. automaticity (p. 225)

6. subliminal (p. 226)

7. visual neglect (p. 227)

8. attention deficit disorder (p. 228)

Mastering the Concepts. Fill in the blanks to create a summary of this section. Answers are on page 141.

The subjective awareness of internal and external events, _____(1), was central to 19th century psychology but lost favor due to the limitations of _____(2). Interest in consciousness is increasing. This chapter considers four adaptive problems: How are priorities set for mental functioning? What are the characteristics and roles of sleep and dreams? How do psychoactive drugs alter awareness? How can alterations in consciousness be induced without drugs?

By directing _____(3) to only some things, the organism sets priorities for mental function, protects mental resources and improves functioning. However, as the _____(4) effect and _____(5) listening experiments show, the unattended message is monitored, and important input does affect behavior. One's name is recognized, and attention unconsciously follows a message continued in the unattended ear.

Divided attention tasks show that _____ (6) can develop for some highly practiced tasks, limiting conscious awareness of that task. Stimuli that do not reach conscious awareness can influence behavior, but it is not clear whether the _____ (7), below threshold, messages supposedly imbedded in advertising and self-help tapes even exist or are effective. In some cases, there is no evidence embedded messages are present. Also, controlled studies found no influence of subliminal messages on behavior beyond that accounted for by a _____ (8) effect.

Right (and sometimes left) parietal lobe damage can cause _____ (9), a disorder in which there is no conscious awareness of the left visual field, although input is processed. Right hemisphere dysfunction also seems to be a central cause of the inability to maintain or control attention, _____ (10) disorder.

Evaluating Your Progress. Select the one best response. Answers are found on page 141. If you make any errors, reread the relevant material before proceeding.

1. Subjects shadow (repeat) the message in one ear while ignoring the message in the other ear in the
   a. visual neglect technique.
   b. dichotic listening technique.
   c. spotlight technique.
   d. subliminal technique.

2. The ability to selectively attend to one message while ignoring others (except for the occurrence of one's name) is known as
   a. visual neglect.
   b. consciousness.
   c. automaticity.
   d. the cocktail party effect.

3. The cocktail party effect and Treisman's "ear-switching" experiment demonstrate that
   a. right parietal lobe brain damage disrupts basic attentional mechanisms.
   b. highly practiced tasks require less attention than less well-practiced tasks.
   c. when more than one message is presented, neither message is understood well.
   d. an unattended message is monitored for important content.

4. A task that can be performed rapidly, effortlessly and without focused attention is considered a(n)
   a. automatic process.
   b. controlled process.
   c. split brain process.
   d. dissociated process.

5. A loss of awareness of the contents of one half of the visual field is known as
   a. visual neglect.
   b. attention deficit disorder.
   c. hypnotic dissociation.
   d. split world disorder.

6. A subliminal message is a message that
    a. motivates you to behave in a certain way.
    b. is extremely appealing and pleasant.
    c. is below the detection threshold.
    d. reduces your attention to the main message.

Sleeping and Dreaming (pp. 229-241)

Mastering the Vocabulary. Define or explain each of the following terms. To check your answers, consult the text pages listed.

1. circadian rhythms (p. 230)

2. biological clocks (p. 230)

3. alpha waves (p. 233)

4. theta waves (p. 233)

5. delta activity (p.233)

6. REM (p. 233)

7. REM rebound (p. 237)

8. wish fulfillment theory (p. 237)

9. manifest content (p. 239)

10. latent content (p. 239)

11. activation-synthesis hypothesis (p. 239)

12. problem solving theory (p. 240)

13. dyssomnias (p. 240)

14. parasomnias (p. 240)

15. insomnia (p. 240)

16. hypersomnia (p. 241)

17. sleep apnea (p. 241)

18. narcolepsy (p. 241)

19. nightmares (p. 241)

20. night terrors (p. 241)

21. sleepwalking (p. 241)

Mastering the Concepts. Fill in the blanks to create a summary of this section. Answers are on page 141.

Sleep, an altered state of consciousness, is an example of a biological rhythm. Because sleep-waking has a 24-hour cycle, it is a _____(11) rhythm. The suprachiasmatic nucleus of the _____(12) may be the _____(13) clock for the sleep cycle, with light playing a key role in pacing the clock.

Brain EEG patterns vary in _____(14), _____(15), regularity and neural synchrony during sleep. Alpha waves are found during relaxation. Stage 1 sleep has mostly _____(16) waves. Irregular EEG patterns called sleep _____(17) and K-complexes occur in State 2 sleep. The deeper sleep of Stages 3 and 4 has slower, synchronous waves called _____(18) activity. The EEG of REM sleep has an irregular pattern similar to a waking state, but the person is deeply asleep. Thus, REM sleep is called _____(19) sleep. If awakened in REM sleep, people usually report they were _____(20). Complete sleep cycles last about _____(21) and are repeated. The length of REM increases with each cycle. The function of sleep is unclear, but it may be restorative or a protective, adaptive response to light-dark cycles and past predators. Sleep deprivation leads to poor functioning.

The function of REM sleep is unclear. REM deprivation has only small psychological effects, but it does lead to REM _____(22), increased REM sleep the next night, and it may impair learning. REM sleep influences neurotransmitter levels. Freud proposed the dreams of REM sleep are a means for _____(23) fulfillment and reflect the contents of the unconsious mind. A dream's manifest content is the actual images of the dream, but the _____(24) content is its hidden meaning. According to the _____(25)-synthesis hypothesis, dreams are the brain's interpretation of random activity. Current concerns, rather than deep-seated problems, might influence these interpretations. REM sleep occurs in many species and in the prenatal period.

Sleep disorders are classified as dyssomnias, or parasomnias. Dyssomnias, troubles in timing, quality, or quantity of sleep, include _____(26), a problem getting to sleep or staying asleep, and hypersomnia, excessive sleepiness. Parasomnias, abnormal events during sleep, include nightmares, _____(27), and sleepwalking. Nightmares are REM dreams, but night terrors and sleepwalking occur in non-REM sleep.

Evaluating Your Progress. Select the one best response. Answers are found on page 142. If you make any errors, reread the relevant material before proceeding.

1. The biological clock that controls circadian rhythms seems to be in the suprachiasmatic nucleus of the
   a. optic nerve.
   b. pituitary gland.
   c. hypothalamus.
   d. reticular activating system.

2. A person whose EEG shows primarily synchronous, high amplitude, very slow-wave delta activity is
   a. awake and concentrating on a task.
   b. awake and very relaxed.
   c. in Stage 4 sleep.
   d. in REM sleep.

3. REM sleep is called paradoxical sleep because
   a. it is the shortest stage of sleep, but it is the most necessary.
   b. dreams with complex plots are likely, but they are usually colorless.
   c. dreams are very likely to occur, but the brain waves are the slowest, highest amplitude type.
   d. the brain waves are similar to those of a waking state, but the person is very deeply asleep.

4. Which is true?
   a. Most people cycle through REM sleep about twice each night.
   b. Heart rate is very slow and regular during REM sleep.
   c. More time is spent in REM sleep near morning than in the first hours of sleep.
   d. REM stands for "restore energy mode."

5. The survival theory of why we sleep suggests that
   a. because we rely on vision, sleeping at night had the adaptive value of keeping us safe.
   b. without sleep our neurotransmitters would be depleted and we couldn't function.
   c. sleep is needed to restore psychological balance through dreaming.
   d. sleep is needed to resynchronize the various biological clocks so they do not drift.

6. Sleepwalking and night terrors usually
   a. occur during REM sleep.
   b. cease when the person gets older.
   c. are symptoms of a psychological problem.
   d. accompanied by sleep apnea.

7. Freud proposed that we dream
   a. for wish fulfillment and to deal with highly disturbing desires.
   b. because we try to interpret the random brain activity generated during sleep.
   c. because we need to restore the supply of brain neurotransmitters.
   d. in order to solve the problems that arose during the day.

Altering Awareness: Psychoactive Drugs (pp. 242-247)

Mastering the Vocabulary. Define or explain each of the following terms. To check your answers, consult the text pages listed.

1. psychoactive drugs (p. 242)

2. tolerance (p. 243)

3. drug dependency (p. 243)

4. withdrawal (p. 243)

5. depressants (p. 243)

6. stimulants (p. 244)

7. opiates (p. 245)

8. hallucinogens (p. 245)

Mastering the Concepts. Fill in the blanks to create a summary of this section. Answers are on page 141.

Mood and consciousness is controlled by neurotransmitters. REM sleep onset is controlled by ACh secretion by neurons in the _____(28). GABA may control the initiation and duration of sleep. Dopamine and norepinephrine are linked to wakefulness and arousal. _____(29) drugs affect mental processes, consciousness, and behavior by changing neurotransmitter balance. Drugs mimic, block, or increase neurotransmitter activity. Use can cause drug dependency, but the underlying cause is unclear. Drug _____(30) can develop, requiring higher doses for an effect, and if drug use ends, withdrawal occurs.

There are four categories of psychoactive drugs. _____(31) depress the nervous system, and include alcohol, barbiturates, and tranquilizers. They increase GABA activity (also dopamine for alcohol), which reduces anxiety, but they can lead to dependency. _____(32) increase neural activity and include caffeine, nicotine, amphetamines, and cocaine. Alertness is increased and mood lifted, primarily by increased norepinephrine and dopamine activity. Dopamine may be the key to the positive feelings produced. _____(33), including morphine, opium, and heroin, elevate mood by depressing nervous system activity, and are likely to cause dependence. _____(34), or psychedelics, include LSD, mescaline, psilocybin, and marijuana and are likely to produce alteration of sensation and perception. LSD seems to mimic serotonin. Side effects include "bad" trips, and impaired concentration and coordination. Drug effects depend on the user's environment, _____(35), physical condition, and familiarity with the drug.

Evaluating Your Progress. Select the one best response. Answers are found on page 142. If you make any errors, reread the relevant material before proceeding.

1. REM sleep begins when acetylcholine (ACh) is secreted by the
    a. hippocampus.
    b. thalamus.
    c. pons.
    d. superchiasmatic nucleus.

2. Repeated use of psychoactive drugs often leads to
    a. increased sensitivity.
    b. tolerance.
    c. withdrawal.
    d. synesthesia.

3. A physical or psychological need for a drug is known as
    a. tolerance.
    b. withdrawal.
    c. synesthesia.
    d. dependency.

4. Which drug is incorrectly assigned to a drug category?
   a. heroin---opiate
   b. diazepam (Valium)---depressant
   c. marijuana---hallucinogen
   d. alcohol---stimulant

5. All of the following drugs are classified as hallucinogens except
   a. mescaline.
   b. marijuana.
   c. psilocybin.
   d. cocaine.

Altering Awareness: Induced States (pp. 247-252)

Mastering the Vocabulary. Define or explain each of the following terms. To check your answers, consult the text pages listed.

1. hypnosis (p. 247)

2. catalepsy (p. 249)

3. hypnotic hypermnesia (p. 249)

4. hypnotic dissociation (p. 250)

5. meditation (p. 251)

Mastering the Concepts. Fill in the blanks to create a summary of this section. Answers are on page 141.

Hypnosis is a social interaction resulting in a heightened state of _____(36). A technique is to suggest the person is getting very relaxed and _____(37) as the person fixates on an object. Hypnosis has assisted in ending unwanted habits, reducing _____(38) during medical procedures, inducing _____(39), the ability to hold an unusual position for a long time, and altering perception.

Evidence that hypnosis can improve memory is poor. Controlled studies find no memory enhancement, and the _____(40) of "recovered" memories and age regression is difficult to verify.

Hilgard suggests that hypnosis involves hypnotic _____(41), a splitting of consciousness into separate parts: a part that acts on the hypnotist's suggestions, and a _____(42) observer with normal awareness. An alternative is that hypnosis involves social _____(43); the subject simply tries to please the hypnotist and plays the hypnotized role. Simulated subjects research and the influence of the subject's _____(44) about hypnosis support this view.

_____(45), a way to self-induce shifts in awareness, is sometimes described as "pure thought" and often involves _____(46) paired with focused concentration on breathing or a mantra to help clear the mind. Research shows meditation reduces arousal and increases _____(47) brain waves, both common to relaxation, and may help reduce anxiety.

Evaluating Your Progress. Select the one best response. Answers are found on page 143. If you miss any questions, reread the relevant material before proceeding.

1. The individual credited with performing a form of hypnosis in 1783 was
    a. Ernest Hilgard.
    b. Anton Mesmer.
    c. Timothy Leary.
    d. Sigmund Freud.

2. Your text defines hypnosis as
    a. "a form of social interaction that produces a heightened state of suggestibility in willing participants."
    b. "an altered state of consciousness the reduces pain, improves memory, and eliminates bad habits."
    c. "a dissociation of consciousness into multiple parts, each with its own level of awareness."
    d. "a technique to self-induce a state of altered awareness, relaxation, and spiritual reflection."

3. Physiological measurements during hypnosis
    a. are most similar to those of a state of relaxation.
    b. are most similar to those of a deep sleep.
    c. show brain wave patterns unique to hypnosis.
    d. show neurotransmitter activity patterns unique to hypnosis.

4. Hilgard's "hidden observer" experiments are used to provide evidence for
    a. catalepsy.
    b. social role playing.
    c. hypnotic hypermnesia.
    d. hypnotic dissociation.

5. The most positive benefit of meditation is its ability to
    a. enhance memory for long-forgotten events.
    b. produce a state of relaxation.
    c. increase physiological arousal.
    d. increase theta waves.

MAKING FINAL PREPARATIONS

Complete these sections without consulting your book or notes. For a more accurate estimate of how well you know this material, wait at least a day or two after studying the chapter before working on the questions. Some of the material you "know" immediately after working with the chapter will be quickly forgotten. Immediate tests will overestimate what you know well.

Short Essay Questions. Write a brief answer to each question. Sample answers are on page 143.

1. Discuss why the development of automaticity is adaptive.

2. Cite the data that show that unattended information is not completely ignored.

3. Discuss the possible adaptive value of sleep.

4. Explain why the effects of psychoactive drugs can vary from person to person or from time to time.

5. Cite the evidence supporting the social role playing view of hypnosis.

6. Discuss the idea that stimuli that do not reach conscious awareness can influence behavior.

Matching. Select the correct definition or description for each item. Answers are on page 144.

_____	1. sleep apnea	**a.**	blending of sensory experiences
_____	2. dependency	**b.**	ability to hold rigid for long periods under hypnosis
_____	3. attention	**c.**	physical symptom caused by cessation of drug use
_____	4. parasomnia	**d.**	brain structure that controls bodily function cycles
_____	5. catalepsy	**e.**	brain waves found in Stage 2
_____	6. alpha waves	**f.**	temporally stopping breathing during sleep
_____	7. biological clock	**g.**	spending more time in REM after deprivation
_____	8. withdrawal	**h.**	particular sound or words used during meditation
_____	9. dichotic listening task	**i.**	selective attention task
_____	10. consciousness	**j.**	internal process that sets mental function priorities
_____	11. hypnotic hypermnesia	**k.**	problems of timing or duration of sleep
_____	12. K-complexes	**l.**	subjective awareness of internal and external events
_____	13. REM rebound	**m.**	abnormal disturbances during sleep
_____	14. mantra	**n.**	brain waves associated with relaxed state
_____	15. synesthesia	**o.**	a physical or psychological need, often for a drug
_____	16. dyssomnias	**p.**	supposed hypnotic memory enhancement

Multiple Choice Pretest 1. Select the one best response. Answers are found on page 144.

1. Automaticity is evaluated by comparing single task performance with a two-task situation known as a
    a. divided attention task.
    b. ear-switching task.
    c. dichotic listening task.
    d. hidden observer task.

2. Liz was told to repeat the message in her right ear and to ignore the message in her left ear. The right ear message was, "Mary had a little lamb, and heard the shattering glass." The left ear message was, "David saw the cars collide, it's fleece was white as snow." Based on Treisman's research, Liz probably said
    a. "Mary had a little lamb, and heard the shattering glass."
    b. "Mary had a little lamb, its fleece was white as snow."
    c. alternate words from each message (Mary saw a cars lamb...).
    d. randomly selected words from each message.

3. Visual neglect and, perhaps, attention deficit disorder seem to be disorders of
    a. the cerebellum.
    b. the occipital lobes.
    c. the hindbrain.
    d. the right hemisphere.

4. K-complexes and sleep spindles are characteristic of
    a. Stage 1 sleep.
    b. Stage 2 sleep.
    c. Stage 4 sleep.
    d. REM sleep.

5. Which of the below is an accurate summary of the research on hypnosis' memory-enhancing properties?
    a. Improvements in memory do occur under hypnosis and cannot be explained by other means.
    b. Although hypnosis is responsible for memory enhancement, this does not include age regression.
    c. Although hypnosis does not improve general memory, the "recovered" memories of traumas in childhood are highly accurate, and can be considered as reliable testimony in criminal trials.
    d. Controlled experiments have not found any memory enhancement due to the properties of hypnosis.

6. Nils is a wimp about dental work, but gas makes him sick, and he's allergic to most painkilling drugs. If he is facing painful dental work, another effective pain reduction technique he could try is
    a. meditation.
    b. hypnosis.
    c. REM deprivation therapy.
    d. alpha wave therapy.

7. Rao is practicing a technique involving the self-induced manipulation of awareness for the purpose of self-reflection and relaxation. Rao is involved in
    a. meditation.
    b. hypnosis.
    c. psychoactive drug use.
    d. sleep.

8. The length of one sleep cycle (Stage 1 through REM sleep) is about
   a. 30 minutes.
   b. 90 minutes.
   c. 2 hours.
   d. 4 hours.

9. Ann has had trouble getting to sleep and staying asleep for the last 6 months. Her likely diagnosis is
   a. sleep apnea.
   b. catalepsy.
   c. hypersomnia.
   d. insomnia.

10. Freud felt that dreams about guns signified sexual concerns and desires. This represents
    a. the dream's manifest content.
    b. the dream's latent content.
    c. the activation-synthesis hypothesis.
    d. the dissociation hypothesis.

11. Sally has taken a drug that is causing her to hear colors and see music. The drug most likely is
    a. LSD.
    b. heroin.
    c. a barbiturate.
    d. alcohol.

12. Phil severely broke his leg in a motorcycle accident. To relieve the pain, his doctor is likely to prescribe
    a. an opiate.
    b. hallucinogens.
    c. amphetamines.
    d. cocaine.

13. A single-blind study of the effectiveness of subliminal message weight loss tapes found that everyone lost weight, even those given tapes without any subliminal messages. This result is best explained as
    a. a placebo effect.
    b. a statistically significant difference.
    c. a difference in motivation between groups.
    d. good evidence that subliminal messages work.

14. Vokey & Read (1985) presented vacation slides in which the word "sex" was visible, but not highly obvious in some of the pictures. On a subsequent memory test recognition was
    a. better for pictures with the word "sex" than pictures without the word "sex."
    b. better for pictures of people with the word "sex" added than pictures of places.
    c. no different for pictures with the word "sex" than pictures without the word "sex."
    d. worse for pictures with the word "sex" than pictures without the word "sex."

Multiple Choice Pretest 2. Select the one best response. Answers are found on page 145.

1. Your 6-year-old son has started sitting up in bed in the middle of the night, screaming and in a state of extreme panic. He usually doesn't respond when you talk to him, but if you do get him to respond, he says he wasn't dreaming. He is probably experiencing
   a. hypersomnia.
   b. sleep apnea.
   c. a night terror.
   d. a nightmare.

2. Tim sat entranced by his favorite TV show. His mother began talking to him, but he showed no awareness that she was even there until she said his name. This is most similar to
   a. attentional neglect.
   b. attention deficit disorder.
   c. the cocktail party effect.
   d. hypnotic hypermnesia.

3. Keno was doing great in his driver's license road test until he started thinking about where he'd go on his first night out. While making his plans he scraped the curb and almost lost control, showing that
   a. Keno probably has visual neglect.
   b. Keno's driving has not yet reached automaticity.
   c. Keno's thinking is an automatic process.
   d. the cocktail party effect relates to driving.

4. Lars is having difficulty concentrating on his schoolwork, is easily distracted, and never seems to be able to finish a task. This is most likely an example of
   a. visual neglect.
   b. delta activity.
   c. the cocktail party effect.
   d. attention deficit disorder.

5. Mia is living in a continuously lighted environment. After several days her sleep cycle probably will
   a. be the same length and timing as it was originally--asleep at 11 p.m., up at 7 a.m.
   b. be the same length, but it will have shifted to a later time--asleep at 3 a.m., up at 1 p.m.
   c. be much shorter, but it will begin at the original time--asleep at 11 p.m., up at 3 a.m.
   d. be much shorter and it will have shifted to an earlier time--asleep at 7 p.m., up at 11 p.m.

6. If you want your studying to be helpful on the exam tomorrow, it is most important that you get
   a. a normal amount of alpha wave presleep time.
   b. a normal amount of Stage 1 and Stage 2 sleep tonight.
   c. a normal amount of Stage 3 and Stage 4 sleep tonight.
   d. a normal amount of REM sleep tonight.

7. A rat will press a response bar hundreds of times if barpressing results in the administration of cocaine. Apparently the pleasurable and reinforcing aspects of the drug are due to cocaine's effect on
   a. endorphins.
   b. serotonin.
   c. dopamine.
   d. GABA.

8. A hypnotized subject has submerged her hand in ice after being given the suggestion that she will feel little pain. Her "hidden observer" has been told to ring a bell in indicate what she (the hidden observer) feels. Based on Hilgard's research, if the person verbally reports a pain level of 4, the hidden observer will report a pain level of
   a. 0 -- hidden observers have no contact with the environment.
   b. 2 -- hidden observers react more strongly to hypnotic suggestions.
   c. 4 -- hidden observers perceive the same things the hypnotized person does.
   d. 8 -- hidden observers perceive what a non-hypnotized person perceives.

9. You dreamed about riding a train into a tunnel. According to the activation-synthesis view, your dream
   a. is really about your need to fulfill an unacceptable sexual desire.
   b. is an attempt by your mind to solve a problem that arose during the last few days.
   c. is your brain's interpretation of the random neural activity generated during sleep.
   d. is an indication of a serious psychological disorder that should be treated.

10. Glenda is using a drug that increases the effectiveness of GABA and dopamine. The drug most likely is
    a. cocaine.
    b. alcohol.
    c. heroin.
    d. LSD.

11. As part of their religious ceremony, the elders of the tribe ate a particular mushroom known to cause "visions" and other intense perceptual effects. The active drug in this mushroom is
    a. mescaline.
    b. marijuana.
    c. psilocybin.
    d. cocaine.

12. Ben feels his eyelids start to sag and he feels very relaxed as he stares at a coin on the table. He is willing to obey commands and might report reduced pain perception. Ben's highly suggestible state is due to
    a. hallucinogenic drugs.
    b. meditation.
    c. sleep deprivation.
    d. hypnosis.

13. People told prior to hypnosis that hypnosis causes rigidity of the arms are likely to show this symptom while hypnotized, even if the hypnotist never suggests rigidity. This supports the view that hypnosis
    a. is a dissociation of consciousness.
    b. is due to an increase in alpha wave activity.
    c. is a kind of social role playing.
    d. is an acetylcholine (ACh) imbalance.

14. Which of the following statements is not an accurate summary of the subliminal perception research?
    a. Stimuli that do not reach conscious awareness cannot have any influence on behavior.
    b. The cause of the apparent success of subliminal self-help tapes is likely a placebo effect.
    c. Embedded words or images related to sex produce no improvements in memory or preferences.
    d. Some subliminal self-help tapes do not appear to even have subliminal messages embedded in them.

15. Sam has been drinking alcohol for many years. He can drink much more now than he could when he first started drinking. This change is an example of
    a. dependency.
    b. catalepsy.
    c. withdrawal.
    d. tolerance.

ANSWERS AND EXPLANATIONS

Mastering the Concepts

1. consciousness (p. 220)	13. biological (p. 231)	25. activation (p. 239)	37. sleepy (p. 248)
2. introspection (p. 220)	14. height (p. 232)	26. insomnia (p. 240)	38. pain (p. 249)
3. attention (p. 222)	15. frequency (p. 232)	27. night terrors (p. 241)	39. catalepsy (p. 249)
4. cocktail party (p. 224)	16. theta (p. 233)	28. pons (p. 242)	40. accuracy (p. 250)
5. dichotic (p. 223)	17. spindles (p. 233)	29. Psychoactive (p. 242)	41. dissociations (p. 250)
6. automaticity (p. 225)	18. delta (p. 233)	30. tolerance (p. 243)	42. hidden (p. 250)
7. subliminal (p. 226)	19. paradoxical (p. 233)	31. Depressants (p. 243)	43. role playing (p. 251)
8. placebo (p. 227)	20. dreaming (p. 234)	32. Stimulants (p. 244)	44. expectations (p. 251)
9. visual neglect (p. 227)	21. 90 minutes (p. 234)	33. Opiates (p. 245)	45. Meditation (p. 251)
10. attention deficit (p. 228)	22. rebound (p. 237)	34. Hallucinogens (p. 245)	46. relaxation (p. 252)
11. circadian (p. 230)	23. wish (p. 237)	35. expectations (p. 247)	47. alpha (p. 252)
12. hypothalamus (p. 230)	24. latent (p. 239)	36. suggestibility (p. 247)	

Evaluating Your Progress

Preview & Setting Priorities for Mental Functioning: Attention

1. **b**
   (p. 223)
   - a. Wrong. Visual neglect is a neuropsychological disorder caused by parietal lobe damage.
   - c. Wrong. Attention is often described as a spotlight, but there is no spotlight technique in research.
   - d. Wrong. Subliminal refers to "below threshold." Input is not subliminal in the case described.

2. **d**
   (p. 224)
   - a. Wrong. Visual neglect is a disorder in which one half of the visual field cannot reach awareness.
   - b. Wrong. Consciousness is the subjective awareness of internal and external events.
   - c. Wrong. Automaticity is fast effortless processing requiring little or no controlled attention.

3. **d**
   (p. 224)
   - a. Wrong. The cocktail party and ear switching research deals with normal attention, not disorders.
   - b. Wrong. This is false, and it does not relate to the selective attention experiments cited.
   - c. Wrong. An attended message is well-processed, and the unattended message is at least monitored.

4. **a**
   (p. 225)
   - b. Wrong. A controlled process requires controlled attention.
   - c. Wrong. Automaticity does not imply a single hemisphere is used for processing.
   - d. Wrong. Dissociation is a splitting into parts. This is not related to automaticity.

5. **a**
   (p. 227)
   - b. Wrong. Attention deficit disorder involves an inability to sustain or control attention.
   - c. Wrong. Hypnotic dissociation is a splitting of consciousness with multiple forms of awareness.
   - d. Wrong. Split world disorder is not an actual condition.

6. **c**   a. Wrong. Subliminal means below threshold. Research shows subliminal messages are ineffective.
  (p. 226) b. Wrong. Subliminal means below threshold. The emotional content is variable.
         d. Wrong. Subliminal means below threshold. Attention is not diverted from the main message.

Sleeping and Dreaming

1. **c**   a. Wrong. Light is important for setting biological clocks, but the clock is not in the optic nerve.
  (p. 230) b. Wrong. Hormones fluctuate in cycles, but the pituitary is not the site of the biological clock.
         d. Wrong. The biological clock influences the RAS, but that is not the clock's location.

2. **c**   a. Wrong. While awake and working on a task, the EEG is asynchronous and high frequency.
  (p. 233) b. Wrong. While awake but relaxed, the EEG is primarily alpha waves.
         d. Wrong. The EEG for REM is similar to waking (asynchronous, high frequency waves).

3. **d**   a. Wrong. This is not a true statement, and the paradox of REM concerns brain waves vs. sleep depth.
  (p. 233) b. Wrong. Dreams are likely, but the paradox of REM concerns brain waves and sleep depth.
         c. Wrong. This is not the paradox, and dreams produce waves similar to a waking state, not delta.

4. **c**   a. Wrong. Most people cycle through four or five times.
  (p. 235) b. Wrong. Heart rate is very irregular and rapid during REM.
         d. Wrong. REM stands for rapid eye movements.

5. **a**   b, c, & d.   Wrong.   These describe sleep as restorative or allowing repair of the system.
  (p. 236)

6. **b**   a. Wrong. These parasomnias are associated with non-REM sleep, usually Stage 4 sleep.
  (p. 241) c. Wrong. These parasomnias usually don't indicate psychological problems, but nightmares might.
         d. Wrong. Hypersomnia involves excessive sleepiness or sleeping too much, not too little.

7. **a**   b. Wrong. This is Hobson & McCarley's activation-synthesis theory.
  (p. 237) c. Wrong. This is a restorative theory of sleep and dreams.
         d. Wrong. This is Cartwright's problem solving theory of dreams.

Altering Awareness: Psychoactive Drugs

1. **c**   a & b. Wrong. These structures are not involved in sleep.
  (p. 242) d.   Wrong. The superchiasmatic nucleus controls circadian rhythms, but not REM sleep onset.

2. **b**   a. Wrong. Continued drug use leads to tolerance, not sensitivity.
  (p. 243) c. Wrong. Withdrawal occurs when drug use is halted.
         d. Wrong. Synesthesia is a bended sensory experience found with hallucinogen use.

3. **d**   a. Wrong. Tolerance is the need to take a higher dose to obtain the same level effect.
  (p. 243) b. Wrong. Withdrawal occurs when a drug dependency is present and the user quits taking the drug.
         c. Wrong. Synesthesia is a blending of sensory experiences most common with hallucinogenic drugs.

4. **d**   a, b, & c.   Wrong.   These are all correct. Alcohol is a depressant, not a stimulant.
  (pp. 243-245)

5. **d**   a, b, & c.   Wrong.   Mescaline, marijuana, and psilocybin are hallucinogens. Cocaine is a stimulant.
  (p. 245)

1. **b**   a. Wrong.   Hilgard, a contemporary psychologist, proposed the dissociation view of hypnosis.
    (p. 247)   c. Wrong.   Timothy Leary was a modern advocate of using LSD to expand consciousness.
               d. Wrong.   Sigmund Freud, the 20th century psychoanalyst, did not originate hypnosis.

2. **a**   b. Wrong.   These are common claims for the uses of hypnosis, but not an accepted definition.
    (p. 247)   c. Wrong.   This is the dissociation theory of hypnosis, but not the accepted definition.
               d. Wrong.   This is a possible definition of meditation, not hypnosis.

3. **a**   b. Wrong.   Brain waves during hypnosis are mostly alpha, not the delta activity of deep sleep.
    (p. 248)   c. Wrong.   Brain waves during hypnosis are mostly alpha, just like the brain waves during relaxation.
               d. Wrong.   Neurotransmitter activity has not been assessed.

4. **d**   a. Wrong.   Catalepsy is a hypnotically-induced state in which a rigid posture is held for long periods.
    (p. 250)   b. Wrong.   The expectancy effect experiments support the social role playing view.
               c. Wrong.   Hidden observer research involves dissociation and pain perception, not memory.

5. **b**   a. Wrong.   Meditation does not enhance memory.
    (p. 252)   c. Wrong.   Physiological arousal is decreased with meditation, not increased.
               d. Wrong.   Meditation is associated with increased alpha, not theta, activity.

MAKING FINAL PREPARATIONS

Short Essay Questions

1. Automaticity involves rapid, effortless processing that requires little or no directed attention. One a task is automatic, it is not a drain on the limited mental resources. Other tasks can be performed at the same time without suffering a reduction in performance. (pp. 225-227)

2. Dichotic listening experiments show that the unattended message does not reach awareness, but is processed. People respond to important information, such as their name, in an unattended message. Also, when the meaningful content of a message is switched to the unattended ear, shadowing switches to follow the meaning, rather than continuing with the "attended" ear. (pp. 224-225)

3. Sleep might serve a restorative function, possibly allowing neurotransmitters to be regenerated. Sleep might have developed to keep early man out of trouble during the time we cannot rely on vision to avoid danger. Also, Freud suggested the dreams of sleep were the means for fulfilling wishes that are too unacceptable to be allowed into consciousness. (pp. 235-237)

4. Several factors other than the chemical composition of a drug determine its effect. The physical condition of the user can modify drug effects, in the case of simple physical differences and concerning whether drug tolerance has developed. Also important are the mental set or expectations of the user and the environment in which the drug is taken. Expectancy can shape the reaction to a drug's effect or even create an effect where there is no drug. Likewise, the environment provides a context that interacts with the drug's actual effects. (pp. 246-247)

5. First, people's behavior while hypnotized is influenced by their expectations or beliefs about hypnosis. They conform their behavior to fit their expectations, including the expectation that people who are hypnotized obey commands. Also, the suggestions made during hypnosis end when the subject believes they are no longer hypnotized, even if no modification of instructions are made by the hypnotist. Finally, most of the phenomena of hypnosis can be achieved by people "simulating" hypnosis (told to act hypnotized). (p. 251)

6. The cocktail party effect and "ear-switching" effect in dichotic listening research both show that unattended (but detectable) information is processed and can influence behavior, even though the "unattended" message usually doesn't reach conscious awareness. The research on subliminal (below threshold) stimuli, however, indicates that it has no effect on behavior other than possible placebo effects. Controlled studies of subliminal advertising and products have not obtained behavior that differed from that of the control group. (pp. 224-227)

Matching

1. **f** (p. 241)   4. **m** (p. 240)   7. **d** (p. 230)   10. **l** (p. 220)   13. **g** (p. 237)   16. **k** (p. 240)
2. **o** (p. 243)   5. **b** (p. 249)   8. **c** (p. 243)   11. **p** (p .249)   14. **h** (p. 251)
3. **j** (p. 222)   6. **n** (p. 233)   9. **i** (p. 223)   12. **e** (p. 233)   15. **a** (p. 245)

Multiple Choice Pretest 1

1. **a**   b. Wrong.   The ear-switching task examines selective attention, not automaticity.
   (p. 226)   c. Wrong.   A dichotic listening task examines selective attention, not automaticity.
                d. Wrong.   The hidden observer task is a test of the dissociation view of hypnosis.

2. **b**   a.   Wrong.   The "split ear" research found people followed a meaningful message across ears.
   (p. 224)   c & d.   Wrong.   Mixing messages occurs only when it retains meaning, not isolated words.

3. **d**   a. Wrong.   Both are associated with the right hemisphere, not the cerebellum.
   (pp. 227,   b. Wrong.   Neither occipital lobe is the usual cite of dysfunction.
   228)   c. Wrong.   The hindbrain is not a likely site for dysfunction in these disorders.

4. **b**   a. Wrong.   Stage 1 sleep EEG is primarily theta waves. Sleep spindles and K-complexes are Stage 2.
   (p. 233)   c. Wrong.   Stage 4 produces delta activity, not sleep spindles or K-complexes.
                d. Wrong.   REM sleep has high frequency, asynchronous waves, but no sleep spindles or K-complexes.

5. **d**   a. Wrong.   Apparent memory enhancement can be accounted for by "normal" conditions.
   (p. 250)   b. Wrong.   Hypnosis itself does not influence memory.
                c. Wrong.   "Recovered" memories are often impossible to verify, can be highly inaccurate, and
                             are not allowed as testimony in many states' criminal proceedings.

6. **b**   a. Wrong.   Meditation causes relaxation, but not pain reduction.
   (p. 249)   c. Wrong.   REM deprivation does not reduce pain perception.
                d. Wrong.   Alpha waves are associated with relaxation, but not pain reduction.

7. **a**   b. Wrong.   Hypnosis is not generally self-induced nor commonly used for self-reflection.
   (p. 251)   c. Wrong.   Drugs might manipulate awareness and allow relaxation and self-reflection, but this would
                             not be considered self-induced because it involves an outside agent, drugs.
                d. Wrong.   Sleep is self-induced and relaxing, and alters awareness. It doesn't involve self-reflection.

8. **b**   a, c, & d.   Wrong.   The five stages of sleep take a total of about 90 minutes to complete.
   (p. 234)

9. **d**   a. Wrong.   Sleep apnea is a disorder in which people quit breathing periodically while asleep.
   (p. 240)   b. Wrong.   Catalepsy is a state in which the limbs of the body may be held rigid for a long time.
                c. Wrong.   Hypersomnia involves excessive sleepiness or sleeping too much, not too little.

10. **b**   a. Wrong.   The manifest content is the actual symbols in the dream, not their interpretation.
    (p. 239)   c. Wrong.   Activation-synthesis is an alternative to Freud's theory.
                d. Wrong.   The dissociation hypothesis proposes that consciousness splits during hypnosis.

11. **a**   b, c & d.   Wrong.   These can produce pleasurable feelings, but synesthesia is most likely with LSD.
(p. 245)

12. **a**   b. Wrong.   Barbiturates elevate mood, but do little to pain sensitivity.
(p. 245)   c. Wrong.   Hallucinogens affect perception, but they do not reduce pain sensitivity.
           d. Wrong.   Cocaine elevates mood, but does not reduce pain sensitivity.

13. **a**   b. Wrong.   There was no difference.
(p. 227)   c. Wrong.   Rather, both groups were probably well motivated to lose weight.
           d. Wrong.   The weight loss didn't differ between groups, so the weight loss can't be due to the tapes.

14. **c**   a, b, & d.   Wrong.   There was no effect of having the word "sex" on the pictures.
(p. 226)

Multiple Choice Pretest 2

1.   **c**   a. Wrong.   Hypersomnia is a tendency to be sleepy much more often than normal.
(p. 241)   b. Wrong.   In sleep apnea the person stops breathing periodically while asleep.
           d. Wrong.   Nightmares are dreams, and they usually do not cause panic and nonresponsiveness.

2.   **c**   a. Wrong.   In attentional (visual) neglect one side of the visual field does not reach consciousness.
(p. 224)   b. Wrong.   In attention deficit disorder the individual cannot sustain attention.
           d. Wrong.   Hypnotic hypermnesia is improved recall under hypnosis.

3.   **b**   a. Wrong.   He'd never drive well if he lacked awareness of half of the visual field (visual neglect).
(p. 225)   c. Wrong.   If thinking were automatic, it would not interfere with driving.
           d. Wrong.   The cocktail party effect shows unattended input is processed. That is not the case here.

4.   **d**   a. Wrong.   Visual neglect involves being unaware of half of the visual field.
(p. 228)   b. Wrong.   Delta activity is a type of brain wave characteristic of deep sleep.
           c. Wrong.   The cocktail party effect is the awareness of important input in an unattended message.

5.   **b**   a, c, & d.   Wrong.   Without light to synchronize the biological clock, the length of sleep remains
(p. 230)   about the same, but shifts its starting time.

6.   **d**   a, b, & c.   Wrong.   Learning and memory are most affected by REM deprivation.
(p. 238)

7.   **c**   a. Wrong.   Endorphins are affected by opiates. Dopamine is the key to cocaine's reinforcing effects.
(p. 244)   b. Wrong.   Serotonin is affected by hallucinogens. Dopamine is the key to cocaine's effects.
           d. Wrong.   Depressants affect GABA. Dopamine is the key to cocaine's effects.

8.   **d**   a, b, & c.   Wrong.   The hidden observer perceives what a non-hypnotized person would perceive.
(p. 250)

9.   **c**   a. Wrong.   This would be a Freudian wish-fulfillment view, not the activation-synthesis approach.
(p. 239)   b. Wrong.   This would be a problem solving approach, not the activation-synthesis approach.
           d. Wrong.   The activation-synthesis view doesn't assign dreams any diagnostic value.

10. **b**   a. Wrong.   Cocaine increases the activity of norepinephrine and dopamine.
(p. 244)   c. Wrong.   Heroin mimics the activity of endorphins.
           d. Wrong.   LSD mimics serotonin.

11.	**c**	a.	Wrong.	The hallucinogen mescaline comes from a cactus, not mushrooms.
	(p. 245)	b.	Wrong.	The hallucinogen marijuana comes from a leafy plant, cannabis sativa, not mushrooms.
		d.	Wrong.	The stimulant cocaine comes from the leaf of the coca plant, not mushrooms.

12.	**d**	a.	Wrong.	Hallucinogens do not increase suggestibility or reduce pain perception.
	(p. 247)	b.	Wrong.	Meditation induces relaxation, but not heightened suggestibility.
		c.	Wrong.	Sleep deprivation causes sagging eyelids, but not pain reduction or suggestibility.

13.	**c**	a.	Wrong.	Hidden observer, not expectancy effect, experiments support the dissociation view.
	(p. 251)	b.	Wrong.	The key aspect of the research is the subject's expectation, not brain waves.
		d.	Wrong.	This is not a view of hypnosis, and ACh has no relation to expectancy effects in hypnosis.

| 14. | **a** | b, c, & d. | Wrong. | These statements are accurate, but events below awareness can have an effect. |
| | (p. 226) | | | |

15.	**d**	a.	Wrong.	Dependency is a need for continued drug use.
	(p. 243)	b.	Wrong.	Catalepsy is the ability to maintain odd postures while hypnotized.
		c.	Wrong.	Withdrawal is the physical reaction to discontinuing drug use.

LANGUAGE ENHANCEMENT GUIDE

CORE TERMS

In the lectures on this chapter you may learn about *illicit* drugs -- that is, illegal drugs (the psychoactive drugs that are used to treat mental illnesses are discussed in chapter 15). You may learn about the *deleterious* (harmful) effects of these drugs on the brain, and about the effects of these drugs on a child *in utero* (in the uterus, before birth). You instructor might also share with you the *prevalence* of their use -- that is, how many people are thought to use them.

An interesting historical note: you may have heard the term *mesmerized*. This is the old term for hypnotized; the person who introduced the technique to western culture was Anton Mesmer.

IDIOMS

221	biological seat of consciousness	specific, physical place where we can find 'consciousness' coming from; no brain part that makes it
222	heightened state of suggestibility	a state in which you are more likely to do what you are told
222	smorgasbord	a great feast or banquet; a wide and wonderful variety
223	her latest escapade	her latest wild adventure or risky behavior
224	a case in point	an example
224	naive (said 'ni-eev')	not sophisticated, not worldly or experienced

225	in the realm of	within the world of; in the same area
225	repertoire (said 'reh-peh-twahr')	usual actions; things you are able to do easily
225	without a hitch	quite easily and without mistakes
228	can manifest itself	can make itself known; can be seen as
231	stay put	stay where they are
231	play havoc with	make a mess of; badly confuse
231	shrug off	not be affected by; take no notice of
231	eavesdrop	to listen in secretly
232	bears a striking similarity	seems very much like
235	a number of plausible hypotheses	several believable theories about how something works
236	venturing forth	going out
237	wreaks havoc	creates a great deal of confusion; messes up
239	in the eye of the beholder	is subjective; depends upon the person who is observing and their particular viewpoint
239	spontaneously activate	to start up completely on their own; suddenly
245	particularly apt	very appropriate; fitting
246	euphoric	very happy and excited
247	fell into disrepute	lost its good reputation; became less well-regarded

WORD PARTS

Here are some words that are made up of word parts, and that you can find in this chapter. After you've looked at these, you can look for others in the chapter that use the same word parts (they are there, but YOU have to find them!)

WORD	WORD PART IT USES	MEANING
synchrony	sys, syl, syn, sym = together, along with chron = time	two things happening at the same time; matched in time

dyssomnia	dys = bad, ill som = sleep	poor sleeping
dissociation	dis = take away, not soc = contact; togetherness	to break two things apart; to prevent contact
cyclic	cycl = round; like a wheel or circle	to go around, to move from stage to stage and then back to the beginning
paradoxical	para = beside, position dox = belief, opinion	two (conflicting) opinions that one believes at the same time
hypersomnia	hyper = overly, too much som = sleep	sleeping too much

Knowing the word parts listed above, you can also create the following words. You can get an idea of their meanings from the word parts they use. You fill in the blanks!

synonymous	syn + nym (name)	_____
parasomnia	_____ + _____	(activities) along with/at the same time as sleep
somnambulism	som + ambul (to walk)	_____
hyperactive	_____	overly active
chronic	_____	lasting a long time, permanent

CHAPTER 7: LEARNING FROM EXPERIENCE

ESTABLISHING LEARNING OBJECTIVES

Use these learning objectives as a preview of the chapter, a guide for active reading, and to evaluate your mastery of the material. Review the relevant objectives as you begin and end your reading of each major section of the chapter.

After studying this chapter you should be able to:

I.   Define learning, and explain how learning is studied.

II. Solve the adaptive problem of recognizing and reacting appropriately to significant events.
   A.   Describe the orienting response and discuss its adaptive value.
   B.   Describe and compare habituation and sensitization.
   C.   Distinguish between short-term and long-term habituation.

III. Solve the adaptive problem of recognizing the relationship between events and responding appropriately.
   A.   Describe the basic elements of classical conditioning.
      1.   Define conditioned stimulus, unconditioned stimulus, conditioned response and unconditioned response, and be able to recognize them in Pavlov's classic experiment.
   B.   Discuss how and why conditioned responding develops.
      1.   Discuss the evidence that suggests that conditioning is more than stimulus substitution.
      2.   Discuss how taste aversions develop and explain how they are both adaptive and troublesome.
   C.   Differentiate among second-order conditioning, stimulus generalization and stimulus discrimination.
   D.   Discuss conditioned inhibition and extinction.
      1.   Describe the process of extinction and what spontaneous recovery indicates about extinction.
      2.   Discuss the adaptive value of conditioned inhibition.

IV. Solve the adaptive problem of recognizing the consequences of a behavior and responding appropriately.
   A.   Define instrumental conditioning, and discuss the law of effect.
   B.   Explain what is meant by the discriminative stimulus.
   C.   Define reinforcement, and differentiate positive and negative reinforcement.
      1.   Explain the response deprivation theory of reinforcement.
      2.   Describe conditioned reinforcers.
   D.   Discuss different schedules of reinforcement, and compare their effects on behavior.
   E.   Discuss how complex behaviors can be acquired through shaping.
      1.   Discuss how superstitious behavior develops.
      2.   Discuss the biological constraints on conditioning.
   F.   Define punishment, and distinguish between positive and negative punishment.
      1.   Discuss the limitations of punishment as a technique for eliminating a behavior.

V.   Solve the adaptive problem of learning without directly experiencing a situation.
   A.   Describe observational learning, and specify the conditions that lead to effective modeling.
   B.   Explain why observational learning is adaptive, and discuss its practical effects.

MASTERING THE MATERIAL

Preview & Learning About Events: Noticing and Ignoring (pp. 260-265)

Mastering the Vocabulary. Define or explain each of the following terms. To check your answers, consult the text pages listed.

1. learning (p. 260)

2. orienting response (p. 263)

3. habituation (p. 263)

4. sensitization (p. 264)

Mastering the Concepts. Fill in the blanks to create a summary of this section. Answers are on page 166.

Learning is a relatively _____(1) change in _____(2), or potential to respond, that results from _____(3). Learning research often uses animals as subjects because of the greater control possible and their simpler learning processes. This chapter examines four adaptive learning problems: How do people notice events? How do they learn about signaling properties of events? How do they learn about the consequences of behavior? How do they learn from others?

Novel stimuli cause _____(4) responses, an automatic shift in attention toward the stimulus. With repeated stimulation _____(5), a reduction in responsiveness, occurs if the stimulus is without serious consequences. Habituation produces selective responding. If the stimulus is intense, sometimes an increase, rather than a decrease, in responsiveness occurs, _____(6). Habituation can be either long-term or short-term, is found throughout the animal world, and is used in modeling the effects of experience.

Evaluating Your Progress. Select the one best response. Answers are found of page 167. If you make any errors, reread the relevant material before proceeding.

1. "A relatively permanent change in behavior, or potential to respond, that results from experience" defines
   a. the orienting response.
   b. performance.
   c. learning.
   d. knowledge.

2. The diners' heads automatically turned toward the kitchen door at the sound of the dishes crashing. Their behavior is an example of
   a. a conditioned response.
   b. an orienting response.
   c. instrumental conditioning.
   d. sensitization.

3. Orienting responses sometimes become more selective and decrease when significant consequences do not follow the unexpected stimulus. This decrease in the tendency to make an orienting response is
   a. habituation.
   b. sensitization.
   c. stimulus generalization.
   d. negative reinforcement.

Learning What Events Signal: Classical Conditioning (pp. 266-277)

Mastering the Vocabulary. Define or explain each of the following terms. To check your answers, consult the text pages listed.

1. classical conditioning (p. 266)

2. unconditioned stimulus (p. 266)

3. unconditioned response (p. 266)

4. conditioned stimulus (p. 266)

5. conditioned response (p. 266)

6. blocking (p. 269)

7. second-order conditioning (p. 272)

8. stimulus generalization (p. 273)

9. stimulus discrimination (p. 274)

10. extinction (p. 275)

11. spontaneous recovery (p. 276)

12. conditioned inhibition (p. 276)

Mastering the Concepts. Fill in the blanks to create a summary of this section. Answers are on page 166.

Organisms learn what events _____(7) through a process known as _____(8) conditioning. A Russian physiologist, _____(9), developed the procedures of classical conditioning after noticing that the dogs in his digestion research began salivating before food was presented. Certain stimuli, _____(10) stimuli (USs), automatically lead to responses known as _____(11) responses (URs). No learning is required. Other stimuli that signal the unconditioned stimulus can acquire an ability to cause a _____(12) response (CR). These stimuli are called _____(13) stimuli (CSs). In Pavlov's experiments food is an unconditioned stimulus for the unconditioned response of salivation. The assistant's footsteps or a bell rung just before food presentation, became conditioned stimuli and elicited a conditioned response of salivation.

To become a CS, a stimulus must provide reliable information about the US. CSs usually must come _____(14) the US (signal the upcoming US) for conditioning to occur. The US usually must follow the CS closely in time; too much delay makes the CS a poor signal. The CS must reliably signal the US; the CS and US should not occur _____(15). Other stimuli that accompany the CS will not become CSs if they provide no new information; _____(16) will occur.

The current signaling approach emphasizes that conditioning is not _____(17). The organism actively seeks information about relationships. This approach does not see the CS as a _____(18) for the US, eliciting a CR very similar to the UR. The characteristics of the CR depend on the characteristics of the CS and the organism's feelings about the US. CRs can be similar to, opposite to, or different from, the URs.

Learning to predict events based on signaling stimuli is very adaptive. Conditioned taste _____ (19), helps prevent consumption of dangerous foods. Organisms that become ill after eating a food, especially an unusual one, develop an aversion to that food and are unwilling to eat it again. In some cases, such as chemotherapy, conditioned taste aversions are not desirable, but can be prevented by giving a distinctive food as a "decoy" or by presenting bland foods unlikely to cause conditioned taste aversion.

Conditioned stimuli can condition other events, a process called _____(20) conditioning, without ever presenting the US. In stimulus _____(21) new stimuli similar to the CS will elicit a CR. "Little Albert" was conditioned to cry when a rat was presented, but other furry items also elicited crying. In contrast, in stimulus _____(22) a new stimulus results in a different response, often after experience shows the new stimulus does not signal the US. If the CS is never again paired with the US, the CS loses its signaling characteristics and _____(23), the loss of the CR, occurs. This is similar to _____(24) but involves a conditioned relationship, not an inborn one. When previously extinguished CRs reappear, spontaneous _____(25) is said to have occurred. In conditioned _____ (26), the CS signals the absence of a US and leads to a reduction of responding.

Evaluating Your Progress. Select the one best response. Answers are on page 167. If you make any errors, reread the relevant material before proceeding.

1. Organisms learn relationships between stimuli that are outside of their control through a process called
   a. instrumental conditioning.
   b. sensitization.
   c. classical conditioning.
   d. habituation.

2. A stimulus that automatically produces an observable response prior to any training is called a(n)
   a. conditioned stimulus.
   b. unconditioned stimulus.
   c. discriminative stimulus.
   d. associate stimulus.

3. In Watson's experiment with Albert, Albert cried when a loud noise was suddenly presented. After presenting a rat just before the noise several times, Watson found that Albert cried when the rat was presented, even if the noise wasn't. In this experiment, the rat was the
   a. unconditioned stimulus.
   b. unconditioned response.
   c. conditioned stimulus.
   d. conditioned response.

4. Stimulus discrimination occurs when
   a. only the unconditioned stimulus elicits the conditioned response.
   b. stimuli that are similar to the conditioned stimulus also elicit the conditioned response.
   c. stimuli other than the conditioned stimulus do not elicit the conditioned response.
   d. an established conditioned stimulus is used to condition a second neutral stimulus.

5. Even though a conditioned response has undergone extinction, it sometimes reappears later without any further training. This reappearance is known as
   a. spontaneous recovery.
   b. second-order conditioning.
   c. sensitization.
   d. generalization.

6. Blocking occurs because the new stimulus
   a. signals the occasions when the unconditioned stimulus won't occur.
   b. adds no new information about the unconditioned stimulus.
   c. is separated from the unconditioned stimulus by too much time.
   d. doesn't provide reliable information about the unconditioned stimulus.

7. Chemotherapy patients find foods eaten prior to therapy are not appealing afterward. This illustrates
   a. second-order conditioning.
   b. conditioned inhibition.
   c. stimulus discrimination.
   d. conditioned taste aversion.

8. If the unconditioned stimulus is never again presented with the conditioned stimulus,
   a. extinction occurs.
   b. blocking occurs.
   c. discrimination occurs.
   d. generalization occurs.

Learning About the Consequences of Behavior: Instrumental Conditioning
(pp. 278-291)

Mastering the Vocabulary. Define or explain each of the following terms. To check your answers, consult the text pages listed.

1. instrumental conditioning (p. 278)

2. law of effect (p. 280)

3. discriminative stimulus (p. 280)

4. reinforcement (p. 281)

5. positive reinforcement (p. 281)

6. negative reinforcement (p. 281)

7. escape conditioning (p. 282)

8. avoidance conditioning (p. 282)

9. conditioned reinforcer (p. 283)

10. schedules of reinforcement (p. 283)

11. partial reinforcement schedule (p. 283)

12. fixed-ratio schedule (p. 283)

13. variable-ratio schedule (p. 285)

14. fixed-interval schedule (p. 285)

15. variable-interval schedule (p. 286)

16. shaping (p. 287)

17. punishment (p. 289)

18. positive punishment (p. 289)

19. negative punishment (p. 290)

Mastering the Concepts. Fill in the blanks to create a summary of this section. Answers are on page 166.

In classical conditioning, events signal outcomes, but in _____(27) or _____(28) conditioning the organism's actions signal outcomes. In the late 1800's, Thorndike proposed the _____(29): Responses followed by a satisfying or pleasant consequence will be _____(30); responses followed by an unsatisfying or unpleasant consequence will be _____(31).

In the 20th century, Skinner proposed that _____(32) stimuli signal when a response will be rewarded, like the CS signaling the US. Stimulus _____(33) occurs when a response is made to stimuli that are similar to the original, and stimulus _____(34) occurs when responding occurs only to one stimulus. Instrumental conditioning once was thought to be a simple association of stimulus and response, but the current view is that the organism learns about the reward, in addition to stimulus and response.

The formal term for the situation in which a "pleasant" consequence "strengthens" a response is _____(35), which is defined as response consequences that increase the likelihood of the response. _____(36) reinforcement is an event, that when presented after a response, increases the likelihood of that response. Response _____(27) theory states an event will be reinforcing if it moves the organism closer to its bliss point, or baseline tendency, for that event. For _____(38) reinforcement, removal of an event after a response increases the likelihood of the response occurring again. Negative reinforcement can involve _____(39) conditioning, in which a response ends an unpleasant event, and _____(40) conditioning, in which a response prevents the occurrence of an unpleasant event. Note that "negative" refers to removing an event, not decreasing the response. All reinforcement increases response likelihood.

Reinforcers can be classified as primary and secondary, or _____(41) reinforcers. Primary reinforcers have intrinsic value (food, water), but secondary reinforcers (money, stars) have acquired (learned) value.

The rules or _____(42) of reinforcement produce individual patterns of response. A _____(43) schedule of reinforcement reinforces every target response. A _____(44) reinforcement schedule reinforces only some responses. A _____(45) schedule requires a certain number of responses for reinforcement and produces steady responding, but a postreinforcement pause can occur with large ratios. If the number of required responses varies around an average, a _____(46) schedule is in effect, and the response rate will be high and steady. _____(47) schedules require a certain amount of time to pass before another response will be reinforced and produces low rates of responding with a scalloped appearance. If the time interval varies, the schedule is a variable interval schedule and produces steady responding.

When reinforcement is ended _____(48) begins, and the organism eventually quits responding. The schedule of reinforcement influences how long responding will continue. Continuous schedules produce _____(49) extinction than partial schedules, and fixed schedules result in _____(50) extinction than variable schedules, apparently due to differences in the discriminability of reinforcement termination.

The method of successive approximations, or _____(51), is used to train an organism to make a desired response. Responses that approximate the desired response are reinforced, and the standards for reinforcement are increased gradually until the final form of the response is required. Accidental or adventitious reinforcement can also modify behavior. This is one cause of superstitious behavior.

Consequences that decrease the likelihood of a response are called punishment. In _____(52) punishment, an aversive event is presented after a response. In _____(53) punishment a positive event is removed after a response. Problems with punishment include judging its strength, the fact that bad behavior is suppressed rather than a good behavior taught, and possibly resentment, aggression, and attempted escape.

Evaluating Your Progress. Select the one best answer. Answers are on page 168. If you make any errors, reread the relevant material before proceeding.

1. Responses followed by pleasant consequences are strengthened; responses followed by unpleasant consequences are weakened. This represents the
   a. principle of extinction.
   b. law of effect.
   c. concept of shaping.
   d. observational learning.

2. A child learns that if she says "please," Dad will usually give her what she wants. The concept at work is
   a. classical conditioning.
   b. instrumental conditioning.
   c. extinction.
   d. sensitization.

3. A pigeon was trained to peck a blue key, but it will also peck the key if it is green. This demonstrates
   a. generalization.
   b. shaping.
   c. extinction.
   d. spontaneous recovery.

4. "Response consequences that increase the likelihood of the response occurring again" describes
   a. shaping.
   b. punishment.
   c. reinforcement.
   d. discrimination.

5. The "positive" and "negative" in positive and negative reinforcement refer to whether
   a. the reinforced response increases or decreases in frequency.
   b. the reinforcer is presented before or after the response.
   c. a stimulus or event is added or removed when a response is made.
   d. the reinforcer has intrinsic value or acquired value.

6. A rat quickly learned to press the bar to turn off an electric shock. This is an example of
   a. positive punishment.
   b. negative punishment.
   c. escape conditioning.
   d. avoidance conditioning.

7. A consequence that decreases a response is
   a. reinforcement.
   b. punishment.
   c. shaping.
   d. generalization.

8. A conditioned reinforcer is a stimulus that
   a. is presented only some of the times a response is made.
   b. identifies the occasions that a response will be followed by a reinforcer.
   c. has acquired, rather than natural, reinforcing characteristics.
   d. produces a very high, continuous rate of responding.

9. If you give your dog a dog biscuit every time you say "sit" and he sits, you are using
   a. a continuous reinforcement schedule.
   b. a partial reinforcement schedule.
   c. secondary reinforcement.
   d. conditioned reinforcement.

10. The situation in which reinforcement is no longer given following a trained response is called
    a. extinction.
    b. conditioned inhibition.
    c. a postreinforcement pause.
    d. shaping.

11. The Brelands tried to teach a raccoon to put a coin in a bank. They found that
    a. raccoons are not responsive to positive reinforcement; they require negative reinforcement.
    b. teaching a raccoon to put a coin in a bank is as easy as teaching a pigeon to peck a key.
    c. the raccoon's natural behavioral tendencies made teaching it the trick very difficult.
    d. classical conditioning doesn't work with raccoons, although operant conditioning does.

12. June is teaching her dog to roll over. At first she gives him a dog treat any time he makes a slight rolling movement, then only for larger rolling movements, and finally, only if he rolls over. She is using
    a. secondary reinforcement.
    b. partial reinforcement.
    c. extinction.
    d. shaping.

13. A reinforcement schedule that reinforces every sixth response is known as a
    a. fixed interval schedule.
    b. variable interval schedule.
    c. fixed ratio schedule.
    d. variable ratio schedule.

14. The schedule of reinforcement that produces high response rates and high resistance to extinction is
    a. continuous reinforcement.
    b. fixed ratio schedule.
    c. fixed interval schedule.
    d. variable ratio schedule.

Learning From Others: Observational Learning (pp. 292-294)

Mastering the Vocabulary. Define or explain each of the following terms. To check your answers, consult the text pages listed.

1. observational learning (p. 292)

2. modeling (p. 292)

Mastering the Concepts. Fill in the blanks to create a summary of this section. Answers are on page 166.

Organisms do not have to be directly involved in behavior to learn about its consequences. Much is learned through _____(54), or social, learning. Here, the organism observes the behavior of others and imitates, or _____(55) it. Observing others being reinforced or punished for a behavior can result in modification of the observer's behavior due to _____(56) reinforcement or punishment. Bandura has shown that children who watched an adult hitting a doll were more likely to hit the doll than children watching an adult play nonviolently. This research raises questions about the impact of TV violence.

Evaluating Your Progress. Select the one best response. Answers are on page 169. If you make any errors, reread the relevant material before you proceed.

1. Much of the concern about the effects of violence on TV is based on the research on
    a. schedules of reinforcement.
    b. orienting responses.
    c. primary vs. secondary reinforcement.
    d. observational learning.

2. Modeling is more likely if the person being observed is reinforced for their behavior. Watching someone be reinforced is called
    a. accidental reinforcement.
    b. vicarious reinforcement.
    c. partial reinforcement.
    d. secondary reinforcement.

3. Another name for observational learning is
    a. instrumental learning.
    b. social learning.
    c. indirect learning.
    d. higher-order learning.

MAKING FINAL PREPARATIONS

Complete these sections without consulting your book or notes.

Matching. Select the correct definition or description for each item. Answers are on page 169.

_____	1. conditioned inhibition	**a.** did Bobo doll experiment on observational learning
_____	2. bliss point	**b.** imitation of observed behavior
_____	3. stimulus substitution view	**c.** developed principles of classical conditioning
_____	4. spontaneous recovery	**d.** proposed the law of effect
_____	5. modeling	**e.** procedure in which reinforcement is given for successive approximation to a response
_____	6. Pavlov	
_____	7. postreinforcement pause	**f.** baseline tendency to respond to events
_____	8. Thorndike	**g.** automatic shift of attention to a novel stimulus
_____	9. Watson & Raynor	**h.** a new CS produces a CR after being paired with an established CS
_____	10. shaping	
_____	11. long-term habituation	**i.** idea that the CS is a literal substitute for the US
_____	12. orienting response	**j.** delayed response after reinforcement in a fixed ratio schedule
_____	13. Bandura	
_____	14. second-order conditioning	**k.** loss in responsiveness for an extended period
_____	15. response deprivation theory	**l.** did "little Albert" study of conditioned fear
_____	16. instrumental conditioning	**m.** reappearance of formerly extinguished CR
		n. idea that an event will be reinforcing if it moves an organism toward its bliss point
		o. learning event signals the absence of the US
		p. operant conditioning

Short Essay Questions. Write a brief answer to each question. Sample answers are on page 169.

1. Compare habituation and classical conditioning extinction.

2. Explain why stimulus generalization might be adaptive, and give an example.

3. Explain why conditioned taste aversions develop. Identify the US, CS, UR, and CR.

4. Explain why variable schedules of reinforcement produce greater resistance to extinction than fixed and continuous schedules.

5. Explain the development of superstitious behavior using conditioning concepts.

6. Discuss the limitations of punishment as a means of behavior modification.

7. Explain the adaptive value of observational learning.

8. Explain why the stimulus substitution view of classical conditioning is incorrect.

Multiple Choice Pretest 1. Select the one best response. Answers are found on page 170.

1. Sensitization is most likely to occur when the orienting stimulus is
   a. rare.
   b. visual.
   c. weak.
   d. intense.

2. Classical conditioning is a process by which organisms learn
   a. by observing the actions of others.
   b. the consequences of their voluntary actions.
   c. the signaling properties of events.
   d. to direct attention to a novel stimulus.

3. In Pavlov's experiments, the food was the
   a. unconditioned stimulus.
   b. unconditioned response.
   c. conditioned stimulus.
   d. conditioned response.

4. After the rat was paired with the noise several times in Watson's Little Albert experiment, Albert cried when the rat was presented alone. Crying to the rat presented alone was the
   a. unconditioned stimulus.
   b. unconditioned response.
   c. conditioned stimulus.
   d. conditioned response.

5. In which situation will the tone be most likely to become a conditioned stimulus for salivation?
   a. Food is presented just before the tone is sounded.
   b. After pairing a light with food, a tone is added to the light: (tone+light)--food
   c. The tone is presented several minutes before the food.
   d. The tone is presented before an established conditioned stimulus, a light.

6. All of the following statements are true concerning conditioned responses except:
   a. A conditioned response is the unconditioned response transferred to a conditioned stimulus.
   b. A conditioned response is sometimes the opposite of the unconditioned response.
   c. The form of the conditioned response is dependent on the characteristics of the conditioned stimulus.
   d. The conditioned response is dependent on how the subject feels about the unconditioned stimulus.

7. One approach to treating alcoholism is to give the person a drug that makes them throw up after they drink alcohol in hopes that alcohol will lose its appeal. This is based on the concept of
   a. conditioned taste aversion.
   b. the blocking procedure.
   c. spontaneous recovery.
   d. second-order conditioning.

8. Wes developed a mild taste aversion for fish after a bout of food poisoning. After several months the taste aversion had disappeared and he was able to eat fish again. However, the taste aversion suddenly reappeared one day. This illustrates
   a. second-order conditioning.
   b. spontaneous recovery.
   c. vicarious reinforcement.
   d. stimulus discrimination.

9. Instrumental conditioning differs from classical conditioning because in instrumental conditioning
   a. an organism's own behavior signals outcomes, but in classical conditioning events signal outcomes.
   b. an organism is learning something, but in classical conditioning no learning occurs.
   c. the principles apply only to animals, but in classical conditioning the principles apply to humans.
   d. discrimination and generalization do not occur, but in classical conditioning they do.

10. A stimulus or event that, when removed following a response, increases the likelihood the response will be made again is a
    a. positive reinforcer.
    b. negative reinforcer.
    c. positive punishment.
    d. negative punishment.

11. Randy had to write an essay and discuss it with his teacher because he said an obscene word in class. His teacher was frustrated when Randy's use of obscenity became more frequent in spite of being made to write an essay each time. In this example, writing the essay and talking to the teacher must be
    a. positive reinforcement.
    b. negative reinforcement.
    c. positive punishment.
    d. negative punishment.

12. Escape and avoidance conditioning involve the use of
    a. positive reinforcement.
    b. negative reinforcement.
    c. positive punishment.
    d. negative punishment.

13. Sam's mother spanks him when he runs into the street, so he quit running into the street. His mother used
    a. positive reinforcement.
    b. negative reinforcement.
    c. positive punishment.
    d. negative punishment.

14. When they behave properly, children at a preschool receive tickets that can later be used to get a grab bag or admission to a party. The tickets are an example of a
    a. variable reinforcer
    b. primary reinforcer.
    c. negative reinforcer.
    d. conditioned reinforcer.

15. Slot machines are set to pay off after some average number of plays (let's guess 150), but a machine might pay off after 30 plays one time and after 270 plays another. This is an example of a
    a. fixed ratio schedule of reinforcement.
    b. fixed interval schedule of reinforcement.
    c. variable ratio schedule of reinforcement.
    d. variable interval schedule of reinforcement.

16. The keypeck record from the pigeon shows long periods of few responses followed by brief periods of very rapid responses, creating a scalloped effect. This bird probably was reinforced for keypecking on a
    a. fixed ratio schedule.
    b. variable ratio schedule.
    c. fixed interval schedule.
    d. variable interval schedule.

17. A response can be taught by reinforcing successive approximations of the response, the technique called
    a. shaping.
    b. partial reinforcement.
    c. discrimination.
    d. sensitization.

18. When asked how they taught their children to be so polite, Dee and Sam replied, "We make sure we are polite to everyone, especially when the children are around. Dee and Sam are using
    a. positive reinforcement to teach politeness.
    b. classical conditioning to teach politeness.
    c. second-order conditioning to teach politeness.
    d. observational learning to teach politeness.

19. The Breland's animal training experiences show that
    a. biological behavioral tendencies limit what behaviors can be conditioned.
    b. reinforcement is a better way to modify behavior than punishment.
    c. behaviors sometimes develop because of accidental reinforcement.
    d. the principles of conditioning work better with animals than with humans.

Multiple Choice Pretest 2. Select the one best response. Answers are found on page 171.

1. Katrina's new apartment is next to the elevator. The day she moved in she found she couldn't study effectively because the elevator bell captured her attention each time it rang. Her behavior in known as
   a. sensitization.
   b. learning.
   c. an orienting response.
   d. habituation.

2. Within a few weeks, Katrina hardly ever noticed the elevator bell. This change can be explained as
   a. habituation.
   b. sensitization.
   c. observational learning.
   d. spontaneous recovery.

3. Pat was bitten by a dog and for months he felt afraid whenever a dog appeared. Eventually, after seeing many dogs without being bitten again, Pat felt no fear when dogs appeared. Pat was "cured" by
   a. spontaneous recovery.
   b. observational learning.
   c. extinction.
   d. conditioned inhibition.

4. Seeing blood always has made Sela feel sick. The movie she saw last week presented a drill-like noise just before the madman butchered each victim. Sela has noticed that she now feels queasy each time she hears the drills at the construction site next door. Sela's problem developed as a result of
   a. instrumental conditioning.
   b. classical conditioning.
   c. observational learning.
   d. extinction.

5. Sam was conditioned to blink when the word "BOO" appeared on the screen. After presenting a tone at the same time as the word "BOO" several times, tone alone did not produce a blink, although the word "BOO" would. This is an example of
   a. extinction.
   b. conditioned inhibition.
   c. second-order conditioning.
   d. blocking.

6. Vic couldn't help grimacing when Don dumped something disgusting on his head. After getting such a wonderful reaction, Don began yelling "Let's party!" and then dumping something on Vic almost every day. After two weeks of this, Vic now grimaces anytime he hears the phrase "Let's party!" even if Don isn't around. In this scenario the unconditioned stimulus is
   a. Don.
   b. Vic's grimace.
   c. the words "Let's party!"
   d. something dumped on Vic's head.

7.   Vic finds he grimaces not only to "Let's party!" but also to "Party down!" This is an example of
     a.   second-order conditioning.
     b.   spontaneous recovery.
     c.   stimulus discrimination.
     d.   stimulus generalization.

8.   A few seconds before your new clock radio sounds its alarm, it makes a tiny click. You've recently
     noticed that you wake up right after the click and before the alarm even though you previously never
     woke up to anything but the alarm itself. The click is acting as a(n)
     a.   unconditioned stimulus.
     b.   conditioned stimulus.
     c.   positive reinforcer.
     d.   blocking stimulus.

9.   Thorndike's law of effect is most similar to what B.F. Skinner would describe as
     a.   stimulus discrimination and stimulus generalization.
     b.   operant conditioning and classical conditioning.
     c.   reinforcement and punishment.
     d.   habituation and sensitization.

10. Xavier has learned that his requests for money are never granted if he asks when his father is frowning,
     but that his requests are granted if his father is smiling. His father's facial expressions are examples of
     a.   shaping stimuli.
     b.   negative reinforcers.
     c.   discriminative stimuli.
     d.   a fixed-interval schedule.

11. Fred complained loudly and unpleasantly to his teacher about his test grade. Although his teacher didn't
     think Fred deserved a higher grade, he gave him one just to avoid having to listen to him complain. If
     Fred complains about test grades more often now, Fred's behavior is being influenced by
     a.   positive reinforcement.
     b.   negative reinforcement.
     c.   positive punishment.
     d.   negative punishment.

12. If Fred's teacher is more likely to change Fred's grade again in order to avoid listening to him complain,
     the teacher's behavior is being influenced by
     a.   positive reinforcement.
     b.   negative reinforcement.
     c.   positive punishment.
     d.   negative punishment.

13. Cal's mother will answer the question, "How long till we get there?" only after 10 minutes have elapsed
     since the last time she answered Cal's question. This represents a
     a.   fixed ratio schedule of reinforcement.
     b.   fixed interval schedule of reinforcement.
     c.   variable ratio schedule of reinforcement.
     d.   variable interval schedule of reinforcement.

14. Who will continue to respond the longest after extinction begins?
    a. Alice, who was previously on a continuous reinforcement schedule.
    b. Bill, who was previously on a variable ratio schedule of reinforcement.
    c. Carl, who was previously on a fixed ratio schedule of reinforcement.
    d. Diedre, who was previously on a fixed interval schedule of reinforcement.

15. Dave loses his dessert when he hits his sister. Dave never hits his sister anymore. This is an example of
    a. positive reinforcement.
    b. negative reinforcement.
    c. positive punishment.
    d. negative punishment.

16. The salesman receives $50.00 for every ten magazine subscriptions he sells. We might think of this as a
    a. variable interval schedule.
    b. variable ratio schedule.
    c. fixed interval schedule.
    d. fixed ratio schedule.

17. Having watched the plumber fix the toilet last time, Dora was able to fix it this time. This illustrates
    a. observational learning.
    b. classical conditioning.
    c. operant conditioning.
    d. second-order conditioning.

18. Seth watched the two shoplifters taken out of the store by the police. He put the CD he had planned to steal back on the shelf and never again tried to take anything without paying. This example illustrates
    a. vicarious punishment.
    b. extinction.
    c. belongingness.
    d. accidental reinforcement.

ANSWERS AND EXPLANATIONS

Mastering the Concepts

1. permanent (p. 260)	15. alone (p. 268)	29. law of effect (p. 280)	43. continuous (p. 283)
2. behavior (p. 260)	16. blocking (p. 269)	30. strengthened (p. 280)	44. partial (p. 283)
3. experience (p. 260)	17. passive (p. 269)	31. weakened (p. 280)	45. fixed ratio (p. 283)
4. orienting (p. 263)	18. substitute (p. 270)	32. discriminative (p. 280)	46. variable ratio (p. 285)
5. habituation (p. 263)	19. aversions (p. 271)	33. generalization (p. 280)	47. Fixed interval (p. 285)
6. sensitization (p. 264)	20. second-order (p. 272)	34. discrimination (p. 280)	48. extinction (p. 284)
7. signal (p. 266)	21. generalization (p. 273)	35. reinforcement (p. 281)	49. faster (p. 286)
8. classical (p. 266)	22. discrimination (p. 274)	36. Positive (p. 281)	50. faster (p. 286)
9. Pavlov (p. 266)	23. extinction (p. 275)	37. deprivation (p. 281)	51. shaping (p. 287)
10. unconditioned (p. 266)	24. habituation (p. 275)	38. negative (p. 281)	52. positive (p. 289)
11. unconditioned (p. 266)	25. recovery (p. 276)	39. escape (p. 282)	53. negative (p. 290)
12. conditioned (p. 266)	26. inhibition (p. 278)	40. avoidance (p. 282)	54. observational (p. 292)
13. conditioned (p. 266)	27. instrumental (p. 278)	41. conditioned (p. 283)	55. models (p. 292)
14. before (p. 267)	28. operant (p. 278)	42. schedules (p. 283)	56. vicarious (p. 293)

Evaluating Your Progress

Preview & Learning About Events: Noticing and Ignoring

1. **c**   a. Wrong.   An orienting response is an *inborn* tendency to shift one's attention toward a novel stimulus.
    (p. 260) b. Wrong.   Performance is any overt behavior, not a change in behavior.
              d. Wrong.   Knowledge is a by-product of learning.

2. **b**   a. Wrong.   There is no conditioned stimulus. This automatic shift of attention is an orienting response.
    (p. 263) c. Wrong.   This was an automatic, not voluntary, response with no reward or punishment.
              d. Wrong.   There is no increased tendency to respond here.

3. **a**   b. Wrong.   Sensitization increases the orienting response. Habituation decreases it.
    (p. 263) c. Wrong.   Stimulus generalization is responding to stimuli similar to the original conditioned stimulus.
              d. Wrong.   There is nothing being removed after a response to increased the likelihood of the response.

Learning What Events Signal: Classical Conditioning

1. **c**   a. Wrong.   Instrumental conditioning involves learning about the consequences or voluntary actions.
    (p. 266) b. Wrong.   Sensitization involves an increased orienting response to a stimulus that is repeated.
              d. Wrong.   Habituation involves the reduction of an orienting response with repeated stimulation.

2. **b**   a. Wrong.   A conditioned stimulus produces a response after training has occurred.
    (p. 266) c. Wrong.   A discriminative stimulus indicates whether a response will be reinforced or not.
              d. Wrong.   Associate stimulus is not a term used in learning and conditioning.

3. **c**   a. Wrong.   The unconditioned stimulus was the loud noise.
    (p. 266) b. Wrong.   The unconditioned response was Albert's crying in response to the noise.
              d. Wrong.   The conditioned response was Albert's crying in response to the rat presented alone.

4. **c**   a. Wrong.   Unconditioned stimuli elicit *unconditioned* responses and are not involved in
    (p. 274)   discrimination.
              b. Wrong.   This describes stimulus generalization, the opposite of discrimination.
              d. Wrong.   This describes second-order conditioning.

5. **a**   b. Wrong.   Second-order conditioning uses a CS to condition another CS. There is no extinction.
    (p. 276) c. Wrong.   Sensitization is an increase in an orienting response, not a return of a CR.
              d. Wrong.   Generalization involves a CR to a new stimulus, not the return of an extinguished CR.

6. **b**   a. Wrong.   This describes conditioned inhibition.
    (p. 269) c. Wrong.   The new stimulus is simultaneous with the old CS, so timing wouldn't be a problem.
              d. Wrong.   The new stimulus and the old CS are paired, so both would be equally reliable sources.

7. **d**   a. Wrong.   Second-order conditioning requires a second CS be conditioned by an established CS.
    (p. 271) b. Wrong.   In conditioned inhibition a CS signal the non-occurrence of a US.
              c. Wrong.   In discrimination, stimuli other than the original CS do not yield the CR.

8. **a**   b. Wrong.   Blocking requires that the US be presented.
    (p. 275) c. Wrong.   Discrimination doesn't occur based on US elimination. It's based on new stimuli.
              d. Wrong.   Generalization occurs when stimuli other than the CS elicit a CR. Not when the US ends.

1. **b**   a. Wrong.   Extinction is the elimination of a response by ending reinforcement or the US.
    (p. 280)   c. Wrong.   Shaping (method of successive approximations) is a method for teaching a response.
               d. Wrong.   Observational learning is learning by observing the responses of others.

2. **b**   a. Wrong.   Classical conditioning is learning a stimulus signals an event, not what outcome follows.
    (p. 278)   c. Wrong.   Extinction occurs when reinforcement or the US is terminated.
               d. Wrong.   Sensitization is the strengthening of an orienting response to stimuli that are repeated.

3. **a**   b. Wrong.   Shaping is a method of training a response, not the generalization of responses.
    (p. 280)   c. Wrong.   Extinction is the elimination of a response when reinforcement or a US is terminated.
               d. Wrong.   Spontaneous recovery is the reemergence of a formerly extinguished response.

4. **c**   a. Wrong.   Shaping is a method for teaching a response that utilizes the reinforcement described here.
    (p. 281)   b. Wrong.   Punishment would decrease the likelihood of the response.
               d. Wrong.   Discrimination involves signals concerning when reinforcement is possible.

5. **c**   a. Wrong.   Response increase or decrease determines reinforcement vs. punishment.
    (p. 281)   b. Wrong.   Reinforcers always come after the response. They're the consequences.
               d. Wrong.   Intrinsic vs. acquired value differentiates primary and secondary (acquired) reinforcement.

6. **c**   a & b. Wrong.   A response is learned (increased), so punishment is not a factor.
    (p. 282)   d.   Wrong.   The rat turns the shock off; it doesn't prevent the shock.

7. **b**   a. Wrong.   Reinforcement increases the response. Punishment decreases it.
    (p. 289)   c. Wrong.   Shaping is a method used to teach a response.
               d. Wrong.   Generalization occurs when a response is made to stimuli other than the original one.

8. **c**   a. Wrong.   This describes a partial reinforcement schedule.
    (p. 283)   b. Wrong.   This describes a discriminative stimulus.
               d. Wrong.   This describes a variable-ratio schedule of reinforcement.

9. **a**   b.   Wrong.   Partial reinforcement schedules reinforce only some, not every, response.
    (p. 283)   c & d. Wrong.   Secondary (conditioned) reinforcers have no intrinsic value, unlike food.

10. **a**   b. Wrong.   In conditioned inhibition, a stimulus signals when a US will not occur.
    (p. 284)   c. Wrong.   A postreinforcement pause is a period of time immediately after a reinforcer has been given
                           in which no responses are made.
               d. Wrong.   Shaping involves reinforcing responses that are increasingly similar to the desired response.

11. **c**   a, b, & d. Wrong.   Their experiences addressed the interaction of natural tendencies and learned
    (p. 289)   relationships, making some relationships easier to learn than others.

12. **d**   a. Wrong.   The dog treat is a primary reinforcer (food).
    (p. 287)   b. Wrong.   She reinforces every "response"--a continuous schedule.
               c. Wrong.   She is giving reinforcement, so extinction is not in effect.

13. **c**   a & b. Wrong.   Interval schedules are based on the *time* elapsing since last reinforcement.
    (p. 283)   d.   Wrong.   A variable ratio requires a variable number of responses, not exactly 6, for example.

14. **d**   a.   Wrong.   Continuous reinforcement does not produce great resistance to extinction.
    (p. 285)   b & c. Wrong.   Fixed schedules, ratio or interval, aren't as resistant to extinction as variable ones.

1. **d**   a, b, & c.   Wrong.   The concern is about violence being learned by watching violence.
    (p. 292)

2. **b**   a. Wrong.   Accidental reinforcement is reinforcement that accidentally follows a response.
    (p. 293)   c. Wrong.   Partial reinforcement involves reinforcing only some, not all, appropriate responses.
                d. Wrong.   Secondary reinforcement involves a reinforcer that has acquired, rather than intrinsic value.

3. **b**   a, c, & d.   Wrong.   Observational learning is sometimes called social learning.
    (p. 292)

MAKING FINAL PREPARATIONS

Matching

1. **o** (p. 276)	4. **m** (p. 276)	7. **j** (p. 284)	10. **e** (p. 287)	13. **a** (p. 293)	16. **p** (p. 278)
2. **f** (p. 281)	5. **b** (p. 292)	8. **d** (p. 278)	11. **k** (p. 264)	14. **h** (p. 272)	
3. **i** (p. 270)	6. **c** (p. 266)	9. **l** (p. 273)	12. **g** (p. 263)	15. **n** (p. 281)	

Short Essay Questions

1.   Habituation is a reduction of an orienting response after a stimulus has occurred repeatedly without significant consequences. Extinction is a reduction of a conditioned response due to repeated absence of the unconditioned stimulus. For both, responses are reduced when stimuli no longer have notable consequences. (pp. 274-275)

2.   Stimulus generalization is adaptive because what is learned with one specific stimulus is transferred to other similar stimuli. Learning is not required for all stimulus variations. This improves interaction with the environment because every variation doesn't require new learning. To open a door with a slightly different knob doesn't require a separate trial and error procedure. Rather than approaching a black snake to see if it bites like the brown one did, the organism can use prior learning to avoid a potentially dangerous situation. (pp. 274-275)

3.   Nausea that occurs following eating or drinking becomes associated with whatever was ingested, particularly new or distinctive items. The illness (US) actually produces the nausea/taste aversion (UR). The food or drink becomes a conditioned stimulus for the conditioned response of nausea/taste aversion. That is: food (CS)—illness (US) ——→nausea (UR) then food (CR) ——→nausea/taste aversion (CR). (p. 271)

4.   It is more difficult to discriminate that extinction has begun because reinforcement has occurred after varying amounts of time or numbers of responses. The organism must recognize that the response is not associated with reinforcement any longer, and that is not as obvious as when reinforcement is delivered after a fixed number of responses or time periods as in continuous and fixed ratio and fixed interval schedules. (pp. 283-287)

5.   When a response is accidentally followed by a common reinforcer, the organism can mistakenly consider the reinforcer a consequence of the response. This will lead to an increased likelihood that the response will be made again. If circumstances cause the response to be followed by the reinforcer again (using a "lucky" pen to take a test and doing well) the behavior will be maintained on a partial reinforcement schedule and be resistant to extinction. (p. 288)

6.   Although punishment can quickly eliminate a response, it has limitations. These include failing to teach an appropriate response (it teaches what not to do, not what to do), being difficult to gauge in terms of intensity, and may cause aggression, escape attempts, and resentment. (pp. 290-291)

7. Observational learning allows learning without the organism directly participating. The organism can quickly, and perhaps more safely, learn the consequences of a behavior. It can learn from the mistakes and success of others and more effectively interact with the environment. (pp. 292-294)

8. Several things indicate the stimulus substitution view is wrong: (1) the characteristics of the CR depends on the properties of the CS; (2) sometimes the CR is opposite to the UR; (3) the occurrence of the CR depends on the organisms feelings about the UCS. If stimulus substitution were correct, the CR would not vary based on these factors; it would simply mimic the UR. (pp.270-272)

Multiple Choice Pretest 1

1. **d**   a, b, & c.   Wrong.   Sensitization occurs for repeated, intense stimuli, regardless of sensory system.
   (p. 264)

2. **c**   a. Wrong.   This describes observational learning.
   (p. 266)   b. Wrong.   This describes respondent (operant) conditioning.
      d. Wrong.   Although not learned, this is most similar to an orienting response.

3. **a**   b. Wrong.   The unconditioned response was the dog's salivation in response to food being presented.
   (p. 266)   c. Wrong.   The conditioned stimulus was the bell, or the footsteps that elicited salivation after training.
      d. Wrong.   The conditioned response was the dog's salivation to the bell or to the footsteps.

4. **d**   a. Wrong.   The noise was the unconditioned stimulus.
   (p. 273)   b. Wrong.   Crying when the noise was presented was the unconditioned response.
      c. Wrong.   The rat was the conditioned stimulus.

5. **d**   a. Wrong.   This is backward conditioning and is unlikely to result in conditioning.
   (p. 267)   b. Wrong.   The tone will not add information, so blocking will occur.
      c. Wrong.   The CS and US usually need to be presented closer together in time.

6. **a**   b. Wrong.   Opposite CRs are possible and are often called compensatory responses.
   (p. 270)   c. Wrong.   Remember that rats freeze to some CRs for shock, but try to cover up others?
      d. Wrong.   Remember a tone--food pairing won't lead to eating if there is a conditioned taste aversion.

7. **a**   b. Wrong.   There is no second neutral stimulus being added here.
   (p. 271)   c. Wrong.   Spontaneous recovery is the reappearance of a CR that has previously been extinguished.
      d. Wrong.   There is no second neutral stimulus being added here.

8. **b**   a. Wrong.   Second-order conditioning uses a CS to establish a new CS.
   (p. 276)   c. Wrong.   Vicarious reinforcement is a reinforcement effect from watching someone be reinforced.
      d. Wrong.   Discrimination involves responding to certain stimuli associated with reinforcement or a US.

9. **a**   b. Wrong.   Both types of conditioning involve learning.
   (p. 278)   c. Wrong.   Both types of conditioning apply to animals and humans.
      d. Wrong.   Discrimination and generalization occur in both types of conditioning.

10. **b**   a. Wrong.   Positive reinforcement is the presentation of an event, not the removal of one.
    (p. 281)   c & d. Wrong.   The response increases, so this isn't punishment of any type.

11. **a**   b. Wrong.   It's reinforcement, but something is added (essay requirement), not removed.
    (p. 281)   c & d. Wrong.   The response (using obscenity) increased, so it isn't punishment.

12. **b**   a.   Wrong.   Escape and avoidance involve *removing* an aversive event and *increasing* a response.
(p. 282)   c & d. Wrong.   Escape and avoidance involve *increasing* a response that results in terminating or
                                          avoiding an aversive event, so punishment is not involved.

13. **c**   a & b. Wrong.   The response (running into street) was reduced, so reinforcement isn't involved.
(p. 289)   d.   Wrong.   An aversive event (spanking) was added, so it's positive punishment.

14. **d**   a. Wrong.   There is no variable reinforcer. Were you thinking of variable schedule of reinforcement?
(p. 283)   b. Wrong.   Primary reinforcers have intrinsic value, like food or water. Tickets must acquire value.
          c. Wrong.   Tickets are given; an aversive event is not taken away if they act properly.

15. **c**   a. Wrong.   Because the requirements for reinforcement is variable, it isn't a fixed schedule.
(p. 287)   b. Wrong.   Payoffs are based on number of plays, not time, and the number isn't constant, so it's not FI.
          d. Wrong.   Payoffs are based on number of plays (responses), not time, so it isn't an interval schedule.

16. **c**   a, b, & d.   Wrong.   A scalloped pattern is characteristic of a fixed interval schedule.
(p. 285)

17. **a**   b. Wrong.   Reinforcing some instances, not changing forms, of a response is partial reinforcement.
(p. 287)   c. Wrong.   Discrimination involves responding only when signal indicate reinforcement is possible.
          d. Wrong.   Sensitization is an increase in a orienting response to a stimulus that is repeated.

18. **d**   a, b, & c.   Wrong.   The key is being a model for politeness, not reinforcing or conditioning it.
(p. 292)

19. **a**   b & c. Wrong.   Although this might be true, it doesn't relate to the cited studies.
(p. 289)   d.   Wrong.   This is not necessarily true and doesn't relate to the cited studies.

Multiple Choice Pretest 2

1. **c**   a. Wrong.   There was no increase in her tendency to divert her attention.
(p. 263)   b. Wrong.   Katrina's behavior did not develop due to experience.
          d. Wrong.   There was no decrease in her tendency to divert her attention.

2. **a**   b. Wrong.   Sensitization would have increased her response to the elevator bell.
(p. 263)   c. Wrong.   Observational learning is learning by watching others. She didn't do this.
          d. Wrong.   Spontaneous recovery is the reappearance of an extinguished conditioned response.

3. **c**   a. Wrong.   Spontaneous recovery is the reappearance of a previously extinguished CR.
(p. 275)   b. Wrong.   Pat didn't learn by observing the behavior of other people.
          d. Wrong.   No stimulus signals when a dog won't bite as required by conditioned inhibition.

4. **b**   a. Wrong.   There is no voluntary response being affected by its consequences here.
(p. 266)   c. Wrong.   Sela didn't learn to be queasy by watching someone else be queasy.
          d. Wrong.   Extinction is the elimination of a response.

5. **d**   a. Wrong.   Extinction is the cessation of the CR. The CR is still occurring to BOO.
(p. 269)   b. Wrong.   Neither CS signalled the absence of the UCS.
          c. Wrong.   In second order conditioning, a new CS produces a CR. No CR was produced here.

6. **d**   a. Wrong.   Don didn't naturally cause Vic to grimace, so he's not the unconditioned stimulus.
(p. 266)   b. Wrong.   Vic's grimace is an unconditioned response to having something dumped on his head.
          c. Wrong.   "Let's party!" became a conditioned stimulus for the conditioned response of grimacing.

7. **d**   a. Wrong.   "Party down!" has not been paired with the CS "Let's party!" for second order conditioning.
(p. 273)   b. Wrong.   Spontaneous recovery is the reappearance of a previously extinguished response.
             c. Wrong.   Discrimination would narrow, not expand, the stimuli acting as a CS for grimacing.

8. **b**   a. Wrong.   The alarm is the unconditioned stimulus for the response of waking up.
(p. 266)   c. Wrong.   A positive reinforcer is a stimulus that, when presented after a response, increases the likelihood of that response occurring again.
             d. Wrong.   Blocking occurs when a second stimulus fails to give new signaling information and fails to become a conditioned stimulus.

9. **c**   a. Wrong.   The law of effect involves the results of an action influencing future action, not signaling
(pp. 280-281)   events prior to a response.
             b. Wrong.   The law of effect involves operant principles, but not classical conditioning.
             d. Wrong.   Habituation and sensitization don't relate to the results of a response, as in the law of effect.

10. **c**   a. Wrong.   Shaping is a method for teaching an organisms to make a response.
(p. 280)   b. Wrong.   Negative reinforcement is an event that, if removed after a response, increases responding.
             d. Wrong.   A fixed-interval schedule is a schedule of reinforcement, not a signal of conditions in which reinforcement might occur.

11. **a**   b.   Wrong.   A response (complaining) led to the presentation of an event (grade change) and
(p. 281)   increased in likelihood.
             c & d.   Wrong.   A response *increased*, not decreased, so punishment isn't involved.

12. **b**   a.   Wrong.   A response (grade change) led to *removal* of an aversive event (Fred's complaints) and
(p. 281)   increased in likelihood.
             c & d.   Wrong.   A response *increased*, not decreased, so punishment isn't involved.

13. **b**   a. Wrong.   This schedule is based on time, so it is an interval schedule (FI 20 sec).
(p. 285)   c. Wrong.   This schedule is based on time, and is fixed, so it is an FI 20 sec schedule.
             d. Wrong.   This schedule is fixed, not variable.

14. **b**   a.   Wrong.   Continuous reinforcement produces the fastest extinction.
(p. 285)   c & d.   Wrong.   Extinction is faster after fixed schedules than after variable schedules.

15. **d**   a & b.   Wrong.   The response (hitting) has decreased, so reinforcement is not involved.
(p. 290)   c.   Wrong.   An event (dessert) is removed, not added, so this is negative punishment, not positive.

16. **d**   a & c.   Wrong.   An interval schedule is based on the time since the last reinforcer, not response
(p. 283)   number.
             b.   Wrong.   Variable schedules reinforce after a variable (average) number of responses.

17. **a**   b & d.   Wrong.   Dora learned by observing. There was no evidence of a conditioned stimulus.
(p. 292)   c.   Wrong.   Dora did not learn plumbing by having responses reinforced and punished.

18. **a**   b. Wrong.   Reinforcement did not occur and then end. The key is observational learning.
(p. 293)   c. Wrong.   Belongingness is the idea that certain relationships are more readily learned than others.
             d. Wrong.   Accidental reinforcement follows a behavior but is not a result of that behavior.

LANGUAGE ENHANCEMENT GUIDE

CORE TERMS

There are a few terms your instructor is likely to use in this chapter without necessarily defining them first. The first is *elicit*, which means "to call forth." If I *elicit* a response from you, I am doing something that causes you to respond. Next, your instructor may use the term **contingent upon**. This means "dependent upon"; you might receive a job offer *contingent upon* graduation from college by a certain date. Finally, you might hear the term **temporal**, as in, "The temporal relationship of the stimulus and the response is important." That means their relation in time -- which comes first, and how close together they happen -- is important.

IDIOMS

260	unfortunate culinary experience	bad experience with cooking or cooked food
260	cut across species	apply to very different animals
262	lie at the heart of	be central to; be a core idea
262	rattling of a tail	the warning sound of the rattlesnake
262	whose fate has already been sealed	who are headed for a sure and bad end
264	relatively modest in intensity	fairly quiet
266	turn of the century	the 1890s through the 1910s (the next turn of the century will be the years around 2000)
272	phonograph turntable	record player
272	metronome	a device that produces a regular ticking sound; used to help musicians perfect their rhythm
273	get the picture	understand
283	haphazard	not organized
288	biological constraints	limits set by one's body and the way it functions
289	appetitive event	interest in eating
292	trial and error	trying different things to see what works

WORD PARTS

Here are some words that are made up of word parts, and that you can find in this chapter. After you've looked at these, you can look for others in the chapter that use the same word parts (they are there, but YOU have to find them!)

WORD	WORD PART IT USES	MEANING
decline	de = down, from, away clin = level, line	to turn down, to angle down from
temporary	temp = time	not lasting long
retraction	re = again tract = to pull	to pull something back again
concur	con = together, with cur = to run, to move through	to agree with
provide	pro = forward, before vid, vis = to see	to place before, to offer
averse	a, an = not, away vers, vert = to turn	to make distasteful, to make one turn away from
distort	dis = take away, not tort = to twist	to twist improperly, to change something's form in a bad way

Knowing the word parts listed above, you can also create the following words. You can get an idea of their meanings from the word parts they use. You fill in the blanks!

recur	re + cur	_____
reverse	_____ + _____	to turn around, to change direction completely
contemporary	_____ + _____	belonging to the same time
revise	re + vis	_____
protracted	_____ + _____	to draw out for a long time
contort	con + tort	_____
distract	_____ + _____	to draw (someone's attention) away from

CHAPTER 8: REMEMBERING AND FORGETTING

ESTABLISHING LEARNING OBJECTIVES

Use these learning objectives as a preview of the chapter, a guide for active reading, and to evaluate your mastery of the material. Review the relevant objectives as you begin and end your reading of each major section of the chapter.

After studying this chapter you should be able to:

I.   Define memory, and describe the role of encoding, storage, and retrieval.

II. Solve the adaptive problem of how to remember information over the short term.
   A. Define sensory memory and distingish it from short-term memory.
   B. Discuss how visual and auditory sensory memories can be measured.
      1. Describe Sperling's research on iconic memory, and discuss what it indicates about the duration and type of code involved in iconic memory.
      2. Identify the type of code and the duration of echoic memory.
      3. Discuss the adaptive value of sensory memory.
   C. Describe the nature of the code used in short-term memory.
   D. Discuss short-term forgeting and evaluate the role of rehearsal.
   E. Discuss why short-term memory has a limited capactiy and explain how chunking can increase memory span.

III. Solve the adaptive problem of how to store information for the long term.
   A. List the kinds of information that are stored in long-term memory.
      1. Define and differentiate episodic memory, semantic memory, and procedural memory.
   B. Compare and contrast the effects of elaboration and distinctiveness on memory.
   C. Discuss how visual imagery can be used to improve memory.
      1. Describe the method of loci, pegword techniques, and linkword systems.
      2. Discuss flashbulb memories.
      3. Evaluate the question of whether mental images are the same as perceptual images.
   D. Explain how and why repetition influences memory.

IV. Solve the adaptive problem of how to retrieve information from memory.
   A. Discuss cue-dependent forgetting and the importance of retrieval cues.
   B. Define the encoding specificity principle and transfer-appropriate processing.
   C. Explain the role of schemas in reconstructive memory.
      1. Provide evidence that long-term memory is reconstructive.
   D. Discuss the differences between implicit and explicity memory.

V.   Solve the adaptive problem of how to update and manage memory.
   A. Discuss forgetting, including the contributions of Ebbinghaus, and explain why forgetting is often adaptive.
   B. Describe the mechanisms that cause forgetting including decay and retroactive and proactive interference.
   C. Discuss motivated forgetting and the case for and against repression.
   D. Discribe retrograde and anterograde amnesia and where in the brain memories might be stored.

MASTERING THE MATERIAL

Preview & Remembering Over the Short Term (pp. 302-312)

Mastering the Vocabulary. Define or explain each of the following terms. To check your answers, consult the text pages listed.

1.   memory (p. 302)

2.   encoding (p. 302)

3.   storage (p. 302)

4.   retrieval (p. 302)

5.   sensory memory (p. 304)

6.   short-term memory (p. 304)

7.   iconic memory (p. 304)

8.   echoic memory (p. 306)

9.   rehearsal (p. 308)

10. memory span (p. 310)

11. chunking (p. 311)

Mastering the Concepts. Fill in the blanks to create a summary of this section. Answers are on page 192.

Memory is the capacity to _____(1) and _____(2) information. Memory involves three processes: _____(3), storage, and _____(4). This chapter considers four adaptive problems: How do we remember over the short term? How do we store information for the long term? How is information recovered appropriately? How do we keep memory current?

_____(5) memory retains a replica of the stimulus for a few seconds to assist perceptual processing. Visual sensory memory is _____(6) memory. By comparing recall in _____(7) and _____(8) procedures, Sperling concluded iconic memory is brief (.5 sec). Recent data suggest only item location is lost quickly. _____(9) memory for audition has a duration of 5-10 seconds.

_____(10) memory, or working memory, briefly stores and manipulates information. Information is mostly recoded in an inner voice, but also includes other information. Errors usually sound like the original input. If short-term memories are not _____(11) they are lost within 10-15 seconds (or 1 or 2 seconds based on recent data) due to _____(12), _____(13) from new input, or both. Short-term memory span is 7, plus or minus 2, and represents memory's _____(14). The time needed to rehearse input might determine the span; memory span is lower for input that takes longer to say. _____(15), rearranging input into meaningful groups, speeds rehearsal and increases memory span.

Evaluating Your Progress. Select the one best response. Answers are on page 192. If you make any errors, reread the relevant material before proceeding.

1. A psychologist who is studying how memories are formed and represented is studying the process of
    a. encoding.
    b. storage.
    c. retrieval.
    d. interference.

2. Sperling's estimate of the duration of iconic memory is
    a. 0.5 second.
    b. 5 seconds.
    c. 15 seconds.
    d. 15 minutes.

3. Sperling concluded that poor whole report performance is caused by
    a. losing a large amount of the stimulus information before it ever enters iconic memory.
    b. an inability to retain all the stimulus array due to iconic memory's very limited storage capacity.
    c. failure to develop adequate retrieval cues for the information in the array.
    d. the fading of information before all of it can be processed and reported.

4. Information in short-term memory can be represented in a variety of forms, but the most common code is
    a. acoustic.
    b. visual.
    c. abstract (not related to any sense).
    d. episodic.

5. Fred thinks forgetting occurs because new items disrupt memories of old items. Fred supports the idea of
   a. information decay.
   b. chunking.
   c. interference.
   d. an inner voice.

6. Organizing input into meaningful units so as to increase the capacity of short-term memory is called
   a. chunking.
   b. the memory span.
   c. cued recall.
   d. rehearsal.

7. A common estimate of the short-term memory span is
   a. 1-5 items.
   b. 5-9 items.
   c. 9-15 items.
   d. more than 20 items.

Storing Information for the Long Term (pp. 312-321)

Mastering the Vocabulary. Define or explain each of the following terms. To check your answers, consult the text pages listed.

1. long-term memory (p. 312)

2. episodic memory (p. 313)

3. semantic memory (p. 313)

4. procedural memory (p. 313)

5. elaboration (p. 314)

6. distinctiveness (p. 314)

7. visual imagery (p. 315)

8. mnemonic devices (p. 315)

9. flashbulb memories (p. 316)

10. method of loci (p. 315)

11. peg-word method (p. 317)

12. linkword system (p. 317)

13. primacy effect (p. 320)

14. recency effect (p. 320)

15. distributed practice (p. 320)

Mastering the Concepts. Fill in the blanks to create a review of this section. Answers are on page 192.

_____(16) memory maintains information for extended periods. Long-term memories can be _____(17) memories, which are memories of personal events, _____(18) memories, factual memories not related to events, or _____ (19) memories, memories about how to do something.

Several techniques improve long-term memory. _____(20) links new items to existing memories, forming connections that act as retrieval cues. One type, _____(21) processing, finds shared properties. Elaboration can increase the _____(22) or uniqueness of the items. Visual _____(23) involves elaboration and distinctiveness and is an important component for many _____(24) devices or memory aids. In the _____(25) technique items are imaged along a path which later acts as a retrieval cue. The _____(26) method uses imagery to link items to memory cues, or pegs, such as a familiar rhyme. The _____(27) system for learning foreign vocabulary uses imagery to link a foreign word with a rhyming known word. Imagery has properties of both memory and perception. Its detail is incomplete, as in memory, but "scanning" and neurological data suggest processes used in perception are also used in imagery.

Emotional content influences memory. _____(28) memories are detailed memories of emotionally significant events. People confidently recall many details, but these memories are not very accurate. This supports the view that remembering is a _____(29) process rather than a direct reproduction.

An item's place in a list affects its recall, producing a _____(30) curve. The first and last items are recalled best, the _____(31) and recency effects. Being more distinctive might produce these effects. Repetition improves memory, but repetitions must be _____(32), spaced over time, rather than massed.

Evaluating Your Progress. Select the one best response. Answers are on page 193. If you make any errors, reread the relevant material before proceeding.

1. Semantic memory includes
    a. events or episodes in one's personal history.
    b. information about how to do something.
    c. a personal memory of a surprising or emotional event.
    d. facts that make little or no reference to one's personal life.

2. Elaboration
    a. increases the number of cues available to assist retrieval.
    b. decreases distinctiveness and thus, reduces the likelihood of retrieval.
    c. involves the simple repetition of an item to be remembered.
    d. adds material that increases the likelihood of interference.

3. Forming images of to-be-remembered items at various places and revisiting those places at retrieval is
    a. the pegword method.
    b. the chunking method.
    c. the method of loci.
    d. the linkword method.

4. The primacy effect in memory is improved recall for items
    a. at the beginning of a list.
    b. at the end of a list.
    c. given relational processing.
    d. that have been repeated.

5. Grady describes his study technique as "distributed practice." This means that he
    a. creates several visual images for each item he needs to learn.
    b. studies for each class a little bit several times a week.
    c. studies the most important material first in each study session.
    d. devotes one long night to studying a single subject.

6. Barry has a detailed memory of what he was doing when he heard that his best friends had been killed in a motorcycle accident. His memory is an example of a(n)
    a. repressed memory.
    b. flashbulb memory.
    c. iconic memory.
    d. procedural memory.

Recovering Information from Cues (pp. 327-329)

Mastering the Vocabulary. Define or explain each of the following terms. To check your answers, consult the text pages listed.

1. free recall (p. 322)

2. cued recall (p. 322)

3. cue-dependent forgetting (p. 322)

4. encoding specificity principle (p. 323)

5. transfer-appropriate processing (p. 324)

6. schema (p. 325)

7. implicit memory (p. 327)

8. explicit memory (p. 327)

Mastering the Concepts. Fill in the blanks to create a summary of this section. Answers are on page 192.

Retrieval is guided by internal or external _____(33). If retrieval cues are presented externally, as in a _____(34) task, recall is better than if no external cues are given, as in free recall. Researchers believe most forgetting is _____(35) forgetting, a failure to access retrieval cues, not loss of input. The _____(36) specificity principle states a cue will be effective only if a link between the cue and the item is developed during encoding. Failure to form a link or to interpret a cue appropriately causes retrieval failure. Links form with _____(37)-appropriate processing, using the same processes at learning as at testing.

Memories are _____(38), not replayed, and _____(39), clusters of related facts, are used to fill in gaps in memory. Although adaptive, this can distort memory. Research also shows that memories are influenced by the form of the _____(40) used in testing. Thus, eyewitness memories can be influenced by the interview itself.

Not all memories are conscious, or _____(41), memories. Remembering without conscious awareness is _____(42) memory. Picture or word fragment _____(43) tests show implicit memory influences behavior, but without the person's awareness. Retrieval cues are important for both types of memory, but conscious strategies are not effective for implicit memory. Implicit memories seem to account for memory _____(44) of deja vu and the false fame effect, and for cryptomnesia.

Evaluating Your Progress. Select the one best response. Answers are on page 193. If you make any errors, reread the relevant material before proceeding.

1   Comparison of free recall and cued recall performance suggests that most memory failures are due to
   a. information no longer being in memory due to decay.
   b. information no longer being in memory due to interference.
   c. repression of the information so that it cannot be brought to consciousness.
   d. a failure to use an appropriate retrieval cue.

2.   Information should be learned using processes that will be used in testing. That is, learners should use
   a. widely distributed practice.
   b. visual imagery mnemonic techniques.
   c. implicit memory, not explicit memory.
   d. transfer appropriate processing.

3.   A retrieval cue must be linked with an memory item at encoding in order to be effective, according to
   a. the primacy effect.
   b. the distinctiveness principle.
   c. the reconstructive memory principle.
   d. the encoding specificity principle.

4.   Which is false concerning schemas and memory?
   a. People are usually aware when schemas are influencing their memories.
   b. Schemas reflect the role of top-down processing in memory.
   c. Schemas can fill in gaps in memory when information is missing.
   d. Schemas can distort memory to be less accurate.

5.   Loftus and Palmer's research on memories for accident details clearly demonstrates that
   a. people routinely can recall minor details with high accuracy because of the visual nature of the event.
   b. people realize what they know about an accident and what they don't know about an accident.
   c. memory is dependent on primarily bottom-up processes.
   d. the way questions about memories are asked significantly influences the memories reported.

6.   Remembering without conscious awareness or willful intent is
   a. schematic memory.
   b. reconstructive memory.
   c. explicit memory.
   d. implicit memory.

7. Remembering is not a literal replay of past events. Instead, it is partly a creative process that blends information from schemas with memories about the event. In other words, long-term memory is
   a. reconstructive.
   b. distinctive.
   c. transfer-appropriate.
   d. primarily iconic.

Updating Memory (pp. 329-336)

Mastering the Vocabulary. Define or explain each of the following terms. To check your answers, consult the text pages listed.

1. forgetting (p. 329)

2. decay (p. 331)

3. retroactive interference (p. 331)

4. proactive interference (p. 331)

5. repression (p. 333)

6. amnesia (p. 334)

7. retrograde amnesia (p. 334)

8. anterograde amnesia (p. 334)

Mastering the Concepts. Fill in the blanks to create a summary of this section. Answers are on page 192.

Forgetting, the loss in _____(45) of stored material, is adaptive because it reduces memory "clutter." By testing relearning after various delays, the _____(46) method, Ebbinghaus developed a "forgetting curve." Most forgetting occurs _____(47) after initial learning and continues gradually.

Forgetting was first attributed to _____(48), a loss due to the passage of time, but current theories emphasize _____(49), disruption caused by other material. When new material disrupts old material,

_____(50) interference occurs. When old material disrupts new material, _____(51) interference occurs. Interference theory suggests material is not necessarily eliminated but becomes harder to access.

Forgetting can occur for emotionally adaptive, or motivated reasons. _____(52), a defense mechanism proposed by Freud in which memories are pushed out of consciousness, may reduce anxiety. Retrieval failure is accepted, but repression's scientific validity is unclear. Apparent cases of repression might be due to reconstructive memory, differential rehearsal, or other factors.

_____(53) is forgetting caused by physical problems. Head injuries can lead to a loss of memory for events that occurred before the injury, _____(54) amnesia. Brain damage also can lead to the loss of memory for events after the injury, _____(55) amnesia. Implicit memory tests show memories might be formed but not be consciously accessible. A cause of this amnesia is _____(56) syndrome, found with alcoholism. The _____(57) is critical for memory, but other brain areas are probably involved.

Evaluating Your Progress. Select the one best response. Answers are on page 194. If you make any errors, reread the relevant material before proceeding.

1.   Ebbinghaus' forgetting curve shows that forgetting occurs
     a. very slowly at first, and then rapidly after a week.
     b. very rapidly at first, and then continues gradually for a long time.
     c. very rapidly at first, but then stops quickly.
     d. at about the same moderate pace for at least the first 6 months, then stops.

2.   If previously learned material disrupts memory for recently learned material _____ has occurred.
     a. retrograde amnesia
     b. anterograde amnesia
     c. retroactive inhibition
     d. proactive inhibition

3.   The view that simply the passage of time, nothing else, causes forgetting to occur is known as
     a. interference theory.
     b. decay theory.
     c. cue-dependence theory.
     d. distinctiveness theory.

4.   Freud proposed that traumatic events are pushed from conscious awareness as a defense mechanism in
     a. anterograde amnesia.
     b. overwriting.
     c. repression.
     d. Korsakoff's syndrome.

5. Korsakoff's syndrome, a disorder due to brain damage from chronic alcoholism, causes
   a. anterograde amnesia.
   b. retrograde amnesia.
   c. repression of drinking memories.
   d. total loss of memory for both old and new pasts.

6. Recent research on anterograde amnesia suggests that the amnesia occurs because
   a. new input is not passed from sensory memory to short-term memory.
   b. the memory span of working memory is reduced drastically, preventing learning.
   c. the storage processes of long-term memory are destroyed, preventing any learning.
   d. new input is stored in long-term memory, but direct conscious retrieval is not possible.

7. The _____ appears to be very important for normal memory activity.
   a. occipital lobe
   b. parietal lobe
   c. pons
   d. hippocampus

MAKING FINAL PREPARATIONS

Complete these sections without consulting your book or notes. For a more accurate estimate of how well you know this material, wait at least a day or two after studying the chapter before working on the questions. Some of the material you "know" immediately after working with the chapter will be quickly forgotten. Immediate tests will overestimate what you know well.

Short Essay Questions. Write a brief answer to each question. Sample answers are on page 194.

1. What is the adaptive value of sensory memory?

2. Compare the characteristics and functions of sensory memory and short-term memory.

3. Nick spent three days before each multiple choice test reading and rereading the text but failed the test. Give at least two responses his instructor might make that are based on principles of memory.

4. How does chunking increase memory span?

5. Explain why memory is described as "reconstructive," and why this might be adaptive.

6. Compare the interference and decay views of forgetting. Which view is currently favored?

7. Why is forgetting adaptive?

Matching. Select the correct definition or description for each item. Answers are on page 195.

_____ 1. Ebbinghaus	a. must recall items without explicit retrieval cues
_____ 2. recognition test	b. studied iconic memory
_____ 3. Sperling	c. accidental plagiarism; implicit memory effect
_____ 4. cryptomnesia	d. must report cued row of stimulus array
_____ 5. relational processing	e. determined forgetting curve
_____ 6. whole report	f. technique to improve retrieval, e.g., pegword
_____ 7. word fragment completion	g. compares time to learn with time to relearn
_____ 8. Peterson & Peterson	h. studied duration of short-term memory
_____ 9. mnemonic device	i. must report entire stimulus array
_____ 10. free recall	j. system that very briefly retains a replica of input
_____ 11. short-term memory	k. implicit memory task
_____ 12. Loftus & Palmer	l. studied the influence the question has on memory
_____ 13. partial report task	m. feeling of familiarity due to implicit memory
_____ 14. savings method	n. must discriminate test item in group of distractors
_____ 15. sensory memory	o. looking for common characteristics; elaboration
_____ 16. deja vu	p. working memory

Multiple Choice Pretest 1. Select the one best response. Answers are on page 195.

1. Memory is the capacity to preserve and recover information. Information is recovered through
   a. encoding processes.
   b. storage processes.
   c. retrieval processes.
   d. transduction processes.

2. Iconic memory and echoic memory are two types of
   a. procedural memory.
   b. short-term memory.
   c. long-term memory.
   d. sensory memory.

3. Mistakes in short-term memory are likely to involve responses that sound like one of the original items even if the items were presented visually. From this, researchers conclude that short-term memory
   a. retains information for 10-15 seconds.
   b. has a limited capacity of 5 to 9 items.
   c. mostly uses an inner voice to code information.
   d. can be disrupted by either decay or interference.

4. The Peterson & Peterson distractor task experiment indicated short-term memory retains information for 10-15 seconds. Recent research suggests this might be incorrect and revises the estimate to
   a. 0.5 second.
   b. 1-2 seconds.
   c. 25-30 seconds.
   d. 30-40 seconds.

5. Kim formed images of the to-be-remembered items with the objects in the nursery rhyme, "One is a bun, two is a shoe, three is a tree..." (a cat in a bun, a chicken wearing shoes, etc.). This illustrates
   a. the method of loci.
   b. a pegword method.
   c. the linkword method.
   d. a distributed practice method.

6. Brenda told Eric the nine streets to take to her apartment. He remembers the first and last streets, but not the ones in between. Eric's problem is similar to
   a. flashbulb memory.
   b. the method of loci.
   c. the serial position effect.
   d. transfer-appropriate processing.

7. Mike couldn't remember his new instructor's name until someone said, "I think it begins with an S." His initial memory failure was clearly an example of
   a. a recency effect.
   b. repression.
   c. encoding specificity.
   d. cue-dependent forgetting.

8. You don't really remember your 14th birthday, but you give a fairly close description by using the season, where you lived, and other schemas. This illustrates the _____ nature of long-term memory.
   a. cue-dependent
   b. transfer-appropriate
   c. reconstructive
   d. highly specific

9. Carl repeats, "555-6739, 555-6739..." Carl is keeping the number in short-term memory by using
   a. rehearsal.
   b. the distractor task.
   c. elaboration.
   d. implicit memory.

10. Compared to iconic memory, echoic memory
    a. has a smaller capacity.
    b. information is less complete.
    c. retains information longer.
    d. is less useful.

11. Recent research suggests that memory span is determined not so much by space limitations, but by
    a. the distinctiveness of the information being placed in memory.
    b. the number of retrieval cues that are developed at input.
    c. the emotional content of the items being placed in memory.
    d. the rate at which items can be rehearsed in the inner voice.

12. To answer the question, "Where did you park this morning?" requires primarily
    a. procedural memory.
    b. semantic memory.
    c. episodic memory.
    d. flashbulb memory.

13. The mnemonic devices known as method of loci, pegword methods, and linkword methods all utilize
    a. imagery.
    b. distributed practice.
    c. episodic memory.
    d. rhymes.

14. You are asked to observe a line-up and to pick out the person who robbed you. This is a form of
    a. recall test.
    b. recognition test.
    c. implicit memory test.
    d. iconic memory test.

15. An example of an implicit memory test is
    a. Sperling's partial report test.
    b. a recognition test.
    c. a cued recall test.
    d. word fragment test.

16. Following a rape, the victim had no memory of the rape, but became very anxious if approached by a man. According to Freud's concept of defense mechanisms and memory, this would be a case of
    a. anterograde amnesia.
    b. proactive interference.
    c. Korsakoff's syndrome.
    d. repression.

17. Football players often have no memory of what happened just before they "get their bell rung" from a hard hit to the head. Their memory loss would be considered
    a. repression.
    b. Korsakoff's syndrome.
    c. retrograde amnesia.
    d. anterograde amnesia.

18. After studying for Exam 2, Al couldn't remember the Exam 1 material. This is most likely an example of
    a. motivated forgetting.
    b. retroactive inhibition.
    c. proactive inhibition.
    d. anterograde amnesia.

19. The current view of forgetting emphasizes
    a. decay.
    b. interference.
    c. repression.
    d. physical problems.

20. You have no memory of being in this restaurant, but as soon as you walk in, you feel like you've been here before. Your deja vu experience is probably linked to a similar location you don't remember, or
    a. a flashbulb memory.
    b. schemas.
    c. implicit memory.
    d. anterograde amnesia.

Multiple Choice Pretest 2. Select the one best response. Answers are on page 196.

1. Sperling found that partial report performance was no better than whole report performance if he delayed the partial report cue until about half a second after the array was removed. From this he concluded that
    a. iconic memory contains a raw, unprocessed, sensory image of the input.
    b. iconic memory contains a fairly complete replica of the sensory input.
    c. iconic memory information disappears in less than a second.
    d. memory span is limited by the time required to repeat it with the inner voice.

2. Sperling found that whole report performance was 30-40% accurate, but immediate partial report performance was nearly perfect. From this he concluded that iconic memory
    a. contains a raw, unprocessed, sensory image of the input.
    b. contains a fairly complete replica of the sensory input.
    c. holds information for less than a second.
    d. uses an acoustic (auditory) code even though the input is visual.

3. Anna yells, "Don't talk to me!" as she reaches for a piece of paper on which to write the important information she just heard. Anna seems to believe that forgetting from short-term memory is caused by
    a. encoding specificity.
    b. decay of information.
    c. transfer appropriate processing.
    d. interference from other input.

4. A short term memory task requires that Chris remember CRLMQ. Chris' most likely error would be
    a. **Z**RLMQ.
    b. **O**RLMQ.
    c. CRLM**S**.
    d. CRLM**O**.

5. Chess masters could recreate legal chessboard positions more accurately than chess novices because
    a. chess masters were older, and that gave them larger memory capacity.
    b. chess masters could code the pieces into meaningful groups to increase capacity.
    c. chess masters could name the individual pieces faster, improving memory capacity.
    d. chess masters were more intelligent, and that gave them better memories.

6. Nakia's argument is based on over ten significant facts, but one is especially important. To be sure that the jurors remember this one fact, Nakia leaves it until last in his closing review. Nakia is relying on
   a. the encoding specificity principle.
   b. the recency effect.
   c. the distributed practice effect.
   d. the primacy effect.

7. Memory for the word "horse" will be best if the person
   a. repeats "horse, horse, horse, horse" several times.
   b. realizes "horse" begins with the letter h and remembers that.
   c. thinks of a rhyme for "horse" such as "course."
   d. identifies "horse" as an animal that is ridden for transportation or fun.

8. Evidence that mental imagery is not really visual includes
   a. comparisons of the brain areas active during mental imagery and visual perception.
   b. data comparing response speed for questions about mental images vs. pictures of objects.
   c. the inability to form a mental image while performing a visually based task.
   d. the accuracy of detail in mental images of familiar objects such as a coin.

9. Based on memory research, which student is most likely to earn the highest grade on the vocabulary test?
   a. Laura, who spent three hours going over her vocabulary note cards the night before the test.
   b. Hannah, who spent only 15 minutes each of the last 12 days going over her vocabulary note cards.
   c. Kristen, who looked at them once, right before walking into the classroom.
   d. Theresa, who studied them for three hours one night two weeks ago.

10. You studied the habitat and leaves of 100 species of trees on your tree hikes. You can name the tree if given those cues. When given bark samples on your quiz, you were lost. Your problem illustrates
   a. encoding specificity.
   b. relational processing.
   c. distinctiveness failure.
   d. retroactive interference.

11. Research on flashbulb memories confirms all of the following except:
   a. Flashbulb memories usually concern emotional or surprising events.
   b. Flashbulb memories are reported with great confidence, even after significant time.
   c. Flashbulb memories are highly accurate because they are like a picture of the event.
   d. Flashbulb memories are influenced by the event's importance to the individual.

12. Students who wait to study until the night before an exam risk poor performance on the exam because
   a. forgetting occurs very rapidly during the first hours after studying.
   b. retroactive interference is likely to occur before the exam.
   c. the anxiety of last minute studying is likely to cause repression.
   d. explicit memories will be fully formed, but not implicit memories.

13. Wanda struggles in college Spanish because her high school French comes out instead. This illustrates
   a. decay theory.
   b. memory overwriting.
   c. retroactive interference.
   d. proactive interference.

14. You are on the jury in a trial involving a fight in a bar. Based on what you know about Loftus & Palmer's research, as you listen to the various eyewitnesses you would be wise to
    a. accept their memories of the event as trustworthy and highly accurate.
    b. accept their memories as highly accurate as long as they are very confident about their memories.
    c. listen very carefully to the questions that are asked each person.
    d. believe absolutely nothing they say because eyewitness testimony is never correct.

15. Firefighters visit schools lecture about what to do in a fire. Some take the process farther and have children "escape" from a smoke-filled fire education trailer. Their approach is based on the principle of
    a. reconstructive remembering.
    b. transfer-appropriate processing.
    c. proactive interference.
    d. cue-dependent forgetting.

16. Lawyers sometimes argue that their clients were picked out of a line-up simply because the witness had seen a photograph of them before. Their argument is related to the "false fame effect" involving
    a. implicit memory.
    b. cue-dependent forgetting.
    c. visual imagery.
    d. cryptomnesia.

17. If your recognition of the mugger is influenced by the clothes, race, or "attitude" of the people in a line-up because they fit your idea of "criminal" you are demonstrating the role of _____ in memory.
    a. schemas
    b. elaboration
    c. interference
    d. encoding specificity

18. People remember more if they sleep 4 hours after learning a list of nonsense syllables than if they engage in normal daily activities for 4 hours. These data are used to support the _____ theory of forgetting.
    a. cue-dependent
    b. decay
    c. interference
    d. encoding specificity

19. After a head injury, Bill seems to have no ability to form new memories and knows only the immediate present and his pre-injury past. Bill is suffering from
    a. anterograde amnesia.
    b. retrograde amnesia.
    c. flashbulb memory.
    d. cue-dependent forgetting.

20. Iris' head injury resulted in very serious anterograde amnesia. Her brain damage most likely includes the
    a. hypothalamus.
    b. hippocampus.
    c. parietal lobe.
    d. cerebellum.

ANSWERS AND EXPLANATIONS

Mastering the Concepts

1. preserve (p. 302)
2. recover (p. 302)
3. encoding (p. 302)
4. retrieval (p. 302)
5. Sensory (p. 304)
6. iconic (p. 304)
7. partial report (p. 305)
8. whole report (p. 306)
9. echoic (p. 306)
10. Short-term (p. 307)
11. rehearsed (p. 308)
12. decay (p. 309)
13. interference (p. 309)
14. capacity (p. 310)
15. Chunking (p. 311)
16. Long-term (p. 312)
17. episodic (p. 313)
18. semantic (p. 313)
19. procedural (p. 313)
20. Elaboration (p. 314)
21. relational (p. 314)
22. distinctiveness (p. 314)
23. imagery (p. 315)
24. mnemonic (p. 315)
25. method of loci (p. 315)
26. pegword (p. 317)
27. linkword (p. 317)
28. Flashbulb (p. 316)
29. reconstructive (p. 316)
30. serial position (p. 320)
31. primacy (p. 320)
32. distributed (p. 320)
33. retrieval cues (p. 322)
34. cued recall (p. 322)
35. cue-dependent (p. 322)
36. encoding (p. 323)
37. transfer (p. 324)
38. reconstructed (p. 325)
39. schemas (p. 325)
40. question (p. 326)
41. explicit (p. 327)
42. implicit (p. 327)
43. completion (p. 327)
44. illusions (p. 328)
45. accessibility (p. 329)
46. savings (p. 330)
47. soon (p. 330)
48. decay (p. 331)
49. interference (p. 331)
50. retroactive (p. 331)
51. proactive (p. 331)
52. Repression (p. 333)
53. Amnesia (p. 334)
54. retrograde (p. 334)
55. anterograde (p. 334)
56. Korsakoff's (p. 334)
57. hippocampus (p. 335)

Evaluating Your Progress

Remembering Over the Short Term

1. **a**   b. Wrong.   Storage is a maintenance, not a representation, process.
(p. 302)   c. Wrong.   Retrieval concerns how information is recovered and is translated into performance.
       d. Wrong.   Interference is a process by which information is "forgotten."

2. **a**   b. Wrong.   Echoic memory is estimated to last 5-10 seconds, iconic memory 0.5 second.
(p. 306)   c. Wrong.   Short-term memory is estimated to last 10-15 seconds, iconic memory 0.5 second.
       d. Wrong.   Anything over about 15-30 seconds is considered long-term memory.

3. **d**   a & b. Wrong.   Sperling concluded iconic memory contains the entire array, but only briefly.
(p. 306)   c.   Wrong.   Retrieval cues aren't used here. They're used for retrieval from long term memory

4. **a**   b. Wrong.   Iconic memory has a visual code; STM is acoustic.
(p. 307)   c. Wrong.   STM errors are acoustic, not abstrac/semantic.
       d. Wrong.   Episodic relates to time-linked memories in LTM, not a STM code.

5. **c**   a. Wrong.   The decay concept is that items are lost simply due to the passage of time.
(p. 309)   b. Wrong.   Chunking is a strategy for organizing material so as to increase memory capacity.
       d. Wrong.   The inner voice is used to encode information in short-term memory, not to forget it.

6. **a**   b. Wrong.   Memory span is the number of items that can be recalled from short-term memory.
(p. 311)   c. Wrong.   Cued recall involves giving retrieval cues to assist the person in recalling information.
       d. Wrong.   Rehearsal is the repetition of input to improve later recall, not to increase capacity.

7. **b**   a, c, & d.   Wrong.   Most people can recall 7, plus or minus 2, items.
(p. 310)

Storing Information for the Long Term

1. **d**
   (p. 313)
   a. Wrong. Semantic memory contains facts not linked to personal events. This is episodic memory.
   b. Wrong. Semantic memory contains facts not linked to personal events. This is procedural memory.
   c. Wrong. Semantic memory contains facts not linked to personal events. This is a flashbulb memory.

2. **a**
   (p. 314)
   b. Wrong. This is the opposite effect.
   c. Wrong. This is simple rehearsal, elaboration expands input.
   d. Wrong. Elaboration improve memory. Interference does not increase.

3. **c**
   (p. 315)
   a. Wrong. Pegword methods link images with a familiar rhyme, not with path locations.
   b. Wrong. Chunking involves regrouping into meaningful units, not imagery.
   d. Wrong. Linkword methods link images of an unfamiliar item and a familiar rhyming item.

4. **a**
   (p. 320)
   b. Wrong. This is the recency effect.
   c. Wrong. The primacy effect relates to serial position, not elaboration.
   d. Wrong. The primacy effect relates to serial position, not rehearsal.

5. **b**
   (p. 320)
   a. Wrong. Distributed practice refers to spacing practice over different times.
   c. Wrong. This relates to the primacy effect, not distributed (spaced) practice.
   d. Wrong. This is massed practice, not distributed (spaced) practice.

6. **b**
   (p. 316)
   a. Wrong. Repressed memories are pushed out of consciousness. Flashbulb memories are accessible.
   c. Wrong. Iconic memories are sensory memories, not part of direct consciousness.
   d. Wrong. Procedural memories are "how to" memories, not memories of what one was doing.

Recovering Information from Cues

1. **d**
   (p. 322)
   a & b. Wrong. Cued recall shows item is present, so it hasn't been eliminated by decay or interference.
   c. Wrong. Repression would not allow cued recall, and most "forgetting" is not due to repression.

2. **d**
   (p. 324)
   a. Wrong. Distributed practice is always good, but it doesn't relate to study-test similarity.
   b. Wrong. Imagery is often good, but it doesn't relate to study-test similarity in processing.
   c. Wrong. An explicit-implicit distinction is not relevant unless the test format will be implicit.

3. **d**
   (p. 323)
   a. Wrong. Primacy refers to improved memory for initial items, not retrieval cue quality.
   b. Wrong. Distinctiveness differentiates one item from another, but key here is initial cue formation.
   c. Wrong. Reconstructive memory refers to the active component of memory, not retrieval cues.

4. **a**
   (p. 325)
   b, c, & d. Wrong. These are all true. People are not always aware of the influence of schemas.

5. **d**
   (p. 326)
   a. Wrong. Memory is not like watching a videotape. Loftus's work emphases it's reconstructive aspect.
   b. Wrong. Loftus showed that people made to think they saw something they didn't.
   c. Wrong. Loftus' work emphasized the top-down (e.g., expectancy, schema) processes.

6. **d**
   (p. 327)
   a. Wrong. Schemas are information structures that influence memory. Key here is "unconscious."
   b. Wrong. Reconstructive means constructed from memories and schemas. Key here is "unconscious."
   c. Wrong. Explicit memory involves conscious, strategic memory processes.

7.   **a**   b. Wrong.   Distinctiveness relates to which information is recalled, but not the description given here.
   (p. 325)   c. Wrong.   Transfer-appropriate processing is learning material in a way similar to the way it will be recalled. This does not relate to the current description.
            d. Wrong.   Iconic refers to sensory memory, not long-term memory.

Updating Memory

1.   **b**   a, c, & d.   Wrong.   Forgetting is very rapid initially, then slows to a very gradual loss.
   (p. 330)

2.   **d**   a & b.   Wrong.   Amnesia is not due to the influence of other learning. It is physically determined.
   (p. 331)   c.   Wrong.   In retroactive inhibition new material interferes with previously learned material.

3.   **b**   a. Wrong.   Interference assumes factors other than time.
   (p. 331)   c. Wrong.   Cue-dependent forgetting concerns whether information is gone vs. difficult to access.
            d. Wrong.   Distinctiveness as an influence on forgetting is not limited to time passing.

4.   **c**   a. Wrong.   If we considered repression amnesia, it would be closer to retrograde than anterograde.
   (p. 333)   b. Wrong.   Overwriting is not a defense mechanism, but proposes old memories are obscured by new.
            d. Wrong.   Korsakoff's syndrome is amnesia caused by brain damage from alcoholism.

5.   **a**   b. Wrong.   Korsakoff's primarily impairs memories for events after the brain damage, not before.
   (p. 334)   c. Wrong.   Repression isn't involved, and the amnesia is not selective to drinking-related events.
            d. Wrong.   Korsakoff's primarily impairs memories for events after the brain damage.

6.   **d**   a, b, & c.   Wrong.   Indirect memory tests show new input is stored in long-term memory. The problem is one of direct, conscious retrieval of new input, not storage failure.
   (p. 335)

7.   **d**   a, b, & c   Wrong.   The hippocampus, not these areas, is an area important for memory functions.
   (p. 335)

MAKING FINAL PREPARATIONS

Short Essay Questions

1.   Sensory memory retains a fairly complete replica of the original sensory input for a short period after the stimulus ends. This allows more time for initial processing and thus, allows more complete processing. Sensory memory may be very important for audition, where stimuli (e.g., speech) must be integrated over time. (p. 304)

2.   Sensory memory contains the original sensory input, its duration is less than a second for vision and 5-10 sec. for audition (although new estimates suggest a longer duration for vision), and it holds the entire stimulus. Short term memory contains processed information, it has a longer duration (about 15 seconds, although new estimates suggest it might be only 1 or 2 seconds), and is limited in its capacity. (pp. 304-311)

3.   The amount of time studied is not always as important as when you study and how you study. First, you should study for shorter periods throughout the entire period before the exam, not just at the end. This is called distributed practice, which is better than massed practice (cramming). Second, by waiting until the last minute you might have learned something one night but have forgotten it by the exam. Most forgetting occurs soon after initial learning. Third, you need to use elaboration to form the rich, distinctive retrieval cues you'll need for the exam; don't just read. Fourth, you should use transfer-appropriate processing--learn the material using the processes you'll use to retrieve it. That is, practice with multiple-choice questions. (pp. 320, 322-324, 330)

4. Research suggests that the memory span is limited by how fast material can be rehearsed. Chunking increases rehearsal speed, thus increasing the amount that can be retained. (p. 311)

5. Long-term memories are not exact versions of the original material. They contain the general idea, but specific details are reconstructed based on expectations and schema. This is adaptive because incomplete memories can be supplemented to allow the organism to act. (pp. 325-326)

6. Decay theory proposes that memories are lost or forgotten spontaneously due to the passage of time. No other processes are involved. Interference theory, currently favored, proposes that memories are disrupted by other processes---loss of distinctiveness as more material enters memory, loss of good retrieval cues as they are reused with other material, new material overwriting old, etc. (pp. 309, 330-332)

7. Forgetting is adaptive because it reduces the "clutter" of memory. Unneeded or outdated information becomes less accessible so other, more important information can be accessed more efficiently. It is usually not necessary to remember every instance of something, and retrieval cues are more selective with less material. (p. 329)

Matching

1. **e** (p. 330)	4. **c** (p. 328)	7. **k** (p. 327)	10. **a** (p. 322)	13. **d** (p. 305)	16. **m** (p. 328)
2. **n** (p. 324)	5. **o** (p. 314)	8. **h** (p. 309)	11. **p** (p. 304)	14. **g** (p. 330)	
3. **b** (p. 305)	6. **i** (p. 306)	9. **f** (p. 315)	12. **l** (p. 326)	15. **j** (p. 304)	

Multiple Choice Pretest 1

1. **c**
   (p. 302)
   a. Wrong. Encoding is the initial formation of memories, not their recovery.
   b. Wrong. Storage processes maintain, rather than recover, information.
   d. Wrong. Transduction is the transformation of physical energy into neural activity.

2. **d**
   (p. 304)
   a, b, & c. Wrong. Iconic and echoic are visual and auditory sensory memory, respectively.

3. **c**
   (p. 307)
   a, b, & d. Wrong. Although true concerning STM, these are not conclusions from the data cited.

4. **b**
   (p. 309)
   a, c, & d. Wrong. Surprise tests suggest forgetting occurs within 1 or 2 seconds.

5. **b**
   (p. 317)
   a. Wrong. Method of loci uses places along a path, not a rhyme.
   c. Wrong. Linkword methods use familiar words and images, not a rhyme.
   d. Wrong. Distributed practice refers to spacing practice, rather than massing it all at once.

6. **c.**
   (p. 320)
   a. Wrong. Flashbulb memories are detailed memories about emotionally important events.
   b. Wrong. The method of loci is a mnemonic technique that improves memory.
   d. Wrong. Related encoding and retrieval processes are not relevant here; serial position is.

7. **d**
   (p. 322)
   a. Wrong. Key here is that he remembered when given a cue, not serial position.
   b. Wrong. Key here is that he remembered when given a cue, not motivated forgetting.
   c. Wrong. Key here is that he remembered when given a cue. No information is given about encoding.

8. **c**
   (p. 325)
   a. Wrong. A "memory" is created (constructed) here, in spite of having no direct retrieval cues.
   b. Wrong. A "memory" is created (constructed) here. Learning vs. testing processes are not key here.
   d. Wrong. This shows memory is not necessarily specific but is constructed .

9.   **a**   b. Wrong.   Carl is rehearsing. Distractor tasks prevent rehearsing short-term memory items.
   (p. 308)   c. Wrong.   Elaboration involves forming connections to other items. Carl isn't doing that.
                d. Wrong.   Implicit memory is remembering without conscious awareness or intent.

10.   **c**   a & b. Wrong.   The primary difference is the duration, not the amount or quality of the information.
   (pp. 304-306) d.   Wrong.   An auditory stimulus is spread over time, not space, so keeping it longer is important.

11.   **d**   a, b, & c.   Wrong.   Recent research centers on the length of time required to rehearse the items. The
   (p. 311)   longer it takes to say an item, the smaller the memory span seems to be.

12.   **c**   a. Wrong.   Procedural memory is "how to" memory.
   (p. 313)   b. Wrong.   Semantic memory involves facts unrelated to one's personal history.
                d. Wrong.   Flashbulb memories are highly detailed memories of emotionally charged events.

13.   **a**   b. Wrong.   Distributed practice refers to spacing practice rather than massing it all at once.
   (p. 315)   c. Wrong.   These do not all use information about events in one's personal past.
                d. Wrong.   Pegwords and linkwords use rhymes, but method of loci doesn't.

14.   **b**   a. Wrong.   You are asked to "recognize" the person, not describe (recall) the person.
   (p. 324)   c. Wrong.   This is an explicit memory test. You are conscious of using memory.
                d. Wrong.   Iconic memory is sensory memory lasting less than one second.

15.   **d**   a, b, & c.   Wrong.   These all require conscious, willful use of memory; they are explicit tests.
   (p. 327)

16.   **d**   a. Wrong.   This isn't a defense mechanism. It is inhibition of new memories, not loss of past ones.
   (p. 333)   b. Wrong.   This isn't a defense mechanism. It is interference of new memories by old ones.
                c. Wrong.   This isn't a defense mechanism. It is a physically caused amnesia due to alcoholism.

17.   **c**   a. Wrong.   Repression is due to emotional trauma, not physical trauma to the brain.
   (p. 334)   b. Wrong.   Korsakoff's syndrome is due to alcoholism and involves problems forming new memories.
                d. Wrong.   Anterograde amnesia is loss of memory for events after the injury, not those before.

18.   **b**   a. Wrong.   Motivated forgetting, like repression, is not likely without anxiety involved.
   (p. 331)   c. Wrong.   If proactive, Alonzo would have trouble with the new material due to the old material.
                d. Wrong.   Even if Alonzo had brain damage, the pattern fits retrograde, not anterograde amnesia.

19.   **b**   a. Wrong.   Decay is given much less emphasis, although some researchers do not rule it out.
   (p. 332)   c. Wrong.   Repression is a special case of forgetting, and its scientific validity is questioned.
                d. Wrong.   Physical problems certainly affect memory, but not the usual forgetting.

20.   **c**   a. Wrong.   Flashbulb memories are conscious memories.
   (p. 327)   b. Wrong.   Schemas are knowledge structures, not unconscious remembering.
                d. Wrong.   Anterograde amnesia is the loss of ability to form new memories.

Multiple Choice Pretest 2

1.   **c**   a & b. Wrong.   This is true concerning iconic memory, but it is not based on the data cited.
   (p. 306)   d.   Wrong.   This statement is true of short-term memory, not iconic memory.

2.   **b**   a & c. Wrong.   This is true concerning iconic memory, but it is not based on the data cited.
   (p. 306)   d.   Wrong.   Short-term memory and echoic memory use acoustic codes, not iconic memory.

3. **d**   a. Wrong.   Key here is Anna's avoidance of new input. New input might interfere with the old.
(p. 309)   b. Wrong.   Anna is avoiding new input that might interfere with the old. Decay is time-based.
            c. Wrong.   Key here is avoiding new, interfering input, not matching encoding and retrieval processes.

4. **a**   b, c, & d.   Wrong.   Short-term memory errors are usually substitutions of similarly sounding items.
(p. 307)

5. **b**   a, c, & d.   Wrong.   Masters were no better if pieces were randomly placed, so knowledge-based
(p. 312)   chunking was key.

6. **b**   a. Wrong.   Encoding specificity relates type of encoding, not position, with later retrieval.
(p. 320)   c. Wrong.   Distributed practice improves memory but isn't related to item position in a list.
            d. Wrong.   A primacy effect is improved memory for the first items presented.

7. **d**   a.   Wrong.   Simple repetition is valuable, but not as much as elaboration.
(p. 314)   b & c.   Wrong.   These involves only limited elaboration.

8. **d**   a. Wrong.   Similarity of activated brain areas supports a common link for imagery and vision.
(p. 319)   b. Wrong.   Speed of response is similar to that expected with "visual" imagery.
            c. Wrong.   This would support the "visual" nature of imagery.

9. **b**   a. Wrong.   Laura massed her practice, which is not the most effective approach.
(p. 320)   c. Wrong.   Kristen has recency going for her, but no repetition. She's likely to forget the middle terms.
            d. Wrong.   Theresa is likely to have forgotten a large percentage of the material.

10. **a**   b. Wrong.   Relational processing is elaboration. Key here are the cues during encoding vs. testing.
(p. 323)   c. Wrong.   Distinctiveness was present. Key here are the cues during encoding vs. testing.
            d. Wrong.   Retroactive = new items disrupt old items. Key here are cues during encoding vs. testing.

11. **c**   a, b, & d.   Wrong.   These are all true statements. Flashbulb memories are not necessarily accurate.
(p. 316)

12. **a**   b. Wrong.   Unless new material is introduced, retroactive interference will be minimal.
(p. 330)   c. Wrong.   Repression is not that common, and it usually involves only traumatic events.
            d. Wrong.   Even if this were true (doubtful!) tests usually emphasize explicit memories.

13. **d**   a. Wrong.   Decay would reduce the impact of French, not cause it to interfere.
(p. 331)   b. Wrong.   In overwriting, new material overwrites (obscures) old memories, the opposite of here.
            c. Wrong.   Retroactive interference here would be the Spanish wiping out the French she knew.

14. **c**   a. Wrong.   Although not completely inaccurate, they can be far from correct.
(p. 326)   b. Wrong.   Confidence does not ensure accuracy of memory.
            d. Wrong.   Although far from perfect, the memories are not entirely inaccurate.

15. **b**   a. Wrong.   Reconstructive memory suggests memories are constructed, not just replayed. Key here,
(p. 324)   though, is learning using the processes to be used during testing, a fire.
            c. Wrong.   Proactive interference is memory disruption caused by previously learned items. Key here,
                        though, is learning using the processes to be used during testing, a fire.
            d. Wrong.   Cue-dependent forgetting occurs when items are in memory but appropriate retrieval cues
                        are not available. Key here is learning using the processes to be used during testing, a fire.

16. **a**   b. Wrong.   The false fame effect involves implicit memory, not ineffective retrieval cues.
(p. 328)   c. Wrong.   The false fame effect involves implicit memory, not visual imagery.
            d. Wrong.   Cryptomnesia is accidental plagiarism. The false fame effect involves implicit memory.

17. **a**   b. Wrong.   Elaboration is the expansion of to-be-remembered items to improve later recovery.
(p. 325)   c. Wrong.   Interference is a possible cause of forgetting.
            d. Wrong.   Encoding specificity relates the cues at encoding with the effective cues for retrieval.

18. **c**   a. Wrong.   Free recall vs. cued recall comparisons support cue-dependent forgetting.
(p. 331)   b. Wrong.   Decay would predict no difference because the time interval was the same.
            d. Wrong.   There's no reason to think encoding differed. The difference is the activity during the delay.

19. **a**   b. Wrong.   Retrograde amnesia disrupts retrieval of old memories, not the forming of new ones.
(p. 334)   c. Wrong.   Flashbulb memories are detailed memories of emotionally-charges event.
            d. Wrong.   Cue-dependent forgetting is forgetting due to having inappropriate retrieval cues.

20. **b**   a, c, & d.   Wrong.   Damage here doesn't usually cause amnesia. Damage to the hippocampus does.
(p. 335)

LANGUAGE ENHANCEMENT GUIDE

CORE TERMS

In this chapter, your instructor will probably talk about the ***practical applications*** of what we know about memory -- that is, how you can use the information day-to-day. And then they might use the term ***pragmatic***. That's another term that means, "to focus on *uses* of something." You could say that a pragmatic person looks for practical applications. You might also hear the term ***implications***, as in, "So what are the *implications* of this research finding?" That means something like, "What does this mean in the real world? How can these findings be applied? What further ideas do they lead to?"

A *pragmatic* person is likely to be interested in ***strategies*** -- ways to actually use something. In a lecture on learning strategies, you are likely to hear three words: ***rote, repetition*** and ***simple rehearsal***. As you can probably guess, they all have to do with practicing something over and over. Those terms will be contrasted with ***elaboration***, which means adding detail. It's **counterintuitive** (not what you'd expect), but the more detail you add to what you want to remember, the better you will remember it. But the key is that the details have to be interesting. So the practical application here is that if you are studying, the more interesting details and examples you can pay attention to, the better you will remember the material!

IDIOMS

302   plight   difficult or dangerous situation

302   albeit   although, even though

302   devoid of   without any

302	depicted visually	shown in a picture
303	fleeting encounter	very brief meeting
304	snapshot	quick picture or photograph; quick impression
306	replicas	copies
308	temporal order of occurrence	the order in which it happened
308	internal repetition	saying it over and over in your mind
313	athletic prowess	skill at sports
314	an involved sequence of events depicting	a complicated mental image of what happened
318	mediocre at best	only average, or even worse
326	undergraduates	college students
326	just prior to	just before
330	cardiopulmonary resuscitation	CPR, a lifesaving technique for heart attacks
330	indefinitely	for an unknown period of time; perhaps for a long time
332	conceivable that	it could be that
333	retain the capacity	keep the ability to
333	in the conventional sense	the usual meaning; the way people usually understand it
333	cast themselves in a positive light	make themselves seem as good as possible

WORD PARTS

Here are some words that are made up of word parts, and that you can find in this chapter. After you've looked at these, you can look for others in the chapter that use the same word parts (they are there, but YOU have to find them!)

WORD	WORD PART IT USES	MEANING
retroactive	retro = back	to act on something in the past
amnesia	a = not mne = memory	lost memory

revert	re = again vert = to turn	to turn back to
retain	re = again tent, tain = to try, touch, keep	to keep back, to hold onto
locate	loc = place	to find
mediocre	med, mid = middle	not very good or very bad
anterograde	ante = back grade = step	to work or step backwards
dysfunction	dys = bad, ill	to not work well
introduce	intro = inward duc = to carry, bring	to bring into
prospective	pro = forward spect = to look	something that might be in the future

Knowing the word parts listed above, you can also create the following words. You can get an idea of their meanings from the word parts they use. You fill in the blanks!

retrograde	retro + grade	_____
contain	con (together) + tain	_____
avert	_____ + _____	to prevent, to turn away
mnemonic	_____	having to do with memory
dislocate	dis (not) + loc	_____
introvert	_____ + _____	one who is turned inward
proactive	pro + active	_____

CHAPTER 9: THOUGHT AND LANGUAGE

ESTABLISHING LEARNING OBJECTIVES

Use these learning objectives as a preview of the chapter, a guide for active reading, and to evaluate your mastery of the material. Review the relevant objectives as you begin and end your reading of each major section of the chapter.

After studying this chapter you should be able to:

I. Solve the adaptive problem of how to communicate with others.
    A. Evaluate the linguistic relativity hypothesis.
    B. Discuss the structure of language and identify its basic units.
        1. Define phonology, syntax, and semantics.
        2. Describe the different levels of language, including surface structure and deep structure.
    C. Discuss some of the factors that contribute to language comprehension.
    D. Trace the major milestones in language development.
    E. Discuss efforts to produce language in nonhuman species.
        1. Describe the language skills of the animals studied.
        2. Discuss the criticisms of the claims that nonhuman species learned a language.

II. Solve the adaptive problem of how to classify or categorize objects.
    A. Define category, and explain how categories are used.
    B. Discuss some of the factors that define category membership.
        1. Discuss the idea that categories have defining features.
        2. Discuss the idea that categorization is based on family resemblance.
    C. Distinguish between prototype and exemplar views of categorization.
    D. Explain the hierarchical organization of categories.

III. Solve the adaptive problem of solving problems effectively.
    A. Distinguish between well-defined problems and ill-defined problems.
    B. List the steps in the IDEAL problem solving technique.
    C. Describe factors that influence how a problem is identified and defined.
        1. Define functional fixedness, and explain its adaptive value.
    D. Compare algorithms and heuristics, and give examples of each.
        1. Describe the means-ends heuristic.
        2. Describe the working backward heuristic.
        3. Describe the searching for analogies heuristic and when analogies will be recognized.

IV. Solve the adaptive problem of making effective decisions.
    A. Define decision making and differentiate it from problem solving.
    B. Discuss framing effects and their influences on decision making.
    C. Describe common decision making heuristics: representativeness, availability, and anchoring and adjustment.
    D. Discuss the pros and cons of using heuristics.

MASTERING THE MATERIAL

Preview & Communicating with Others (pp. 344-355)

Mastering the Vocabulary. Define or explain each of the following terms. To check your answers, consult the text pages listed.

1. thinking (p. 344)

2. linguistic relativity hypothesis (p. 346)

3. grammar (p. 348)

4. phonology (p. 348)

5. syntax (p. 348)

6. semantics (p. 348)

7. phonemes (p. 348)

8. morphemes (p. 349)

9. surface structure (p. 350)

10. deep structure (p. 350)

11. pragmatics (p. 351)

Mastering the Content. Fill in the blanks to create a summary of this section. Answers are on page 216.

Thinking, or _____(1), involves the processes used to mentally manipulate knowledge and is the focus of study for the field of cognitive _____(2). This chapter examines four adaptive problems concerning thinking: How do individuals communicate? How do they categorize things? How do people solve problems? How do people make decisions?

The linguistic _____(3) hypothesis states language determines thought, but people with limited languages perceive and learn like people with rich languages. Language influences thought (often through memory) but doesn't determine it. To be a language, the communication system must have _____(4), rules for combining symbols to convey meaning. Grammar involves three parts: _____(5), rules for combining sounds, _____(6), rules for combining words, and semantics, rules for meaning. Words are composed of phonemes, the smallest speech sounds, and _____(7), the smallest units of meaning. Words are combined using syntax to form phrases and sentences. Language can be ambiguous because one surface structure can have multiple _____(8) structures, according to Chomsky. These meanings are evaluated by top-down processes including _____(9), the practical knowledge used to judge a speaker's intent.

The universal stages of development suggest language is not entirely determined by _____(10). Babies coo at 3-5 weeks, _____(11) by 4-6 months, produce single words by 1 year, and multiple words by 2 years. Environment affects language after _____(12), shaping accent and specific words. Early speech is described as _____(13) speech because it omits all unimportant words (Give cup.). The tendency to _____(14) (runned) may indicates children automatically learn language production rules, and supports the role of genetic preparedness for language development. Nonhuman primates have learned to communicate with _____(15) or plastic symbols. Not all researchers agree this is _____(16).

Evaluating Your Progress. Select the one best response. Answers are on page 216. If you make any errors, reread the relevant material before proceeding.

1. The linguistic relativity hypothesis suggests that
    a. sentences with the same surface structure can have different deep structures.
    b. an individual's language determines their thoughts and perceptions.
    c. grammar is the central requirement for a communication system to be a language.
    d. nonhuman primates acquire "language" very differently than humans.

2. If you are studying the practical knowledge used to comprehend a speaker's intentions, you are studying
    a. linguistic relativity.
    b. grammar.
    c. pragmatics.
    d. phonology.

3. The intended meaning of "Visiting relatives can be a pain" is unclear because it has two
    a. phonemes.
    b. morphemes.
    c. surface structures.
    d. deep structures.

4. English has about 40-45 basic speech sounds that are known as
   a. phonemes.
   b. morphemes.
   c. the surface structure.
   d. the deep structure.

5. Most psychologists believe that
   a. the linguistic relativity hypothesis is accurate.
   b. nonhuman species have acquired a formal language.
   c. there is a strong genetic component in language development.
   d. one-word language does not communicate meaning or intent.

6. Most children first use single words at about
   a. 4-6 months.
   b. 12 months.
   c. 18 months.
   d. 24 months.

7. Telegraphic speech omits
   a. verbs.
   b. nouns.
   c. articles.
   d. intonation or stress ("?," "!")

8. Which of the following is not an accurate statement concerning language in nonhuman species?
   a. Chimps have learned to make two-word communications.
   b. Chimps have used new, unique word combinations to describe objects.
   c. Chimps have learned language skills by watching other chimps using language.
   d. Chimps have learned to understand sign language but not spoken language.

Classifying and Categorizing (pp. 356-362)

Mastering the Vocabulary. Define or explain each of the following terms. To check your answers, consult the text pages listed.

1. category (p. 356)

2. defining features (p. 356)

3. family resemblance (p. 358)

4. prototypes (p. 358)

5. category exemplars (p. 358)

6. basic-level categories (p. 360)

Mastering the Concepts. Fill in the blanks to create a summary of this section. Answers are on page 216.

A _____(17) is a class of objects that belong together, and that allows inferences about members' characteristics and predictions about the future. Categories are defined in terms of _____(18) features and family _____(19). Using fixed features can work poorly for _____(20) categories with fuzzy _____(21). Members of natural categories have features that are _____(22), not defining. In a family resemblance approach, members share many, but not all, of a set of critical features.

Psychologists differentiate the idea of _____(23), or most representativeness member, and category _____(24), examples of the category, as means for assigning category membership. The exemplar view suggests all members of the category are stored and used for comparison. The prototype view suggests items are compared to a stored prototype, not the actual members of the category. Because more information is available than prototypes would predict, researchers tend to favor the exemplar view.

Categories are structured in _____(25). _____(26) categories are the first to be learned and give the most useful information. Higher categories, _____(27), are less descriptive.

Evaluating Your Progress. Select the one best response. Answers are on page 217. If you make any errors, reread the relevant material before you proceed.

1. The defining features and family resemblance approaches differ because the defining features approach
   a. requires the object to have all the defining features, but family resemblance doesn't.
   b. uses prototypes, but family resemblance uses category exemplars to assign membership.
   c. is used best with natural concepts, but family resemblance is used best with mathematical concepts.
   d. applies to non-living objects, but family resemblance applies to living objects.

2. Prototype theory proposes that new objects are classified based on a comparison to
   a. each of the individual examples of members of the category.
   b. a list of critical features that define the category.
   c. the abstract "best" example of a category.
   d. the superordinate characteristics of the category.

3. The category level that generates the most useful information, is used most, and is first to be learned is
   a. prototype.
   b. superordinate.
   c. basic-level category.
   d. fuzzy category.

Solving Problems (pp. 362-370)

Mastering the Vocabulary. Define or explain each of the following terms. To check your answers, consult the text pages listed.

1. well-defined problem (p. 363)

2. ill-defined problem (p. 363)

3. functional fixedness (p. 365)

4. mental sets (p. 365)

5. algorithms (p. 366)

6. heuristics (p. 366)

7. means-ends analysis (p. 367)

8. working backward (p. 367)

9. searching for analogies (p. 369)

Mastering the Concepts. Fill in the blanks to create a summary of this section. Answers are on page 216.

Problems are situations in which there is some uncertainty about how to reach a goal. _____(28) defined problems have a clear goal, a starting point, and a way to evaluate success. _____(29) defined problems do not have clear goals, starting points, or ways to evaluate the outcome. The IDEAL Problem Solver outlines effective problem solving: _____(30) the problem; _____(31) the problem efficiently; _____(32) a variety of strategies; Act on the problem strategy; and _____(33) back and evaluate the strategy. Problem representation is critical, but _____(34), habits of perception and thought, can distort the process. People treat objects and their functions in a fixed and typical way, functional _____(35).

Strategies for solving problems include _____(36), step-by-step instructions that guarantee a solution, and _____(37), "rules of thumb" that are helpful but do not guarantee success. Algorithms are useful only for certain _____(38) problems. Heuristics can be inaccurate, but they allow rapid, logical, decisions. One heuristic is _____(39) analysis, in which actions are chosen to reduce distance to the goal. This often includes breaking a larger problem down into _____(40). The working _____(41) heuristic begins at the goal and works toward the start. In the searching for _____(42) heuristic, similar past problems guide the solution. The difficulty recognizing similar problems is reduced by _____(43) with a type of problem, hints, and initial failure on the past problems. Looking back and evaluating the solution is critical.

Evaluating Your Progress. Select the one best response. Answers are on page 217. If you make any errors, reread the relevant material before you proceed.

1. A problem with a specific goal, a specific starting place, and a good way to evaluate a solution is
   a. a well-defined problem.
   b. a heuristic.
   c. a means-ends analysis.
   d. an ill-defined problem.

2. IDEAL is Bransford & Stein's
   a. classification system for different types of problems.
   b. steps to follow for effective problem solving.
   c. artificial intelligence (computer program) problem solver.
   d. algorithm for solving ill-defined problems.

3. The tendency to see objects in a fixed and typical way is known as
   a. means-ends analysis.
   b. the availability heuristic.
   c. anchoring.
   d. functional fixedness.

4. The concept that is most closely related to functional fixedness is
   a. mental set.
   b. IDEAL.
   c. algorithm.
   d. well-defined problem.

5. "Look for similarities between the current problem and a previous problem, and solve the current problem using the procedures that were successful before." This represents
   a. the representativeness heuristic.
   b. the availability heuristic.
   c. the working backward heuristic.
   d. the searching for analogies heuristic.

6. Heuristics are
   a. step-by-step instructions for how to solve a problem.
   b. general guidelines or strategies for solving a problem.
   c. strategies that guarantee a correct solution.
   d. only useful with a well-defined problem.

7. Selecting actions to reduce the gap between the current starting point and the desired goal describes
   a. the representativeness heuristic.
   b. the availability heuristic.
   c. the searching for analogies heuristic.
   d. the means-ends heuristic.

Making Decisions (pp. 370-375)

Mastering the Vocabulary. Define or explain each of the following term. To check your answers, consult the text pages listed.

1. decision making (p. 370)

2. framing (p. 370)

3. representativeness heuristic (p. 371)

4. availability heuristic (p. 372)

5. conjunction error (p. 372)

6. anchoring and adjustment (p. 373)

Mastering the Concepts. Fill in the blanks to create a summary of this section. Answers are on page 216.

Decision making, choosing from among a set of alternatives, is affected by beliefs and perceptions. How alternatives are presented, their _____(44), is important. Selection is not necessarily rational and based on the _____(45). Perception of possible gain leads to risk avoidance; possible loss leads to risk in order to avoid loss. Personal interpretation of the situation, rather than objective information is critical.

Heuristics can lead to inaccurate evaluations. The _____(46) heuristic, in which alternatives are compared to a prototype, causes decisions that disregard objective facts. Base rates are often ignored. This also causes the _____(47) error, in which a combination of traits is judged more common than a single trait (A+B > A). In the _____(48) heuristic, estimates are inflated if many examples of the concept can be generated easily. In the _____(49) and adjustment heuristic, the starting point is influential. Low starting values lead to _____(50) estimates than higher starting values. Heuristics can distort decisions, but they allow _____(51), often effective, decisions with less than full information.

Evaluating Your Progress. Select the one best response. Answers are on page 217. If you make any errors, reread the relevant material before proceeding.

1. When treatment outcomes are described in terms of deaths, doctors make different decisions than if treatment outcomes are described in terms of survival. In other words, the decision is influenced by
   a. framing.
   b. the representativeness heuristic.
   c. the availability heuristic.
   d. conjunction errors.

2. If people always acted rationally, decisions would be based on
   a. a means-ends analysis.
   b. the representativeness heuristic.
   c. anchoring and adjustment.
   d. expected value.

3. Judging the probability of an event based on the event's similarity to a typical or average event is
   a. the expected value of the event.
   b. the availability heuristic.
   c. the representativeness heuristic.
   d. the conjunction error.

4. Using the ease with which examples of an situation come to mind to judge an event's probability is
   a. the expected value.
   b. anchoring and adjustment.
   c. the representativeness heuristic.
   d. the availability heuristic.

5. In the anchoring and adjustment heuristic, decisions are influenced by
   a. the ease of recalling a similar event.
   b. initial estimates or starting points.
   c. ideas about what the typical case is like.
   d. the way the problem is presented.

6. The conjunction error and ignoring the base rate are caused by
   a. the framing effect.
   b. the availability heuristic.
   c. the representativeness heuristic.
   d. the anchors and adjustment heuristic.

MAKING FINAL PREPARATIONS

Complete these sections without consulting your book or notes. For a more accurate estimate of how well you know this material, wait at least a day or two after studying the chapter before working on the questions. Some of the material you "know" immediately after working with the chapter will be quickly forgotten. Immediate tests will overestimate what you know well.

Short Essay Questions. Write a brief answer to each question. Sample answers are on page 218.

1. Cite some reasons why most researchers believe language has a strong genetic component.

2. Summarize the language capabilities of nonhuman species.

3. Compare the prototype and category exemplar theories of categorization, and explain why researchers tend to favor the exemplar theory.

4. Why are mental sets such as functional fixedness generally adaptive?

5. Define heuristics and discuss their limitations and adaptive value.

Matching. Select the correct definition or description for each item. Answers are on page 218.

_____ 1. algorithm	**a.**	idea that language dictates thought
_____ 2. exemplars	**b.**	rules of thumb or general strategies
_____ 3. thinking	**c.**	rules used in language to communicate meaning
_____ 4. expected value	**d.**	most representative member of category
_____ 5. linguistic relativity	**e.**	rules for how sounds combine to form words
_____ 6. mental sets	**f.**	rules for how words are combined
_____ 7. framing	**g.**	processes of mental manipulation of knowledge
_____ 8. semantics	**h.**	step-by-step rules that guarantee a correct solution
_____ 9. decision making	**i.**	processes used to choose from among alternatives
_____ 10. prototype	**j.**	well-established habits of perception and thought
_____ 11. anchors	**k.**	specific category members stored in memory
_____ 12. syntax	**l.**	(probability of outcome) X (value of outcome)
_____ 13. heuristics	**m.**	manner in which problem is presented
_____ 14. phonology	**n.**	starting points that influence decisions or estimates

Multiple Choice Pretest 1. Select the one best response. Answers are on page 219.

1. Rosch examined the color perception of the Dani, a tribe with only 4 color words. She found
   a. they perceive color like English speakers, as predicted by the linguistic relativity hypothesis.
   b. they perceive color like English speakers, in opposition to the linguistic relativity hypothesis.
   c. they don't perceive color like English speakers, as predicted by the linguistic relativity hypothesis.
   d. they don't perceive color like English speakers, in opposition to the linguistic relativity hypothesis.

2. In the word "unmade," "un" and "made" represent
   a. phonemes.
   b. morphemes.
   c. the surface structure.
   d. the deep structure.

3. Pierre's babbling has begun to sound like French in rhythm and common sounds. Pierre is probably
   a. about 5 weeks old.
   b. about 4 months old.
   c. about 8 months old.
   d. about 1 year old.

4. All of the following support a strong genetic component in language development except:
   a. Language development proceeds through the same stages all around the world.
   b. Children use grammatical forms (runned) that have not been reinforced.
   c. All children show the same changes in vocalization until 6 months old.
   d. Between 6 and 18 months, children develop the accent associated with their future native language.

5. Which of the following is true concerning attempts to teach nonhuman species language?
   a. A few chimps have learned spoken language, although their pronunciation is poor.
   b. Chimps have learned to use single words, but they cannot progress to the two-word stage.
   c. Chimps can use symbols to communicate only if the symbols look like the objects they represent.
   d. Researchers have reported that chimps can produce new word combinations.

6. If an animal must bark and have four legs and a tail to be a dog, the category is defined in terms of
   a. family resemblance.
   b. a prototype.
   c. exemplars.
   d. defining features.

7. If a new object is compared to several individual examples of a category, membership is based on
   a. prototypes.
   b. category exemplars.
   c. the availability heuristic.
   d. fuzzy boundaries.

8. The level of category that provides the most useful and predictive description of an object is known as
   a. a superordinate category.
   b. a prototype category.
   c. a well-defined category.
   d. a basic-level category.

9. In IDEAL, the A stands for
   a. Allocate.
   b. Algorithm.
   c. Answer.
   d. Act.

10. A paper-and-pencil maze has six starting positions, only one of which leads to the pot of gold. Cliff visually followed the path leading away from the pot of gold until he had an idea about which path he should choose. Cliff used the problem solving approach known as
    a. means-ends analysis.
    b. searching for analogies.
    c. working backward.
    d. anchoring and adjustment.

11. All of the following are true concerning algorithms except:
    a. They guarantee a correct solution if properly followed.
    b. They are step-by-step rules or procedures for solving a problem.
    c. They guarantee the most rapid solution to a problem.
    d. They are more useful with well-defined problems than with ill-defined problems.

12. Functional fixedness is likely to be a problem during the problem-solving stage of
    a. identifying the problem.
    b. problem representation.
    c. acting on a chosen strategy.
    d. evaluating the effectiveness of the strategy.

13. Which is false concerning the searching for analogies heuristic?
    a. Many people fail to recognize analogous problems if the surface characteristics are different.
    b. Greater experience with a particular type of problem has little effect on recognizing analogies.
    c. Hints that two problems are related improves problem solving performance.
    d. Having failed before finally solving the earlier problem can make solving the new problem easier.

14. In contest #1, Alice has a 10% chance of winning $1000. In contest #2, she has an 80% chance of winning $50. If she enters only one contest, the rational choice is _____. Based on research, she's likely to enter _____.
    a. #1; #1
    b. #1; #2
    c. #2; #2
    d. #2; #1

15. People usually decide that coin tosses of HHHTTT are less likely than HTHTTH because HHHTTT doesn't seem like an outcome that could be due to chance (random). This demonstrates
    a. the availability heuristic.
    b. the representativeness heuristic.
    c. functional fixedness.
    d. anchoring and adjustment.

16. Leo used to eat tuna often, but after a case of botulism made headlines, he decided tuna was too risky. His decision appears to have been influenced by
    a. a framing effect.
    b. functional fixedness.
    c. the representativeness heuristic.
    d. the availability heuristic.

17. In the anchoring and adjustment heuristic, the "anchor" is the
    a. initial estimate or starting point.
    b. middle or typical score or estimate.
    c. final estimate or last alternative.
    d. most common similar event that is recalled.

Multiple Choice Pretest 2. Select the one best response. Answers are on page 220.

1. Mary threw the ball. The ball was thrown by Mary. These sentences have the same
    a. surface structure.
    b. deep structure.
    c. phonemes.
    d. pragmatics.

2. The word "cat" has _____ morphemes.
    a. 0
    b. 1
    c. 2
    d. 3

3. A clear example of overgeneralization is
    a. "Daddy sees the mouses."
    b. "Mommy danced."
    c. "The cow was kicked by the horse."
    d. "Da-da-da-da."

4. At what age do children typically begin to use single, simple words?
    a. 4 months
    b. 8 months
    c. 1 year
    d. 2 years

5. Overgeneralization demonstrates that
    a. language development is strongly influenced by the environment.
    b. children develop language by imitating their parents.
    c. children have a natural inclination to acquire the rules of language.
    d. language development is not as universal as the biological view of language development requires.

6. Ruth identifies an object as a peach if it is very similar to some ideal peach. Ruth seems to use
   a. category exemplars.
   b. defining features.
   c. prototypes.
   d. basic-level categories.

7. Deanne is three years old. She is the just learning the concept of categorization. She classifies large, four-legged objects that go "moo" as cows. Her categories are going to be primarily
   a. subordinate categories.
   b. median categories.
   c. basic-level categories.
   d. superordinate categories.

8. Bob has broken his term paper assignment into subgoals that will take him closer to his final goal: collect reference material; develop outline; write rough draft; revise to final draft. He will attack each subgoal one by one. This problem solving approach is most similar to
   a. means-ends analysis.
   b. searching for analogies.
   c. working backward.
   d. framing.

9. Evan had replaced his lawnmower's spark plug to get it running smoothly. When his car started running poorly, he remembered the lawnmower and tried changing his car's sparkplugs. His strategy was most representative of
   a. a means-ends analysis.
   b. working backward.
   c. searching for analogies.
   d. framing.

10. If Fonda follows the kit's step-by-step instructions, the boards will become a bookcase. The instructions represent
    a. heuristics.
    b. analogies.
    c. an algorithm.
    d. prototypes.

11. You wear your raincoat if the forecast calls for a 40% chance of rain, but you don't wear it if the forecast is a 60% chance of getting no rain. Your behavior illustrates the importance of
    a. the availability heuristic.
    b. expected value.
    c. framing.
    d. mental set.

12. You can easily remember the times that changing an answer was an error. If your memories of bad outcomes influence you to avoid changing answers, you are using
    a. the availability heuristic.
    b. the working backward heuristic.
    c. an algorithm.
    d. the representativeness heuristic.

13. An example of a well-defined problem would be
    a. getting a vase to your mother by her birthday.
    b. understanding the meaning of life.
    c. selecting the best college to attend.
    d. finding the person who will be a good spouse.

14. Monty is considering different approaches to a problem. He is working on the _____ in IDEAL.
    a. I
    b. D
    c. E
    d. A

15. Never considering using a dime to tighten a screw when no screwdriver is available is an example of
    a. the working backward heuristic.
    b. the availability heuristic.
    c. a means-ends analysis.
    d. functional fixedness.

16. At first, people came through Tamara's gate at the fair in groups of two or three. Later, group size increased substantially. The same number of people went through Nick's gate, but in the opposite pattern---many large groups at first, then dwindling. Tamara estimated the crowd at 2000, but Nick estimated 7000. The difference in their estimates can best be explained by
    a. the representativeness heuristic.
    b. the availability heuristic.
    c. the anchoring and adjustment heuristic.
    d. the working backward heuristic.

17. "If you don't know the answer to a test question, choose the longest answer." This is an example of
    a. an algorithm.
    b. a heuristic.
    c. an ill-defined problem.
    d. a prototype.

18. Ted is 20 years old, 6 foot 2, and weighs 275 lbs. You decided that Ted is more likely to be a college student and football player than just a college student. This decision illustrates
    a. functional fixedness.
    b. a framing effect.
    c. a conjunction error.
    d. means-ends failure.

19. The adaptive value of heuristics is that they
    a. always produce rational, highly accurate decisions.
    b. keep decision-making objective and fact-oriented.
    c. allow reasonable, quick decisions from limited facts.
    d. provide step-by-step instructions that reduce cognitive demands.

ANSWERS AND EXPLANATIONS

Mastering the Concepts

1. cognition (p. 344)
2. science (p. 344)
3. relativity (p. 346)
4. grammar (p. 348)
5. phonology (p. 348)
6. syntax (p. 348)
7. morphemes (p. 349)
8. deep (p. 350)
9. pragmatics (p. 351)
10. experience (p. 351)
11. babble (p. 351)
12. 6 months (p. 351)
13. telegraphic (p. 352)
14. overgeneralize (p. 353)
15. sign language (p. 354)
16. language (p. 354)
17. category (p. 356)
18. defining (p. 356)
19. resemblance (p. 358)
20. natural (p. 356)
21. boundaries (p. 357)
22. characteristic (p. 357)
23. prototypes (p. 358)
24. exemplars (p. 358)
25. hierarchies (p. 359)
26. Basic-level (p. 360)
27. superordinates (p. 360)
28. Well- (p. 363)
29. Ill- (p. 363)
30. Identify (p. 363)
31. Define (p. 363)
32. Explore (p. 363)
33. Look (p. 364)
34. mental set (p. 365)
35. fixedness (p. 365)
36. algorithms (p. 366)
37. heuristics (p. 366)
38. well-defined (p. 366)
39. means-ends (p. 367)
40. subgoals (p. 367)
41. backward (p. 368)
42. analogies (p. 369)
43. experience (p. 368)
44. framing (p. 370)
45. expected value (p. 371)
46. representativeness (p. 371)
47. conjunction (p. 372)
48. availability (p. 372)
49. anchoring (p. 373)
50. lower (p. 373)
51. economical (p. 374)

Evaluating Your Progress

Preview & Communicating with Others

1. **b** (p. 346) — a, c, & d. Wrong. Although these are true statements, they don't relate to linguistic relativity, the idea that language determines thought.

2. **c** (p. 351)
   - a. Wrong. Linguistic relativity is the idea that language determines thought and perception.
   - b. Wrong. The rules of language = grammar.
   - d. Wrong. The rules for combining sounds = phonology.

3. **d** (p. 350)
   - a. Wrong. Phonemes are the smallest speech sound units. Having two is normal.
   - b. Wrong. Morphemes are the smallest units of meaning. Having two is normal.
   - c. Wrong. A sentence has one surface structure (specific word order); two deep structures is a problem.

4. **a** (p. 348)
   - b. Wrong. Morphemes are the smallest units of meaning in language. Phonemes are sound units.
   - c & d. Wrong. These are grammatical characteristics of sentences, not speech sounds.

5. **c** (p. 351)
   - a. Wrong. Rosch's Dani study damaged the credibility of linguistic relativity.
   - b. Wrong. There are significant questions about chimp "language."
   - d. Wrong. Single words combined with gestures and intonation have clear meanings.

6. **b** (p. 352)
   - a. Wrong. Babbling begins at about 4-6 months.
   - c. Wrong. Children usually have several words at 18 months.
   - d. Wrong. Children begin putting 2 words together at about 2 years.

7. **c** (p. 352) — a, b, & d. Wrong. Telegraphic speech has 2+ words and intonation, but no articles or prepositions.

8. **d** (p. 354) — a, b, & c. Wrong. These are true, but chimps have limited vocabularies and learn slowly.

Classifying and Categorizing

1.   **a**   b. Wrong.   Defining features give a clear definition, so prototypes (and exemplars) are not relevant.
(p. 358)   c. Wrong.   Defining features are not very appropriate for natural categories (with fuzzy boundaries).
             d. Wrong.   Defining features are inappropriate for natural categories, including non-living ones.

2.   **c**   a. Wrong.   This describes exemplar theory. A prototype is the "best" example.
(p. 358)   b. Wrong.   This describes the critical features definition of categories. "Best" = prototype.
             d. Wrong.   Superordinate is the most general category. A prototype is the "best " example.

3.   **c**   a. Wrong.   A prototype is not a type of category, it is the most representative member of a category.
(p. 360)   b. Wrong.   Superordinate categories are high level categories that are less useful.
             d. Wrong.   Fuzzy is not a category level; it is a description of a type of boundary.

Solving Problems

1.   **a**   b. Wrong.   Heuristics are "rules of thumb," not a type of problem.
(p. 363)   c. Wrong.   Means-ends analysis is a way to solve problems, not a type of problem.
             d. Wrong.   Ill-defined problems lack one or more of the listed characteristics.

2.   **b**   a, c, & d.   Wrong.   IDEAL describes basic steps (not an algorithm) for effective problem solving.
(p. 363)

3.   **d**   a. Wrong.   Means-ends analysis is a problem-solving heuristic.
(p. 365)   b. Wrong.   In this heuristic, decisions are based on the ease of generating examples.
             c. Wrong.   An anchor is an initial estimate that influences later estimates.

4.   **a**   b, c, & d.   Wrong.   Functional fixedness is the tendency to think of objects and their functions in a
(p. 365)   fixed, typical way---a mental set--which is often an obstacle.

5.   **d**   a. Wrong.   The representativeness heuristic uses the idea of a typical case, not similar problems.
(p. 369)   b. Wrong.   The availability heuristic is to use ease of recalling examples, not to look for similar cases.
             c. Wrong.   Working backward from a goal is not mentioned.

6.   **b**   a. Wrong.   Heuristics are "rules of thumb," not specific instructions.
(p. 366)   c. Wrong.   Heuristics don't guarantee a solution; algorithms do.
             d. Wrong.   Heuristics can be useful with ill-defined problems. Algorithms need well-defined problems.

7.   **d**   a. Wrong.   The representativeness heuristic uses ideas of the "representative" case to make decisions.
(p. 367)   b. Wrong.   The availability heuristic involves basing estimates on the ease of generating examples.
             c. Wrong.   Searching for analogies involves looking for similar problems were solved previously.

Making Decisions

1.   **a**   b. Wrong.   Key to this question is the wording of the outcomes, not how representative they are.
(p. 370)   c. Wrong.   Key here is the wording of the outcomes, not how easily an example is generated.
             d. Wrong.   Key to this question is the wording of the outcomes, not misestimating a conjunction.

2.   **d**   a. Wrong.   Means-ends analyses are not best in all cases.
(p. 371)   b. Wrong.   The representativeness heuristic is not always the most rational approach.
             c. Wrong.   Anchoring and adjustment is not possible in all cases.

3. **c**   a. Wrong.   Expected value = probability of outcome X outcome value. Key here is the comparison to
(p. 371)   the average or typical event.
       b. Wrong.   The availability heuristic bases estimates on ease of generating an example.
       d. Wrong.   The failure to see conjunctions as less likely than single characteristics is not relevant here.

4. **d**   a. Wrong.   Expected value is not used to estimate probabilities.
(p. 372)   b. Wrong.   Anchoring and adjustment involve using an initial estimate or starting point, not memory.
       c. Wrong.   Representativeness involves similarity to a prototype, not ease of recall.

5. **b**   a. Wrong.   This describes the availability heuristic.
(p. 373)   c. Wrong.   This describes the representativeness heuristic.
       d. Wrong.   This describes the framing effect.

6. **c**   a, b, & d.   Wrong.   Conjunction error and base rate occur because the alternative matches a
(p. 372)   preconceived typical case, leading to an overestimation of likelihood.

MAKING FINAL PREPARATIONS

Short Essay Questions

1. Language development occurs in the same sequence and at approximately the same rate across the world, as predicted by a biological component. Deaf infants vocalize the same as hearing infants until about 6 months. The grammar of children differs from adults' and would not be predicted from an environmental view. Overgeneralization of rules occurs, causing the production of word forms that would not have been reinforced. Development occurs rapidly and when children can't handle abstract concepts. (pp. 351-353)

2. Chimps and other nonhuman primates have been taught to use sign language or plastic symbol keys to communicate. Some have developed significant vocabularies, produced multiple-word constructions, generated novel constructions, and possibly learned to do this by watching other chimps. The process is difficult and slow, and the "language" is quite abnormal compared to a child's language. This, plus the anecdotal nature of the data, cause some to question whether their communication should be considered true language. (pp. 353-355)

3. Prototype theory proposes that new items are compared to a prototype, an ideal example of the category. The category exemplar theory proposes that all the members of the category are stored in memory and are used to compare to new items. Researchers favor the exemplar theory because people seem to have more information available about the category than prototype theory would predict. (pp. 358-359)

4. Mental sets develop as a result of experience in the world. They reflect the way the world often works. Thus, they provide a rapid, and usually accurate, means of representing information. (p. 365)

5. Heuristics are "rules of thumb" or general strategies used in reasoning and problem solving. They give guidance, not explicit instructions, and though they often lead to good answers, they don't guarantee success. Organisms don't always have time to evaluate all possible strategies. Heuristics afford a means for making economical, rapid, and fairly accurate responses even with incomplete information. (pp. 366, 374)

Matching

1. **h** (p. 366)   4. **l** (p. 371)   7. **m** (p. 370)   10. **d** (p. 358)   13. **b** (p. 366)
2. **k** (p. 358)   5. **a** (p. 346)   8. **c** (p. 348)   11. **n** (p. 373)   14. **e** (p. 348)
3. **g** (p. 344)   6. **j** (p. 365)   9. **i** (p. 370)   12. **f** (p. 348)

Multiple Choice Pretest 1

1. **b**
(p. 346)
- a. Wrong. The finding is true, but this does not support the linguistic relativity hypothesis.
- c & d. Wrong. The Dani perceive color like English speakers, refuting linguistic relativity.

2. **b**
(p. 349)
- a. Wrong. Phonemes are the smallest speech sounds (\n\). Here, these are units of meaning.
- c & d. Wrong. Sentences, not words, have surface and deep structures.

3. **c**
(p. 351)
- a. Wrong. Babbling doesn't begin by 5 weeks. Cooing does.
- b. Wrong. Babbling begins now, but similarity to a specific language occurs at about 6 months.
- d. Wrong. Pierre would probably be using words at one year.

4. **d**
(p. 351)
- a, b, & c. Wrong. These all support a genetic view.

5. **d**
(pp. 354)
- a. Wrong. This is false. Attempts to teach spoken language were totally unsuccessful.
- b. Wrong. This is false. Washoe and others do combine "words."
- c. Wrong. This is false. The symbols can be abstract (triangle = banana).

6. **d**
(p. 356)
- a. Wrong. Family resemblance does not require all attributes to be present.
- b. Wrong. A prototype is an ideal member, but other members don't have to have all attributes.
- c. Wrong. Exemplars are the particular members of a category, not really a way to define it.

7. **b**
(p. 358)
- a. Wrong. A prototype is an ideal member, and each category has only one.
- c. Wrong. The availability heuristic bases estimates on the ease of generating examples.
- d. Wrong. Fuzzy boundaries are characteristics of natural categories, not examples of members.

8. **d**
(p. 360)
- a. Wrong. Superordinate categories are too general to contain much information.
- b. Wrong. Prototypes are not category levels.
- c. Wrong. Well-defined category is not a category level.

9. **d**
(p. 363)
- a, b, & c. Wrong. A stands for Act on the strategy.

10. **c**
(p. 368)
- a. Wrong. Cliff worked backward from the goal. He did not use subgoals.
- b. Wrong. There were no analogous problems here. He worked backward from the goal.
- d. Wrong. Anchoring and adjustment is an estimation procedure. There were no estimates required.

11. **c**
(p. 366)
- a, b, & c. Wrong. These are true. Algorithms do not always give quick solutions, only correct ones.

12. **b**
(p. 364)
- a, c, & d. Wrong. Functional fixedness influences how the problem's components are represented.

13. **b**
(p. 368)
- a, c, & d. Wrong. These are all true, but experience is very helpful in recognizing analogies.

14. **b**
(p. 371)
- a. Wrong. #1 is rational (expected value = $1000 X .10 = 100), but people avoid risk (choose #2).
- c & d. Wrong. #2 is not the rational choice. Expected value = .80 X $50 = $40.

15. **b**
(p. 371)
- a. Wrong. Availability is based on ease of generating examples, not similarity to a typical outcome.
- c. Wrong. Key here is the comparison to typical randomness, not an object's usual function.
- d. Wrong. Starting points are not relevant; comparison to a representative situation is.

16. **d**   a. Wrong.   Framing effects involve the influence of wordings. Key here is decision based on publicity.
(p. 372)   b. Wrong.   Functional fixedness involves not seeing new uses. Key here is the publicity.
           c. Wrong.   The representativeness heuristic involves decisions based on similarity to a standard
                       example. Key here is the publicity.

17. **a**   b, c, & d.   Wrong.   An initial estimate or starting point is the anchor. Adjustments are made from
(p. 373)   there.

Multiple Choice Pretest 2

1. **b**   a. Wrong.   Each has a different word order (surface structure) but the same meaning (deep structure).
(p. 350)   c. Wrong.   Each has different phonemes (speech sounds).
           d. Wrong.   Sentences don't have pragmatics (knowledge use to understand intent), the listener does.

2. **b**   a, c, & d.   Wrong.   Cat has 1 morpheme (meaning unit) and 3 phonemes(\k\ \a\ \t\ ).
(p. 349)

3. **a**   b. Wrong.   The grammatical rule has been properly applied (danced).
(p. 353)   c. Wrong.   The grammar is fine. A 4-year-old might misunderstand this, however.
           d. Wrong.   This is babbling, not the overgeneralization of a grammatical rule.

4. **c**   a, b, &d.   Wrong.   First words develop at about 1 year.
(p. 352)

5. **c**   a & b.   Wrong.   Environmental reinforcement models for overgeneralization are not likely.
(p. 353)   d.   Wrong.   Overgeneralization is used to support the natural predisposition for language.

6. **c**   a. Wrong.   Using exemplars requires comparing the object to all memories of each peach she's seen.
(p. 358)   b. Wrong.   Using defining features requires comparing the object to a list of specific features.
           d. Wrong.   Basic-level categories describe a level in the hierarchy, not a way to assign categories.

7. **c**   a. Wrong.   Basic-level categories are acquired first.
(p. 360)   b. Wrong.   Median is not a valid level. Basic-level categories are acquired first.
           d. Wrong.   Basic-level categories are acquired first. Cow is not a superordinate category.

8. **a**   b. Wrong.   There is no consideration of analogous problems. Key here was attacking subgoals.
(p. 367)   c. Wrong.   Bob worked from "start" toward a goal, not the reverse. Key here were the subgoals.
           d. Wrong.   Framing is the way a problem is stated. Key here were the subgoals.

9. **c**   a, b, & d.   Wrong.   The key here is Evan's use of a successful solution from an analogous problem.
(p. 369)

10. **c**   a. Wrong.   Heuristics are rules of thumb, not detailed instructions. Key here is "step-by-step."
(p. 366)   b. Wrong.   Analogies are similarities between problems. Key here is "step-by-step."
           d. Wrong.   Prototypes are ideal members of a category. Key here is "step-by-step."

11. **c**   a. Wrong.   There is no difference in the ability to generate examples. Key here is the wording.
(p. 370)   b. Wrong.   Expected value is not relevant. Key here is the different wording of the forecast.
           d. Wrong.   Habits are not relevant. Key here is the different wording of the forecast.

12. **a**   b. Wrong.   You didn't work backward from a goal. You used memories to influence a decision.
(p. 372)   c. Wrong.   There is no step-by-step process ensuring a correct outcome.
           d. Wrong.   The emphasis here was the ease of recalling cases of making an error.

13.	**a**	b, c, & d.	Wrong.	These have no easily defined or evaluated goal.
(p. 366)				

14.	**c**	a.	Wrong.	I = Identify the problem. Monty is Exploring different strategies.
(p. 363)		b.	Wrong.	D = Define the problem. Monty is Exploring different strategies.
		d.	Wrong.	A = Act on the problem strategy. Monty is Exploring different strategies.

15.	**d**	a.	Wrong.	Working backward is beginning at the goal. Key here is being limited to standard functions.
(p. 365)		b.	Wrong.	The availability heuristic is based on ease of recalling examples, not standard function.
		c.	Wrong.	Means ends analysis is a heuristic involving finding the means to get closer to the goal. Key here is being limited to standard functions.

16.	**c**	a.	Wrong.	There's no mention of differing ideas of a typical crowd. Key is the initial flow.
(p. 373)		b.	Wrong.	If ease of recall is used, estimates would use last crowd pattern, not first.
		d.	Wrong.	If worked backward, estimates would be reversed.

17.	**b**	a.	Wrong.	This doesn't guarantee a correct solution, so it can't be an algorithm.
(p. 366)		c.	Wrong.	This isn't a problem at all; it's a strategy for solving a problem.
		d.	Wrong.	Prototypes are the most representative members of categories, not a strategy.

18.	**c**	a.	Wrong.	Functional fixedness involves considering only the object's usual function. Key here is selecting two attributes, rather than one as most likely.
(p. 372)		b.	Wrong.	The way the problem was posed was not important. Key here is selecting two attributes.
		d.	Wrong.	Means-ends analysis is a problem solving, not a decision-making procedure.

19.	**c**	a.	Wrong.	Heuristics do not always produce rational or highly accurate decisions.
(p. 374)		b.	Wrong.	Heuristics involve subjective factors (memory, interpretation, "typical").
		d.	Wrong.	Heuristics don't give step-by-step instructions.

LANGUAGE ENHANCEMENT GUIDE

CORE TERMS

In discussing thought, your instructor may talk about *logic*, and how illogical some of our thinking is. We often commit logical *fallacies* -- errors in clear thinking, such as making unfounded assumptions. You may be urged by your instructor to think *critically*. That means questioning your own assumptions as well as those that others make.

In discussing language your instructor may use the terms *bilingual* or *multilingual*. The word part *bi* means two, and the word part *multi* means many, so a *bilingual* person speaks two languages, and a *multilingual* person speaks many. Your instructor might also use the term *non-native*, meaning someone who was not born or raised in the country that they are now in. A *non-native* American may take *ESL* (English as a Second Language) classes to improve their speaking and writing skills.

IDIOMS

344	a devious soul	a person who is willing to trick others for his own gain
344	internally based psychological phenomena	things that happen within peoples' minds
344	rationales	reasons
345	knack	special talent or skill
345	*homo sapiens*	human beings
345	to woo	to convince someone to mate with or marry
346	idiosyncrasies	quirks; strange personality characteristics; odd behaviors
347	sole determinant	that only reason something else exists
349	decipher	decode; tell what something means
349	nuances	subtle clues that help you understand what someone or something really means
349	to bolster	to increase the support for something
350	trivial	of little importance
353	fine-tune their articulation skills	get better at speaking clearly
353	arbitrary symbols	symbols chosen more or less randomly to stand for other things
353	surrogate children	adopted children
353	effectively mute	unable to speak
354	the jury is still out	it has not yet been definitely decided
355	follow rigid scripts	follow very specific rules about how to behave
356	"redneck"	a term for a person who lives in the country and has very conservative political and cultural views
366	an arsenal of strategies	a collection of ways to attack a problem
367	it's hardly expedient	it is not a very good idea
369	ticket scalping	buying tickets, and then selling them for a higher price

WORD PARTS

Here are some words that are made up of word parts, and that you can find in this chapter. After you've looked at these, you can look for others in the chapter that use the same word parts (they are there, but YOU have to find them!)

WORD	WORD PART IT USES	MEANING
structure	struct = to build	something that has been built
superficial	super = over, above, outside fic, fac = face	outer expression; an appearance that doesn't reflect the inner reality
conclusion	con = together clud, clus = to close	to come together finally; to have a final idea
illogical	il = not, wrong log = reason	not reasonable
influence	in = in flu = to flow	to have an affect on; to have power over
conjunction	con = together junct = to join	something that joins things together; a point of joining
egocentric	ego = self center = center	self-centered
prescribe	pre = before scribe = to write	to write down directions for what someone is to do

Knowing the word parts listed above, you can also create the following words. You can get an idea of their meanings from the word parts they use. You fill in the blanks!

instruct	_____ + _____	to fill someone with sets of ideas
construct	con + struct	_____
confluence	con + flu	_____
concentric	_____ + _____	coming in toward the center
inscribe	in + scribe	_____
preclude	pre + clud	_____

CHAPTER 10: INTELLIGENCE

ESTABLISHING LEARNING OBJECTIVES

Use these learning objectives as a preview of the chapter, a guide for active reading, and to evaluate your mastery of the material. Review the relevant objectives as you begin and end your reading of each major section of the chapter.

After studying this chapter you should be able to:

I.   Solve the conceptual problem of defining intelligence.
     A. Describe the psychometric approach to conceptualizing intelligence, including Spearman's two-factor theory.
         1. Describe how Galton applied the psychometric approach in measuring intelligence.
         2. Explain Spearman's two-factor theory, and discuss its contribution.
         3. Define and compare fluid intelligence and crystallized intelligence.
     B. Explain the cognitive approach to conceptualizing intelligence.
         1. Explain how and why speed might be useful in predicting performance on mental tests.
     C. Discuss Gardner's theory of multiple intelligences.
         1. Explain why a multiple intelligences approach has been proposed and its impact.
         2. List and describe Gardner's seven kinds of intelligence.
     D. Explain Sternberg's triarchic theory of intelligence.
         1. List and describe Sternberg's three types of intelligence.

II. Solve the practical problem of measuring individual differences.
     A. Describe the components of a good test: reliability, validity, and standardization.
     B. Describe the intelligence quotient (IQ) and how it is interpreted.
         1. Describe the purpose of Binet and Simon's IQ test and how IQ is computed.
         2. Define deviation IQ, and discuss its advantages.
     C. Explain how mental retardation and giftedness are defined.
         1. Describe the behavioral characteristics of individuals with high or low IQ scores.
     D. Discuss the validity of IQ tests and the effects of labeling.
         1. Describe how the validity of intelligence tests is evaluated and the outcome of the evaluation.
         2. Discuss the idea that most tests measure a narrow type of intelligence and lead to labeling effects.
     E. Discuss creativity and emotional intelligence.

III. Solve the practical problem of discovering the sources of intelligence.
     A. Evaluate the stability of IQ, and discuss why IQ might change across the lifespan.
     B. Discuss how twin studies are used to evaluate genetic contributions to intelligence.
         1. Explain heritability, and describe the heritability of intelligence.
     C. Discuss environmental influences on intelligence.
         1. Discuss factors that might account for group differences in intelligence test scores.
     D. Explain how genetic and environmental factors interact to determine intelligence.

MASTERING THE MATERIAL

Preview & Conceptualizing Intelligence (pp. 384-394)

Mastering the Vocabulary. Define or explain each of the following terms. To check your answers, consult the text pages listed.

1. intelligence (p. 384)

2. psychometrics (p. 386)

3. factor analysis (p. 386)

4. g (general intelligence) (p. 387)

5. s (specific intelligence) (p. 387)

6. fluid intelligence (p. 388)

7. crystallized intelligence (p. 388)

8. multiple intelligences (p. 392)

9. triarchic theory (p. 392)

Mastering the Concepts. Fill in the blanks to create a summary of this section. Answers are on page 238.

Intelligence is a concept used to account for individual _____(1) in mental test performance and purposive _____(2) to the environment. This chapter considers three conceptual and practical problems: How should intelligence be conceptualized? How can it be measured? What are the sources of intelligence?

The _____(3) approach proposes intelligence is a capacity that can be measured with mental tests. _____(4) proposed that some single intellectual ability causes _____(5) performance across a variety of psychological and physical tests. _____(6) is a mathematical technique to find relationships between scores on several tests. _____(7) concluded two factors explain test performance: *g*, or

_____(8) intelligence, and *s*, or a _____(9) factor. Spearman's _____(10) theory has been criticized, with Thurstone proposing seven "_____(11) mental abilities" instead. Modifications of general intelligence include hierarchical models, with *g* at the top above lower-level sub-factors, such as Cattell and Horn's _____(12) and crystallized intelligence.

The _____(13) approach proposes the speed and type of internal processes, not just test performance must be considered. The _____(14) signal and _____(15) analysis are used to do this. Computer programs have been developed to mimic intelligence or expert thinking.

Gardner's theory of _____(16) intelligences proposes seven different intelligences, rather than one general intelligence. Based on case studies of exceptional talents, the theory includes traditional types of intelligence (logical-mathematical) that are measured by conventional tests and others (bodily-kinesthetic, musical, intrapersonal) that are not. Although many agree with a broad view of intelligence, some view Gardner's theory as a study of talents, not intelligence, and criticize its lack of scientific support.

Sternberg's recent _____(17) theory proposes three components and includes not only information processing activities, but also adaptive and practical components. _____(18) intelligence refers to analytical skills and information processing, the skills measured by most psychometric tests. _____(19) intelligence applies to coping with new tasks. _____(20) intelligence involves the ability to adapt to the environment, or "street smarts." Triarchic theory is limited by the difficulty of defining and measuring the practical and creative components.

Evaluating Your Progress. Select the one best response. Answers are on page 239. If you make any errors, reread the relevant material before proceeding.

1. Spearman proposed that intelligence can be accounted for by
   a. general intelligence and a test-specific factor.
   b. fluid intelligence and crystallized intelligence.
   c. verbal intelligence and spatial intelligence.
   d. analytical intelligence and practical intelligence.

2. If you are very high in Spearman's *g* factor, you would be expected to
   a. perform very well on a wide variety of mental tests.
   b. perform very well on general knowledge tests, but poorly on more specific tests.
   c. have some special skill such as musical ability or artistic talent.
   d. have great insight into your own feelings and emotions.

3. "Intelligence is a mental capacity that is measured by analyzing performance on mental tests" describes
   a. the multiple intelligences approach.
   b. the triarchic theory of intelligence.
   c. the psychometric approach.
   d. the cognitive approach.

4.   Thurstone suggested that intelligence can be accounted for by _____ primary mental abilities.
     a.   2
     b.   3
     c.   5
     d.   7

5.   Fluid intelligence is best described as
     a.   the natural ability to solve problems and reason.
     b.   bodily-kinesthetic intelligence.
     c.   knowledge and mental ability acquired from experience.
     d.   practical intelligence.

6.   The _____ approach to intelligence proposes that understanding intelligence requires an
     understanding of the information processing routines involved in intelligent thought, not just test scores.
     a.   multiple intelligences
     b.   psychometric
     c.   triarchic
     d.   cognitive

7.   Bodily-kinesthetic intelligence and intrapersonal intelligence are included in
     a.   Thurstone's primary mental abilities theory of intelligence.
     b.   Sternberg's triarchic theory of intelligence.
     c.   Gardner's multiple intelligences theory.
     d.   Spearman's two-factor theory of intelligence.

8.   According to the triarchic theory, a person who does well on traditional intelligence tests is high in
     a.   analytical intelligence.
     b.   general intelligence.
     c.   practical intelligence.
     d.   creative intelligence.

Measuring Individual Differences (pp. 395-405)

Mastering the Vocabulary.   Define or explain each of the following terms. To check your answers, consult
the text pages listed.

1.   achievement tests (p. 395)

2.   aptitude tests (p. 395)

3.   reliability (p. 395)

4.   validity (p. 396)

5. content validity (p. 396)

6. predictive validity (p. 396)

7. construct validity (p. 397)

8. standardization (p. 397)

9. intelligence quotient (p. 397)

10. mental age (p. 398)

11. deviation IQ (p. 399)

12. mental retardation (p. 400)

13. gifted (p. 400)

14. tacit knowledge (p. 402)

15. creativity (p. 404)

16. emotional intelligence (p. 405)

Mastering the Concepts. Fill in the blanks to create a summary of this section. Answers are on page 238.

Psychological tests measure individual differences. Some, _____(21) tests, measure current status. Others, _____(22) tests, measure the ability to learn. Regardless of what is measured, all good tests need _____(23), _____(24), and standardization. Reliability is a measure of _____(25) and often is evaluated in terms of _____(26) reliability, the correlation of scores from two separate testings. Validity is a measure of whether the test measures what it is supposed to measure. _____(27) validity evaluates whether the test provides a broad measure of the characteristic. _____(28) validity evaluates how well the test predicts future behavior. _____(29) validity measures how well the test relates to a theoretical view or concept. Standardization is the use of _____(30) procedures on all occasions.

The most famous index of intelligence is the intelligence _____(31) or IQ. Binet and Simon developed an intelligence test to identify children who would have difficulty in school. A child's _____(32) was determined based on a comparison of his or her performance with the performance of children of specific ages. A child with a mental (not actual) age of 8 scores as well as an average 8-year-old. Later, Terman developed the formula, (_____(33) age / _____(34) age) X 100 = IQ, which creates an "average" score of 100.

Modern tests compute a _____(35) IQ, based on a score's location in the distribution for others of the same age, to avoid problems created by comparisons based on mental age. Most people have IQs between _____(36). Scores below 70 suggest mental _____(37); scores above 130 suggest _____(38). Mental retardation is caused by both genetic and environmental influences and varies from mild to profound.

Major intelligence tests (Stanford-Binet, WAIS, WISC) are valid for predicting _____(39) success, and to some extent, job performance. In response to criticisms that previous tests failed to broadly sample intelligence, _____(40) items were included in the Weschler tests. Testing dangers include the impact of _____(41) and misinterpretation.

Standard intelligence assessments focus on well-defined, academic material, and do not predict job success well. Wagner & Sternberg suggest job performance can be predicted by evaluating _____(42) knowledge, unspoken practical "know how" that is rarely taught, but is gained through _____(43) people's behavior. Tacit knowledge is assessed using scenarios of decision-making situations. Criticisms of the tacit knowledge concept include questions about its _____(44) validity, its separate identity, and its ability to predict job performance better than general intelligence can.

_____(45) is the ability to generate original, useful ideas. Creativity is not highly correlated with traditional IQ scores. _____(46) intelligence is the ability to perceive, understand, and express emotion in useful ways, and might be a better predictor of social or career success than IQ.

Evaluating Your Progress. Select the one best response. Answers are on page 239. If you make any errors, reread the relevant material before proceeding.

1. A reliable test is a test that
   a. gives approximately the same result from one administration to the next.
   b. is administered the same way each time it is given.
   c. accurately predicts a future outcome.
   d. measures what it is supposed to measure.

2. High scores on the new test used to select new candidates for the police academy accurately predict high achievement on the job two years later. This finding provides evidence that the new test is
   a. an achievement test.
   b. reliable.
   c. standardized.
   d. valid.

3. An IQ of 100 corresponds to
   a. very high intelligence.
   b. average intelligence.
   c. borderline retardation.
   d. significant retardation.

4. Binet's original IQ test was designed to
   a. identify children who would do poorly in traditional schools.
   b. quantify the genetic determinant of intelligence.
   c. quantify the environmental determinants of intelligence.
   d. predict job success in adulthood.

5. Ed, age 10, has a raw score of 110. To compute his deviation IQ score the psychologist will
   a. compare the location of 110 relative to the average score in the 10-year-olds' distribution.
   b. find the age associated with an average score of 110 and compare that "mental age" to Ed's age.
   c. test Ed twice and compute the difference between the two scores.
   d. compare this test score with other ratings (from teachers, parents, etc.) of his intelligence.

6. Lee has been classified as mentally retarded. Lee's IQ score is probably
   a. between 90 and 100.
   b. between 85 and 90.
   c. below 70.
   d. below 50.

7. Based on comparisons of intelligence test scores and later school performance, psychologists conclude
   a. intelligence tests have good construct validity.
   b. intelligence tests have poor construct validity.
   c. intelligence tests have good predictive validity.
   d. intelligence tests have poor predictive validity.

8. Tacit knowledge is best described as
   a. innate.
   b. "book learning."
   c. practical "know how."
   d. "hard-wired."

9. Which is true concerning creativity?
   a. Creativity is highly correlated with IQ.
   b. Creativity is not really measured by intelligence tests.
   c. Creativity requires the ability to understand and express emotion.
   d. Creativity is also known as tacit knowledge.

Discovering the Sources of Intelligence: The Nature-Nurture Issue (pp. 406-413)

Mastering the Vocabulary. Define or explain the following terms. To check your answers, consult the text pages listed.

1. heritability (p. 409)

2. reaction range (p. 413)

Mastering the Concepts. Fill in the blanks to create a summary of this section. Answers are on page 238

Strong genetic determinants predict stable intelligence, whereas strong environmental determinants predict changing intelligence. Some evidence suggests fast habituation in infancy relates to intelligence, but reliable measurements of intelligence cannot be obtained until age _____(47). A longitudinal study found _____(48) in IQ throughout adulthood, but a slight decline begins at age 60. _____(49) intelligence, basic information processing, declines but _____(50) intelligence, acquired knowledge, remains constant or increases.

Twin studies suggest that genetic factors are important determinants of intelligence. _____(51) twins have the most similar IQs, even if reared apart. Twin studies indicate _____(52), the amount of the variation in IQ scores within a population that is due to genetics, may be 50 - 70%. Still, separated twins have less similar IQs than twins reared together, showing that _____(53) influences intelligence.

Racial differences in IQ occur, but why is unclear. They reflect average IQs, and cannot be applied to individuals. Economic differences exist and these environmental factors are hard to separate from genetic factors. Test _____(54) can contribute to the difference, but they do not account for all of it. Studies of minority children adopted into advantaged homes find higher IQs than the racial average, supporting an _____(55) factor. Most see IQ resulting from an _____(56) of genetics and environment. Genetics may establish a reaction range in which IQ is pushed up or down by environmental factors.

Evaluating Your Progress. Select the one best response. Answers are on page 240. If you make any errors, reread the relevant material before proceeding.

1. According to the Seattle Longitudinal study, the first modest reductions in intelligence occur at age
   a. 40.
   b. 50.
   c. 60.
   d. 70.

2. Based on previous research, IQ scores should be most similar for
   a. same-sex fraternal twins raised together.
   b. identical twins raised apart.
   c. fathers and biological sons living together.
   d. nontwin siblings raised together.

3. If a trait has high heritability, we can conclude that
   a. much of the change in the trait over time can be attributed to genetics.
   b. much of the variability of the trait within a population can be attributed to genetics.
   c. much of any between-group differences found for the trait can be attributed to genetics.
   d. much of an individual's score for the trait can be attributed to genetics.

4. Which is true concerning racial differences in IQ?
   a. The range of IQ scores for a race is much greater than the difference in IQ scores between races.
   b. The heritability of intelligence is high, so racial differences in IQ must be due to genetic differences.
   c. The racial differences in IQ almost entirely are due to racially biased intelligence tests.
   d. Research shows that the racial difference in IQ almost entirely is due to poverty.

5. The concept of _____ states that genetics set limits on intelligence and that the environment determines the specific level of intelligence within those limits.
   a. heritability
   b. construct validity
   c. predictive validity
   d. reaction range

MAKING FINAL PREPARATIONS

Complete these sections without consulting your book or notes. For a more accurate estimate of how well you know this material, wait at least a day or two after studying the chapter before working on the questions. Some of the material you "know" immediately after working with the chapter will be quickly forgotten. Immediate tests will overestimate what you know well.

Short Essay Questions. Write a brief answer to each question. Sample answers are on page 240.

1. Explain what is meant by general intelligence and why Spearman proposed this concept.

2. Discuss the major contributions and limitations of the multiple intelligences theory and the triarchic theory.

3. Explain why standardization is necessary in a good test.

4. Define validity, and discuss the apparent validity of intelligence tests.

5. Discuss the possible dangers of IQ labeling.

6. Discuss the stability of intelligence in adulthood, including the roles of fluid and crystallized intelligence.

7. Summarize the current thought concerning the role of genes and the environment as determinant of intelligence, citing evidence relevant to each factor.

Matching. Select the correct definition or description for each item. Answers are on page 241.

_____ 1. Sternberg	a. used for standard comparison of scores
_____ 2. achievement test	b. proposed 7 primary mental abilities instead of *g*
_____ 3. crystallized intelligence	c. technique for evaluating information processing
_____ 4. Galton	d. revised Binet's test and developed IQ formula
_____ 5. heritability	e. intelligence based on acquired knowledge
_____ 6. aptitude test	f. basic reasoning & information processing skill
_____ 7. fluid intelligence	g. proposed triarchic theory
_____ 8. test-retest reliability	h. proposed multiple intelligences theory
_____ 9. componential analysis	i. index of trait variability in a group due to genetics
_____ 10. Spearman	j. measures current status of knowledge
_____ 11. Thurstone	k. proposed two-factor theory
_____ 12. practical intelligence	l. one of first to use the psychometric approach
_____ 13. Terman	m. actual age that best fits a child's test performance
_____ 14. mental age	n. similarity of scores on two administrations of a test
_____ 15. norm group	o. "street smarts" in triarchic theory
_____ 16. Gardner	p. measures ability to learn

Multiple Choice Pretest 1. Select the one best response. Answers are on page 241.

1. The psychometric approach to intelligence
   a. examines the environmental and biological factors that determine intelligence.
   b. uses factor analysis to measure relationships between scores on mental tests.
   c. measures the speed of neural processing in the brain to predict intelligence.
   d. uses reaction times and error rates on mental tests to predict intelligence.

2. Thurstone's theory of primary mental abilities suggests
   a. a high score on one primary mental ability will be accompanied by high scores on the others.
   b. that differences in intelligence are best described by 3 factors or abilities.
   c. the primary mental abilities are fairly independent abilities.
   d. most musicians would score high in the musical primary mental ability.

3. Crystallized intelligence is best described as
   a. the natural ability to solve problems and reason.
   b. the ability to adapt to an environment ("street smarts").
   c. the ability to infer other people's moods and motivations.
   d. knowledge and mental ability acquired from experience.

4. The brain activity that is used to indirectly measure speed of neural transmission is the
   a. g wave.
   b. P100 signal.
   c. alpha wave.
   d. triarchic complex.

5. Gardner's theory of multiple intelligences has been criticized for all of the following except:
   a. It is primarily descriptive.
   b. It really deals with talents, not intelligences.
   c. It is supported by little scientific evidence.
   d. It broadens the way intelligence is conceptualized.

6. Analytical, practical, and creative intelligence are part of
   a. Spearman's general intelligence theory.
   b. Gardner's multiple intelligences theory.
   c. Sternberg's triarchic intelligence theory.
   d. Thurstone's primary mental abilities theory.

7. Tara got about the same score on the SAT the two times she took it last year. This indicates the SAT
   a. is standardized.
   b. has high construct validity.
   c. has high content validity.
   d. is reliable.

8. To evaluate the content validity of a new test for depression, a psychologist might check to see if
   a. it predicts who will develop depression within the next six months.
   b. its scores tend to vary the way an accepted theory of depression would predict.
   c. it samples a wide range of behaviors associated with depression.
   d. it gives about the same result if taken twice in a relatively short period of time.

9. Lance is 6 and scored as well as the average 9-year-old. Terman would compute his IQ score to be
   a. 150
   b. 130
   c. 103
   d. 67

10. Approximately 68% of the population has a deviation IQ score of
    a. 100.
    b. at or below 130.
    c. 85 - 115.
    d. 70 - 130.

11. Mica's on the job experiences have allowed him to develop a good understanding of how to identify good workers and other management skills. Mica probably will score high on tests of
    a. *g*.
    b. intrapersonal intelligence.
    c. analytic intelligence.
    d. tacit knowledge.

12. To be classified as "gifted," an individual must have an IQ at or above approximately
    a. 115.
    b. 130.
    c. 145.
    d. 160.

13. Terman's study of gifted children found
    a. they grew up to be more likely to commit suicide than "normal" people.
    b. they were less socially adept and more withdrawn than "normal" people.
    c. they were more likely to be divorced than "normal" people.
    d. they were more successful in adult occupations than "normal" people.

14. Intelligence tests are most valid for predicting
    a. academic performance.
    b. success in a career.
    c. changes in fluid and crystallized intelligence.
    d. the ability to adapt to environmental demands.

15. The earliest time at which reliable estimates of IQ can be obtained is
    a. sometime between age 6 months and 1 year.
    b. sometime between age 2 and 3 years.
    c. sometime between age 4 and 7 years.
    d. sometime between age 8 and 12 years.

16. The heritability for intelligence is estimated to be
    a. 70 - 90%.
    b. 50 - 70%.
    c. 30 - 50%.
    d. 10 - 30%.

17. Sternberg and Wagner suggest that tacit knowledge is a good predictor of
    a. job success.
    b. IQ.
    c. satisfaction in life.
    d. academic performance.

18. Gardner's interpersonal and intrapersonal intelligences are most similar to the new idea of
    a. emotional intelligence.
    b. creativity.
    c. tacit knowledge.
    d. fluid intelligence.

Multiple Choice Pretest 2. Select the one best response. Answers are on page 242

1. Positive correlations between scores on several very different mental tests support
   a. Gardner's multiple intelligences theory.
   b. Sternberg's triarchic theory of intelligence.
   c. Spearman's two-factor theory of intelligence.
   d. Cattell's concept of crystallized and fluid intelligence.

2. In modern psychometric theories, general intelligence is considered
   a. a totally worthless concept without support from any data.
   b. at the top of a hierarchy of factors that are involved in intelligence.
   c. one of three equally important factors that are involved in intelligence.
   d. to be the sole factor determining differences in performance on mental tests.

3. Verbal fluency, numerical ability, spatial ability, memory, perceptual speed, and reasoning are
   a. Spearman's special abilities (s).
   b. Thurstone's primary mental abilities.
   c. Gardner's multiple intelligences.
   d. Sternberg's triarchic intelligences.

4. Jill, age 20, scores high in crystallized intelligence. Jill probably
   a. inherited her crystallized intelligence from her parents.
   b. has had a great deal of education.
   c. will show a large drop in crystallized intelligence by age 60.
   d. has very fast reaction times.

5. Hank can quickly size up a situation and turn it to his advantage, making him a very successful businessman. In terms of the triarchic theory of intelligence, Hank is high in
   a. analytical intelligence.
   b. creative intelligence.
   c. practical intelligence.
   d. intrapersonal intelligence.

6. Pat's raw score is 120, which corresponds to a score one standard deviation above the mean for her age group. Her deviation IQ score must be
   a. 90
   b. 100
   c. 115
   d. 135

7. A psychologist uses neural transmission speed to study intelligence. This approach is a
   a. psychometric approach.
   b. cognitive approach.
   c. multiple intelligences approach.
   d. triarchic approach.

8. To allow meaningful comparisons of scores across individuals, a test must be
   a. high in predictive validity.
   b. high in content validity.
   c. an aptitude test.
   d. standardized.

9. Which is not a reason why researchers question the use of the P100 signal to evaluate intelligence?
   a. The relationship is a correlation.
   b. Differences in the P100 signal account for a small part of the differences in intelligence scores.
   c. Researchers are not sure what the P100 signal actually measures.
   d. People differ in the amount of time required for the P100 signal to appear.

10. Clinical psychologists need to be skilled at reading people's emotions and motivation. They need high
    a. general intelligence (g).
    b. creative intelligence.
    c. interpersonal intelligence.
    d. intrapersonal intelligence.

11. The deviation IQ was developed to avoid the problems created by
    a. using "mental age" as the critical comparison.
    b. a lack of predictive validity for the Stanford-Binet IQ test.
    c. a lack of reliability in the Stanford-Binet IQ test.
    d. the complex mathematics involved in computing the IQ score.

12. An individual with an IQ of 60 would be expected to
    a. eventually graduate from high school and become fully self-supporting.
    b. develop academic skills at the 6th grade level and become self-supporting.
    c. develop academic skills at the 2nd grade level and become semi-independent.
    d. have limited speech and be able to learn only simple tasks.

13. By developing intelligence tests that include a wider variety of tasks (e.g., WISC, WAIS) to reflect multiple intelligences, psychologists are addressing the criticisms of intelligence tests'
    a. content validity.
    b. predictive validity.
    c. standardization.
    d. reliability.

14. Assume Jason and Diane have identical reaction ranges, but Jason's IQ is 100 and Diane's is 120. According to the reaction range concept, these differences are due to
    a. random variation in test scores.
    b. genetic differences.
    c. environmental differences.
    d. heritability differences.

15. Scarr and Weinberg have found that the average IQ of African American children raised in white, middle-class homes is higher than the average IQ of all African Americans. From this we can conclude
    a. genetic differences between races cause racial differences in IQ.
    b. racially biased tests are the cause of the racial differences in IQ.
    c. discrimination is the cause of the racial differences in IQ.
    d. environmental factors may contribute to the racial differences in IQ.

16. A genetic determinant of intelligence would be supported most by high correlations between IQ scores for
    a. identical twins raised together.
    b. identical twins raised apart.
    c. fraternal twins raised together.
    d. fraternal twins raised apart.

17. During adulthood, fluid intelligence usually _____, and crystallized intelligence _____.
    a. stays the same or increases; stays the same or increases
    b. stays the same or increases; decreases
    c. decreases; decreases
    d. decreases; stays the same or increases

18. Having no styrofoam packing materials, Pat used popcorn instead. Pat probably would score high in
    a. analytic thinking.
    b. crystallized intelligence.
    c. fluid intelligence.
    d. creativity

19. Most psychologists believe that intelligence is determined by
    a. genetics, almost exclusively.
    b. the environment, almost exclusively.
    c. a significant interaction of genetics and environment.
    d. some yet-to-be-discovered factor.

ANSWERS AND EXPLANATIONS

Mastering the Concepts

1. differences (p. 384)
2. adaptation (p. 384)
3. psychometric (p. 386)
4. Galton (p. 386)
5. similar (p. 386)
6. Factor analysis (p. 386)
7. Spearman (p. 387)
8. general (p. 387)
9. specific (p. 387)
10. two-factor (p. 387)
11. primary (p. 387)
12. fluid (p. 388)
13. cognitive (p. 389)
14. P100 (p. 390)

15. componential (p. 391)
16. multiple (p. 391)
17. triarchic (p. 393)
18. Analytical (p. 393)
19. Creative (p. 393)
20. Practical (p. 394)
21. achievement (p. 395)
22. aptitude (p. 395)
23. reliability (p. 395)
24. validity (p. 396)
25. consistency (p. 395)
26. test-retest (p. 396)
27. Content (p. 396)
28. Predictive (p. 396)

29. Construct (p. 397)
30. the same (p. 397)
31. quotient (p. 397)
32. mental age (p. 398)
33. mental (p. 399)
34. chronological (p. 399)
35. deviation (p. 399)
36. 85 and 115 (p. 399)
37. retardation (p. 400)
38. giftedness (p. 400)
39. academic (p. 401)
40. nonverbal (p. 401)
41. labels (p. 401)
42. tacit (p. 402)

43. observing (p. 402)
44. scientific (p. 402)
45. Creativity (p. 404)
46. Emotional (p. 405)
47. 4 - 7 years (p. 407)
48. stability (p. 407)
49. fluid (p. 408)
50. crystallized (p. 408)
51. Identical (p. 409)
52. heritability (p. 409)
53. environment (p. 410)
54. biases (p. 411)
55. environmental (p. 412)
56. interaction (p. 412)

Evaluating Your Progress

Preview & Conceptualizing Intelligence

1. **a**   b. Wrong.   These are Cattell and Horn's units of intelligence.
    (p. 387)   c. Wrong.   These are 2 of Gardner's 7 multiple intelligences.
                d. Wrong.   These are 2 of the 3 types of intelligence in the triarchic theory.

2. **a**   b, c, & d.   Wrong.   General intelligence (g) is an broad ability, but not limited to general information.
    (p. 387)

3. **c**   a & b.   Wrong.   These approaches do not emphasize mental tests.
    (p. 386)   d.   Wrong.   The cognitive approach uses speed and analysis processes, not mental test scores.

4. **d**   a, b, & c. Wrong.   There are 7 primary mental abilities.
    (p. 387)

5. **a**   b. Wrong.   This is one of Gardner's intelligences, not Cattell's fluid intelligence.
    (p. 388)   c. Wrong.   This is one of the triarchic intelligences, not Cattell's fluid intelligence.
                d. Wrong.   This is one of the triarchic intelligences, not Cattell's fluid intelligence.

6. **d**   a. Wrong.   The multiple intelligences view stresses the many types of intelligence.
    (p. 389)   b. Wrong.   The psychometric view stresses using test score patterns.
                c. Wrong.   The triarchic view stresses multiple types, including practical sorts.

7. **c**   a, b, & d.   Wrong.   These do not include bodily-kinesthetic or intrapersonal intelligence.
    (p. 392)

8. **a**   b. Wrong.   General intelligence is not part of the triarchic theory.
    (p. 393)   c. Wrong   Practical intelligence is the ability to adapt to the environment or "street smarts."
                d. Wrong.   Creative intelligence is the ability to deal with new tasks or situations quickly.

Measuring Individual Differences

1. **a**   b   Wrong.   This describes standardization.
    (p. 395)   c & d.   Wrong.   These describe aspects of validity.

2. **d**   a. Wrong.   Achievement tests measure current status. Predictive validity is demonstrated here.
    (p. 396)   b. Wrong.   Reliability doesn't involve predictions (predictive validity does), just consistency if retested.
                c. Wrong.   Standardization doesn't use prediction (predictive validity does), only constant conditions.

3. **b**   a, c, & d.   Wrong.   IQ of 100 is always average intelligence (mental age = chronological age).
    (p. 399)

4. **a**   b, c, & d.   Wrong.   The French government wanted to identify "dull" children who needed a different
    (p. 398)   academic experience.

5. **a**   b   Wrong.   This is how Terman's original IQ was computed.
    (p. 399)   c & d.   Wrong.   These have nothing to do with IQ computations.

6. **c**   a, b, & d.   Wrong.   Mental retardation is assigned when IQ is below 70. IQ of 70-130 is normal.
    (p. 400)

7. **c**   a & b. Wrong. These data don't really address content validity, only predictive validity.
  (p. 396)   d.   Wrong. Tests scores and school performance are strongly correlated.

8. **c**   a. Wrong. Tacit knowledge is mostly acquired through experience.
  (p. 402)   b. Wrong. Tacit knowledge is not taught directly in school or elsewhere.
              d. Wrong. Hard-wired implies innate, which is incorrect. Tacit knowledge is acquired.

9. **b**   a. Wrong. The correlation of creativity & IQ is low.
  (p. 405)   c. Wrong. This is emotional intelligence.
              d. Wrong. Tacit knowledge is implicit, practical "know-how."

Discovering the Sources of Intelligence: The Nature-Nurture Issue

1. **c**   a, b, & d. Wrong. Intelligence is quite stable throughout, but limited declines occur after age 60.
  (p. 407)

2. **b**   a, c, & d. Wrong. The stronger the genetic link, the higher the correlation, even if environment
  (p. 409)   differs.

3. **b**   a, c, & d. Wrong. Heritability is an index of the *variability* of a trait *within* a group that is due to
  (p. 409)   genetic factors.

4. **a**   b. Wrong. Remember, heritability only pertains to within-group differences in IQ.
  (p. 410)   c. Wrong. Racial differences remain even when biased questions are removed.
              d. Wrong. Data supports environmental influence, but does not limit it to poverty-related factors.

5. **d**   a.   Wrong. Heritability involves the variability in IQ within a population accounted for by genes.
  (p. 413)   b & c. Wrong. Validity is a characteristic of a test, not an influence on behavior.

MAKING FINAL PREPARATIONS

Short Essay Questions

1. Spearman considered general intelligence to be the primary intellectual ability responsible for individual differences in IQ. Spearman analyzed performance on several different mental tests using factor analysis and found that people who performed well on one test usually performed well on most other tests. That is, one common ability (he called general intelligence) seemed to control performance. (p. 387)

2. Both Gardner's multiple intelligences theory and Sternberg's triarchic theory broadened what intelligence is conceptualized to be. They included aspects of behavior that previous theories had not and extended intelligence to include interpersonal and "real world," nonacademic abilities. These additions are difficult to define or test scientifically, and critics ask whether they are part of intelligence or only specific talents. (pp. 391-394)

3. Standardization, maintaining the same procedures for all administrations of the test, is needed if scores are to be compared across individuals or groups. If procedures differ, differences in IQ scores could be due to the procedural differences rather than individual differences in intelligence. (p. 397)

4. Validity is an assessment of how well a test measures what it is supposed to measure. Intelligence tests are considered to be valid, at least relating to academic performance. They predict academic performance well (job success less so), giving them good predictive validity. Researchers have questioned their content validity, but the Weschler tests added performance scales so that a broader range of activities are sampled. (pp. 396, 401)

5. Labels of "smart" or "slow" are difficult to change and lead to different treatment. Teachers treated "smart" children with more respect and expose them to more opportunities than "slow" children, further delaying possible advancement of the "slow" children. Mislabeling due to misuse of IQ tests resulted in immigration laws designed to keep out "defective" groups early in the 20th century. (pp. 403-404)

6. The Seattle Longitudinal study suggests that IQ remains quite steady throughout adulthood, with only a slight decline after age 60. Individual differences are large in later years, possibly due to physical problems. Fluid intelligence seems to decline, but crystallized intelligence remains constant or increases. (pp. 406-408)

7. Intelligence is determined by an interaction of genes and environment. Genetic factors are supported by twin studies that show genetic similarity predicts IQ similarity. Even if environments differ, identical twins have more similar IQs than same-sex fraternal twins reared together. Adoption studies of minority children reared in "advantaged" homes find they have higher IQs than average, supporting environmental factors. (pp. 408-413)

Matching

1. **g** (p. 393)	4. **l** (p. 386)	7. **f** (p. 388)	10. **k** (p. 386)	13. **d** (p. 398)	16. **h** (p. 391)
2. **j** (p. 395)	5. **i** (p. 409)	8. **n** (p. 396)	11. **b** (p. 387)	14. **m** (p. 398)	
3. **e** (p. 408)	6. **p** (p. 395)	9. **c** (p. 391)	12. **o** (p. 394)	15. **a** (p. 397)	

Multiple Choice Pretest 1

1. **b**   a.   Wrong.   The conceptualization, not origin, of intelligence is key to the psychometric approach.
    (p. 386) c & d. Wrong.   These describe the cognitive approach.

2. **c**   a. Wrong.   The factors are fairly independent, so one test scores doesn't predict another.
    (p. 388) b. Wrong.   Thurstone proposed 7 primary mental abilities, not 3.
              d. Wrong.   Gardner proposed musical ability, not Thurstone.

3. **d**   a. Wrong.   This is fluid intelligence, as opposed to crystallized intelligence.
    (p. 388) b. Wrong.   This is Sternberg's practical intelligence.
              c. Wrong.   This is Gardner's interpersonal intelligence.

4. **b**   a & d. Wrong.   These are not types of brain activity.
    (p. 390) c.   Wrong.   Alpha waves are associated with relaxation, not mental activity.

5. **a**   b, c & d.   Wrong.   IQ = (mental age/chronological age) X 100 = (9/6) X 100 = 150.
    (p. 399)

6. **c**   a. Wrong.   100 is the mean, which means 50% of the scores are at or below 100.
    (p. 399) b. Wrong.   About 98% of the scores fall at or below 130.
              d. Wrong.   About 96% of the scores fall between 70 and 130.

7. **d**   a, b, & c.   Wrong.   These are all points of criticism.
    (p. 393)

8. **c**   a, b, & d.   Wrong.   These are part of Sternberg's theory.
    (p. 393)

9. **d**   a. Wrong.   A test is standardized if it is *administered* the same way for all people, every time.
    (p. 395) b. Wrong.   A test has construct validity if it taps into a theoretical construct.
              c. Wrong.   A test has content validity if it samples broadly from the domain of interest.

10. **c**   a. Wrong. This describes predictive validity.
    (p. 396)   b. Wrong. This describes construct validity.
                d. Wrong. This describes reliability.

11. **d**   a. Wrong. These are tacit knowledge skills, which do not relate to *g*.
    (p. 402)   b. Wrong. Intrapersonal intelligence is insight about one's own feelings and emotions.
                c. Wrong. Analytic intelligence involves standard intelligence skills.

12. **b**   a, c, & d.   Wrong.   The usual score is 130 or above.
    (p. 400)

13. **d**   a, b, & c.   Wrong.   Gifted children are at least as stable and sociable as "normals."
    (p. 400)

14. **a**   b, c, & d.   Wrong.   Intelligence tests were designed for, and currently are evaluated in terms of
    (p. 401)   predicting academic performance. They do not predict career success well.

15. **c**   a, b, & d.   Wrong.   Reliability is poor in infancy and toddlerhood, but good by early school-age.
    (p. 407)

16. **b**   a, c, & d.   Wrong.   The most common estimate is 50%, but some suggest 70% is more accurate.
    (p. 410)

17. **a**   b, c, & d.   Wrong.   Tacit knowledge is correlated with job success.
    (p. 402)

18. **a**   b. Wrong. Inter-and intra-personal intelligence deals with emotions, not novel ideas.
    (p. 405)   c. Wrong. Not practical "know how."
                d. Wrong. Basic reasoning skills.

Multiple Choice Pretest 2

1.   **c**   a & b.   Wrong.   Correlations support a single factor view of intelligence. These are multifactor.
    (p. 387)   d.   Wrong.   Correlations would have nothing to say about the fluid vs. crystallized issue.

2.   **b**   a & d.   Wrong.   General intelligence hasn't been discarded or accepted totally.
    (p. 388)   c.   Wrong.   Triarchic theory proposes 3 aspects of intelligence, but none is *g*.

3.   **b**   a. Wrong. These are closer to skills within general intelligence than special abilities.
    (p. 388)   c. Wrong. Gardner proposed musical, bodily-kinesthetic, logical-mathematical, linguistic, spatial,
                           interpersonal, & intrapersonal intelligences.
                d. Wrong. Sternberg proposed analytical, practical, and creative intelligences.

4.   **b**   a. Wrong. Fluid intelligence is related to biological factors. Crystallized is related to experience.
    (p. 388)   c. Wrong. Crystallize intelligence doesn't decline significantly with aging.
                d. Wrong. Fluid intelligence, a more biologically based ability, might be related to reaction times.

5.   **c**   a. Wrong. Analytical intelligence involves traditional mental skills and reasoning.
    (p. 394)   b. Wrong. Creative intelligence involves learning novel tasks quickly.
                d. Wrong. Intrapersonal intelligence is not part of the triarchic theory.

6. **c**   a. Wrong. Pat's score is above the mean, but 90 is below the mean of 100.
(p. 399)   b. Wrong. Pat's score is above the mean, but 100 is the mean.
               d. Wrong. 135 is more than 2 standard deviations above; 1 standard deviation = 15 deviation IQ pts.

7. **b**   a. Wrong. The psychometric approach uses mental test performance, not neural response.
(p. 389)   c. Wrong. Multiple intelligences is studied by looking at cases of exceptional talent.
               d. Wrong. The triarchic approach studies processing, not neural transmission speed.

8. **d**   a, b, & c.   Wrong.   Comparisons rely on standardization to avoid confounding variables.
(p. 397)

9. **d**   a, b, & c.   Wrong.   These are all reasons for caution in using the P100 signal to predict intelligence.
(p. 390)   The individual differences in P100 are the reason it might be useful.

10. **c**   a. Wrong. General intelligence involves basic mental skills, not social skills.
(p. 393)   b. Wrong. Creative intelligence involves coping well with new tasks, not social skills.
               d. Wrong. Intrapersonal intelligence involves insight into one's own emotions, not other people's.

11. **a**   b & c.   Wrong.   The Stanford-Binet has good reliability and validity.
(p. 399)   d.   Wrong.   Deviation IQ is no less complex a computation.

12. **b**   a. Wrong. People with IQs of 60 are unlikely to progress past a 6th grade level.
(p. 400)   c. Wrong. This describes IQs of 35-50, moderate retardation. IQ = 60 is mild retardation.
               d. Wrong. This describes IQs of 20-35, severe retardation. IQ = 60 is mild retardation.

13. **a**   b. Wrong. Broad sampling relates to content validity, not predicting some criterion behavior.
(p. 396)   c. Wrong. Broad sampling relates to content validity, not using the same procedures for all people.
               d. Wrong. Broad sampling relates to content validity, not whether there is test-retest similarity.

14. **c**   a, b, & d.   Wrong.   Genetic factors set the reaction range, but the specific IQ in that range is due to
(p. 413)   the environmental factors. With equal ranges, IQ difference are environmental.

15. **d**   a.   Wrong.   The data address environmental influences, not genetic factors in racial differences.
(p. 412)   b & c.   Wrong.   The data don't address these issues, only predictions concerning environmental factors

16. **b**   a. Wrong. If raised together, both environment and genes are the same, so either could be critical.
(p. 409)   c. Wrong. This would support environmental factors (genes different, same environment).
               d. Wrong   This would favor neither--both genes and environment differs.

17. **d**   a, b, & c. Wrong.   Fluid intelligence decreases, while crystallized intelligence remains stable.
(p. 408)

18. **d**   a. Wrong. Analytic thinking involves traditional intellectual skills. Key here is the unusual, new idea.
(p. 404)   b. Wrong. Crystallized intelligence is acquired abilities. Key here is the unusual, new idea.
               c. Wrong. Fluid intelligence involves inborn reasoning abilities. Key here is the unusual, new idea.

19. **c**   a, b, & d.   Wrong.   Data clearly show both environment and genes influence intelligence.
(p. 412)

Language Enhancement Guide

Core Terms

One of the central questions about intelligence is whether it is one thing or many things. So you are likely to hear terms like *comprehensive, multifaceted,* and *multimodal.* A *comprehensive* test covers all the relevant material, so a comprehensive intelligence test would have many questions of different kinds. *Multifaceted* and *multimodal* are very similar; a multifaceted test would have many different parts, and a multimodal one would measure something in many different ways. In terms of an intelligence test, both mean that the test uses different means to study intelligence.

Also, your instructor may talk about various levels of education, but may use unfamiliar terms. *Primary* school is from kindergarten to about 6th grade. *Secondary* is from about 6th grade up through high school. *Higher education* is all that follows graduation from high school. *Undergraduates* are regular college students, seeking bachelor's degrees. *Graduate students* are pursuing master's degrees or doctorates, and we would say that they are in graduate school. Finally, *postgraduate* work is academic work one can do even after receiving a doctorate.

Idioms

384	cocky grin	a smile that says that he is very self-confident
384	furrowed brows	wrinkled foreheads, meaning that they are worried
384	oblivious to the exploits	not aware of what other peoples' adventures
384	secret caches	valuable things hidden away in various spots
385	cartography school	a school for map-makers
385	granted that	given that; let's assume that
386	in a more rigorous way	with more standardization, more careful control, etc.
386	mathematically inclined	very good at and interested in math
389	socioeconomic classes	your social level, based upon your income and racial background
390	central tenets	main ideas
391	via	by way of
392	*savant*	short for *idiot savant,* a person with low mental ability except in one spectacular area

394	with ringing precision	exactly and perfectly
397	rigid adherence	sticking very carefully to the rules
399	appropriate curriculum adjustments	helpful changes in what is being taught to a child
402	champion	to support, to speak out in support of
402	cut and dried	easy to understand; clear and simple
402	intuitively plausible	immediately easy to understand; fitting in with your assumptions
402	indices	scales; indicators
401	socially adept	good at making friends and talking with people
401	bookworm	someone who reads a lot
406	airtight	perfect; impossible to damage
407	test battery	group of tests
409	irrespective	no matter which one

WORD PARTS

Here are some words that are made up of word parts, and that you can find in this chapter. After you've looked at these, you can look for others in the chapter that use the same word parts (they are there, but YOU have to find them!)

WORD	WORD PART IT USES	MEANING
triarchic	tri = three arch = rule	rule of threes
concept	con = together cept = to take	a group of ideas, or an idea that explains several things
psychometric	psych = mind meter = to measure	tools and techniques for measuring the mind and its abilities
predict	pre = before dict = to say	to foretell
excel	ex = out of cel = to move	to move beyond, to pass up

component	com = together pon, pos = to put	a part of some larger whole
multiple	mult = many	several, many
logical	log = reason	reasonable; clearly thought
compelling	com = together pel, puls = to push, throw, drive	very interesting combination of ideas; something that demands attention

Knowing the word parts listed above, you can also create the following words. You can get an idea of their meanings from the word parts they use. You fill in the blanks!

multiply	multi + ply (to fold over)	_____
precept	_____ + _____	a basic rule; a foundational idea on which one builds
monarch	mon (one) + arch	_____
composition	com + pos	_____
dictate	_____	to say to someone
propulsion	pro (forward) + puls	_____
psychological	_____ + _____	_____

CHAPTER 11: MOTIVATION AND EMOTION

ESTABLISHING LEARNING OBJECTIVES

Use these learning objectives as a preview of the chapter, a guide for active reading, and to evaluate your mastery of the material. Review the relevant objectives as you begin and end your reading of each major section of the chapter.

After studying this chapter you should be able to:

I. Solve the adaptive problem of activating behavior.
    A. Discuss the role of instincts and drives in activating behavior.
    B. Explain incentive motivation and discuss how it activates behavior.
    C. Distinguish between achievement motivation and intrinsic motivation.
    D. Describe Maslow's hierarchy of needs, and discuss how each need influences behavior.

II. Solve the adaptive problem of meeting the biological need for food.
    A. Discuss internal factors that influence when and why we eat.
        1. Describe the role of glucose and insulin levels in hunger and eating.
        2. Discuss the role of the hypothalamus and other brain areas in the control of eating.
    B. Discuss external factors that influence when and why we eat.
    C. Explain how body weight is regulated, including the concept of a set point.
    D. Discuss the eating disorders anorexia nervosa and bulimia nervosa.

III. Solve the adaptive problem of meeting the biological need for sexual activity.
    A. Describe the characteristics of the sexual response cycle.
    B. Describe the role that hormones play in human and animal sexual.
    C. List some external influences on sexual behavior.
    D. Discuss the factors that influence mate selection.
    E. Discuss the factors that may determine sexual orientation.

IV. Solve the adaptive problem of expressing and experiencing emotion.
    A. Identify the basic components of an emotion and discuss their adaptive value.
    B. Discuss the evidence for and against basic emotions.
        1. Discuss the cross-cultural research concerning facial expressions and emotion.
        2. Explain the facial-feedback hypothesis.
    C. Discuss the role that arousal plays in the emotional experience.
        1. Explain the basic logic behind using physiological arousal to signal lying.
        2. Discuss the limitations and problems of polygraph exams.
    D. Describe the subjective experiences of anger and happiness.
    E. Differentiate among the James-Lange, Cannon-Bard, and two-factor theories of emotion.
        1. Describe Schachter & Singer's research and the resulting conclusions.

Psychology 1215.

MASTERING THE MATERIAL

Preview & Activating Behavior (pp. 422-430)

Mastering the Vocabulary. Define or explain each of the following terms. To check your answers, consult the text pages listed.

1. motivation (p. 422) - The set of factors that initiate and direct behavior, usually toward some goal.

2. emotions (p. 422) Psychological events involving (1) a physiological reaction, usually arousal; (2) some kind of expressive reaction, such as a distinctive facial expression; and (3) some kind of subjective exp. such as the conscious feeling of being happy or sad.

3. instinct (p. 424) → Unlearned characteristic patterns of responding that are controlled by specific triggering stimuli in the world; they are not thought to be an important factor in explaining goal directed behavior in humans.

4. drive (p. 425) - A psychological state that arises in response to an internal physiological need, such as hunger or thirst.

5. homeostasis (p. 425) - The process through which the body maintains a steady state, such as a constant internal temperature or an adequate amount of fluids.

6. incentive motivation (p. 426) - External factors in the environment — such as money, an attractive person, or tasty food — that exert pulling effects on peoples' actions.

7. achievement motive (p. 426) - An internal drive or need for achievement that is possessed by all individuals to varying degrees. Whether people will work for success on any given task depends on (1) their expectations about whether they will be successful and (2) how much they value succeeding at the task.

8. intrinsic motivation (p. 428) → Goal-directed behavior that seems to be entirely self-motivated.

9. need hierarchy (p. 429) → The idea popularized by Maslow that human needs are prioritized in a hierarchy. Some needs, especially physiological ones, must be satisfied before others, such as the need for achievement or self-actualization can be pursued.

Mastering the Concepts. Fill in the blanks to create a summary of this section. Answers are on page 263.

Motivation, the set of factors that _initiate_ (1) and direct behavior toward a goal, and emotion are closely linked. Emotions include a _physiological_ (2) reaction, a _subjective_ (3) experience, and an expressive reaction. Four adaptive problems are discussed: What factors activate goal-directed action? What factors create hunger and control eating? What factors promote sexual behavior? How and why do emotions occur?

Motivation is the result of both internal and external events. _Instincts_ (4), unlearned characteristic responses, are internal motivators that influence animal, and possibly human, behavior. The concept of

_____drive_____ (5), a psychological state due to an internal physiological need, replaced instinct for human motivation. Drives maintain _homeostasis_(6), but unlike instincts, drives are flexible in format.

_____Incentive,_____ (7) motivation involves the value of an external factor. Internal and external factors interact, as in the case of _achievment_(8) motivation, a drive for success or achievement. Experience with failure, cultural attitudes, and other external factors influence achievement behaviors.

_____Intrinsic_____ (9) motivation, self-motivated behavior without external reward or homeostatic influence, can be reduced by rewards. Explanations include a loss of _control_ (10) when rewarded and the possibility the _reward_ (11) is perceived to be the source of motivation (overjustification). This occurs only if rewards are _expected_ (12), so the promise of reward might be critical, not the reward itself.

Maslow proposed a _hierarchy_(13) that prioritizes needs. _Physiological_(14) and safety needs are most basic, and _self-actualization_(15), reaching one's full potential, is the final need. Maslow's hierarchy is criticized for its lack of scientific rigor, but it has had wide impact.

Evaluating Your Progress. Select the one best response. Answers are on page 263. If you make any errors, reread the relevant material before proceeding.

1. Which is true concerning the current view of human instincts?
   a. Instincts play no role in goal-directed human behavior.
   b. Instincts are not a widely applied explanation for goal-directed human behavior.
   c. Seventeen instincts account for much goal-directed human behavior.
   d. Twelve instincts account for much goal-directed human behavior.

2. A psychological state that arises in response to an internal physiological need is
   a. an instinct.
   b. an emotion.
   c. homeostasis.
   d. drive.

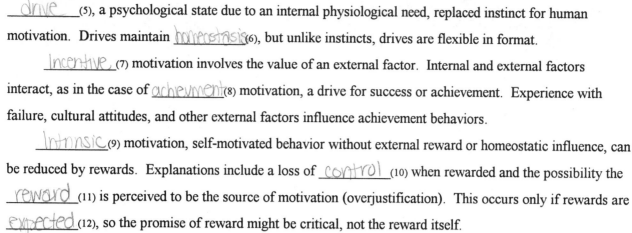

3. Incentives differ from drives because
   a. incentives involve physiological needs, but drives do not.
   b. incentives "pull" behavior, but drives "push" behavior.
   c. incentives are unlearned, but drives are learned.
   d. incentives are internal, but drives are external.

4. Homeostasis is
   a. the process through which the body maintains a steady state.
   b. an internal drive or need for success.
   c. goal-directed behavior that seems to be entirely self-motivated.
   d. a psychological state that arises in response to an internal physiological need.

5. People who work hard to accomplish some task are said to be high in
    a. self-actualization.
    b. achievement motivation.
    c. intrinsic motivation.
    d. homeostasis.

6. Beverly spends every spare minute playing her violin. This behavior is best explained in terms of
    a. intrinsic motivation.
    b. the two-factor theory.
    c. need for homeostasis.
    d. a musical drive.

7. The most important and most accepted aspect of Maslow's hierarchy of needs is
    a. the idea that need for self-actualization is the most important need of all.
    b. the clear definitions given for newly proposed needs.
    c. the idea that some needs are more important or basic than others.
    d. the suggestion that need for achievement is the most important need of all.

8. Jim is open, spontaneous, and generally has fulfilled his potential. Maslow would say he has achieved
    a. self-actualization.
    b. incentive motivation.
    c. homeostasis.
    d. his set point.

Meeting Biological Needs: Hunger and Eating (pp. 431-437)

Mastering the Vocabulary. Define or explain each of the following terms. To check your answers, consult the text pages listed.

1. glucose (p. 431)

2. insulin (p. 432)

3. ventromedial hypothalamus (p. 432)

4. lateral hypothalamus (p. 432)

5. set point (p. 435)

6. obesity (p. 435)

7. anorexia nervosa (p. 436)

8. bulimia nervosa (p. 436)

Mastering the Content. Fill in the blanks to create a summary of this section. Answers are on page 263.

Internal conditions, including stomach contents, are monitored to control eating. Receptors monitor blood
glucose (16), a sugar required for energy production. As levels increase, hunger decreases.
Insulin (17), a pancreatic hormone required for glucose utilization, also is monitored. The glucose-insulin
interaction is critical, but other internal factors (body fat level) are important.

The hypothalamus (18) is important in the control of eating. Damage to the ventromedial (19) hypothalamus
results in overeating; stimulation of this area inhibits eating. Damage to the lateral (20) hypothalamus
inhibits eating; stimulation initiates eating. These areas were once considered the satiety and initiation centers
for eating, but recent data suggest the situation is more complex. Other data suggest the brainstem (21) and
hippocampus (22) also are involved in eating behavior. Eating is also influenced by learned eating habits (23),
the presence of food cues, and other external factors.

Both internal and external factors regulate weight. The set point (24) theory states that individuals
have a natural weight the body tries to maintain. Genetic (25) factors may control the number of fat cells
and metabolic (26) rate to establish the set point. Excessive body fat, obesity (27), is not just a matter of
poor willpower. Metabolic rate, set point, cultural habits, and stress also influence eating and weight control.

Culturally-influenced "ideal" weights and inaccurate body images affect eating. Anorexia (28)
nervosa, in which an abnormally low weight is maintained, can include the perception of being fat even while
starving. Bulimia (29) nervosa, in which binge eating (30) is followed by purging, has serious medical
consequences and is most common in women with an obsessive desire to be thin.

Evaluating Your Progress. Select the one best response. Answers are on page 264. If you make any errors,
reread the relevant material before proceeding.

1. Hunger increases as the blood level of glucose decreases.
    a. fat.
    b. salt.
    c. glucose.
    d. estrogen.

2. The part of the brain once thought to be the satiety center (to control the termination of eating) is the
    a. hippocampus.
    b. brainstem.
    c. ventromedial hypothalamus.
    d. lateral hypothalamus.

3. The current view of the role of the hypothalamus in the control of eating is that
    a. the ventromedial hypothalamus stops eating, and the lateral hypothalamus initiates eating.
    b. the ventromedial hypothalamus initiates eating, and the lateral hypothalamus stops eating.
    c. the ventromedial and lateral hypothalamus are involved in eating, but their exact roles are unclear.
    d. the ventromedial and lateral hypothalamus are not involved in the control of eating at all.

4. The set point is
    a. the fixed amount of glucose needed for cellular activity.
    b. the natural weight the body tries to maintain.
    c. the insulin level that stimulates a desire to eat.
    d. the weight that is viewed as ideal in a specific culture.

5. Anorexia nervosa is an eating disorder
    a. most common in young men.
    b. in which the person eats massive quantities of food at one time.
    c. characterized by an irrational fear of being overweight.
    d. that is most common in middle-aged women.

Meeting Biological Needs: Sexual Behavior (pp. 437-443)

Mastering the Vocabulary. Define or explain each of the following terms. To check your answers, consult the text pages listed.

1. excitement phase (p. 438)

2. plateau phase (p. 438)

3. orgasmic phase (p. 438)

4. resolution phase (p. 438)

5. sexual scripts (p. 441)

6. sociobiology (p. 441)

7.   sexual orientation (p. 442)

Mastering the Concepts. Fill in the blanks to create a summary of this section. Answers are on page 263.

Sexual behavior ensures continuation of the species and may lead to companionship, love and protection. The sexual response follows a fixed sequence. In the _excitement_(31) phase, physiological arousal begins, leading to erection in men and lubrication in women. In the _plateau_ (32) phase, these processes continue to develop, but slowly. Sexual release occurs during the _orgasmic_(33) phase, then arousal returns to normal in the _resolution_ (34) phase. Men have a _refractory_ (35) period in which further sexual response is impossible.

Animals' sexual behavior is controlled by _hormones_(36) and limited to a period of fertility. Human sexual behavior is mostly under the control of the _individual_ (37), although estrogens and androgens are influential. Loss of sex hormones does not necessary eliminate all sexual motivation in humans. Touch and other external stimuli affect human sexual behavior. Animals respond to certain scents or _pheromones_ (38), but little evidence supports an unlearned response in humans.

Exactly how, when, and why people have sex is influenced by _sexual scripts_(39), learned tendencies and attitudes. Some sex differences in sexual scripts are cross-cultural. Men do not link sex and marriage, are more likely to engage in _short-term_(40) strategies, and prefer young, attractive partners, not financially secure partners. _Sociobiology_ (41) suggests these differences arise from evolutionary problems related to reproduction.

A person's sexual _orientation_(42) involves whether the same or different sex is found sexually and emotionally attractive. _Homosexuals_(43) are predominantly attracted to the same sex; _Heterosexual_(44) are predominantly attracted to the opposite sex. Orientation should be considered a continuum, rather than distinct categories. Homosexuality once was thought to be caused by a dominant mother and passive father. Recent research refutes this and suggests _biological_ (45) factors influence orientation. Differences in the _hypothalamus_(46) have been found. Twin studies support a _genetic_ (47) factor, and a "gay gene" has been proposed. _Correlational_(48) data complicates interpretation, and genetic factors clearly are not the entire story.

Evaluating Your Progress. Select the one best response. Answers are on page 264. If you make any errors, reread the relevant material before proceeding.

1.   The role of sex hormones in the sexual behavior of humans can be described as
     a.   highly important. They strictly determine when people seek sexual activity.
     b.   moderately important. They don't have total control, but they are more important than other factors.
     c.   minimally important. Hormones have some influence, but the individual maintains active control.
     d.   totally unimportant. Hormones have no influence on sexual behavior.

2. Cross-cultural studies show that in most cultures
   a. men are more likely than women to pursue short-term sexual strategies.
   b. men place less value on their long-term partner's attractiveness than women.
   c. women place less value on the financial status of a prospective partner than men.
   d. men are less concerned than women with having a younger sexual partner.

3. The sociobiology view suggests that differences in men's and women's sexual attitudes and rituals reflect
   a. different sex hormones that influence male and female sexual behaviors.
   b. resolution of gender-specific reproductive problems present throughout history.
   c. short-term cultural differences that influence current sexual scripts.
   d. basic cognitive differences in men and women.

4. The learned programs that instruct people on how, why, and what to do in their sexual interactions are
   a. sexual phases.
   b. sexual orientations.
   c. sexual pheromones.
   d. sexual scripts.

5. Recent research suggests that homosexuality is at least partially determined by
   a. sexual molestation during early childhood.
   b. having a domineering mother and passive father.
   c. single parent families with no father or other role model present.
   d. biological factors.

Expressing and Experiencing Emotion (pp. 444-455)

Mastering the Vocabulary. Define or explain each of the following terms. To check your answers, consult the text pages listed.

1. facial-feedback hypothesis (p. 446)

2. polygraph test (p. 449)

3. James-Lange theory (p. 451)

4. Cannon-Bard theory (p. 453)

5. two-factor theory (p. 454)

Mastering the Concepts. Fill in the blanks to create a summary of this section. Answers are on page 263.

Emotions involve a physiological (49) reaction, an expressive reaction, and subjective (50) experience. Ekman found six basic emotions (fear, happiness, surprise, sadness, anger, and disgust/contempt) associated with cross-cultural facial (51) expressions, suggesting a genetic origin of the expression of emotion. The facial feedback (52) hypothesis suggests input from facial muscles influence emotion. Others view basic emotions as shared components of many emotions. The emotion of disgust (53) is often food-related, but relates to general "contamination." Disgust is not innate, and may be irrational due to "sympathetic magic."

Performance declines at very low and high levels of arousal. Arousal found with emotion is the basis of polygraph (54) tests. Lying is assumed to lead to emotionality, which causes physiological changes. Lying is inferred if arousal differs on relevant and control questions. Problems include the ease of "beating" the test and a high "false positive "(55) rate. Certain events (being restrained, expectations violated) are linked to emotion (e.g., anger), but emotion is also influenced by social comparisons (56) and adaptation level.

Different theories of emotion handle the three components of emotion differently. The commonsense (57) view states a stimulus causes an emotion, which causes physical changes. The James-Lange (58) theory states a stimulus causes physical changes, which cause an emotion. This theory requires different physical patterns for each emotion and a reduction of emotion if feedback about physical changes is eliminated. Some research supports this idea, but more complete confirmation is still needed. The Cannon-Bard (59) theory states a stimulus independently produces both the emotional experience and physical changes. The two-factor (60) theory, currently the most accepted theory, states the stimulus causes physical changes, but the emotion is the result of cognitive appraisal or interpretation of the physical changes in context. This is supported by Schachter & Singer's data showing expectations about physical reactions affect emotion.

Evaluating Your Progress. Select the one best response. Answers are on page 265. If you make any errors reread the relevant material before proceeding.

1. Jess' heart was racing, she felt afraid, and she was screaming. Her screams represent the emotion's
   a. physiological response.
   b. expressive reaction.
   c. subjective experience.
   d. unconscious experience.

2. There is not complete agreement about what the "basic" emotions are, but the most common choices are
   a. anger, fear, happiness, and sadness.
   b. surprise, anger, happiness and fear.
   c. disgust, sadness, fear, and happiness.
   d. jealousy, disgust, fear, sadness, and happiness.

3. Research on disgust suggests
   a. typical patterns of disgust are found even in infancy.
   b. disgust first develops at about age 12.
   c. disgust is influenced by cultural beliefs.
   d. disgust is limited to situations of possible contamination.

4. The facial feedback hypothesis states that
   a. feedback from facial muscles to the brain is used to determine what emotion is being experienced.
   b. people evaluate the emotional impact they have on someone by watching their facial expressions.
   c. people tend to adopt the facial expressions shown by the other people around them.
   d. facial feedback causes sympathetic nervous system arousal that is unique to one emotion.

5. Which of the following best represents the relationship between performance and level of arousal?
   a. As arousal increases, performance increases.
   b. As arousal increases, performance decreases.
   c. As arousal increases, performance decreases and then increases.
   d. As arousal increases, performance increases and then decreases.

6. The basic assumption behind the polygraph exam is that lying causes
   a. a specific pattern of physiological activity that is distinct from other situations.
   b. increased emotionality which is accompanied by physiological reactions.
   c. delayed response time to relevant questions.
   d. changes in vocal intensity during responses to relevant questions.

7. Dan believes that a specific emotion is experienced because a stimulus has caused specific physical changes to occur. Dan's view of emotion is most similar to
   a. the commonsense view.
   b. the James-Lange theory.
   c. the Cannon-Bard theory.
   d. the two-factor theory.

8. According to the Cannon-Bard theory, emotions are
   a. the result of specific patterns of physiological arousal.
   b. determined by a cognitive appraisal process.
   c. determined by the feedback from the facial muscles.
   d. independent of the physiological changes.

9. The two-factor theory is very different from other approaches because it
   a. adds a cognitive component to the experience of emotion.
   b. places more emphasis on the physiological patterns than other theories.
   c. proposes emotions precede any physiological changes.
   d. proposes that emotions are independent of physiological changes.

10. The most commonly accepted theory of emotion today is
   a. the commonsense view.
   b. the James-Lange theory.
   c. the Cannon-Bard theory.
   d. the two-factor theory. the two-factor theory = emotion.

MAKING FINAL PREPARATIONS

Complete these sections without consulting your book or notes.

Matching. Select the correct definition or description for each item. Answers are on page 266.

_____	1. Cannon-Bard	a.	sexual/emotional attraction to same or different sex
_____	2. incentive motivation	b.	external factor that exerts a pulling effect on actions
_____	3. sympathetic magic	c.	did research on recognition of emotional expression
_____	4. James-Lange	d.	unlearned behaviors controlled by triggering stimuli
_____	5. sexual orientation	e.	measurement of physiological activity to detect lies
_____	6. polygraph	f.	proposed need hierarchy
_____	7. intrinsic motivation	g.	proposed independent physical & emotional reaction
_____	8. instinct	h.	added cognitive evaluation to the emotion sequence
_____	9. refractory period	i.	second stage in sexual response cycle
_____	10. belongingness needs	j.	third level in need hierarchy
_____	11. Ekman	k.	self-motivated goal directed behavior
_____	12. Maslow	l.	theory that social behavior should be understood from evolutionary or genetic perspective
_____	13. plateau phase	m.	idea that objects in contact acquire "like" properties
_____	14. motivation	n.	set of factors that initiate and direct behavior
_____	15. sociobiology	o.	proposed body reactions precede and drive emotion
_____	16. Schachter & Singer	p.	time when stimulation can't result in sexual arousal

Short Essay Questions. Write a brief answer to each question. Sample answers are on page 266.

1. Compare incentive motivation and drive.

2. Describe how external factors influence eating behavior.

3. Discuss the possible determinants of the weight set point.

4. Compare the determinants of sexual behavior for animals and humans.

5. Describe the three basic components of all emotions.

6. Explain the basic assumption of polygraph exams, and discuss why polygraphs are not always accurate.

257

7.   Discuss how expectations and adaptation level influence happiness.

Multiple Choice Pretest 1. Select the one best response. Answers are on page 266.

1.   The idea of human instincts has been replaced by the concept of
      a.   incentives.
      b.   intrinsic motivation.
      c.   drive.
      d.   emotion.

2.   Ben just ate a large dinner and wishes he could discreetly loosen his belt, but when the dessert cart rolls by, he selects a beautiful piece of cheesecake. Taking the dessert is an example of the power of
      a.   drives.
      b.   instincts.
      c.   incentives.
      d.   needs.

3.   Children will be most likely to show high achievement motivation and attempt to accomplish a task if
      a.   they have a history of failing at the task, driving up their need to achieve.
      b.   their parents show they value the task.
      c.   they are never rewarded for doing the task.
      d.   they are working at the lowest levels of Maslow's hierarchy.

4.   Bill begs to help rake leaves each fall. This year his father tells him he will get an extra $5 in allowance each week if he keeps the leaves raked. According to research on intrinsic motivation, it's likely that
      a.   because of the reward, Bill will be even more enthusiastic about raking the leaves.
      b.   because of the reward, Bill will be less enthusiastic about raking the leaves.
      c.   Bill will initially be less enthusiastic, but will increase in enthusiasm after about three weeks.
      d.   Bill's enthusiasm about raking leaves won't change, because this is a case of intrinsic motivation.

5.   Deanna's parents are worried about her refusal to eat. She weighs 80 lbs., but still thinks she is too fat for a 5 ft-5 inch 17-year-old. A health professional should advise her parents that
      a.   Deanna probably has anorexia nervosa, a serious eating disorder that often can lead to death.
      b.   Deanna probably has bulimia nervosa, a serious eating disorder with serious medical consequences.
      c.   Deanna will begin eating again when she reaches her normal set point.
      d.   Deanna is just going through a growth spurt that is nothing to worry about.

6.   A snarling dog approached Rob suddenly. He began to sweat, his heart beat more rapidly, and his muscles tensed. According to the James-Lange theory, Rob first felt the emotion of fear
      a.   right after seeing the dog and before physiological arousal began.
      b.   at the same time as the physiological arousal began.
      c.   right after the physiological arousal began.
      d.   right after he evaluated or appraised the physiological arousal.

7. Of the following needs, the one that is most basic in Maslow's hierarchy and the first to be satisfied is
    a. self-actualization.
    b. belongingness.
    c. self-esteem.
    d. safety.

8. Destruction to the lateral hypothalamus causes
    a. abnormal sexual behavior.
    b. bulimia nervosa.
    c. loss of emotional response.
    d. reduction of eating and body weight.

9. Brain areas that have been linked to the control of eating include the
    a. brainstem and hippocampus.
    b. cerebellum and pons.
    c. amygdala and midbrain.
    d. parietal lobe and occipital lobe.

10. A person's set point is determined by
    a. cultural attitudes.
    b. willpower.
    c. genetics.
    d. food preferences.

11. According to Masters and Johnson, increased heart rate and blood pressure and penile erection begins in
    a. the orgasmic phase.
    b. the resolution phase.
    c. the excitement phase.
    d. the plateau phase.

12. For humans, sexual motivation is best described as
    a. a hormone-based drive.
    b. incentive motivation.
    c. a process of self-actualization.
    d. a physiological need.

13. When exposed to sexually explicit images, women
    a. are less likely than men to report sexual arousal, and show no physiological signs of arousal.
    b. are less likely than men to report sexual arousal, but show physiological arousal similar to men.
    c. are as likely as men to report sexual arousal, but show few physiological signs of arousal.
    d. are as likely as men to report sexual arousal, and show physiological arousal similar to men.

14. Autopsies on the brains of homosexual and heterosexual men found differences in the
    a. hypothalamus.
    b. hippocampus.
    c. frontal lobes.
    d. temporal lobes.

15. Psychologists who believe that there are 4-6 basic emotions support their argument with
    a. twin studies showing identical emotional reactions to a stimulus.
    b. the fact that all babies show emotions very early.
    c. the cross-cultural data on recognition of facial expressions.
    d. the results of polygraph exams.

16. When shown a picture of a modern American experiencing an emotion, a New Guinea tribesman would
    a. have no idea what emotion the American was experiencing.
    b. be able to identify anger and fear, but not any other emotions.
    c. be able to identify sadness, fear and anger, but would confuse happiness and surprise.
    d. be able to identify happiness, surprise, fear, sadness, anger, and disgust/contempt.

17. Dot's friend tells her, "Smile. You'll feel better." Her advice is consistent with the
    a. Cannon-Bard theory.
    b. the two-factor theory.
    c. the facial feedback hypothesis.
    d. the James-Lange theory.

18. Most courts do not accept polygraph exams as evidence for all of the following reasons except
    a. polygraph exams result in a significant number of innocent people being declared liars.
    b. lying does not necessarily produce physiological reactions.
    c. physiological reactions can occur for reasons other than lying.
    d. estimates of "truthful" physiological reactions cannot be obtained.

19. Firecrackers suddenly go off behind Kim. To explain Kim's fear, the Cannon-Bard theory would suggest
    a. the firecrackers make Kim feel afraid, and being afraid makes her heart beat rapidly.
    b. the firecrackers make Kim feel afraid and make her heart beat rapidly.
    c. Kim feels afraid because she appraised the situation as dangerous.
    d. Kim is afraid because her heart is beating rapidly.

20. In Schachter & Singer's experiment, the subjects most likely to adopt the mood of the accomplice were
    a. the subjects given a stimulant and then told that the drug would cause arousal symptoms.
    b. the subjects given a stimulant but not told that the drug would cause arousal symptoms.
    c. the subjects given saline solution and then told that the "drug" would cause arousal symptoms.
    d. the subjects given saline solution and not told that the "drug" would cause arousal symptoms.

Multiple Choice Pretest 2. Select the one best response. Answers are on page 268.

1. The actor gained 25 pounds for a film role. To keep his weight high throughout the months of filming, the actor had to eat more than he really wanted. After completing the film, he resumed eating normally, and the weight gradually disappeared. The actor's experience would be explained best in terms of
    a. anorexia nervosa.
    b. a disorder of the ventromedial hypothalamus.
    c. the weight set point.
    d. a glucose-insulin imbalance.

2. A male stickleback fish sees a form with a red belly enter the area and immediately attacks. This will occur the first, and every other time a red-bellied form is seen. This behavior is an example of
   a. an instinct.
   b. a drive.
   c. incentive motivation.
   d. homeostasis.

3. Tad hasn't eaten in 12 hours. The psychological state that will cause him go to the pantry for food is
   a. a need.
   b. incentive motivation.
   c. a drive.
   d. intrinsic motivation.

4. Jill pulls on a sweater when she begins to feel chilly. Her behavior is best explained in terms of
   a. incentive motivation.
   b. instinct.
   c. homeostasis.
   d. set point.

5. School breakfast programs make sure children aren't hungry so that they will be interested and able to focus on learning and academic achievement. The view of motivation that is most similar to this is
   a. incentive motivation theory.
   b. Schachter & Singer's two-factor theory.
   c. Maslow's hierarchy of needs.
   d. intrinsic motivation theory.

6. Charlene frequently eats a half-gallon of ice cream, two bags of cookies, a bucket of fried chicken, half a cake and three bags of potato chips in one evening. Afraid of gaining weight, but unable to stop eating, she vomits and uses laxatives to get rid of the food. Charlene's eating habits are characteristic of
   a. a lateral hypothalamic lesion or tumor.
   b. diabetes, an insufficiency of insulin.
   c. anorexia nervosa.
   d. bulimia nervosa.

7. In some cultures premarital sex is strictly forbidden, and married couples have sex essentially fully clothed. Other cultures encourage sexual experimentation and have no problems with nudity. According to Gagnon and Simon, these differences are best explained in terms of different
   a. hormones.
   b. genes.
   c. sexual scripts.
   d. sexual orientations.

8. Performing in front of an audience always increases arousal levels, but performing in a championship match increases arousal a bit further. Which performer is most likely to experience poorer performance in the championship than in non-championship competition?
   a. Becky, who has very low arousal under non-championship conditions.
   b. Gail, who has moderate arousal under non-championship conditions.
   c. Hattie, who has fairly high arousal under non-championship conditions.
   d. All of the performers are equally likely to experience poorer championship performance.

9. The overjustification explanation of the effect of rewards on intrinsic motivation states that
   a. people conclude they do the task because of the reward, not because they naturally enjoy doing it.
   b. people perceive rewards as ways of controlling their behavior.
   c. people begin to think they are doing the task in order to please someone else besides themselves.
   d. people remember the past cases in which they have failed and earned no reward, so they quit trying.

10. Sue's blood glucose level is high due to insufficient insulin production. Sue is probably experiencing
    a. a constant feeling of hunger leading to overeating and weight gain.
    b. a loss of appetite leading to undereating and weight loss.
    c. frequent binge and purge episodes to maintain a constant weight.
    d. an obsessive fear of being too fat.

11. Leroy suddenly began eating a lot and gaining weight. In the unlikely event a brain tumor is to blame, we should suspect the tumor is in the
    a. midbrain.
    b. lateral hypothalamus.
    c. ventromedial hypothalamus.
    d. frontal lobe.

12. Ten minutes after he reached orgasm, Chuck is mentally responding to his partner's advances, but his body isn't responding. Chuck's limitation is probably due to the fact that he
    a. is in the plateau phase of sexual response.
    b. is in the resolution phase of sexual response.
    c. is in the pre-excitement phase of sexual response.
    d. has depleted his testosterone supply.

13. Brain and twin studies are consistent with the idea that sexual orientation is partially determined by biological or genetic factors, but a cause-effect relationship has not been established because
    a. the brain and twin studies data are correlational.
    b. the brain and twin studies do not match other recent data that show no biological factor.
    c. not all of the identical twins have the same orientation.
    d. sexual orientation is too difficult to classify.

14. A rare disorder involving the facial nerves leaves the face expressionless. According to the facial feedback hypothesis, people with this disorder
    a. should be unable to recognize the facial expressions of other people.
    b. should not understand the concept of emotion at all.
    c. should experience less emotion themselves.
    d. should not show social comparison effects.

15. Babies show a wide range of emotional expressions, and emotional facial expressions are identified across cultures. These data support the idea that
    a. there are 10 basic emotions.
    b. the expression of emotion has a biological or genetic component.
    c. cognitive appraisal is an important part of the emotional experience.
    d. feedback from facial muscles is used to interpret an emotional experience.

16. Hal was smiling and he said he felt unbelievably happy. The missing component of the emotion is
    a. a physiological response.
    b. a subjective experience.
    c. an expressive reaction.
    d. a cognitive reaction.

17. The James-Lange theory predicts that
    a. if physiological feedback is eliminated, emotions should be eliminated, or at least reduced.
    b. expectations about a stimulus or situation should influence the emotion experienced.
    c. fear will produce the same general pattern of physical changes as anger.
    d. physical changes will be slower to occur than the emotional experience.

18. Juan meets a woman as he emerges from climbing three flights of stairs. According to the two-factor theory, Juan will be most likely to report the emotion of sexual attraction or "love at first sight" if
    a. his physiological pattern is specific to love rather than exercise.
    b. he attributes his increased heart rate to the woman, rather than to the stairs.
    c. he receives feedback that he is smiling.
    d. he expects his heart rate to increase as a result of climbing the stairs.

ANSWERS AND EXPLANATIONS

Mastering the Concepts

1. initiate (p. 422)	16. glucose (p. 431)	31. excitement (p. 438)	46. hypothalamus (p. 443)
2. physiological (p. 422)	17. Insulin (p. 432)	32. plateau (p. 438)	47. genetic (p. 443)
3. subjective (p. 422)	18. hypothalamus (p. 432)	33. orgasmic (p. 438)	48. Correlational (p. 443)
4. Instincts (p. 424)	19. ventromedial (p. 432)	34. resolution (p. 438)	49. physiological (p. 444)
5. drive (p. 425)	20. lateral (p. 432)	35. refractory (p. 438)	50. subjective (p. 444)
6. homeostasis (p. 425)	21. brainstem (p. 433)	36. hormones (p. 439)	51. facial (p. 444)
7. Incentive (p. 426)	22. hippocampus (p. 433)	37. individual (p. 439)	52. feedback (p. 446)
8. achievement (p. 426)	23. habits (p. 434)	38. pheromones (p. 440)	53. disgust (p. 447)
9. Intrinsic (p. 428)	24. set point (p. 435)	39. sexual scripts (p. 441)	54. polygraph (p. 449)
10. control (p. 428)	25. Genetic (p. 435)	40. short-term (p. 441)	55. positive (p. 449)
11. reward (p. 428)	26. metabolic (p. 435)	41. Sociobiology (p. 441)	56. comparisons (p. 450)
12. expected (p. 429)	27. obesity (p. 435)	42. orientation (p. 442)	57. commonsense (p. 451)
13. hierarchy (p. 429)	28. Anorexia (p. 436)	43. Homosexuals (p. 442)	58. James-Lange (p. 451)
14. Physiological (p. 429)	29. Bulimia (p. 436)	44. Heterosexuals (p. 442)	59. Cannon-Bard (p. 453)
15. self-actualization (p. 429)	30. binge eating (p. 436)	45. biological (p. 443)	60. two-factor (p. 454)

Evaluating Your Progress

Preview & Activating Behavior

1. **b**   a, c, & d.   Wrong.   Although human instincts might exist, the difficulty of identifying true instincts
   (p. 424)   has caused them to lose favor as an explanation of human behavior.

2. **d**   a. Wrong.   An instinct is a characteristic behavioral response to an external stimulus.
(p. 425)   b. Wrong.   Emotions are not responses to internal physiological needs.
             c. Wrong.   Homeostasis is the process by which the body maintains a steady state.

3. **b**   a. Wrong.   Drives involve physiological needs, incentives do not.
(p. 426)   c. Wrong.   Incentives can be learned, and drives are usually unlearned.
             d. Wrong.   Incentives are external, and drives are usually internal.

4. **a**   b. Wrong.   This is a definition of achievement motivation. Achievement is not a physiological state.
(p. 425)   c. Wrong.   This is a definition of intrinsic motivation. Homeostasis is physically motivated.
             d. Wrong.   This is a definition of drive. Homeostasis is not a psychological state.

5. **b**   a. Wrong.   Self-actualization involves fulfilling your ultimate potential in life.
(p. 426)   c. Wrong.   Intrinsic motivation is self-motivated behavior, such as painting a picture for pleasure.
             d. Wrong.   Homeostasis is the process by which the body maintains a stable state.

6. **a**   b. Wrong.   This is a theory of emotion, not motivation.
(p. 428)   c. Wrong.   There is no physiological imbalance here.
             d. Wrong.   Drives are psychological states resulting from physiological needs.

7. **c**   a. Wrong.   Self-actualization and its position are not entirely accepted.
(p. 430)   b. Wrong.   Critics complain about the lack of clear definition and testability.
             d. Wrong.   Achievement is not given as the most important.

8. **a**   b, c, & d.   Wrong.   Maslow used "self-actualization" to describe the state of fulfilling potential.
(p. 430)

Meeting Biological Needs: Hunger and Eating

1. **c**   a, b, & d.   Wrong.   Glucose levels are critical for controlling hunger.
(p. 431)

2. **c**   a. Wrong.   The hippocampus might be involved in eating, but it wasn't the proposed satiety center.
(p. 432)   b. Wrong.   The brainstem might be involved in eating, but it wasn't the proposed satiety center.
             d. Wrong.   The lateral hypothalamus was the proposed "start-up" center.

3. **c**   a. Wrong.   This was the original view, but current research suggests the situation is not so simple.
(p. 432)   b. Wrong.   This the opposite of the original, not discarded, view.
             d. Wrong.   Both areas of the hypothalamus are involved, but their roles are not clear.

4. **b**   a, c, & d.   Wrong.   Set point refers to a weight the body tries to maintain.
(p. 435)

5. **c**   a & d.   Wrong.   Anorexia is most common in young women.
(p. 436)   b.   Wrong.   Binge eating is not common to anorexia. Self-starvation is.

Meeting Biological Needs: Sexual Behavior

1. **c**   a. Wrong.   Even the absence of sex hormones does not necessarily prevent sexual behavior.
(p. 439)   b. Wrong.   For humans, sexual behavior is primarily determined by personal control.
             d. Wrong.   Hormone levels can reduce sexual behavior in some cases or increase it.

2.   **a**   b, c, & d.   Wrong.   These are all opposite from the actual data.
   (p. 441)

3.   **b**   a, c, & d.   Wrong.   Sociobiology stresses looking at behavior from an evolutionary perspective.
   (p. 441)

4.   **d**   a. Wrong.   Sexual phases are the 4 stages of sexual response.
   (p. 441)   b. Wrong.   Sexual orientations involve the type (sex) of sexual partner selected.
              c. Wrong.   Pheromones are scents that control some animal and insect sexual behavior.

5.   **d**   a, b, & c.   Wrong.   Recent research does not confirm these hypotheses.
   (p. 443)

Expressing and Experiencing Emotion

1.   **b**   a. Wrong.   Her heart racing is the physiological response.
   (p. 444)   c. Wrong.   Her feeling of fear is the subjective experience.
              d. Wrong.   There is no unconscious experience in emotion.

2.   **a**   b, c, & d.   Wrong.   Although surprise and disgust are universally recognized, they are not as
   (p. 444)   commonly included as fear, sadness, happiness and anger.

3.   **c**   a & b.   Wrong.   Disgust doesn't arise until at least age 4.
   (p. 447)   d.   Wrong.   Disgust can involve contact with unsavory people, bizarre sex, etc.

4.   **a**   b, c, & d.   Wrong.   These do not represent the facial feedback hypothesis which states feedback from
   (p. 446)   facial muscles is used to interpret the emotion being experienced.

5.   **d**   a. Wrong.   At high levels of arousal, performance decreases.
   (p. 448)   b. Wrong.   Performance decreases only at high levels of arousal; it increases otherwise.
              c. Wrong.   This is backward.

6.   **b**   a. Wrong.   Lying doesn't produce changes that are unlike the changes with other emotional events.
   (p. 449)   c. Wrong.   Physiological behavior, not response time is measured during a polygraph exam
              d. Wrong.   Physiological behavior, not vocal intensity is measured during a polygraph exam.

7.   **b**   a. Wrong.   Commonsense view would say stimulus---> emotion---> physical changes.
   (p. 451)   c. Wrong.   Cannon-Bard proposes simultaneous emotion and physical change.
              d. Wrong.   The two-factory theory includes a cognitive evaluation, which is absent here.

8.   **d**   a. Wrong.   This is the James-Lange view.
   (p. 453)   b. Wrong.   This is the two-factor theory.
              c. Wrong.   This is the facial feedback hypothesis.

9.   **a**   b. Wrong.   The James-Lange theory places most emphasis on physical change.
   (p. 454)   c. Wrong.   Two-factor theory has emotion following physical change.
              d. Wrong.   This is the Cannon-Bard theory, not two-factor theory.

10. **d**   a, b, & c.   Wrong.   These are not popular at all. The two-factor theory is accepted.
   (p. 454)

MAKING FINAL PREPARATIONS

Matching

1. **g** (p. 453)	4. **o** (p. 451)	7. **k** (p. 428)	10. **j** (p. 429)	13. **i** (p. 438)	16. **h** (p. 454)
2. **b** (p. 426)	5. **a** (p. 442)	8. **d** (p. 424)	11. **c** (p. 444)	14. **n** (p. 422)	
3. **m** (p. 447)	6. **e** (p. 449)	9. **p** (p. 438)	12. **f** (p. 429)	15. **l** (p. 441)	

Short Essay Questions

1. A drive is a psychological state that arises in response to an internal physiological need and pushes the organism into action. Incentive motivation is an external factor that exerts a pulling effect on action. Thus, they differ both in origin and method of activation of behavior. (pp. 425-426)

2. External factors include the incentive value of the food itself, cultural practices, social factors, and cultural ideas of beauty. Food is reinforcing and provides an incentive to eat. Cultural practices influence when and what we eat, and how the culture defines beauty may direct eating behavior in order to attain that standard. Finally, eating is associated with social situations. (pp. 433-434)

3. The weight set point is the standard weight the body tries to maintain and is probably genetically determined. Metabolic rate controls how efficiently calories are utilized. The number of fat cells present varies and constrains weight gain and loss. (p. 435)

4. Hormones control animal sexual behavior but only minimally influence humans. Animals mate during fertile periods, and their sexual behavior is highly specific in form, both determined by hormones. Some animals respond to pheromones, scents which activate sexual behavior. For humans, if hormones are not present, sexual activity often declines, but the normal rhythm of hormones exerts minimal changes in sexual activity. Humans control the timing and form of their sexual behavior. Pheromones exert no clear effect. (pp. 439-441)

5. Emotions involve (1) physiological reaction, an arousal manifest in changes in heart rate, blood pressure, etc.; (2) expressive reactions, such as facial expressions, postures, or vocalization; and (3) subjective reaction, internal thoughts and feelings of fear, sadness, etc. (p. 444)

6. Polygraph exams are based on the idea that lying leads to emotionality which, in turn, produces increased physiological arousal that can be measured. Thus, by comparing responses to control and relevant questions, a lie can be inferred. However, polygraphs can be very inaccurate because they are easy to beat, lying doesn't always produce an emotional state, and other factors besides lies can produce physiological arousal. Also, there is a strong tendency to make false positive errors, to call a truthful answer a lie. (p. 449)

7. Happiness can be produced when expectations are exceeded, or can be eliminated when expectations are not met. How high one's expectations are affects the likelihood of being happy. People also become accustomed to certain conditions, and deviations from that adaptation level produce increases or decreases in happiness. (p. 450)

Multiple Choice Pretest 1

1. **c**
    (p. 425)
    a. Wrong. Incentives are external motivators, instincts and drives are internal.
    b. Wrong. Intrinsic motivation is self-motivation, not a response to some state or stimulus.
    d. Wrong. Emotions can act as motivators, but they did not replace the concept of instinct.

2. **c**
    (p. 426)
    a. Wrong. Ben isn't hungry; there is no need to eat. The appearance of the dessert is an incentive.
    b. Wrong. Humans don't have a characteristic, unlearned response to cheesecake.
    d. Wrong. Needs are states of deprivation. Ben has just eaten and has no need for more food.

3. **b**
    (p. 427)
    a. Wrong.   This reduces the chance they will try, even if they have high achievement motivation.
    c. Wrong.   Rewards can reduce intrinsic motivation, but they can act as incentives for achievement.
    d. Wrong.   The lowest levels concern bodily needs, not achievement.

4. **b**
    (p. 428)
    a & d.   Wrong.   Expectation of rewards reduces intrinsic motivation.
    c.   Wrong.   The reward will further decrease intrinsic motivation, not begin to have less effect.

5. **a**
    (p. 436)
    b.   Wrong.   Bulimia is characterized by relatively stable weight, but binge eating and purging.
    c & d.   Wrong.   Refusal to eat, excessive weight loss, and distorted body image characterizes anorexia.

6. **c**
    (p. 451)
    a. Wrong.   This is the commonsense view. James-Lange uses stimulus--physical change--emotion.
    b. Wrong.   This is the Cannon-Bard theory. James-Lange uses stimulus--physical change--emotion.
    d. Wrong.   This is the two-factor theory. James-Lange uses stimulus--physical change--emotion.

7. **d**
    (p. 429)
    a.   Wrong.   This is the last need to be addressed.
    b & c.   Wrong.   These are some of the last needs to be addressed.

8. **d**
    (p. 432)
    a. Wrong.   Other areas of the hypothalamus are important for sexual behavior.
    b. Wrong.   Although weight loss occurs, it is not due to the binge-purge cycle of bulimia.
    c. Wrong.   The lateral hypothalamus is not involved in emotion.

9. **a**
    (p. 433)
    b, c, & d.   Wrong.   These areas are not involved in the control of eating.

10. **c**
    (p. 435)
    a, b, & d.   Wrong.   These influence eating patterns, but not the set point.

11. **c**
    (p. 438)
    a. Wrong.   This is the phase in which orgasm occurs.
    b. Wrong.   During resolution, arousal subsides to normal. This is the last phase.
    d. Wrong.   The plateau phase follows initial arousal and includes changes related to reproduction.

12. **b**
    (p. 440)
    a & d.   Wrong.   There is no physiological need for sex, and hormones are not critical.
    c.   Wrong.   Self-actualization does not involve sexual behavior.

13. **b**
    (p. 440)
    a.   Wrong.   Women show similar physiological reactions to explicit material.
    c & d.   Wrong.   Women are less likely to report being aroused by explicit material.

14. **a**
    (p. 443)
    b, c, & d.   Wrong.   An area in the hypothalamus was smaller in homosexuals than in heterosexuals.

15. **c**
    (p. 444)
    a & b.   Wrong.   Data such as these would only support a biological origin, not 4-6 basic emotions.
    d.   Wrong.   Polygraph data have no relation to the idea of 6 basic emotions.

16. **d**
    (p. 444)
    a, b, & c.   Wrong.   Cross-cultural data show recognition of facial expressions of 6 "basic" emotions.

17. **c**
    (p. 446)
    a. Wrong.   Key here is the idea that one's expression affects subjective experience of emotion, not that physiological and subjective components are simultaneous but independent.
    b. Wrong.   Key here is the idea that one's expression affects subjective experience, not that physiological responses are interpreted to yield a particular emotion.
    d. Wrong.   Key here is the idea that one's expression affects subjective experience, not that specific patterns of physiological activity identify an emotion.

18. **d**   a, b, & c. Wrong. These are all problems. "Truthful" estimates are obtainable from measurements
    (p. 449)   for control questions.

19. **b**   a. Wrong. This is the commonsense view.
    (p. 453)   c. Wrong. This is the two-factor view.
               d. Wrong. This is the James-Lange view.

20. **b**   a.   Wrong. Only subjects not expecting arousal, but experiencing arousal, adopted the mood.
    (p. 454)   c & d. Wrong. Saline did not produce arousal, and thus, little or no evidence of emotion.

Multiple Choice Pretest 2

1. **c**   a, b, & d. Wrong. Key here is the difficulty maintaining a high weight and later, the weight loss
    (p. 435)   when eating normally. His body tried to maintain its natural weight (set point).

2. **a**   b. Wrong. Drives are responses to internal physiological needs.
    (p. 424)   c. Wrong. Incentive motivation is goal-directed behavior that is self-motivated.
               d. Wrong. Homeostasis is a process by which the body maintains a steady state.

3. **c**   a. Wrong. A need (physiological) causes the drive (psychological) that gets him to look for food.
    (p. 425)   b. Wrong. Incentive motivation involves external factors "pulling" behavior, not a psychological state.
               d. Wrong. He seeks food because of a biological need. Intrinsic motivation is not a response to a need.

4. **c**   a. Wrong. The sweater is a means to an end, not the cause of the behavior.
    (p. 425)   b. Wrong. Sweaters do not naturally cause a person to put them on.
               d. Wrong. Set point relates to weight control, not temperature.

5. **c**   a & d. Wrong. Key here is addressing physiological needs before other, higher needs--Maslow's view.
    (p. 429)   b.   Wrong. Two-factor theory is a theory of emotion. Key here is prioritizing needs--Maslow's
                               idea.

6. **d**   a. Wrong. Damage to the lateral hypothalamus would probably cause her to quit eating.
    (p. 436)   b. Wrong. Diabetes would keep glucose high, leading to less hunger and less eating.
               c. Wrong. Anorexia nervosa involves self-starvation.

7. **c**   a. Wrong. Hormones do not determine sexual attitudes or behaviors in humans.
    (p. 441)   b. Wrong. Genes do not determine sexual attitudes such as these.
               d. Wrong. Sexual orientation relates to heterosexuality, homosexuality, bisexuality, etc.

8. **c**   a. Wrong. Increases from low arousal will probably not push arousal past optimal levels.
    (p. 448)   b. Wrong. Increases from moderate arousal are less likely to hurt than increases from high levels.
               d. Wrong. Performance increases as arousal moves from low to moderate, but then decreases.

9. **a**   b & c. Wrong. These are alternative explanations, but not the overjustification explanation.
    (p. 428)   d.   Wrong. This describes learning to be helpless, an achievement motivation situation.

10. **b**   a. Wrong. High glucose levels inhibit eating.
    (p. 431)   c. Wrong. Glucose inhibits eating and does not cause bulimic episodes.
               d. Wrong. Although high glucose inhibits eating, it doesn't cause anorexia nervosa.

11. **c**   a & d. Wrong. These areas do not control eating.
    (p. 432)   b.   Wrong. Damage to this area usually results in reduction of intake and weight loss.

12. **b**
(p. 438)
a. Wrong. Stimulation produces arousal during the plateau phase. Key here is the recent orgasm.
c. Wrong. This is not a true phase of sexual response. Key here is the recent orgasm.
d. Wrong. One episode of sexual activity does not deplete testosterone. Key here is the recent orgasm.

13. **a**
(p. 443)
b, c, & d. Wrong. The brain and twin studies were correlational and can't prove cause-effect. Data for other factors wouldn't eliminate biological factors as *partial* determinants.

14. **c**
(p. 446)
a & b. Wrong. Facial expression affects one's own experience, not the interpretation of others'.
d. Wrong. Social comparison, using other's emotion to judge your own, doesn't rely on expression.

15. **b**
(p. 445)
a. Wrong. These data don't support a certain number of basic emotions, and 4-6, not 10, is accurate.
c. Wrong. These data don't relate to the two-factor theory. Cognitive factors are not involved here.
d. Wrong. These data don't relate to facial feedback hypothesis. No mention of feedback is made.

16. **a**
(p. 444)
b & d. Wrong. Feeling happy is the subjective (or cognitive) reaction.
c. Wrong. Smiling is an expressive reaction.

17. **a**
(p. 451)
b. Wrong. This is predicted by the two-factor theory. James-Lange doesn't include expectations.
c. Wrong. James-Lange predicts different physical responses for each different emotion.
d. Wrong. James-Lange has physical changes leading to emotion, not following emotion.

18. **b**
(p. 454)
a. Wrong. Two-factor theory doesn't require different physical patterns for different emotions.
c. Wrong. Two-factor theory isn't based on facial expression feedback.
d. Wrong. Here, the heart rate would be attributed to the stairs, rather than attraction to a woman.

LANGUAGE ENHANCEMENT GUIDE

CORE TERMS

This chapter will approach the subject of emotions and motivation *objectively;* that is, it will not refer to individual experiences, but to what people in general experience. Psychologists are interested in the *universality* of motivation and emotions -- the behaviors, facial expressions, and so on that are common to people all around the world. You will probably find yourself comparing what you read about emotions with your *subjective,* personal experience.

IDIOMS

422	meltdown	step-by-step breakdown with dangerous results
422	"fix"	a dose of an illegal drug
422	junkie	drug addict
423	shy away	move away to avoid

431	optimal level	best level for good performance
447	feelers	antennae
447	akin to contagion	like a communicable disease (for example, a cold virus)
447	have no conception	have no idea
447	notions	ideas
448	rates skyrocket	rates go up very high quickly
449	send up a red flag	draw notice and make one cautious
449	mundane	ordinary, unexciting
450	blowing off steam	expressing anger, such as yelling
450	utopian bliss	perfect happiness in a perfect world
451	amorous attentions	flirting, mating activities
451	Holy Grail	a very valuable thing that is sought but not often found (refers to the cup Christ used at the Last Supper, which legendary knights went on quests to find)
453	mounted an influential attack	attacked in a way that caused others to agree with the attacker

WORD PARTS

Here are some words that are made up of word parts, and that you can find in this chapter. After you've looked at these, you can look for others in the chapter that use the same word parts (they are there, but YOU have to find them!)

WORD	WORD PART IT USES	MEANING
emote	e, ef, ec = out mot, mov = to move	to express emotions
compel	com = together pel, puls = drive, push, throw	to urge, force
consume	con = together sum = to take, use, waste	to use up

resist	re = again, back sist, stet, sta = to stand	to hold against, withstand
external	ext, extra = outer	outside
degrade	de = down, from, away grad = step, degree, walk	to become less good, healthy, etc.
disrupt	dis = bad, not, apart rupt = to tear, break	to break apart
transformation	trans = across form = shape	to change the shape of something
satiate	sat = enough, sufficient	to have enough, to stop seeking
aversion	a = not, away vers, vert = to turn	strong dislike
polygraph	poly = many graph = to write	a machine that records many different variables, such as heart rate, respiration rate, and skin conductivity (sweating).

Knowing the word parts listed above, you can also create the following words. You can get an idea of their meanings from the word parts they use. You fill in the blanks!

demote	de + mot	_____
dissatisfied	dis + sat	_____
consist	_____ + _____	to make up all together; to add up to
desist	de + sist	_____
extrovert	_____ + _____	one who is turned outward; friendly person
repulsive	re + puls	_____

CHAPTER 12: PERSONALITY

ESTABLISHING LEARNING OBJECTIVES

Use these learning objectives as a preview of the chapter, a guide for active reading, and to evaluate your mastery of the material. Review the relevant objectives as you begin and end your reading of each major section of the chapter.

After studying this chapter you should be able to:

I.   Solve the practical problem of defining and measuring personality.
    A. Describe the psychometric approach to personality.
        1. Describe Cattell's source traits.
    B. Identify Eysenck's three primary dimensions of personality as well as the "Big Five" personality dimensions.
        1. Explain why different researchers find different numbers of traits.
        2. Explain why the "Big Five" concept is popular.
    C. Discuss Allport's distinction between cardinal traits and central traits.
    D. Discuss the advantages and disadvantages of self-report inventories and projective personality tests.
        1. Describe three self-report inventories, how they are used, and their strengths and weaknesses.
        2. Compare projective tests to self-report inventories and identify their strengths and weaknesses.

II. Solve the practical problem of determining how personality develops.
    A. Discuss Freud's psychodynamic theory of personality and mind.
        1. Define conscious, preconscious, and unconscious mind, and describe their role in Freud's theory.
        2. Define id, ego, and superego, and describe their relationship to each other and to behavior.
    B. Explain defense mechanisms, the stages of psychosexual development, and provide a critical evaluation of Freud's theory.
        1. Describe repression, projection, sublimation, and reaction formation.
        2. Describe Jung's, Horney's, and Adler's versions and the current view of psychodynamic theory.
    C. Discuss and evaluate humanistic approaches to personality, including the specific proposals of Carl Rogers and Abraham Maslow.
        1. Compare the humanistic and psychodynamic approaches.
        2. Describe Roger's theory, and discuss the role of the self-concept, positive regard, and congruence.
        3. Describe Maslow's theory, and discuss the role of self-actualization and the hierarchy of needs.
        4. Discuss the criticisms of the humanistic approach to personality.
    D. Describe and evaluate cognitive-behavioral theories of personality; show how cognitions and the environment interact to produce behavior.
        1. Explain the role of classical conditioning, instrumental conditioning, and observational learning.
        2. Describe how expectations and beliefs influence behavior or personality.
        3. Discuss the criticisms of the cognitive-behavioral approach.

III. Solve the conceptual problem of resolving and person-situation debate.
    A. Describe the person-situation debate.
    B. Evaluate the evidence for within and across situation consistency.
    C. Define self-monitoring behavior.
    D. Discuss the role that genetic factors play in personality.

MASTERING THE MATERIAL

Preview & Conceptualizing and Measuring Personality (pp. 464-472)

Mastering the Vocabulary. Define or explain each of the following terms. To check your answers, consult the text pages listed.

1. personality (p. 464)

2. trait (p. 464)

3. trait theories (p. 466)

4. Big Five (p. 467)

5. cardinal traits (p. 469)

6. central traits (p. 469)

7. secondary traits (p. 469)

8. self-report inventories (p. 470)

9. 16 Personality Factor (p. 470)

10. NEO-PI-R (p. 470)

11. Minnesota Multiphasic Personality Inventory (MMPI) (p. 470)

12. projective personality test (p. 471)

13. Rorschach test (p. 471)

14. Thematic Apperception Test (p. 471)

Mastering the Concepts. Fill in the blanks to create a summary of this section. Answers are on page 288.

_____(1) is one's particular pattern of psychological characteristics. Personality _____(2), tendencies to behave in a particular way, establish an identity. Three conceptual and practical problems are addressed: How should traits be conceptualized and measured? How do traits develop? Are traits independent of the environment?

Trait theories, systems for assessing individual _____(3), use a _____(4) approach in which responses on questionnaires are used to identify traits. _____(5) analysis identifies related behaviors that reflect a disposition or trait. Cattell identified 16 _____(6) traits that vary between two opposites (e.g., reserved-outgoing). Eysenck proposed three superfactors: extroversion, how sociable one is; _____(7), how moody or anxious; and psychoticism, how uncaring or cruel. Most psychologists support the _____(8) traits: extroversion, _____(9), conscientiousness, neuroticism, and openness to experience. Allport, studying individuals rather than group data, proposed three levels of traits. _____(10) traits are very dominant traits. _____(11) traits are less dominant but enduring. Secondary traits are situation-specific.

There are two main types of personality tests. _____(12) inventories are paper-and-pencil tests involving true-false questions or ratings. These include the 16 Personality Factor, which measures Cattell's 16 primary factors, the NEO-PI-R, which measures the Big 5, and the very popular _____(13), which is also used to diagnose disorders. Self-report inventories are _____(14) tests whose strengths are reliability, standardization, validity and ease of scoring. _____(15) tests, such as the Rorschach test and the _____(16), allow unrestricted responses, often to an ambiguous stimulus. Critics of projective tests cite poor reliability and validity. Critics of inventories cite subject bias and poor predictive validity.

Evaluating Your Progress. Select the one best response. Answers are on page 288. If you make any errors, reread the relevant material before proceeding.

1. Cattell proposed 16 basic personality traits (timid--venturesome, relaxed--tense) he called
   a. cardinal traits.
   b. central traits.
   c. source traits.
   d. secondary traits.

2. In Eysenck's trait approach, a person strong in neuroticism is likely to
   a. be irritable and moody.
   b. sociable and outgoing.
   c. cooperative with others.
   d. rude to other people.

3. Currently, the most popular trait theory is
   a. the Big 5 traits.
   b. Eysenck's three superfactors.
   c. Allport's trait theory.
   d. Cattell's 16 factor theory.

4. "Occasional" traits in Allport's theory are called
   a. secondary traits.
   b. source traits.
   c. central traits.
   d. cardinal traits.

5. Allport's trait theory was developed based on
   a. the factor analysis of tests from large groups of people.
   b. cross-cultural testing of groups of people with many languages.
   c. comparing the Rorschach test results of normal and disturbed groups.
   d. detailed studies of particular individuals.

6. All of the following are self-report inventories except
   a. the MMPI.
   b. the NEO-PI-R.
   c. the Rorschach test.
   d. the 16 Personality Factor test.

7. Self-report personality inventories
   a. allow complete freedom in how the person responds.
   b. use a true-false or rating scale format in most cases.
   c. use an unstructured or ambiguous stimulus in most cases.
   d. use a subjective scoring technique.

Determining How Personality Develops (pp. 471-487)

Mastering the Vocabulary. Define or explain each of the following terms. To check your answers, consult the text pages listed.

1. psychodynamic theory (p. 474)

2. conscious mind (p. 474)

3. preconscious mind (p. 474)

4. unconscious mind (p. 474)

5. id (p. 474)

6. superego (p. 474)

7. ego (p. 475)

8. defense mechanisms (p. 475)

9. repression (p. 475)

10. projection (p. 476)

11. reaction formation (p. 476)

12. sublimation (p. 476)

13. oral stage (p. 477)

14. anal stage (p. 477)

15. phallic stage (p. 477)

16. latency period (p. 478)

17. genital stage (p. 478)

18. collective unconscious (p. 478)

19. humanistic psychology (p. 479)

20. self-concept (p. 480)

21. positive regard (p. 480)

22. conditions of worth (p. 480)

23. incongruence (p. 480)

24. self-actualization (p. 481)

25. cognitive-behavioral theories (p. 484)

26. social learning theory (p. 485)

27. locus of control (p. 485)

28. self-efficacy (p. 486)

29. reciprocal determinism (p. 487)

Mastering the Concepts. Fill in the blanks to create a summary of this section. Answers are on page 288.

Freud's _____(17) theory proposes behavior is influenced by unconscious forces, and that the mind includes the conscious mind, holding current thoughts, the _____(18) mind, containing inactive but accessible memories, and the _____(19) mind, containing memories, urges, and conflicts that are inaccessible, but still influence behavior. Items in the unconscious are symbolically revealed in _____(20).

Freud suggested personality has three parts. The _____(21), residing in the unconscious, is driven by innate urges and the need for immediate gratification. It operates by the _____(22) principle, without regard to morals. The _____(23) contains morals defined by parents and society and acts as a conscience. It follows an _____(24) principle. The _____(25) operates by the _____(26) principle. It tries to satisfy the id while staying within the limits set by the superego.

To reduce anxiety, the ego uses _____(27) mechanisms. The most important is _____(28), burying uncomfortable, often sexual, thoughts in the unconscious where they still affect behavior. In _____(29) unacceptable ideas are attributed to others. Reaction formation involves transforming anxiety-producing thoughts into an _____(30) form of behavior (e.g., hate to floods of affection). In _____(31) unacceptable behaviors are channeled into socially acceptable forms.

Freud proposed psychosexual stages of development, each associated with an _____(32) zone of the body. In the first year, the _____(33) stage, sexual gratification is obtained by the mouth. The second year begins the _____(34) stage, and gratification is obtained by passing feces. The _____(35) stage begins at age 3 and is focused on the genitals. At this time sexual feelings are directed toward the opposite sex parent, which causes the conflict of the _____(36) complex (boys) or Electra complex (girls). Failure to resolve this conflict causes later sexual problems. After age 5 and until puberty, sexuality is suppressed, and the _____(37) stage focuses on friendships. At puberty, sexuality reemerges in an adult form in the _____(38) stage. Failure to satisfy the needs (or overindulgence) of a stage leads to a _____(39) and adult behavior characteristic of that childhood stage. An oral fixation retains excessive oral activities (e.g., smoking); anal fixation results in excessive neatness or messiness.

Adler, Jung, and Horney, disagreed with Freud's emphasis on sexuality. Adler viewed feeling of _____(40) as the force behind behavior. Jung replaced sexuality with a general life force and added the idea of a _____(41) unconscious that contains _____(42), symbols passed down through generations. Horney argued against the concept of penis envy and for a balanced view of women. Freud's theory has lost much of its influence. Unconscious influences, defense mechanisms, and conflict between personal and societal demands are accepted. Criticisms include a lack of scientific rigor and testability, and continued concern about his view of women.

The _____(43) approach stresses people's positive qualities and potential for growth. Actions are influenced by the environment and a person's _____(44) of reality. Rogers stressed the need for a _____(45) self-concept which develops when _____(46) is given without conditions of worth. Maslow believed that inappropriate behavior results from being unable to satisfy basic needs and self-actualization. Self-schemas, multiple senses of self, influence interpretation and reactions to situations. Critics argue humanistic theories are vague, incomplete, based on subjective data, and too optimistic, but this approach remains very popular.

The cognitive-_____(47) approach emphasizes learning/conditioning and cognitive factors. Classically conditioned or reinforced behaviors become "traits." Social learning theory states traits come from _____(48) other's behavior, especially if the behavior is reinforced. The cognitive-behavioral view also considers people's beliefs. Some people see outcomes based on chance, an _____(49) locus of control, while others feel they control the outcome, an _____(50) locus of control. Feelings of competence, or _____(51) also effect behavior. Critics argue cognitive-behavioral theories are insufficient and focus too much on the situation and too little on biological factors and the person as a whole.

Evaluating Your Progress. Select the one best response. Answers are on page 289. If you make any errors, reread the relevant material before proceeding.

1. According to Freud, the part of the mind that contains inactive, but accessible, thoughts is the
    a. preconscious mind.
    b. conscious mind.
    c. unconscious mind.
    d. collective unconscious mind.

2. According to Freud, the ego
    a. operates according to the reality principle.
    b. is located entirely in the unconscious mind.
    c. contains society's rules about right and wrong.
    d. desires immediate, total satisfaction of needs.

3. The defense mechanism of repression
    a. transforms an anxiety-producing desire into a behavior that expresses the opposite desire.
    b. channels an inappropriate behavior into a more socially appropriate one.
    c. attributes an unacceptable thought or desire to someone else.
    d. submerges troubling thoughts deep into the unconscious mind.

4. The correct order of Freud's psychosexual stages is
    a. oral, phallic, anal, latency, genital.
    b. oral, anal, phallic, latency, genital.
    c. oral, genital, anal, phallic, latency.
    d. oral, anal, latency, genital, phallic.

5. Each of Freud's stages of development are based on the
    a. body region that provides pleasure or sexual gratification.
    b. defense mechanism that the ego tends to employ the most.
    c. part of the personality that is dominant at that time (ego, id, superego).
    d. level of congruence that has been achieved for the self-concept at that time.

6. According to Freud, when the needs of a particular psychosexual stage are frustrated
    a. incongruence is likely to develop.
    b. a fixation will occur.
    c. the Oedipal complex will occur.
    d. the id will be overwhelmed by the superego.

7. After watching the baseball team win the game on a double-play, B.J. said, "I don't think I'd ever want to be a professional athlete. Whether you win or lose is a matter of luck. You can practice all you want and be the best player, but if the other guy is luckier, he wins the game." B.J. would be described as having
    a. high self-efficacy.
    b. internal locus of control.
    c. unmet conditions of worth.
    d. external locus of control.

8.   Which of the following is false?
   a.   Despite some criticism, Freud's theory gained influence during the past several decades.
   b.   Many of the important and unique concepts in Freud's theory lack scientific rigor.
   c.   Many of the important and unique concepts in Freud's theory are almost impossible to test.
   d.   Freud's theory is very male-oriented and views women as weaker psychologically.

9.   The theory that stresses the human's capacity for self-awareness, choice, responsibility and growth is
   a.   the cognitive-behavioral theory of personality.
   b.   the humanistic theory of personality.
   c.   the social learning theory of personality.
   d.   the psychodynamic theory of personality.

10.   The humanistic theorist, Carl Rogers, suggests that for a healthy personality to develop
   a.   the Electra or Oedipal complex must be resolved.
   b.   love should be given only when the person is acting appropriately.
   c.   the self-concept must be congruent.
   d.   conditions of worth must be present.

11.   The cognitive-behavioral approach to personality emphasizes
   a.   the importance of a congruent self-concept.
   b.   biological urges that drive behavior.
   c.   learning and expectations.
   d.   the innate goodness of human nature.

Resolving the Person-Situation Debate (pp. 488-492)

Mastering the Vocabulary.   Define or explain each of the following terms. To check your answers, consult the text pages listed.

1.   person-situation debate (p. 488)

2.   self-monitoring (p. 489)

Mastering the Concepts. Fill in the blanks to create a summary of this section. Answers are on page 288.

   The person-situation debate involves the question of whether behavior is _____(52) across situations, as a definition of personality based on enduring traits requires. Mischel found behavior was fairly _____(53) across situations. Within similar situations, Hartshorne & May found consistent behavior, supporting a cognitive-behavioral view. Inconsistency might be due to the number of observations, or it might reflect a personality trait, _____(54). Those high in this trait monitor the situation and change their behavior to fit it; those low in the trait act consistently regardless of the context. Cantor suggests personality should be viewed as strategies for solving _____(55) tasks rather than as traits. When life tasks (situations) change, behavior (personality) might change and appear inconsistent.

Twin studies of personality traits support a strong _____(56) factor. Although the environment is very influential, genetic influences are stronger, at least for some traits. This allows enduring traits.

Evaluating Your Progress. Select the one best response. Answers are on page 290. If you make any errors, reread the relevant material before proceeding.

1. Mischel's research concerning the person-situation debate found that
   a. people's behavior is not very consistent across different situations.
   b. people's behavior is not very consistent within a particular situation.
   c. genetic factors cause very consistent behavior across different situations.
   d. genetic factors cause very consistent behavior within a situation.

2. People who evaluate the situation and change their behavior to fit it
   a. are high self-monitors.
   b. are low self-monitors.
   c. have an internal locus of control.
   d. have an external locus of control.

3. If a person's life task changes, Nancy Cantor suggests we should expect
   a. locus of control will change.
   b. the tendency to self-monitor will change.
   c. behavior will change.
   d. conditions of worth will change.

4. Twin studies suggest that personality
   a. is determined entirely by genetics.
   b. is determined entirely by the environment or experience.
   c. is determined by both the environment and genetics, but genetics play a greater role.
   d. is determined by both the environment and genetics, with each equally important.

MAKING FINAL PREPARATIONS

Complete these sections without consulting your book or notes. For a more accurate estimate of how well you know this material, wait at least a day or two after studying the chapter before working on the questions. Some material you "know" immediately after working with the chapter will be quickly forgotten. Immediate tests will overestimate what you know well.

Short Essay Questions. Write a brief answer for each question. Sample answers are on page 290.

1. Compare source traits and superfactors.

2. Compare projective personality tests and self-report inventories.

3. Explain the Oedipal and Electra complexes and their role in personality development.

4. Compare the psychodynamic and humanistic views of personality.

5. Explain Ron's very quiet personality in terms of instrumental conditioning.

6. Discuss the criticism of the cognitive-behavioral approach to personality and behavior.

7. Explain how psychologists resolve the person-situation debate.

Matching. Select the correct definition or matching accomplishment for each. Answers are on page 291.

_____	1. Karen Horney	**a.** found three trait superfactors of personality
_____	2. Raymond Cattell	**b.** humanistic theorist stressing self-concept
_____	3. Gordon Allport	**c.** found inconsistency of behavor across situations
_____	4. Alfred Adler	**d.** neo-Freudian against idea of penis envy in women
_____	5. Hans Eysenck	**e.** neo-Freudian who proposed inferiority complex
_____	6. Carl Jung	**f.** found 16 source traits of personality
_____	7. Walter Mischel	**g.** stressed observational learning and self-efficacy
_____	8. Albert Bandura	**h.** proposed cardinal, central, & secondary traits
_____	9. Abraham Maslow	**i.** neo-Freudian who added collective unconscious
_____	10. Carl Rogers	**j.** psychodynamic theorist stressing sexuality
_____	11. Sigmund Freud	**k.** projective personality test
_____	12. Rorschach	**l.** humanistic theorist proposing self-actualization
_____	13. Electra complex	**m.** expectations people believe others place on them
_____	14. positive regard	**n.** girl's anxiety over sexual attraction to father
_____	15. reciprocal determinism	**o.** beliefs, behavior, environment affect what's learned
_____	16. conditions of worth	**p.** idea that people value others' approval

Multiple Choice Pretest 1. Select the one best response. Answers are on page 291.

1. Beth completed a personality inventory intended to identify "normal" personality traits. The test assessed the personality trait dimensions of shrewd vs. forthright, tense vs. relaxed, dominant vs. submissive, and other dimensions. The test was probably the
   a. Rorschach test.
   b. 16 Personality Factor test.
   c. MMPI (Minnesota Multiphasic Personality Inventory).
   d. NEO-PI-R.

2. The Big 5 traits are extroversion, neuroticism, openness to experience, agreeableness, and
   a. conscientiousness.
   b. psychoticism.
   c. hysteria.
   d. intelligence.

3. Allport proposed that most people can be described in terms of 5-10 representative traits known as
   a. cardinal traits.
   b. source traits.
   c. secondary traits.
   d. central traits.

4. Jerry is telling a story about a rather ambiguous picture he was shown. He is taking
   a. a self-monitoring test.
   b. the MMPI.
   c. a self-report personality inventory.
   d. a projective test.

5. Critics of self-report inventories such as the MMPI have complained that
   a. it is easy for subjects to bias their answers to make themselves look good.
   b. the scoring procedures are much too subjective.
   c. two people scoring the same test often give different interpretations.
   d. they allow too much freedom in the person's response.

6. Tom feels anxious anytime he is out in public, but he can't figure out why. According to Freud, Tom's anxiety probably originates with some past conflict now hidden in
   a. the preconscious mind.
   b. the unconscious mind.
   c. the superego.
   d. the reaction formation.

7. As a young boy, Rick would spy on the girls in locker rooms and peep in neighbors' windows to satisfy his need to look at female bodies. As an adult, Rick is a professional photographer, a profession that allows him great opportunities to look at beautiful women. Freud might suggest that his choice of profession is an example of
   a. repression.
   b. sublimation.
   c. reaction formation.
   d. projection.

8. According to Freud, the superego
   a. is present at birth and motivates most early behavior.
   b. operates completely in the unconscious mind.
   c. follows the idealistic principle.
   d. requires immediate gratification.

9. Bill, age 21, is a true slob. His sink is always full of dirty dishes, and his apartment is filled with trash. Freud would probably suggest that Bill is fixated at
   a. the oral stage.
   b. the anal stage.
   c. the phallic stage.
   d. the latency stage.

10. According to Freud's psychosexual stages view of development, children from about age 5 to puberty are
   a   in the phallic stage and are undergoing the Oedipal or Electra complex.
   b. in the genital stage and are deriving sexual pleasure in more direct ways with the opposite sex.
   c. in the latency stage and are forming solid friendships rather than seeking sexual gratification.
   d. in the anal stage and are deriving pleasure from expelling or retaining feces.

11. Adler proposed that the important factor in abnormal personality development is
   a. developing irrational, rather than rational, beliefs.
   b. developing incongruence and conditions of worth during childhood.
   c. how people deal with a basic sense of inferiority.
   d. having many models of unhealthy personalities during childhood.

12. Karen Horney disagreed with Freud's view that women are dissatisfied with their sex and that they have
   a. the Oedipus complex.
   b. weak superegos.
   c. an inferiority complex.
   d. penis envy.

13. Carl Rogers, the humanistic theorist believes that people have an inborn need for
   a. conditions of worth.
   b. incongruence.
   c. defense mechanisms.
   d. positive regard.

14. The view that personality traits are influenced by genetic factors is supported by higher correlations on the MMPI for
   a. identical twins reared together than for identical twins reared apart.
   b. identical twins reared apart than for fraternal twins reared together.
   c. fraternal twins reared together than for fraternal twins reared apart.
   d. fraternal twins reared apart than for identical twins reared apart.

15. According to Maslow, people are inherently good and only act aggressively or unkindly when
   a. they have reached self-actualization.
   b. they have not satisfied their basic survival needs.
   c. the conflict between the id and superego gets out of control.
   d. they undergo peak experiences.

16. The humanistic view of personality and behavior has been criticized for all of the following except
    a. proposing humans have control over their behavior, rather than being driven by animalistic urges.
    b. the fact that many of the concepts in their theories are vague and not clearly developed.
    c. the problem of testing a theory that emphasizes subjective experiences.
    d. the highly optimistic view that all humans will achieve lofty goals if not blocked in their pursuit.

17. To explain Ted's very aggressive personality, a social learning theorist probably would suggest that
    a. Ted learned to be aggressive by watching people be reinforced for aggression.
    b. Ted's natural biological inheritance includes strong urges to be aggressive.
    c. Ted has been frustrated in his attempt to reach full self-actualization.
    d. Ted has a very strong internal locus of control and low self-efficacy.

18. The idea that beliefs, behavior, and the environment interact to shape what is learned from experience is
    a. self-efficacy.
    b. self-actualization.
    c. reciprocal determinism.
    d. conditions of worth.

19. Based on Hartshorne and May's research on dishonesty, if Kim stole a dollar from a classmate
    a. Kim will probably steal money from another classmate if given the opportunity.
    b. Kim will probably steal again and is likely to cheat on tests at school.
    c. Kim will show dishonest behavior in all aspects of life from childhood to adulthood.
    d. Kim is no more likely to steal again or show dishonesty in any aspect of life than any other person.

20. Nancy Cantor suggests that life tasks are useful for understanding
    a. self-efficacy.
    b. self-monitoring.
    c. locus of control.
    d. behavioral consistency.

Multiple Choice Pretest 2. Select the one best response. Answers are on page 292.

1. Peter is usually reserved and quiet, but when he goes to a football game he screams at the officials when they make a call he dislikes. Allport would say that Peter's aggressiveness is an example of
    a. a source trait.
    b. a central trait.
    c. a secondary trait.
    d. a cardinal trait.

2. "How can you use that test?" Ed asked. "Don't you know that two psychologists are probably going to give two different interpretations, and the validity is poor?" The test being used probably is
    a. the 16 Personality Factor.
    b. the Rorschach test.
    c. the NEO-PI-R.
    d. the MMPI.

3. Harry is cooperative, polite, and concerned about cleanliness. In Eysenck's view, Harry is low in
   a. extroversion.
   b. neuroticism.
   c. conscientiousness.
   d. psychoticism.

4. Aysa is sympathetic, warm, trusting, and cooperative. Aysa's NEO-PI-R scores should be high on
   a. extroversion.
   b. neuroticism.
   c. agreeableness.
   d. conscientiousness.

5. The Big 5 traits are more popular than Cattell's or Eysenck's traits because the Big 5
   a. aren't sex-biased and the Cattell's and Eysenck's approaches are biased.
   b. have been found consistently in many cultures and using many languages.
   c. were identified by studying individuals instead of using factor analysis of group data.
   d. give a more specific, fine-tuned description of personality than either Cattell's or Eysenck's traits.

6. To diagnose Fritz's psychological problem, a psychologist is most likely to have him take
   a. the MMPI.
   b. the 16 Personality Factor test.
   c. the NEO-PI-R.
   d. any of the above; all are primarily used to diagnose mental disorders.

7. Stan drinks, uses drugs, and has unprotected sex whenever the opportunity arises with no consideration of the appropriateness or consequences of his behavior. Freud would say Stan's behavior demonstrates
   a. how sublimation operates.
   b. the power of projection.
   c. the influence of the id.
   d. a very strong superego.

8. Roy, age 4, has unconscious sexual feelings for his mother. Roy is currently in Freud's
   a. oral stage.
   b. genital stage.
   c. anal stage.
   d. phallic stage.

9. Jung proposed that the collective unconscious contains
   a. all the forbidden desires and traumas accumulated over the person's life.
   b. the id, but not the ego or superego.
   c. a driving force to overcome inferiority and to achieve superiority.
   d. archetypes, symbols of enduring concepts passed from one generation to the next.

10. The aspect of Freud's psychodynamic theory that is least accepted today is
    a. the role of unconscious influences in behavior.
    b. the concept of defense mechanisms.
    c. the impact of the need to satisfy biological processes and the demands of society.
    d. his views on the nature and role of human sexuality.

11. Lester is always accusing his wife of being attracted to other men, but in reality, it is Lester who has frequent thoughts about having affairs with other women. Freud might suggest that Lester is dealing with the anxiety that these unacceptable wishes create by using the defense mechanism of
    a. repression.
    b. sublimation.
    c. projection.
    d. reaction formation.

12. Cal thinks he is very smart and creative, but in college he has gotten mediocre grades and has gotten no praise for his papers or presentations. Carl Rogers might predict Cal will become anxious because of
    a. incongruence.
    b. the elimination of conditions of worth.
    c. self-actualization.
    d. high self-efficacy.

13. Dr. Geltic believes personalities are made, not born. That is, a specific personality is the result of conditioning and an interpretation of how the world works. Dr. Geltic's view is most similar to that of
    a. psychodynamic theory.
    b. humanistic theory.
    c. neo-Freudian theory.
    d. cognitive-behavioral theory.

14. A humanistic theorist would agree with all of the following except:
    a. Behavior is influenced by the individual's own view of the world.
    b. The environment influences the growth process, but it cannot stop it entirely.
    c. Every person is unique and individual whole.
    d. Behavior is motivated primarily by unconscious, biological urges.

15. Lee is very nervous about her promotion. She's not at all sure she can handle the job. Lee seems to have
    a. an internal locus of control.
    b. an external locus of control.
    c. low self-efficacy.
    d. high self-efficacy.

16. The person-situation debate is important for personality theory because
    a. personality is defined in terms of enduring (consistent) psychological characteristics.
    b. none of the current theories have a component that suggests consistent behavior should occur.
    c. personality theories propose factors that supposedly apply to all people, not just a few.
    d. personality theories are intended to explain individual differences, not behavior common to everyone.

17. May believes business success is determined by how hard people work to be a success. May has
    a. low self-efficacy.
    b. high self-efficacy.
    c. internal locus of control.
    d. external locus of control.

18. The person most likely to be a low self-monitor is
    a. Ben, who thinks he passed the chemistry test because he worked very hard to learn the material.
    b. Lynn, who dresses conservatively at work but dresses in wild outfits when going out socially.
    c. Eva, who is as loud and boisterous when dining at a fancy restaurant as when playing racquetball.
    d. Mort, who is very insecure and tries to please whomever he is with at the moment.

19. Iva sees herself as a mother, a teacher, and a wife. These different views are her
    a. self-schemas.
    b. conditions of worth.
    c. self-efficacy.
    d. congruences.

ANSWERS & EXPLANATIONS

Mastering the Concepts

1. Personality (p. 464)	15. Projective (p. 471)	29. projection (p. 476)	43. humanistic (p. 479)
2. traits (p. 464)	16. TAT (p. 471)	30. opposite (p. 476)	44. interpretation (p. 480)
3. differences (p. 466)	17. psychodynamic (p. 474)	31. sublimation (p. 476)	45. congruent (p. 480)
4. psychometric (p. 466)	18. preconscious (p. 474)	32. erogenous (p.477)	46. positive regard (p. 480)
5. Factor (p. 466)	19. unconscious (p. 474)	33. oral (p. 477)	47. behavioral (p. 484)
6. source (p. 466)	20. dreams (p. 474)	34. anal (p. 477)	48. modeling (p. 485)
7. neuroticism (p. 467)	21. id (p. 474)	35. phallic (p. 477)	49. external (p. 485)
8. Big 5 (p. 467)	22. pleasure (p. 474)	36. Oedipus (p. 477)	50. internal (p. 485)
9. agreeableness (p. 467)	23. superego (p. 474)	37. latency (p. 478)	51. self-efficacy (p. 486)
10. Cardinal (p. 469)	24. idealistic (p. 475)	38. genital (p. 478)	52. consistent (p. 488)
11. Central (p. 469)	25. ego (p. 475)	39. fixation (p. 477)	53. inconsistent (p. 488)
12. Self-report (p. 470)	26. reality (p. 475)	40. inferiority (p. 478)	54. self-monitoring (p. 489)
13. MMPI (p. 470)	27. defense (p. 475)	41. collective (p. 478)	55. life (p. 490)
14. objective (p. 471)	28. repression (p. 475)	42. archetypes (p. 478)	56. genetic (p. 491)

Evaluating Your Progress

Preview & Conceptualizing and Measuring Personality

1. **c**   a, b, & d.   Wrong.   These are Allport's types of traits.
    (p. 466)

2. **a**   b.   Wrong.   This relates to the extroversion trait.
    (p. 468)   c & d.   Wrong.   These relate to the psychoticism trait.

3. **a**   b, c, & d.   Wrong.   These are not the most popular.
    (p. 467)

4. **a**   b. Wrong.   Source traits are Cattell's idea.
    (p. 469)   c. Wrong.   Central traits are "representative" traits.
                d. Wrong.   Cardinal traits are "dominant" traits.

5. **d**   a, b, & c.   Wrong.   Allport used an ideographic (case study) approach, not group data.
    (p. 469)

6. **c**   a, b, & d.   Wrong.   These are self-report inventories; the Rorschach is a projective test.
    (p. 471)

7. **b**   a. Wrong.   The true-false or rating scale limits the possible responses. Projective tests are open-ended.
    (p. 470)   c. Wrong.   The items are specific. Projective tests use ambiguous stimuli.
               d. Wrong.   Self-reports are scored objectively. Projective tests use subjective scoring.

Determining How Personality Develops

1. **a**   b. Wrong.   The conscious mind has active, current thoughts.
    (p. 474)   c. Wrong.   The unconscious contains only inaccessible information.
               d. Wrong.   The collective unconscious is Jung's idea, and it's inaccessible.

2. **a.**   b & d.   Wrong.   These answers describe the id.
    (p. 475)   c.   Wrong.   This answer describes the superego.

3. **d**   a. Wrong.   This is reaction formation. Repression pushes forbidden desires into the unconscious.
    (p. 475)   b. Wrong.   This is sublimation. Repression pushes forbidden desires into the unconscious.
               c. Wrong.   This is projection. Repression pushes forbidden desires into the unconscious.

4. **b**   a, c, & d.   Wrong.   The correct order is oral, anal, phallic, latency, genital.
    (p. 477)

5. **a**   b, c, & d.   Wrong.   Freud proposed psychosexual stages, based on the part of the body from which
    (p. 477)   sexual pleasure is derived at a particular time.

6. **b**   a. Wrong.   Incongruence is a term from humanistic personality theories.
    (p. 477)   c. Wrong.   Freud believed all boys face the Oedipal complex during the phallic period.
               d. Wrong.   Failure to satisfy the needs of a psychosexual stage results in fixation, not a strong superego.

7. **d**   a. Wrong.   Key here is the feeling about luck vs. effort (locus of control), not competency.
    (p. 485)   b. Wrong.   Internal locus of control would emphasize the importance of one's own effort, not luck.
               c. Wrong.   Key here is luck vs. effort (locus of control), not others' expectations.

8. **a**   b, c, & d.   Wrong.   These are all true, but Freud's theory has *lost* influence.
    (p. 479)

9. **b**   a. Wrong.   This approach stresses learning and thought. Humanistic theory stresses growth.
    (p. 479)   c. Wrong.   This approach stresses observational learning. Humanistic theory stresses growth.
               d. Wrong.   Freud's theory takes a very negative, deterministic view. Humanistic theory stresses growth.

10. **c**   a. Wrong.   This is a Freudian concept, not humanistic.
    (p. 480)   b. Wrong.   This describes conditional love, which is not healthy.
               d. Wrong.   Conditions of worth lead to an incongruent self-concept, an unhealthy situation.

11. **c**   a & d.   Wrong.   These are stressed in humanistic theories.
    (p. 484)   b.   Wrong.   This is a Freudian view.

1. **a**   b.   Wrong.   Mischel didn't address consistency within a situation. That's Hartshorne & May.
    (p. 488)   c & d.   Wrong.   Mischel didn't address genetic factors. He found inconsistent behavior across situations

2. **a**   b.   Wrong.   Low self-monitors do not alter their behavior to fit a situation.
    (p. 489)   c & d.   Wrong.   Locus of control is the perceived source of control, not behavioral consistency.

3. **c**   a & b.   Wrong.   Life tasks don't influence these personality styles.
    (p. 490)   d.   Wrong.   Life tasks don't involve one's perception of what is expected of them by others.

4. **c**   a. Wrong.   Fraternal twins reared apart were less similar than fraternal twins reared together.
    (p. 492)   b. Wrong.   Identical twins reared apart were more similar than fraternals reared together.
               d. Wrong.   For some traits at least, identical twins were no less similar if raised apart.

MAKING FINAL PREPARATIONS

Short Essay Questions

1. Cattell's source traits are 16 trait dimensions that account for individual differences in behavior. Eysenck, using a different version of factor analysis found 3 superfactors (neuroticism, psychoticism, and extroversion) that he felt described the basics of personality. Source traits provide a finer analysis than do superfactors. (pp. 466-467)

2. Projective tests do not constrain the possible answers and often involve ambiguous stimuli, allowing the unconscious to project its contents onto the answer. Interpretation of responses is partly subjective. Self-report inventories ask the individual to rate themselves. Questions are direct and involve limited response options (true-false, etc.). Scoring is objective, but subjects may bias their answers to look good. (pp. 470-472)

3. Freud felt that children in the phallic stage had unconscious sexual desires for the opposite sex parent. This causes anxiety known as the Oedipus complex for boys and the Electra complex for girls. Failure to resolve this conflict results in sexual problems in adulthood. (pp. 477-478)

4. The psychodynamic view is based on negative, animalistic biological urges, conflicts, and anxiety. Unconscious sexuality and aggression battle the need to be moral. The humanistic view is a positive view of people that stresses their innate goodness, control over their behavior, self-awareness, and potential for growth. In this view, people strive to achieve their full potential. (p. 479)

5. An instrumental conditioning view of personality would suggest that Ron often was reinforced when quiet in the past. He learned that the consequences of being quiet is reinforcement, so he continued his quiet ways. (p. 484)

6. The cognitive-behavioral approach has been criticized as being insufficient. By focusing on what is learned about particular situations, this approach ignores the person as a whole. Also, biological influences are neglected. (p. 487)

7. Psychologists solve the debate by assuming that both the person and the situation must be considered because people interact with situations. Current conditions will influence behavioral traits, causing some traits to appear in one context and not in others. Also, some situations can force modification of behavior. (p. 491)

Matching

Multiple Choice Pretest 1

1. **b**
    (p. 470)
    a. Wrong. The Rorschach is a projective test, not a personality inventory.
    c. Wrong. The MMPI is used to diagnose disorders, not normal personality traits.
    d. Wrong. The NEO-PI-R measures the Big 5.

2. **a**
    (p. 468)
    b Wrong. This is one of Eysenck's 3 superfactors, not one of the Big 5.
    c. Wrong. This is an MMPI scale, not one of the Big 5.
    d. Wrong. This is one of Cattell's 16 factors.

3. **d**
    (p. 469)
    a. Wrong. Allport's cardinal traits are single traits that dominate all of a person's behavior.
    b. Wrong. Source traits are Cattell's 16 personality traits.
    c. Wrong. Allport's secondary traits are noticeable only occasionally.

4. **d**
    (p. 471)
    a. Wrong. This is not a test; it's a trait. Tests using unstructured answers are projective tests.
    b & c. Wrong. Self-report inventories do not allow unstructured responses like projective tests.

5. **a**
    (p. 471)
    b. Wrong. Self-report tests are objective, often scored by computer. Projective test scoring is subjective.
    c. Wrong. Inter-scorer differences is a problem of projective tests.
    d. Wrong. Self-report tests limit responses (e.g., true/false). Projective tests are open-ended.

6. **b**
    (p. 474)
    a. Wrong. Hidden conflicts are kept in the unconscious mind.
    c. Wrong. The superego defines and strives for ideal behavior.
    d. Wrong. Reaction formation is a defense mechanism, not a storehouse for conflicts.

7. **b**
    (p. 476)
    a. Wrong. Nothing is being forgotten/repressed. Key here is the socially acceptable outlet for his urges.
    c. Wrong. There is no opposite behavior. Key here is the socially acceptable outlet for his urges.
    d. Wrong. There is no transfer of his urges. Key here is the socially acceptable outlet for his urges.

8. **c**
    (p. 474)
    a. Wrong. The superego is acquired from experience.
    b. Wrong. Only the id operates totally in the unconscious.
    d. Wrong. The id requires immediate gratification.

9. **b**
    (p. 477)
    a. Wrong. Oral fixations involve oral activities (eating, smoking...), not issues of order or disorder.
    c. Wrong. A phallic fixation would involve sexual relationships or sexual orientation, not being a slob.
    d. Wrong. A fixation in latency might involve a disinterest in sex, not issues of order or disorder.

10. **c**
    (p. 478)
    a. Wrong. The phallic stage runs from about age 3 to 5.
    b. Wrong. The genital stage runs from puberty to adulthood.
    d. Wrong. The anal stage runs from the second year of life to about age 3.

11. **c**
    (p. 478)
    a. Wrong. This is Horney's view. Adler stressed overcoming inferiority.
    b. Wrong. This is Roger's humanistic view. Adler stressed overcoming inferiority.
    d. Wrong. This is a social learning view. Adler stressed overcoming inferiority.

12. **d**   a. Wrong.   Freud proposed the Oedipus complex for men, not women.
(p. 478)   b. Wrong.   This is not one of Freud's views. Horney took issue with Freud's concept of penis envy.
            c. Wrong.   Freud didn't propose the inferiority complex; Horney disliked his concept of penis envy.

13. **d**   a & b.   Wrong.   These are not needs; they inhibit growth.
(p. 480)   c.   Wrong.   This a Freudian concept, not a needed condition in Rogers' theory.

14. **b**   a & c.   Wrong.   These are accurate data, but they support an environmental component.
(p. 492)   d.   Wrong.   These are inaccurate data, but they would support an environmental component

15. **b**   a. Wrong.   Self-actualization involves fulfilling a potential, associated with positive behavior.
(p. 481)   c. Wrong.   This is a Freudian concept, not something Maslow would consider.
            d. Wrong.   Peak experiences relate to self-actualization and the associated positive behavior.

16. **a**   b, c, & d.   Wrong.   These are all points of criticism. Personal control is widely favored.
(p. 483)

17. **a**   b. Wrong.   This is a Freudian view. Social learning theory stresses observational learning.
(p. 485)   c. Wrong.   This is a humanistic view. Social learning theory stresses observational learning.
            d. Wrong.   This is a more cognitive view. Social learning theory stresses observational learning.

18. **c**   a. Wrong.   Self-efficacy is the belief a person holds about their own ability to perform a task.
(p. 487)   b. Wrong.   Self-actualization is the ingrained desire to reach one's true potential.
            d. Wrong.   Conditions of worth are the expectations that people believe others place on them.

19. **a**   b & c.   Wrong.   Dishonesty is likely to reoccur in similar situations, but not in different situations.
(p. 489)   d.   Wrong.   Dishonesty is likely to reoccur in similar situations.

20. **d**   a & c.   Wrong.   Life tasks pertain to behavioral consistency.
(p. 490)   b.   Wrong.   Self-monitoring and life tasks affect consistency, but don't explain self-monitoring.

Multiple Choice Pretest 2

1. **c**   a. Wrong.   Cattell proposed source traits.
(p. 469)   b. Wrong.   Central traits are representative of most behavior; Peter's trait is more restricted.
            d. Wrong.   Cardinal traits are very dominant; Peter's trait is very restricted.

2. **b**   a, c, & d.   Wrong.   These are criticisms of projective tests (Rorschach), not self-report inventories.
(p. 472)

3. **d**   a. Wrong.   Extroversion relates to sociability.
(p. 468)   b. Wrong.   Neuroticism relates to moodiness and irritability.
            c. Wrong.   This is the Big 5 trait, not Eysenck's, showing dependability, productivity, etc.

4. **c**   a. Wrong.   A person high in extroversion is talkative, sociable, fun-loving and affectionate.
(p. 468)   b. Wrong.   A person high in neuroticism is moody, fed up, and irritable.
            d. Wrong.   A person high in conscientiousness is ethical, dependable, productive, and purposeful.

5. **b**   a. Wrong.   Sex bias is not an issue for these approaches.
(p. 468)   c. Wrong.   The Big 5 did come from factor analysis. Allport used an ideographic approach.
            d. Wrong.   The most fine-tuned description is Cattell's 16 factor approach.

6. **a**   b, c, & d.   Wrong.   The 16 PF and NEO-PI-R are used for describing *normal* personality.
   (p. 471)

7. **c**   a.   Wrong.   Sublimation channels behavior in socially appropriate forms.
   (p. 479)   b.   Wrong.   Projection involves transferring one's own problems to someone else.
            d.   Wrong.   The superego demands behavior follow moral rules be socially appropriate.

8. **d**   a, b, & c.   Wrong.   Roy is experiencing the Oedipus complex, a hallmark of the phallic stage,
   (p. 477)   involving children ages 3-5.

9. **d**   a.   Wrong.   One's personal traumas are placed in the personal unconscious.
   (p. 478)   b.   Wrong.   The collective unconscious contains symbols passed on through the generations.
            c.   Wrong.   Adler stressed inferiority/superiority, not Jung.

10. **d**   a, b, & c.   Wrong.   These are all well-accepted. His views of sexuality are not.
    (p. 479)

11. **c**   a.   Wrong.   He's attributing (projecting) his feelings to someone else, not "forgetting" them.
    (p. 476)   b.   Wrong.   He's attributing his feelings to his wife, not channeling them to acceptable forms.
             d.   Wrong.   He's attributing (projecting) his feelings to his wife, not acting in an opposite way to them.

12. **a**   b, c, & d.   Wrong.   These are good situations. Key here is the incongruence between his self-concept
    (p. 480)   and his experiences.

13 **d**   a, b, & c.   Wrong.   These theories all emphasize inborn tendencies, not conditioning and
    (p. 484)   interpretation.

14. **d**   a, b, & c.   Wrong.   These are all characteristic of the humanistic view of behavior. The view that
    (p. 480)   behavior is motivated by unconscious urges is a Freudian view.

15. **c**   a & b.   Wrong.   Lee's concern is about her ability, not whether her efforts make a difference.
    (p. 486)   d.   Wrong.   High self-efficacy involves high confidence in one's ability to do the job.

16. **a**   b.   Wrong.   Cognitive-behavioral theories tend to emphasize the situation, but most theories assume
    (p. 488)   some general tendencies would be present---the person side of the debate.
             c.   Wrong.   The debate questions behavioral consistency across situations, not across people.
             d.   Wrong.   The debate questions consistency across situations, not across people.

17. **c**   a & b.   Wrong.   Nothing is said about how May feels about her own personal chance for success.
    (p. 485)   d.   Wrong.   An external locus of control focuses on luck or external factors, not personal effort.

18. **c**   a.   Wrong.   Ben has an internal locus of control, but we can't tell about self-monitoring.
    (p. 489)   b & d.   Wrong.   Lynn and Mort adjust their behavior to fit the situation--high self-monitoring.

19. **a**   b.   Wrong.   Conditions of worth are the expectations that people believe other place on them, not their
    (p. 482)   own views of themselves.
             c.   Wrong.   Self-efficacy is one's feeling of competency or incompetency for the task.
             d.   Wrong.   Congruence is a match between one's self-concept and one's experiences.

LANGUAGE ENHANCEMENT GUIDE

CORE TERMS

In the lectures on this chapter and those that follow, you are likely to hear several related terms that all have to do with way of organizing ideas. First of all, this process of organizing and classifying ideas can be called 'creating a *taxonomy*.' A familiar taxonomy might be the one that you learned in biology class, classifying different organisms into species. To explain complex concepts like personality (or intelligence or development) we construct a *model* -- a tentative description that shows all the parts we know about and how they relate. There are different kinds of models. One kind is a *hierarchy*, a sort of pyramid or stair-step which has the most basic element at the bottom, and climbs to the more rare or special elements. Maslow's hierarchy works this way. So does a hierarchy of people in a business, or a school. A second common kind of model is a *matrix*. A matrix is a set of boxes arranged in rows and columns -- you might call it a chart. The matrix has a vertical *axis* and a horizontal *axis*, and it allows you to neatly classify things in relation to one another; you just sort them into the cell to which they belong. Imagine a chart that has 'height' along one side and 'weight' along the bottom. You could put each of your friends into a box between those lines, depending upon their height and weight. The plural of axis is a*xes,* and they are also sometimes called *dimensions.*

By the way, using models is a terrific way to study. Sometimes the models are already drawn for you, in the illustrations in the book. That's almost a shame, because it is so helpful to draw them for yourself. To check whether you really understand a concept in the book, you might want to try to reproduce a model that has been described and drawn for you -- such as Freud's model of the personality, or Maslow's hierarchy of needs. How well you do at filling in the various parts will show you exactly what you know well, and where you need to do a little more studying. Try it!

IDIOMS

464	strict sensibilities	very strong sense of what is proper
464	smoking ebullition	boiling activity
464	thesis	main idea
464	seem like a given	seem obvious
466	brooding	worrying, especially for a long time without much action
466	an opposing pole	an opposite
471	fit the bill	be ideal for a position; be appropriate
471	a testament to	provide evidence for; tell about; support
474	manifest	open, obvious, visible
474	latent	hidden, underneath, to be revealed

475	rears its ugly head	shows itself
475	dark recesses	back corners; hidden places
476	harboring	keeping, holding
476	anti-Semite	one who hates Jews
477	cauldron	big pot
478	coining	making for the first time
478	intellectual heir	someone who will carry on one's ideas
482	the nineteenth century	the 1800s
483	social conditions of worth	messages from those around you about what is good or bad about you
488	strikes at the core of	gets at the most important part of
489	rock the foundation of	disturb the most basic assumptions of
489	chameleon-like	able to change one's appearance instantly; able to change one's behavior to fit in or meet expectations (refers to a lizard that can change its body color for camouflage)

WORD PARTS

Here are some words that are made up of word parts, and that you can find in this chapter. After you've looked at these, you can look for others in the chapter that use the same word parts (they are there, but YOU have to find them!)

WORD	WORD PART IT USES	MEANING
psychodynamic	psych = mind dyna, dyno = power	the actions of the mind; that which powers the mind
controversial	contra, contro = against vers, vert = to turn	a dispute; raising arguments against
infer	in = in, into fer = bring into, bear, yield	to carry over a truth from one point to another
presumed	pre = before sum = bring together, add, take	to take for granted; assume to be true

intermediate	inter = between med = middle	being or happening in the middle between two ends
irrational	ir, il, im, in = not rat, ratio = thought	unreasonable, illogical
proposed	pro = before, forth pos = to put	to suggest, put forward
erogenous	ero = sexual love gen = birth, race, kind, origin	coming from sexual love
retention	re = again, back tent, tain = to hold	to hold back
contradict	contra = against dict = to say	to say the opposite as another says
constrain	con = together strain = to bind	to limit freedom, confine

Knowing the word parts listed above, you can also create the following words. You can get an idea of their meanings from the word parts they use. You fill in the blanks!

psychogenic	psych + gen	_____
restrain	_____ + _____	to hold back, to prevent from further movement
prefer	pre + fer	_____
invert	_____ + _____	to turn over; to change into the opposite direction
interpose	inter + pos	_____
mediate	_____	to stand between, to help opposites connect

CHAPTER 13: SOCIAL PSYCHOLOGY

ESTABLISHING LEARNING OBJECTIVES

Use these learning objectives as a preview of the chapter, a guide for active reading, and to evaluate your mastery of the material. Review the relevant objectives as you begin and end your reading of each major section of the chapter.

After studying this chapter you should be able to:

I. Solve the adaptive problem of social cognition, interpreting the behavior of others.
   A. Discuss how physical attractiveness and social schemas influence our impressions of others.
   B. Explain stereotypes and discuss their role in producing and maintaining prejudice.
      1. Describe self-fulfilling prophecy, and discuss how it can influence behavior.
      2. Define and discuss prejudice.
   C. Discuss how we attribute causality to the behavior of others, listing the biases and errors that we show.
      1. Define attribution, and describe the covariation model of attribution.
         a. Explain the role of consistency, distinctiveness, and consensus in attribution.
      2. Compare internal and external attributions, and describe when each is most likely to occur.
         a. Describe the fundamental attribution error and the self-serving bias.
   D. Define attitude and discuss how attitudes are formed and changed.
      1. Describe the cognitive, affective, and behavioral components of attitudes.
      2. Explain how exposure, conditioning, and observational learning influence attitudes.
      3. Describe the central route and the peripheral route to persuasion.
      4. Define cognitive dissonance, and discuss the research on its effect on attitudes.
      5. Describe the self-perception theory of the relationship between behavior and attitude.

II. Solve the adaptive problem of how social influence affects behavior.
   A. Define and discuss social facilitation and interference.
   B. Describe the bystander effect, and the concept of diffusion of responsibility.
   C. Discuss how behavior changes when we're in a group setting, including the concepts of social loafing, deindividuation, and conformity.
      1. Describe Asch's research on conformity, and discuss the factors that increase conformity.
      2. Describe cross-cultural differences in attitudes about the individual versus the group.
   D. Discuss group decision-making, including group polarization and groupthink.
   E. Describe the Milgram experiment and explain what it indicates about the power of authority.

III. Solve the adaptive problem of establishing relations with others.
   A. Discuss the factors that influence our perception of facial attractiveness.
   B. Explain how proximity, similarity, and reciprocity influence liking and loving.
   C. Define the components of romantic love and discuss the triangular theory of love.

MASTERING THE MATERIAL

Preview & Interpreting the Behavior of Others: Social Cognition (pp. 500-515)

Mastering the Vocabulary. Define or explain each of the following terms. To check your answers, consult the text pages listed.

1. social psychology (p. 500)

2. social cognition (p. 502)

3. social schema (p. 503)

4. stereotypes (p. 503)

5. self-fulfilling prophecy (p. 504)

6. prejudice (p. 505)

7. attributions (p. 506)

8. external attribution (p. 507)

9. internal attribution (p. 507)

10. fundamental attribution error (p. 507)

11. self-serving bias (p. 509)

12. attitude (p. 509)

13. elaboration likelihood model (p. 511)

14. source characteristics (p. 512)

15. cognitive dissonance (p. 513)

16. self-perception theory (p. 514)

Mastering the Concepts. Fill in the blanks to create a summary of this section. Answers are on page 313.

_____(1) psychology is the study of how people perceive, influence and relate to other people. Three adaptive problems are discussed: How do people interpret the behavior of others? How do people behave in the presence of others? How do people establish relations with other people?

Social _____(2) is the study of how people use cognitive processes to understand other people and themselves. Impressions of other people are influenced by that person's physical appearance and the observer's _____(3) about the person. Expectations are based on _____(4), knowledge structures about social experiences, and influence action.

_____(5) are schemas about the traits and behavior of people that belong to a group, especially groups based on race, gender, or _____(6). Stereotypes cause self-fulfilling _____(7) effects in which expectations lead to behaviors which causes the person to behave in ways matching the expectations. Stereotypes can be adaptive heuristics, but they can lead to rigid interpretations and an emphasis on _____(8) between, rather than within, groups. They increase the likelihood of prejudice and discrimination. Prejudice is reduced with repeated, _____(9) social interactions with representative individuals from the group.

According to Kelly's covariation model, inferences about the cause of a behavior, _____(10), are based on events occurring with a behavior, and the consistency, distinctiveness, and _____(11) of the relationship. _____(12), or situational, attributions are likely if these factors are strong. If consistency is high, but the others are low, an _____(13), trait-based, attribution is made. The _____(14) attribution error is a bias to make internal attributions about a someone else's behavior. The _____(15) bias is the tendency to make internal attributions about one's successes, but external ones about failures. Attribution biases allow quick decisions but possibly inaccurate decisions.

_____(16), beliefs held about something, have three parts: a _____(17) part involving knowledge; an _____(18) part involving feelings; and a _____(19) part involving a predisposition to act. Attitudes guide behavior, influence perceptions, and serve a defensive function. Attitudes develop through mere _____(20), classical and instrumental conditioning, and _____(21) learning.

The elaboration likelihood model of attitude change or _____(22) states change can occur through a _____(23) route where the content of a persuasive message is processed, or through a peripheral route where superficial cues are influential and the message is not processed directly. In peripheral processing _____(24) characteristics and heuristics are important influences. Festinger's cognitive _____(25) theory states behavior inconsistent with attitude creates _____(26) that the person seeks to reduce, usually by changing the attitude. People asked to lie changed their attitudes more if paid little to lie than if paid a lot. Bem's self-perception theory states people use their _____(27) to infer their _____(28). The _____(29) technique shows that people who behave in small ways implying an attitude later engage in larger behaviors implying the attitude because self-perception is triggered. Low balling works similarly.

Evaluating Your Progress. Select the one best response. Answers are on page 313. If you make any errors, reread the relevant material before proceeding.

1. Dan's first impression of his new roommate will be most strongly influenced by his roommate's
    a. name.
    b. apparent intelligence.
    c. physical appearance.
    d. first words.

2. When one's expectations about a person actually cause that person to behave in the expected way,
    a. a self-fulfilling prophecy effect has occurred.
    b. a social schema has been violated.
    c. a fundamental attribution error has been made.
    d. cognitive dissonance has developed.

3. The most common types of stereotypes are based on race, age, and
    a. gender.
    b. intelligence.
    c. hair color.
    d. occupation.

4. Kelly's covariation model of attribution states that attributions are influenced by
    a. originality, familiarity, and personality.
    b. intelligence, mood, and age.
    c. race, age, and gender.
    d. consensus, distinctiveness, consistency.

5. If everyone that ate the mushrooms got sick, the relationship has
    a. high distinctiveness.
    b. high consistency.
    c. high consensus.
    d. low consistency.

6. When the surgeon's patient died, the intern decided the surgeon was incompetent. This illustrates
   a. an internal attribution.
   b. an external attribution.
   c. self-serving bias.
   d. cognitive dissonance.

7. The fundamental attribution error is the tendency to make
   a. internal attributions about oneself for good outcomes, and external attributions for bad outcomes.
   b. external attributions about oneself for bad outcomes, and external attributions for bad outcomes.
   c. external attributions about other people's behavior more readily than external attributions.
   d. internal attributions about other people's behavior more readily than external attributions.

8. When people explain their successes in terms of their personal characteristics, but explain their failures in terms of environmental events or situations, they are demonstrating
   a. the fundamental attribution error.
   b. the self-serving bias.
   c. self-perception theory.
   d. a self-fulfilling prophecy effect.

9. The affective component of an attitude is
   a. the person's feelings about the object of the attitude.
   b. the person's thoughts about the object of the attitude.
   c. the person's strength of commitment to the object of the attitude.
   d. the person's behavioral predispositions concerning the object of the attitude.

10. An example of mere exposure as a means of attitude formation is
    a. liking a car because the music in the ads makes you feel happy.
    b. liking a brand of shoes because an athlete endorses them.
    c. liking a song after hearing it several times.
    d. liking a charity because it wrote you a nice thank you letter.

11. The central route of persuasion involves
    a. focusing attention on processing the persuasive message.
    b. superficial cues in the persuasive message that are not processed directly.
    c. basing attitudes on emotional responses to an ad or persuasive message.
    d. creating a state of tension as a result of mismatched attitudes and behavior.

12. Attitudes shift due to the tension produced by attitudes and behaviors that do not match, according to
    a. the elaboration likelihood theory.
    b. the cognitive dissonance theory.
    c. the self-perception theory.
    d. the triangular theory.

13. Festinger paid some subjects $1 and some $20 to lie about a boring task. Others were not asked to lie. Festinger found the greatest positive shift in attitudes about the task occurred in the subjects
    a. paid $20 to lie.
    b. paid $1 to lie.
    c. paid $20 or $1 (equal shift, but greater than non-liars).
    d. not asked to lie.

14. The alternative to cognitive dissonance theory is Bem's self-perception theory, which states
    a. behaviors and attitudes that don't match create a tension that the person seeks to reduce.
    b. people give more emphasis to internal factors when explaining someone else's behavior.
    c. people examine their behavior and infer their attitudes based on those behaviors.
    d. attitudes form either from evaluation of the message or based on superficial cues in the message.

Behaving in the Presence of Others: Social Influence (pp. 516-527)

Mastering the Vocabulary. Define or explain each of the following terms. To check your answers, consult the text pages listed.

1. social influence (p. 516)

2. social facilitation (p. 516)

3. social interference (p. 517)

4. altruism (p. 517)

5. bystander effect (p. 518)

6. diffusion of responsibility (p. 519)

7. social loafing (p. 519)

8. deindividuation (p. 520)

9. conformity (p. 520)

10. in-group (p. 521)

11. group polarization (p. 522)

12. groupthink (p. 523)

13. obedience (p. 525)

Mastering the Concepts. Fill in the blanks to create a summary of this section. Answers are on page 313.

Social _____(30) involves how behavior is affected by the presence of others. Audiences enhance performance, social _____(31), or disrupt performance, social _____(32). Task difficulty influences whether performance improves or declines; difficult or new tasks are disrupted because the audience increases arousal.

In the _____(33) effect the presence of others inhibits helping behavior because of _____(34) of responsibility. Helping increases if the person has watched others be helpful. Diffusion of responsibility can explain _____(35), working less hard when in a group, and might influence _____(36), a depersonalization that can lead to destructive behavior.

People in groups often show _____(37), behavior that shifts toward the group norm. Asch's research shows that people will give a wrong answer if everyone else does so, especially if the group contains 3-5 people for whom the person has respect or a sense of identification, as in an _____(38). In _____(39) social influence, conformity is an attempt to get approval or avoid rejection, but in _____(40) social influence, the group is a source of information. Because one's sense of self varies across cultures, attitudes about conformity might also vary.

Group decisions differ from those of individuals. With time, a group decision grows more extreme, the group _____(41) effect. Close-knit groups make bad decisions because they value obtaining a consensus more than considering all the facts, a situation known as _____(42).

As shown by Milgram's research, orders given by an authority often lead to _____(43). Sixty-five percent of Milgram's subjects followed the experimenter's orders and gave what they thought were severe shocks to another person. Obedience is reduced when the prestige of the setting or the authority is low, and when the authority figure _____(44) the room. This study has been criticized as _____(45).

Evaluating Your Progress. Select the one best response. Answers are on page 314. If you make any errors, reread the relevant material before you proceed.

1. Zajonc suggests that social facilitation and interference effects occur because an audience
   a. decreases arousal and causes the most recent response to occur.
   b. decreases arousal and causes the most dominant response to occur.
   c. increases arousal and causes the most recent response to occur.
   d. increases arousal and causes the most dominant response to occur.

2. In the bystander effect
   a. performance of a task improves when there are a large number of observers.
   b. people are reluctant to help someone if a large number of observers are present.
   c. confidence in a decision becomes stronger if the decision is made in front of an audience.
   d. one person in a group task doesn't do his or her fair share of the work.

3. Decisions about the invasion of Cuba and the launching of the Challenger space shuttle were disastrous because the group was most concerned about reaching a consensus and ignored dissenting views and information. This close-mindedness and overestimation of the uniformity of opinion is known as
   a. group polarization.
   b. groupthink.
   c. social loafing.
   d. informational social influence.

4. The bystander effect is explained in terms of
   a. increased arousal created by the presence of other people.
   b. greater obedience that is created by being a bystander in a group.
   c. the feeling that responsibility is shared by the other people present.
   d. the feeling that one shares certain characteristics with other members of a group.

5. Social psychologists explain social loafing in terms of
   a. increased arousal created by the presence of other people.
   b. greater obedience that is created by being in a group.
   c. the feeling that responsibility for the task is shared by the other people present.
   d. the feeling that one shares certain characteristics with other members of a group.

6. An individual will be most likely to conform if
   a. the group contains 10 people or more, rather than 4 or 5 people.
   b. the individual shares common features with the group members.
   c. at least one person in the group does not conform.
   d. the group is made up of people the person doesn't respect.

7. Normative social influence stimulates conformity based on
   a. the desire to receive approval from others and to avoid rejection.
   b. the information the group can give about an unfamiliar situation.
   c. the power exerted by an authority figure.
   d. the perception that group members share the responsibility for a decision.

8. Group polarization involves the tendency
   a. to act like the other members of the group because they have important information.
   b. for a group decision to grow more extreme with increasing time.
   c. for a group to emphasize reaching a consensus rather than considering dissenting views.
   d. to separate into leaders and loafers in groups working on a specific project.

9. In Milgram's experiment on obedience, 65% of the people
   a. refused to begin the experiment after hearing they would have to shock someone.
   b. began the experiment, but quit when then were faced with actually having to shock someone.
   c. participated in most of the experiment, but quit when the "learner" started screaming with pain.
   d. participated in the entire experiment, giving the highest level of shocks to the "learner."

Establishing Relations with Others (pp. 528-535)

Mastering the Vocabulary. Define or explain each of the following terms. To check your answers, consult the text pages listed.

1. reciprocity (p. 533)

2. passionate love (p. 534)

3. companionate love (p. 534)

Mastering the Concepts. Fill in the blanks to create a summary of this section. Answers are on page 313.

Physical appearance influences social relations. An evolutionary view of attractiveness predicts attractiveness should be related to _____(46) capacity (youth and health) and be similar across cultures. Attractive faces tend to be _____(47) or prototypical faces. Although cross-cultural similarities in attractiveness exist, culture-specific attitudes are important also.

Primary determinants of relationships include _____(48), the physical distance between the people's homes, _____(49), the number of shared interests or characteristics, and _____(50), a tendency to return the feelings directed toward a person. Physical nearness encourages relationships through mere exposure or a sense of connectedness developing from repeated contact. Similarity influences relationships by _____(51) the person's beliefs, because people dislike others that do not share their views, or because personal characteristics limit the range of choices.

Love can be _____(52) love, which is an intense desire, or _____(53) love, which is a less intense, but a more enduring feeling of trust and warmth. Sternberg's _____(54) theory of love classifies love based on three dimensions: passion or erotic attraction, _____(55) or the sharing of feelings, and _____(56) to remaining in the relationship. Passion may develop first, but often fades. Commitment and intimacy develop later, but are more likely to endure.

Evaluating Your Progress. Select the one best response. Answers are on page 315. If you make any errors, reread the relevant material before proceeding.

1. The most accurate summary of research on facial attractiveness is:
   a. Universal, innate factors entirely determine what types of faces are most attractive.
   b. Culture factors entirely determine what types of faces are most attractive.
   c. Both universal and culturally-specific factors determine what faces are most attractive.
   d. Attractiveness is entirely an individual matter, there is little consistency in choices.

2.	Interpersonal attraction is primarily determined by
	a.	proximity, similarity, and reciprocity.
	b.	income, proximity and attractiveness.
	c.	reciprocity, education, and attractiveness.
	d.	income, education, and attractiveness.

3.	Ralph Waldo Emerson wrote in *Friendship*, "To have a friend, you must be a friend." He seems to be referring to the determinant of love and friendship that social psychologists call
	a.	similarity.
	b.	proximity.
	c.	reciprocity.
	d.	conformity.

4.	The type of love that is most likely to lead to self-disclosure and enduring feelings of trust and warmth is
	a.	passionate love.
	b.	companionate love.
	c.	empty love.
	d.	infatuated love.

5.	Sternberg's triangular view of love is based on
	a.	proximity, similarity, and reciprocity.
	b.	growth, duration, and arousal.
	c.	loving, liking, and desiring.
	d.	passion, intimacy, and commitment.

MAKING FINAL PREPARATIONS

Complete these sections without consulting your book or notes. For a more accurate estimate of how well you know this material, wait at least a day or two after studying the chapter before working on the questions. Some material you "know" immediately after working with the chapter will be quickly forgotten. Immediate tests will overestimate what you know well.

Short Essay Questions. Write a brief answer to each question. Sample answers are on page 315.

1.	Explain the adaptive value of stereotypes and their disadvantages.

2.	Compare Festinger's cognitive dissonance theory and Bem's self-perception theory.

3.	Compare social facilitation and social interference and explain why each occurs.

4.	Describe the bystander effect and give one primary explanation.

5. Explain why similarity might promote friendship.

6. Compare passionate and companionate love.

Matching. Select the correct definition or description for each item. Answers are on page 316.

_____	1. reciprocity	**a.**	proposes central & peripheral route to attitude
_____	2. social interference	**b.**	beliefs about traits of a particular group
_____	3. elaboration likelihood model	**c.**	enhanced performance in the presence of others
_____	4. obedience	**d.**	tendency to return feeling shown toward oneself
_____	5. social cognition	**e.**	positive or negative evaluation about something
_____	6. Daryl Bem	**f.**	expectation leads to behavior matching expectation
_____	7. social facilitation	**g.**	attribution by consistency, distinctiveness, consensus
_____	8. Solomon Asch	**h.**	proposed self-perception theory of attribution
_____	9. foot-in-the-door technique	**i.**	compliance in response to an authority
_____	10. Stanley Milgram	**j.**	get attitude shift by inducing attitude-consistent act
_____	11. stereotypes	**k.**	impaired performance in the presence of others
_____	12. self-fulfilling prophecy	**l.**	knowledge structures relating to social experiences
_____	13. Leon Festinger	**m.**	conducted obedience experiments
_____	14. social schemas	**n.**	proposed theory of cognitive dissonance
_____	15. attitude	**o.**	conducted conformity experiments
_____	16. covariation model	**p.**	study of how thoughts help people understand people

Multiple Choice Pretest 1. Select the one best response. Answers are on page 316.

1. An evolutionary approach to attractiveness would suggest people are attracted to people
   a. who look like them (share the same gene pool).
   b. who are youthful and healthy looking.
   c. who have unusual features.
   d. who fit their cultural definition of beauty.

2. Research indicates that when people first see an attractive person, they tend to assume the person is
   a. less intelligent than people with an average appearance.
   b. more self-centered than people with an average appearance.
   c. better adjusted than people with an average appearance.
   d. greater trouble-makers than people with an average appearance.

3. Stereotypes often can cause people to
   a. underestimate differences that exist between groups.
   b. overestimate differences that exist within groups.
   c. make rigid interpretations of people.
   d. make external attributions about a person's behavior.

4. In Kelly's covariation model of attribution, behaviors that occur only in one situation have
   a. high consensus.
   b. high distinctiveness.
   c. low consistency.
   d. low consensus.

5. According to Kelly's covariation model, internal attributions are most likely when there is
   a. low consistency, high consensus, and high distinctiveness.
   b. low consistency, low consensus, and low distinctiveness.
   c. high consistency, high consensus, and high distinctiveness.
   d. high consistency, low consensus, and low distinctiveness.

6. The view that persuasion can involve a central route or a peripheral route is
   a. the cognitive dissonance theory.
   b. the elaboration likelihood model.
   c. the self-perception theory.
   d. the social schema model.

7. Who would experience the most cognitive dissonance, according to Festinger?
   a. Harry, who buys drinks for his friends.
   b. Ron, who drives an ugly car he was given as a gift.
   c. Walter, a vegetarian, who eats chicken at a dinner at his boss' house.
   d. Pete, who smokes cigarettes, knowing they are bad for his health.

8. Social facilitation is most likely to occur when
   a. the task being performed is easy.
   b. the task being performed is moderately difficult.
   c. the task being performed is very difficult.
   d. the task being performed is very difficult and not well practiced.

9. Dee is most likely to get help quickly if she has an accident where there are
   a. 1 or 2 witnesses.
   b. 5-10 witnesses.
   c. 10-20 witnesses.
   d. 20-40 witnesses.

10. The football player, playing injured, dropped the ball on a key play. The coach told the player he dropped the ball because he "didn't have the heart of a winner." The coach's behavior illustrates
    a. the self-serving bias.
    b. a self-fulfilling prophecy.
    c. the fundamental attribution error.
    d. cognitive dissonance.

11. George attributed his success in chemistry to his great intelligence, but when he failed physics it was because the teacher was impossible to understand. George's behavior best demonstrates
    a. the fundamental attribution error.
    b. a self-fulfilling prophecy.
    c. elaboration likelihood.
    d. a self-serving bias.

12. Nancy hates cigarettes. She knows they cause lung disease, and she feels ill when she smells them, so she refuses to sit in any area in which smoking is allowed. The cognitive component of this attitude is
    a. hating the cigarettes.
    b. knowing they cause lung disease.
    c. feeling ill when she smells them.
    d. refusing to sit in a smoking section.

13. Rob barely sings the national anthem when he is in a large group. Rob's behavior is most similar to
    a. the bystander effect.
    b. group polarization.
    c. groupthink.
    d. social loafing.

14. Everyone thinks blue carpet is a great idea except Don, but Don votes for it too. Don is demonstrating
    a. group polarization.
    b. conformity.
    c. obedience.
    d. social facilitation.

15. Ed's conformity is an example of informational social influence if
    a. he is afraid that by acting different he will be rejected.
    b. he questions his own opinion and thinks the group knows more than he does.
    c. he admires the group members and wants them to admire him.
    d. he is responding to the demands of a powerful authority figure.

16. The fraternity president began the meeting by stating that all new pledges should be required to live in the fraternity house for one year and that fees should be increased 25% to raise the money needed for a new game room. The group knew that this move might cause a reduction in the number of people willing to join, but they chose to ignore this and other possible problems and concentrated only on getting a consensus. Their behavior illustrates
    a. informational social influence.
    b. social interference.
    c. group polarization.
    d. groupthink.

17. If Milgram's experiment were repeated today, obedience would be expected to decrease if
    a. an ordinary looking woman was in charge.
    b. the person giving the orders stayed in the room with the "teacher."
    c. the experiment was conducted at a famous research facility.
    d. the authority calmly replied to the "teacher's" concerns about the other person, "Please continue. You have no other choice; you must go on."

18. Rose has just moved to a new city. Her first friends are most likely to be people
    a. who live near her in her apartment building.
    b. she talks with at the grocery store.
    c. who ride the bus with her to work.
    d. she passes on her morning walks.

19. Mike and Carol share an incredibly strong need to be with each other and strong emotional arousal when together. Their relationship is an example of
    a. companionate love.
    b. empty love.
    c. passionate love.
    d. friendship.

Multiple Choice Pretest 2. Select the one best response. Answers are on page 317.

1. Jill had heard that Sue, her freshman "little sister," was unfriendly. As a result, Jill made no effort to be friendly. Hurt by Jill's coldness, Sue wasn't friendly either, confirming Jill's expectations. This illustrates
    a. cognitive dissonance.
    b. social interference.
    c. a self-fulfilling prophecy effect.
    d. the self-serving bias.

2. Erin thinks all fraternity members are heavy-drinking, woman-chasing animals who stay up all night partying rather than studying. Erin's beliefs are an example of
    a. a stereotype.
    b. a fundamental attribution error.
    c. a self-serving bias.
    d. cognitive dissonance.

3. Before deciding Dan's failing grade was due to his lack of knowledge rather than the nature of the test, you asked how his classmates did on the exam. Your decision emphasized
    a. consistency.
    b. consensus.
    c. distinctiveness.
    d. expectation.

4. When Pat was late, Lee decided Pat's tardiness was due to car trouble. Lee's decision is an example of
    a. the fundamental attribution error.
    b. the self-serving bias.
    c. an external attribution.
    d. an internal attribution.

5. According to the fundamental attribution error, Anne will explain her favorite politician's loss by saying,
    a. "He just didn't have the campaign skills necessary to get his ideas across."
    b. "His opponent ran a dirty campaign that turned the voters away from the real issues."
    c. "He didn't have big money behind him, so he couldn't buy the advertising time he needed to win."
    d. "The voters were determined to get rid of all the incumbents, no matter how good they were."

6. If being given a free mug when you buy a particular brand of coffee-maker improves your attitude about that brand, your attitude change was influenced by
    a. mere exposure.
    b. observational learning.
    c. classical conditioning.
    d. instrumental conditioning.

7. Sid is a Indianapolis Pacers basketball fan. He knows the team's win-loss record and the achievements of the individual players. He buys season tickets every year, and gets angry at any one who says they aren't the best. The behavioral component of Sid's attitude is
   a. knowing the team's win-loss record.
   b. knowing the achievements of the individual players.
   c. buying season tickets every year.
   d. getting angry at people who disagree with him.

8. Candidate Smith distributes summaries of his views and accomplishments. Candidate Smith is using
   a. cognitive dissonance as a means of persuasion.
   b. instrumental conditioning as a means of persuasion.
   c. the central route as a means of persuasion.
   d. the peripheral route as a means of persuasion.

9. Kit, a volunteer, and Tom, a paid staff member, are working on Candidate Smith's campaign. Although Candidate Smith has been revealed to have a minor criminal record, both Kit and Tom have continued to work for him. How are Kit's and Tom's attitudes about Candidate Smith likely to have changed, according to cognitive dissonance theory?

   a. both Kit's and Tom's attitudes decreased, but Kit's decreased more.
   b. both Kit's and Tom's attitudes decreased, but Tom's decreased more.
   c. both Kit's and Tom's attitudes decreased an equal amount.
   d. Kit's attitude decreased, but Tom's attitude increased.

10. A House of Representatives committee quickly reached a consensus that some changes, generally minor, needed to be made to the immigration laws. After a lengthy, well-balanced discussion, they produced a quite radical bill that would almost stop immigration. Their decision appears to be an example of
    a. groupthink.
    b. social facilitation.
    c. normative social influence.
    d. group polarization.

11. Georgia just met a woman who is like a twin sister. She likes the same things Georgia likes, she looks a little like Georgia, and she often starts to say the same thing as Georgia. Based on the research on interpersonal relationships, Georgia will probably
    a. feel really creepy about finding someone so similar to her and will avoid her in the future.
    b. very quickly become lasting friends with this person.
    c. become friends for a short while before becoming bored with someone so like her.
    d. become friends for a short while before the small differences cause her to lose interest.

12. Ben realized that every time he had an open elective, he took a psychology class. Based on his observation, Ben has decided he must like psychology. Ben's attitude is best explained by
    a. self-perception theory.
    b. cognitive dissonance theory.
    c. the fundamental attribution error model.
    d. the elaboration likelihood model.

13. A victory rally Fred attended turned into a wild riot by hundreds of students, Fred included. Afterward, Fred said, "It was weird. I didn't feel like me. I just felt like a part of the crowd, and everybody else was tearing up the Quad, so I did too. Fred seems to have experienced
    a. group polarization.
    b. social facilitation.
    c. deindividuation.
    d. reciprocity.

14. Kit saw a boy fall out of the tree in the crowded park, but he was reluctant to help. This is similar to
    a. the group polarization effect.
    b. the self-fulfilling prophecy effect.
    c. the mere presence effect.
    d. the bystander effect.

15. All of Nan's friends ride bikes to school. Nan hates bikes, but she wants her friends' approval, so she starts riding a bike to school. Nan's conformity seems to involve
    a. group polarization.
    b. obedience.
    c. normative social influence.
    d. informational social influence.

16. All of the following should reduce groupthink and group polarization except
    a. having an understanding that these effects can influence even the most intelligent group.
    b. having a very strong, opinionated leader.
    c. assigning one member the job of "devil's advocate" to bring up dissenting information.
    d. delaying any statement of opinion by the leader until late in the discussions.

17. Sal and Carol tell each other their innermost thoughts and feelings. They score high on the dimension of
    a. passion.
    b. commitment.
    c. intimacy.
    d. companionship.

18. Sternberg suggests that
    a. passion is the first dimension to develop, but is unlikely to be maintained.
    b. commitment is the first dimension to develop, but is unlikely to be maintained.
    c. intimacy develops only if passion is also present.
    d. commitment requires both passion and intimacy in order to be maintained.

19. He knew it might cause a fire, but Jacob used the wire the foreman told him to use. Jacob's behavior is best explained in terms of
    a. social loafing.
    b. social interference.
    c. obedience.
    d. normative social influence.

20. Research by Langlois and Roggman found that people tended to rate as most attractive pictures of
    a. people who look similar to themselves.
    b. people who have very distinctive features.
    c. people who were blends of many other people.
    d. people who had asymmetrical faces.

ANSWERS AND EXPLANATIONS

Mastering the Concepts

1. Social (p. 500)
2. cognition (p. 502)
3. expectations (p. 502)
4. social schemas (p. 503)
5. Stereotypes (p. 503)
6. age (p. 504)
7. prophecy (p. 504)
8. differences (p. 505)
9. widespread (p. 506)
10. attributions (p. 506)
11. consensus (p. 507)
12. External (p. 507)
13. internal (p. 507)
14. fundamental (p. 507)

15. self-serving (p. 509)
16. Attitudes (p. 509)
17. cognitive (p. 510)
18. affective (p. 510)
19. behavioral (p. 510)
20. exposure (p. 510)
21. observational (p. 511)
22. persuasion (p. 511)
23. central (p. 511)
24. source (p. 512)
25. dissonance (p. 513)
26. tension (p. 513)
27. behavior (p. 514)
28. attitudes (p. 514)

29. foot-in-the-door (p. 514)
30. influence (p. 516)
31. facilitation (p. 516)
32. interference (p. 517)
33. bystander (p. 518)
34. diffusion (p. 519)
35. social loafing (p. 519)
36. deindividuation (p. 520)
37. conformity (p. 520)
38. in-group (p. 521)
39. normative (p. 522)
40. informational (p. 522)
41. polarization (p. 522)
42. groupthink (p. 523)

43. obedience (p. 525)
44. leaves (p. 527)
45. unethical (p. 527)
46. reproductive (p. 529)
47. average (p. 530)
48. proximity (p. 532)
49. similarity (p. 532)
50. reciprocity (p. 533)
51. validating (p. 532)
52. passionate (p. 534)
53. companionate (p. 534)
54. triangular (p. 534)
55. intimacy (p. 534)
56. commitment (p. 534)

Evaluating Your Progress

Preview & Interpreting the Behavior of Others: Social Cognition

1. **c**   a, b, & d.   Wrong.   First impressions are most strongly influenced by physical appearance.
    (p. 502)

2. **a**   b. Wrong.   Expectations are upheld, not violated.
    (p. 504)   c. Wrong.   The fundamental attribution error is making internal attributions about other's behavior.
               d. Wrong.   Cognitive dissonance is tension produced when attitudes and actions don't match.

3. **a**   b, c, & d.   Wrong.   Although stereotypes can include these, race, age, and gender are most common.
    (p. 504)

4. **d**   a, b, & c.   Wrong.   These are not part of the covariation model.
    (p. 507)

5. **c**   a.   Wrong.   There is no information about whether people get sick only after eating mushrooms.
    (p. 507)   b & d. Wrong.   There is no information about whether the same reaction has occurred before.

6. **a**   b. Wrong.   Incompetence is an internal trait, not an external situation.
    (p. 507)   c. Wrong.   The intern isn't making attributions about himself and gains nothing here.
               d. Wrong.   There is no tension due to a mismatch of attitude and behavior here.

7. **d**   a. Wrong.   This is self-serving bias. Fundamental attribution error involves attributions for others.
    (p. 507)   b. Wrong.   Fundamental attribution error deals with attributions about others, not oneself.
                c. Wrong.   This is the opposite pattern found with fundamental attribution error.

8. **b**   a. Wrong.   Attributions in this question are for people's own behavior, not someone else's.
    (p. 509)   c. Wrong.   Nobody is examining their own behavior to determine what their beliefs are here.
                d. Wrong.   Nobody's expectations are resulting in later behavior that matches their expectations.

9. **a**   b. Wrong.   This answer describes the cognitive component. Affect concerns emotions.
    (p. 510)   c. Wrong.   This is not considered a component of an attitude, and affect concerns emotions.
                d. Wrong.   This answer describes the behavioral component. Affect concerns emotions.

10. **c**   a. Wrong.   This is classical conditioning in action.
    (p. 510)   b. Wrong.   This is a heuristic in action.
                d. Wrong.   This is instrumental conditioning in action.

11. **a**   b & c. Wrong.   These involve the peripheral route of persuasion.
    (p. 511)   d.   Wrong.   This describes cognitive dissonance.

12. **b**   a. Wrong.   Elaboration likelihood proposes central and peripheral routes to persuasion, not tension.
    (p. 513)   c. Wrong.   Self-perception theory states we use behavior to infer our attitudes. Tension isn't involved.
                d. Wrong.   The triangular theory is Sternberg's theory of love.

13. **b**   a, c, & d. Wrong.   Those paid $1 had the greatest shift in attitude.
    (p. 513)

14. **c**   a. Wrong.   This describes the cognitive dissonance theory.
    (p. 514)   b. Wrong.   This describes the fundamental attribution error.
                d. Wrong.   This describes the elaboration likelihood model.

Behaving in the Presence of Others: Social Influence

1. **d**   a, b, & c. Wrong.   Arousal is increased, causing the best learned, dominant response to occur.
    (p. 517)

2. **b**   a. Wrong.   This describes social facilitation.
    (p. 518)   c. Wrong.   This describes the group polarization effect.
                d. Wrong.   This describes social loafing.

3. **b**   a. Wrong.   The decision didn't become more extreme. Key here is the suppression of dissenting views.
    (p. 523)   c. Wrong.   The decision didn't involve some members working less. Key is suppression of dissension.
                d. Wrong.   The decision didn't involve conformity because the group knew more.

4. **c**   a. Wrong.   This is the explanation of social facilitation and social interference.
    (p. 519)   b. Wrong.   Obedience isn't relevant; the person is reluctant to help due to diffusion of responsibility.
                d. Wrong.   This describes an in-group. In the bystander effect the key is diffusion of responsibility.

5. **c**   a. Wrong.   This is the explanation of social interference or social facilitation.
    (p. 519)   b. Wrong.   Obedience is not involved in a person not working as hard in a group.
                d. Wrong.   This describes an in-group feeling, not social loafing.

6. **b**   a. Wrong.   Group sizes above 5 don't increase conformity further, and can decrease it.
    (p. 521)   c. Wrong.   One person dissenting dramatically decreases conformity in others.
               d. Wrong.   Conformity is decreased if the group is not respected.

7. **a**   b. Wrong.   This answer describes informational social influence as a factor in conformity.
    (p. 522)   c. Wrong.   Normative social influence is just being like the group to avoid rejection.
               d. Wrong.   Acting like others (the norm) reduces rejection. Diffusion of responsibility isn't an issue.

8. **b**   a. Wrong.   This describes informational social influence.
    (p. 522)   c. Wrong.   This describes groupthink.
               d. Wrong.   Group polarization involves the nature of group decisions, not social loafing.

9. **d**   a, b, & c.   Wrong.   Most people were distressed, but continued to the highest shock level.
    (p. 527)

Establishing Relations with Others

1. **c**   a. Wrong.   Culture is influential.
    (p. 531)   b. Wrong.   Universal tendencies have been found.
               d. Wrong.   General tendencies have been found.

2. **a**   b, c, & d.   Wrong.   Income, education, and attractiveness are not primary determinants.
    (pp. 532-533)

3. **c**   a, b, & d.   Wrong.   The quote suggests one person must act friendly for another to be friendly--
    (p. 533)   reciprocity.

4. **b**   a.   Wrong.   Passionate love is usually low in commitment and enduring trust and warmth.
    (p. 535)   c & d.   Wrong.   Fatuous and infatuated love are low in intimacy (self-disclosure).

5. **d**   a, b, & c.   Wrong.   The side of the triangle are passion, intimacy, and commitment.
    (p. 534)

MAKING FINAL PREPARATIONS

Short Essay Questions

1. Stereotypes act as "rules of thumb" for how to organize the social world and how to act with new people. Stereotypes can be relatively accurate, although not always. The danger of stereotypes is that they lead to more rigid behavior that emphasizes differences between groups rather than differences within groups. (pp. 503-504)

2. Festinger's cognitive dissonance is a tension created by a mismatch of attitudes and behavior. The person then tries to reduce dissonance, mostly by adjusting the attitude to match the behavior. Bem's theory doesn't involve dissonance. Bem suggests that rather than trying to reconcile existing attitudes and behavior, people determine their attitude on the spot by examining their recent behavior. "If I did this, I must like that." (pp. 512-515)

3. The presence of other people can improve (social facilitation) or impair (social interference) performance. These effects occur due to the increased arousal an audience produces. If the task is easy and well-learned, performance improves because arousal tends to result in the dominant response being made. If the task is difficult or new, the dominant response is not usually desired, leading to impaired performance. (pp. 516-517)

4. The bystander effect is the reluctance to help when other people are present. The primary explanation is that responsibility for helping (or the consequences of not helping) are shared by all present, a diffusion of responsibility. Thus, the person feels less responsible for helping; someone else can help. (pp. 517-519)

5. Similarity might promote friendship because similar views validate our views, which is valued. We might associate with similar people to avoid associating with people who don't agree with us. Physical factors might limit the range of possible mates. Unattractive people might be limited to other unattractive people as companions, and economic or social similarity can restrict exposure to different people. (pp. 532-533)

6. Passionate love involves an intense erotic attraction to, and longing for, another person. It includes intimacy, but commitment is low. Companionate love has less passion, but is high in intimacy and commitment. (pp. 533-534)

Matching

1. d (p. 553)	4. i (p. 525)	7. c (p. 516)	10. m (p. 525)	13. n (p. 512)	16. g (p. 506)
2. k (p. 517)	5. p (p. 502)	8. o (p. 521)	11. b (p. 503)	14. l (p. 503)	
3. a (p. 511)	6. h (p. 514)	9. j (p. 514)	12. f (p. 504)	15. e (p. 509)	

Multiple Choice Pretest 1

1. **b**   a, c, & d.   Wrong.   Evolutionary theory stresses reproductive and protective value.
   (p. 529)

2. **c**   a, b, & d.   Wrong.   Physical attractiveness is associated with positive first impressions.
   (p. 502)

3. **c**   a & b.   Wrong.   These are the opposite of what happens.
   (p. 505)   d.   Wrong.   If anything, stereotypes would discourage attributing a behavior to external events.

4. **b**   a & d.   Wrong.   Consensus involves whether other people show the behavior in the situation.
   (p. 508)   c.   Wrong.   Consistency involves whether the behavior occurs every time the situation is present.

5. **d**   a & b.   Wrong.   These patterns are not strongly associated with a particular attributions.
   (p. 508)   c.   Wrong.   This pattern is associated with external attributions.

6. **b**   a. Wrong.   Cognitive dissonance theory states that attitudes shift to conform to discrepant behavior.
   (p. 511)   c. Wrong.   Self-perception theory states that behavior is used to infer attitudes.
             d. Wrong.   A social schema model concerns the knowledge base that influences social experiences.

7. **d**   a. Wrong.   Harry's doing something nice to people he likes--no dissonance.
   (p. 513)   b. Wrong.   Rod doesn't have to like a free car--little or no dissonance.
             c. Wrong.   Walter can justify eating meat because it's dinner with the boss--no dissonance.

8. **a**   b, c, & d.   Wrong.   Social facilitation is less likely as task difficulty increases.
   (p. 517)

9. **a**   b, c, & d.   Wrong.   Reluctance to help increases as the number of people present increases.
   (p. 518)

10. **c**
(p. 507)
a. Wrong. Self-serving bias has to do with attributions about one's own behavior, not someone else's.
b. Wrong. The coach is making an attribution, not letting expectations affect his behavior.
d. Wrong. The coach is making an attribution. There is no mismatch of belief and behavior.

11. **d**
(p. 509)
a. Wrong. George's attributions concern his own behavior, not someone else's behavior.
b. Wrong. George is making attributions, not letting expectations cause behavior matching expectations.
c. Wrong. George is making attributions, not dealing with attitude change issues.

12. **b**
(p. 510)
a. Wrong. This is the attitude itself, not one of the components.
c. Wrong. This is the affective component.
d. Wrong. This is the behavioral component.

13. **d**
(p. 519)
a. Wrong. The bystander effect is the reluctance to help if others are present.
b. Wrong. Group polarization is the tendency to make more extreme decisions in a group.
c. Wrong. Groupthink is the tendency to emphasize consensus rather than facts in a group.

14. **b**
(p. 520)
a. Wrong. Group polarization causes extreme decisions. Don going along with the group is key here.
c. Wrong. Obedience is following an order. Don wasn't ordered to do anything.
d. Wrong. Social facilitation is improved performance in the presence of others.

15. **b**
(p. 522)
a, c, & d. Wrong. These all involve wanting approval or avoiding rejection--normative social influence.

16. **d**
(p. 523)
a. Wrong. There is no conformity based on information value. Key is the rush to consensus.
b. Wrong. Performance does not decrease due to an audience. Key is the rush to consensus.
c. Wrong. The decision did not become more extreme with time. Key is the rush to consensus.

17. **a**
(p. 527)
b. Wrong. Obedience is high if the authority figure remains in the room.
c. Wrong. Obedience is high is the setting is prestigious or official.
d. Wrong. This is what Milgram's experimenter said, and obedience was high.

18. **a**
(p. 532)
b, c, & d. Wrong. Proximity is a primary determinant of friendship.

19. **c**
(p. 534)
a, b, & d. Wrong. These do not involve the intense arousal of passionate love.

Multiple Choice Pretest 2

1. **c**
(p. 504)
a. Wrong. Cognitive dissonance would occur if Jill's actions and attitudes didn't match.
b. Wrong. Social interference is impaired performance due to the presence of others.
d. Wrong. Self-serving bias is making internal attributions for your success, external ones for failures.

2. **a**
(p. 503)
b. Wrong. Fundamental attribution error is attributing the cause of a behavior to internal traits.
c. Wrong. Self-serving bias is making internal attributions for your success, external one's for failure.
d. Wrong. Cognitive dissonance is a tension caused by attitudes and behaviors not matching.

3. **b**
(p. 507)
a. Wrong. If you decide based on whether Dan always fails, consistency is involved.
c. Wrong. If you decide based on whether Dan only failed this exam, distinctiveness is involved.
d. Wrong. Checking what other people did involves consensus. Expectancy is not a factor.

4. **c**   a. Wrong.   Fundamental attribution error is a bias to make internal attributions, not external ones.
(p. 507)   b. Wrong.   Lee is making an attribution about Pat, not himself. Lee gains nothing here.
          d. Wrong.   Car trouble is an event, not a trait, so the attribution is external, not internal.

5. **a**   b, c, & d.   Wrong.   These are all external attributions. Fundamental attribution error is a bias to
(p. 507)   make internal attributions about someone else.

6. **d**   a. Wrong.   Key here was the free mug, a reward. Mere exposure doesn't involve more than exposure.
(p. 511)   b. Wrong.   There is nobody being observed buying the brand. Key here is the reward of the mug.
          c. Wrong.   Key here is the free mug reward, not a signal for a pleasant emotion.

7. **c**   a & b.   Wrong.   These are cognitive components.
(p. 510)   d.   Wrong.   These are affective components.

8. **c**   a. Wrong.   There is no mismatch of behavior and attitude here. Key is his use of direct information.
(p. 511)   b. Wrong.   There is no reward here. Key is his use of direct information.
          d. Wrong.   He is using direct information, not superficial content.

9. **b**   a.   Wrong.   Tom can justify his behavior because he is paid, so no dissonance occurs.
(p. 513)   c & d.   Wrong.   Kit has more dissonance. She is freely supporting Smith, so her attitude will remain
                            more positive.

10. **d**   a, b, & c.   Wrong.   Key to this question is the more extreme position reached with continued
(p. 522)   discussion--group polarization.

11. **b**   a, c, & d.   Wrong.   Similarity is a strong determinant of friendship.
(p. 532)

12. **a**   b. Wrong.   Ben is basing his attitude on his behavior, not changing it due to dissonance.
(p. 514)   c. Wrong.   Fundamental attribution error predicts internal attributions for others' behavior.
          d. Wrong.   Ben's attitude is based on an evaluation of his past behavior, not central or peripheral
                      routes.

13. **c**   a. Wrong.   Key here is not feeling like an individual, not a more extreme decision after discussion.
(p. 520)   b. Wrong.   There was no improved performance due to an audience here.
          d. Wrong.   Fred did not return the feelings shown toward him. Key here is not feeling individual.

14. **d**   a. Wrong.   This doesn't involve a group making a more extreme decision than an individual.
(p. 518)   b. Wrong.   This doesn't involve expectations leading to behavior matching those expectations.
          c. Wrong.   This doesn't involve forming an attitude based on simple exposure to the item.

15. **c**   a. Wrong.   Group polarization is a shift to an extreme position, not a tendency to conform.
(p. 522)   b. Wrong.   Nan was not ordered to ride a bike, she just wanted to avoid rejection.
          d. Wrong.   Nan is not gaining information from the group, she just wants approval.

16. **b**   a, c, & d.   Wrong.   These reduce the problems, according to Janis, but the leader should be impartial,
(p. 524)   not opinionated, according to Janis.

17. **c**   a. Wrong.   Passion involves intense erotic feelings.
(p. 534)   b. Wrong.   Commitment is a decision to remain in the relationship.
          d. Wrong.   Companionship is not a dimension.

18. **a**   b. Wrong.   Commitment takes time to develop.
  (p. 535)   c. Wrong.   Friendship has intimacy, but not necessarily passion.
           d. Wrong.   Empty love has commitment, but neither passion nor intimacy.

19. **c**   a. Wrong.   Jacob didn't work less in a group. Key here is Jacob obeying an authority's orders.
  (p. 525)   b. Wrong.   Jacob's performance didn't suffer due to an audience. Jacob obeyed an authority.
           d. Wrong.   Jacob didn't conform his behavior to the norm of a group. He obeyed an authority.

20. **c**   a, b, & d.   Wrong.   Blended, prototypical faces were preferred.
  (p. 530)

LANGUAGE ENHANCEMENT GUIDE

CORE TERMS

In the lectures on social psychology, your instructor may refer to *pro-social* behaviors, such as *philanthropy*. These are behaviors that help others; *philanthropy*, for example, is donating money or other goods to help mankind.

Your instructor may also use the terms *legal, ethical* and *moral*. These terms are not quite interchangeable. Something that is *illegal* breaks a specific law in a society; something that is *unethical* breaks the principles that guide conduct in a profession, such as those research psychologists must follow in designing their studies. Finally, something that is *immoral* violates public standards for good behavior.

One term that you may hear in the lecture on conformity and obedience is *compliance*. Psychologists make a careful distinction between these three terms. Conformity is doing what you see others like you do, like dressing in clothes like those your friends wear. Obedience is doing what you are told to do by an authority figure. Compliance is sort of in-between; it is doing what you are asked to do (either explicitly or implicitly) by others around you who are *not* in a position of authority.

IDIOMS

500	itching for	wanting, restlessly waiting for
500	spearheaded by	led by, directed by
500	shortcomings	faults
500	save one	except one
500	locale	location
502	under the rubric of	classified with, under the heading of

502	judging a book by its cover	making assumptions about someone or something based upon its outward appearance
503	seedy characters	people who are unattractive or seem to be likely to cause trouble
506	channel surfing	flipping from one television (TV) channel to another
506	sour disposition	unpleasant personality
507	demeanor	personality, behavior
508	bearing down on your bumper	coming closer and closer to the back of your car
508	tailgated	followed very closely by another car
508	switch gears	change topics or approaches to a topic
510	engenders	causes
510	landlord	owner of a rented property, such as a house or apartment
510	pet deposit	money some landlords require pet owners to pay in order to keep their pets in the house with them
510	classified ads	short advertisements in newspapers
512	anecdotes	short story of an incident
514	measly	tiny, inconsequential, nearly worthless
516	underling	employee
517	risen to the occasion	performed well when the situation called for it
517	"choke"	to seize up, to fail to perform when the situation requires
519	unanimity	complete agreement of all members of a group
521	rigged	set up an event so that the outcome is certain
524	watershed event	an event that serves as a critical point or dividing line
524	devil's advocate	a person who deliberately takes a contrary position in an argument, especially to test the others' case
525	toe the line	do what everyone else does; conform
525	laced with	containing a small amount of an additive

525	billed as	described or advertised as
526	via intercom	by way of a room-to-room communication device
527	three-plus decades	more than 30 years
528	paramount	most important
531	a looming visual configuration	something large that you can look up and see
533	con job	a swindle; a deception
533	ulterior motive	a hidden reason or motivation
534	unrequited	unrewarded; unreturned
534	bedrock	foundation, basis

WORD PARTS

Here are some words that are made up of word parts, and that you can find in this chapter. After you've looked at these, you can look for others in the chapter that use the same word parts (they are there, but YOU have to find them!)

WORD	WORD PART IT USES	MEANING
apathy	a = not path = feeling	feeling nothing
attractive	a, ad = to, toward tract = to pull	having the power to draw others closer; pleasing
dissonance	dis = not son = sound	conflict; harsh, disagreeable sound
engenders	en = into, in gen = beginning, birth	that which begins something else; starts; gives birth to
exposure	ex = out of, away from pos, pon = place, set, put	left visible; left out in the open
expressing	ex = out of, away from press = to press, send out	showing, sending out
inclined	in = in, into, toward clin, lin = line, level	angled toward, tending toward

prejudice	pre = before jud = to judge, decide	a decision made before evidence is presented
project	pro = forward ject = to throw	send out beforehand; that which goes before
prototypical	proto = first typ = kind	first of its kind
speculate	pect, spec, spect = to look at	to think about; to see what is happening or about to happen

Knowing the word parts listed above, you can also create the following words. You can get an idea of their meanings from the word parts they use. You fill in the blanks!

sympathy	sym (together) + pathy	_____
expect	_____ + _____	to look forward to, to see ahead
inject	in + ject	_____
contract	_____ + _____	that which pulls or ties together
propose	pro + pos	_____
atypical	_____ + _____	not like others of its kind
prospect	pro + spect	_____

CHAPTER 14: PSYCHOLOGICAL DISORDERS

ESTABLISHING LEARNING OBJECTIVES

Use these learning objectives as a preview of the chapter, a guide for active reading, and to evaluate your mastery of the material. Review the relevant objectives as you begin and end your reading of each major section of the chapter.

After studying this chapter you should be able to:

I.   Solve the conceptual problem of defining abnormality.
    A. Discuss and evaluate the various criteria that have been proposed to define abnormality.
        1. Compare the concepts of abnormality and insanity, and describe the criteria for insanity.
    B. Explain how the medical model classifies and categorizes abnormality.
    C. Discuss effects of diagnostic labeling.

II. Solve the conceptual problem of classifying psychological disorders.
    A. Describe the DSM-IV, and discuss the pros and cons of this multiaxial system.
    B. Identify and describe the common anxiety disorders.
        1. Compare the symptoms of generalized anxiety disorder, panic disorder, and specific phobias.
        2. Describe obsessive-compulsive disorder.
    C. Identify and describe the somatoform disorders.
        1. Compare hypochondriasis, somatization disorder, and conversion disorder.
    D. Identify and describe the common dissociative disorders.
        1. Compare dissociative amnesia and dissociative fugue.
        2. Describe dissociative identity disorder, and discuss why this disorder is controversial.
    E. Identify and describe the common mood disorders.
        1. List the symptoms of a major depressive episode.
        2. Describe bipolar disorder.
        3. Discuss the evidence concerning a link between mania and creativity.
    F. Identify and describe the characteristics of schizophrenia.
        1. Differentiate positive and negative symptoms and give examples of each.
    G. Identify and describe the common personality disorders.
        1. Compare paranoid, dependent, and antisocial personality disorders.
        2. Explain why personality disorders are not listed as Axis I disorders.

III. Solve the practical problem of understanding the origin of psychological disorders.
    A. Explain how biological and genetic factors can contribute to psychological disorders.
        1. Describe the role of neurotransmitters in schizophrenia and mood disorders.
        2. Describe the evidence of structural problems in the brain contributing to psychological disorders.
        3. Describe the evidence for a genetic predisposition for schizophrenia and mood disorders
    B. Discuss how maladaptive thoughts can contribute to psychological disorders.
        1. Describe the types of attributions that are characteristic of psychological disorders.
        2. Explain the learned helpless theory of depression.
    C. Discuss how environmental factors can contribute to psychological disorders.

MASTERING THE MATERIAL

Preview & Conceptualizing Abnormality: What is Abnormal Behavior? (pp. 544-551)

Mastering the Vocabulary. Define or explain each of the following terms. To check your answers, consult the text pages listed.

1. statistical deviance (p. 546)

2. cultural deviance (p. 546)

3. emotional distress (p. 546)

4. dysfunction (p. 547)

5. insanity (p. 548)

6. medical model (p. 549)

7. diagnostic labeling effects (p. 550)

Mastering the Concepts. Fill in the blanks to create a summary of this section. Answers are on page 338.

Three conceptual and practical problems are explored: How should abnormal behavior be defined? How can psychological disorders be classified? What are the underlying causes of psychological disorders?

Abnormality can be defined in terms of _____(1) deviance or infrequency, _____(2) deviance, emotional _____(3), or _____(4), a breakdown in normal functioning. Any one definition is insufficient to define abnormality, and some disorders involve exaggerations of normal behavior. Normal and abnormal behavior are considered to form a continuum, not clear-cut categories.

_____(5) is a legal concept and is usually defined based on the person's ability to understand whether an action is right or wrong. The insanity defense began in the 1800's in the M'Naughten case. It is used in only 1% of felony cases and is successful only 26% of the time.

The _____(6) views abnormality as a symptom of a disease. Support for this includes _____(7) abnormalities found in some disorders and the fact that disorders can be classified in terms of symptoms.

Criticisms focus on a lack of identifiable physical causes for some disorders, the idea that some problems are "problems in living," and the stigma of diagnostic _____ (8). Rosenhan's pseudopatient study shows that once labeled, behavior is viewed differently. Expectation affects interpretation.

Evaluating Your Progress. Select the one best response. Answers are on page 338. If you make any errors, reread the relevant material before proceeding.

1.   Behaviors that violate the accepted rules might be classified as abnormal using the criterion of
     a.   statistical deviance.
     b.   cultural deviance.
     c.   dysfunction.
     d.   emotional distress.

2.   Who is most likely to be considered psychologically abnormal?
     a.   Fred, who cried for two days nonstop after hearing his father died.
     b.   Nathan, who screams obscenities at the umpires at the baseball game.
     c.   Tom, who sits immobile for hours in his room for no apparent reason.
     d.   Roy, who can calculate the day of the week for any date in the last 1200 years.

3.   The primary criterion for a judgment of insanity is whether the person
     a.   violated the cultural norms for behavior due to a "mental disease."
     b.   acted in dysfunctional or maladaptive ways due to a "mental disease."
     c.   showed intense emotional distress due to a "mental disease."
     d.   had no understanding of the wrongfulness of the behavior due to a "mental disease."

4.   That some psychological disorders can be treated with drugs that affect neurotransmitters, and the ability to reliably classify many psychological disorders in terms of measurable symptoms are facts that support
     a.   the legal definition of insanity.
     b.   the medical model of abnormality.
     c.   the need to consider the context of a behavior before declaring a person psychologically abnormal.
     d.   the need for more than one type of deviance to declare a person psychologically abnormal.

5.   The Rosenhan pseudopatient study is important because it showed
     a.   psychologists are incompetent in most cases.
     b.   patients in mental hospitals receive inhumane treatment
     c.   the medical model of psychological disorders is most appropriate.
     d.   expectations and labels influence the interpretation of behavior.

Classifying Psychological Disorders: DMS-IV (pp. 552-566)

Mastering the Vocabulary. Define or explain each of the following terms. To check your answers, consult the text pages listed.

1.   DSM-IV (p. 552)

19. manic state (p. 562)

20. schizophrenia (p. 563)

21. personality disorders (p. 565)

22. paranoid personality disorder (p. 565)

23. dependent personality disorder (p. 565)

24. antisocial personality disorder (p. 565)

Mastering the Concepts. Fill in the blanks to create a summary of this section. Answers are on page 338.

DSM-IV is a _____(9) system based on objective, measurable criteria without reference to therapy. Axis I, clinical syndromes, and Axis II, _____(10) disorders, classify abnormal behavior. Axis III notes _____(11) conditions, Axis IV notes _____(12) problems, and Axis V evaluates daily functioning.

Persistent and intense anxiety that interferes with behavior characterizes _____(13) disorders. In _____(14) anxiety disorder, the anxiety is free-floating and causes difficulty sleeping, digestive problems and other physical problems. In _____(15) disorder, anxiety is sudden, relatively brief, but intense. If an attack occurs in public, the person can develop _____(16), a fear of going into public places. Obsessive-compulsive disorder involves obsessions, persistent _____(17), and compulsions, a need to perform an action. A specific, irrational fear is found in specific _____(18) disorder.

_____(19) disorders focus on the body. In hypochondriasis, normal bodily reactions are interpreted as serious medical conditions. In somatization disorder, the focus is on _____(20) symptoms with no physical cause, rather than a possible disease. In _____(21) disorder, the person has a true symptom but no real physical disorder, such as paralysis even though the nervous system is normal.

The _____(22) disorders involve a separation of conscious awareness from memories. Dissociative amnesia involves memory loss not due to head injury. Dissociative _____(23) involves a loss of memory for identity and a flight from the home. Dissociative _____(24) disorder involves more than one personality. This disorder is controversial, and not all psychologists accept it.

The mood disorders involve prolonged, disabling disruptions of emotional state, including depressive disorders and _____(25) disorder. A major depressive episode involves behavioral changes, low mood, and a pessimistic outlook. A milder, more chronic depression is dysthymic disorder. _____(26) depression is disthymic disorder with a major depressive episode. In bipolar disorder, mood swings from depression to a _____(27) of hyperactivity and abnormal thought. The risk factors for suicide include depression, sudden _____(28), suicidal thinking and suicidal thoughts.

Andreasen found a higher rate of _____(29) among creative people, and descriptions of creative episodes resemble _____(30) states. Research by Weisberg on the composer Schumann, suggests that although _____(31) increases during manic states, the _____(32) of the product does not improve.

_____(33) involves disordered thoughts, emotion, and behavior. Symptoms are classified as _____(34) if they involve an excess or added behavior, and _____(35) if they involve a deficit. Schizophrenia often involves hallucinations, perceptions without a sensory cause, and _____(36), thoughts with inappropriate content. Speech can be disordered, emotions can be flat, and bizarre postures may be held for long periods, _____(37).

Axis II describes personality disorders, chronic patterns of behavior that lead to impaired social function. People with _____(38) personality disorder show a pervasive distrust of others, _____(39) personality disorder involves the need to be taken care of, and _____(40) personality disorder involves no respect for social customs and an absence of guilt. Personality disorders do not respond well to treatment, and some psychologists argue they are not true disorders, only extreme personalities.

Evaluating Your Progress. Select the one best response. Answers are on page 338. If you make any errors, reread the relevant material before proceeding.

1. The purpose of the DSM-IV is
   a. to provide a definition of insanity that is based on objective criteria.
   b. to indicate the appropriate treatment for common psychological disorders.
   c. to provide an objective classification system for psychological disorders.
   d. to eliminate the problems associated with diagnostic labeling effects.

2. Axis III and Axis IV of DSM-IV involve
   a. an evaluation of the person's current level of adaptive functioning.
   b. the medical and psychosocial context in which the behavioral symptoms should be considered.
   c. objective and measurable definitions of all the major clinical syndromes.
   d. evaluation of pervasive behavioral characteristics such as mental retardation and personality.

3. The disorders characterized by persistent, intense apprehension that interferes with functioning are the
   a. schizophrenias.
   b. mood disorders.
   c. anxiety disorders.
   d. dissociative disorders.

4. Cindy is unrealistically terrified of snakes and will not walk across a yard for fear a snake will be there. Cindy's likely diagnosis is
   a. panic disorder.
   b. obsessive-compulsive disorder.
   c. manic state.
   d. specific phobic disorder.

5. A strong need to perform some behavior, usually in a repetitive manner, is
   a. a phobia.
   b. an obsession.
   c. a delusion.
   d. a compulsion.

6. A difference between hypochondriasis and somatization disorder is that in hypochondriasis
   a. there is no physical symptom, but in somatization disorder there is a physical symptom.
   b. the symptoms are chronic, but in somatization the symptoms are brief, but intense.
   c. the presumed disease causes anxiety, but in somatization disorder the symptoms cause anxiety.
   d. the person is lying about the symptoms, but in somatization the person is telling the truth.

7. Dissociative fugue most specifically involves
   a. a loss of personal identity that is accompanied by flight from the home.
   b. mood shifts from deep depression to a manic state.
   c. free-floating anxiety that is chronic.
   d. the alternation of two or more apparently distinct identities or personalities.

8. Bipolar disorder is characterized by
   a. hallucinations and language disorders.
   b. alternation between depression and a manic state.
   c. a chronic, relatively low intensity, agitated depression.
   d. two or more personalities.

9. All of the following are characteristic of schizophrenia except
   a. disordered thoughts.
   b. disordered language.
   c. inappropriate emotions.
   d. multiple personalities.

10. Tina thinks that she is Joan of Arc. This is an example of
    a. a hallucination.
    b. a delusion.
    c. catatonia.
    d. dysthymia.

11. Andreasen's research found that creative people
     a. have a lower incidence of bipolar disorder than control subjects.
     b. have a higher incidence of bipolar disorder than control subjects.
     c. have a lower incidence of schizophrenia than control subjects.
     d. have a higher incidence of schizophrenia than control subjects.

12. Axis II personality disorders differ from Axis I clinical syndromes because personality disorders
     a. generally seem to be due to a specific brain dysfunction, unlike the clinical syndromes.
     b. are caused by environmental stressors, and clinical syndromes are mostly brain disorders.
     c. are more ingrained and inflexible, and are resistant to treatment, unlike the clinical syndromes.
     d. come and go without treatment much more often than the clinical syndromes.

Understanding Psychological Disorders: Biological, Cognitive, or Environmental?
(pp. 567-573)

Mastering the Vocabulary. Define or explain each of the following terms. To check your answers, consult the text pages listed.

1. bio-psycho-social perspective (p. 567)

2. learned helplessness (p. 571)

Mastering the Content. Fill in the blanks to create a summary of this section. Answers are on page 338.

The bio-psycho- social perspective recognizes the multiple causes of abnormality. Signs of abnormal brain chemistry or brain structures and evidence for a genetic component to disorders support a biological explanation of some psychological disorders. Schizophrenia may involve an excess of _____(41) or an interaction between dopamine and serotonin. Drugs that affect dopamine affect the symptoms of schizophrenia. Schizophrenia is associated with low activity in the frontal lobes and enlarged _____(42). For mood disorders, the monoamine neurotransmitters _____(43), norepineprine and dopamine may be involved. The true role of these biological abnormalities is unclear, however.

There is a strong _____(44) predisposition for schizophrenia and mood disorders. Concordance rates for identical twins with schizophrenia are very high and also very high for mood disorders. Children whose parents have these disorders are at greater risk, even if adopted into healthy homes.

Thought patterns may also be a determinant of mood disorders. People prone to depression tend to make attributions that are _____(45), stable, and global. If repeated failures occur, learned _____(46) can occur, leading to passive behavior and depression.

Evidence suggests some disorders may be learned. _____(47) might be classically conditioned, and abnormal behaviors, if reinforced, can be acquired through _____(48) conditioning. Observational learning, watching others, can contribute to the development of phobias.

Evaluating Your Progress. Select the one best response. Answers are on page 339. If you make any errors, reread the relevant material before proceeding.

1. The neurotransmitter that seems to be involved in schizophrenia is
   a. dopamine.
   b. norepinephrine.
   c. acetylcholine.
   d. epinephrine.

2. If one identical twin develops schizophrenia, the other twin's odds of developing schizophrenia are
   a. 1 in 100.
   b. 1 in 50.
   c. 1 in 20.
   d. 1 in 2.

3. The data concerning genetic influences on mood disorders shows that
   a. mood disorders have no significant genetic component.
   b. mood disorders have a significant genetic component, but it is weaker than that for schizophrenia.
   c. mood disorders have a genetic component at least as strong as that for schizophrenia.
   d. mood disorders are almost entirely due to genetic factors.

4. Instead of pointing to genetic determinants, some psychologists suggest depression is a matter of
   a. maladaptive attributions.
   b. defective parenting.
   c. classical conditioning.
   d. poor diet and too little sleep.

5. Research with monkeys suggests that a disorder likely to develop due to learning is
   a. schizophrenia.
   b. dissociative disorder.
   c. bipolar disorder.
   d. specific phobic disorder.

6. Which neurotransmitter in affected by Prozac, an antidepressant, and may be involved in mood disorders?
   a. serotonin
   b. acteylcholine
   c. GABA
   d. lithium carbonate

MAKING FINAL PREPARATIONS

Complete these sections without consulting your book or notes. For a more accurate estimate of how well you know this material, wait at least a day or two after studying the chapter before working on the questions. Some material you "know" immediately after working with the chapter will be quickly forgotten. Immediate tests will overestimate what you know well.

Short Essay Questions. Write a brief answer to each question. Sample answers are on page 340.

1. Identify the 4 types of criteria for abnormality and discuss why classifying abnormal behavior is difficult.

2. Discuss the purpose of Axes III, IV, and V of the DSM-IV.

3. Explain how insanity differs from psychological abnormality.

4. Compare generalized anxiety disorder and specific phobic disorder.

5. Explain what positive and negative symptoms are, and give an example of each.

6. Explain how classical conditioning, instrumental conditioning and observational learning could influence the development of specific phobic disorder.

Matching. Select the correct definition or description for each item. Answers are on page 340.

_____	1. dependent personality disorder	**a.**	belief that others are plotting against you
_____	2. catatonia	**b.**	disorder with thought, emotion, & behavior defects
_____	3. double depression	**c.**	chronic behavior causing impaired social function
_____	4. delusion of persecution	**d.**	lack of emotion
_____	5. anxiety disorders	**e.**	disorders that focus on the body
_____	6. dysthymic disorder	**f.**	involves excessive need to be taken care of
_____	7. delusion of grandeur	**g.**	chronic, moderate depression
_____	8. personality disorders	**h.**	tendency to hold strange postures for a long time
_____	9. dissociative disorder	**i.**	sense of helplessness after repeated failures
_____	10. flat affect	**j.**	prolonged and disabling disruption of emotion
_____	11. mood disorders	**k.**	major depressive episode added to dysthymia
_____	12. somatoform disorders	**l.**	the thought you are someone famous
_____	13. learned helplessness	**m.**	disorders with separation of awareness & memory
_____	14. schizophrenia	**n.**	disorders with excessive, prolonged apprehension

Multiple Choice Pretest 1. Select the one best response. Answers are on page 340.

1. If a behavior is classified as abnormal because it occurs infrequently, abnormality is being defined by
    a. cultural deviance.
    b. dysfunction.
    c. emotional distress.
    d. statistical deviance.

2. Which of the following is true concerning the insanity defense in felony cases?
    a. It is attempted in about 25% of felony cases, and it is successful in about 50% of those attempts.
    b. It is attempted in about 25% of felony cases, and it is successful in about 5% of those attempts.
    c. It is attempted in about 1% of felony cases, and it is successful in about 75% of those attempts.
    d. It is attempted in about 1% of felony cases, and it is successful in about 25% of those attempts.

3. Criticisms of the medical model of psychological disorders include
    a. that the medical model sees many disorders as problems with living.
    b. that the medical model puts too much emphasis on cultural context.
    c. the fact that behavioral symptoms allow reliable classification of many disorders.
    d. the fact that some mental disorders have no well-defined physical cause.

4. Diagnostic labeling effects involve
    a. giving inappropriate diagnoses to individuals who psychological disorders.
    b. treating a person differently because they have a history of psychological disorder.
    c. spontaneous improvements in a person's symptoms after being given a name for their problem.
    d. excusing criminal behavior by blaming it on psychological problems.

5. Axis I of the DSM-IV
    a. includes the criteria used to define major clinical syndromes.
    b. is used to note major medical conditions that might affect diagnosis.
    c. is used to note environmental problems that might affect diagnosis and treatment.
    d. involves a global assessment of the person's current adaptive functioning.

6. Chris has been having repeated attacks of sudden, overwhelming anxiety in which his heart races and he feels like he's going to die. His doctor has found no physical problem. Chris' diagnosis would likely be
    a. generalized anxiety disorder.
    b. specific phobic disorder.
    c. somatoform disorder.
    d. panic disorder.

7. Excessive and chronic worrying lasting for at least 6 months and not related to any specific source is characteristic of
    a. generalized anxiety disorder.
    b. panic disorder.
    c. specific phobic disorder.
    d. conversion disorder.

8. Terri cannot see, although there is nothing physically wrong with her eyes. Terri's problem might be
   a. hypochondriasis.
   b. dissociative fugue.
   c. panic disorder.
   d. conversion disorder.

9. Which is not a positive symptom of schizophrenia?
   a. flat affect
   b. catatonia
   c. delusions
   d. disorganized speech

10. Gary shifts between two other apparently distinct personalities, but he has only incomplete knowledge of his alternate selves. Gary's diagnostic classification would probably be
    a. schizophrenia.
    b. dissociative identity disorder.
    c. somatization disorder.
    d. bipolar disorder.

11. For two months Lenny has been sleeping little. He is extremely restless, can't concentrate, and feels worthless and low. He doesn't even get dressed most days. Lenny's problem would be classified as
    a. schizophrenia.
    b. conversion disorder.
    c. obsessive-compulsive disorder.
    d. major depressive episode.

12. We know that schizophrenia is not entirely due to genetic factors because
    a. children raised apart from their schizophrenic parents have a greater rate of schizophrenia than their adoptive siblings.
    b. children raised apart from their schizophrenic parents have the same rate of schizophrenia as their adoptive siblings.
    c. the concordance rate for fraternal twins is very low.
    d. the concordance rate for identical twins is not 100%.

13. A pervasive and long-term distrust of others, without thought or emotional disorders, are symptoms of
    a. antisocial personality disorder.
    b. dependent personality disorder.
    c. paranoid personality disorder.
    d. multiple personality disorder.

14. An imbalance of the monoamines (serotonin, norepinephrine, dopamine) seems to be involved in
    a. antisocial personality disorder.
    b. mood disorders.
    c. somatoform disorders.
    d. dissociative disorders.

15. People prone to depression are likely to make attributions about failures that are
    a. global, stable, and internal.
    b. global, unstable, and internal.
    c. specific, unstable, and external.
    d. specific, stable, and external.

16. Theresa always gets a lot of attention when she screams because she sees a spider. If she develops a spider phobia, an appropriate explanation will be that the phobia was acquired through
    a. classical conditioning.
    b. instrumental conditioning.
    c. observational learning.
    d. learned helplessness.

17. Weisberg's study of Schumann's musical compositions indicated that during his manic periods, Schumann
    a. produced more compositions.
    b. produced better compositions.
    c. produced neither more nor better compositions.
    d. produced both more and better compositions.

Multiple Choice Pretest 2. Select the one best response. Answers are on page 342.

1. Becoming a good chemist is so important to Dot that she constantly studies her chemistry. She sleeps and eats little, she has no friends, and she is failing her other classes. Dot's behavior would be considered abnormal based on
    a. insanity.
    b. dysfunction.
    c. cultural deviance.
    d. personal distress.

2. Ike heard voices telling him the children had put the worm in his brains. He planned for weeks how he would kill them and hide their bodies. His insanity defense failed. The jury must have decided
    a. he did not have serious psychological problems.
    b. he met the cultural deviance and statistical criteria, but not the dysfunction or distress criteria.
    c. he was capable of understanding the wrongfulness of his actions.
    d. a medical problem caused his thought disorders, not a psychological one.

3. Max repeatedly worries that there will be an electrical fire, so he checks each light switch and electrical outlet and appliance several times a day. The checking is repetitive and ritualistic. Max rarely goes out because of his need to check the house. Max's problem is
    a. specific phobic disorder.
    b. dissociative disorder.
    c. obsessive-compulsive disorder.
    d. panic disorder.

4. Laura thinks psychological disorders are caused by a disease that can be cured with an appropriate treatment. Laura believes in
    a. the medical model.
    b. the DSM-IV.
    c. insanity.
    d. the Rosenhan study.

5. A past political candidate became emotional and had tears in his eyes while talking about the difficulties of his campaign. Because he had a history of depression, this incident received more negative attention than similar behavior by other candidates without histories of depression. The different reactions to the behavior seems to be an example of
    a. dissociation.
    b. learned helplessness.
    c. a diagnostic labeling effect.
    d. maladaptive attributions.

6. Mark woke up and found he didn't know who he was or what he did for a living. The doctor he consulted could find no evidence of a stroke or other physical problem. Mark's problem is probably
    a. dissociative identity disorder.
    b. dissociative fugue.
    c. dissociative amnesia.
    d. conversion disorder.

7. Abe worries unrealistically about everything all the time. He shows high autonomic nervous system activity and a variety of chronic medical complaints. Abe probably would be diagnosed as having
    a. panic disorder.
    b. generalized anxiety disorder.
    c. agoraphobia.
    d. obsessive-compulsive disorder.

8. Fran suffered a panic attack at the store one day, and since then, she has found it very difficult to leave her home without being overwhelmed by anxiety. Her intense fear of going out is characteristic of
    a. obsessive-compulsive disorder.
    b. agoraphobia.
    c. generalized anxiety disorder.
    d. conversion disorder.

9. Yan, who has a history of depression, is likely to explain being laid off from work by saying,
    a. "It was just luck, I guess. I was one of the most recently hired, so I'm the first to go."
    b. "That foreman never liked me, no matter how hard I worked."
    c. "I'm just incompetent. I was rotten in school, and now I'm rotten in my job."
    d. "I wasn't very good at my job yet. I'll get more training, and this won't happen again."

10. Woody Allen's characters often interpret minor physical symptoms as major diseases. A headache means a brain tumor and an irregular heart beat means a heart attack. This type of behavior is characteristic of
    a. somatoform disorders.
    b. dissociative disorders.
    c. anxiety disorders.
    d. personality disorders.

11. Last month Kiesha's mood was very low, she felt worthless and considered suicide. This month Kiesha has been racing around in a hyperactive state making great plans, none of which are realistic or have been completed. She says she feels great, but her thinking isn't normal, and she tends to jump from one idea to another. Kiesha's symptoms are consistent with
    a. dissociative fugue.
    b. dysthymic disorder.
    c. bipolar disorder.
    d. double depression.

12. Clark hears voices in his head and thinks the CIA is watching him. His thoughts are generally disordered, his emotions are inappropriate, and he makes bizarre movements. His behavior is so maladaptive that he has been hospitalized several times. Clark is probably classified as having
    a. bipolar disorder.
    b. generalized anxiety disorder.
    c. dissociative identity disorder.
    d. schizophrenia.

13. Walter has spent his life stealing people's money in fake investment schemes. He has never felt remorse, and has no respect for laws or moral values. A prison psychologist is likely to classify him as having
    a. schizophrenia.
    b. a personality disorder.
    c. dissociative disorder.
    d. conversion disorder.

14. Opal is being treated with a drug that influences the levels of the monoamines, especially serotonin. Opal's psychological disorder is probably
    a. schizophrenia.
    b. a mood disorder.
    c. conversion disorder.
    d. a dissociative disorder.

15. Bob's neurological work-up showed enlarged ventricles in his brain, and low levels of activity in his frontal lobes. The psychological disorder Bob has is probably
    a. bipolar disorder.
    b. obsessive-compulsive disorder.
    c. schizophrenia.
    d. dissociative identity disorder.

16. Adam and Wilma both have schizophrenia. Their child, Thea, was raised in a healthy adoptive family without contact with Wilma and Adam. The likelihood that Thea will develop schizophrenia is
    a. equal to the general population's likelihood.
    b. equal to her adoptive siblings' likelihood.
    c. much higher than her adoptive siblings' likelihood.
    d. almost 100%.

17. Which of the following is true concerning mental disorders and creativity?
    a. Highly creative people have a higher incidence of some mental disorders than average people.
    b. Highly creative people have a lower incidence of some mental disorders than average people.
    c. Highly creative people produce much better quality work while in a manic state.
    d. Highly creative people produce much poorer quality work while in a manic state.

ANSWERS AND EXPLANATIONS

Mastering the Concepts

1. statistical (p. 546)
2. cultural (p. 546)
3. distress (p. 546)
4. dysfunction (p. 547)
5. Insanity (p. 548)
6. medical model (p. 549)
7. neurotransmitter (p. 549)
8. labeling (p. 550)
9. classification (p. 552)
10. personality (p. 552)
11. medical (p. 552)
12. psychosocial (p. 552)
13. anxiety (p. 553)
14. generalized (p. 554)
15. panic (p. 554)
16. agoraphobia (p. 555)
17. thoughts (p. 555)
18. phobic (p. 556)
19. Somatoform (p. 557)
20. body (p. 557)
21. conversion (p. 558)
22. dissociative (p. 558)
23. fugue (p. 558)
24. identity (p. 558)
25. bipolar (p. 560)
26. Double (p. 562)
27. manic state (p. 562)
28. stress (p. 563)
29. bipolar disorder (p. 560)
30. manic (p. 560)
31. productivity (p. 561)
32. quality (p. 561)
33. Schizophrenia (p. 563)
34. positive (p. 564)
35. negative (p. 565)
36. delusions (p. 564)
37. catatonia (p. 565)
38. paranoid (p. 565)
39. dependent (p. 565)
40. antisocial (p. 565)
41. dopamine (p. 567)
42. ventricles (p. 568)
43. serotonin (p. 568)
44. genetic (p. 569)
45. internal (p. 570)
46. helplessness (p. 571)
47. Phobias (p. 572)
48. instrumental (p. 573)

Evaluating Your Progress

Preview & Conceptualizing Abnormality: What is Abnormal Behavior

1. **b**
   (p. 546)
   a. Wrong. Statistical deviance involves behaviors that occur infrequently, not disruptive behavior.
   c. Wrong. Dysfunction involves maladaptive behavior that might or might not violate rules.
   d. Wrong. Emotional distress involves personal feelings of emotional discomfort.

2. **c**
   (p. 547)
   a & b. Wrong. The context changes the interpretation of the behaviors.
   d. Wrong. Statistically deviant, but that alone isn't enough to declare psychological abnormality.

3. **d**
   (p. 548)
   a, b, & c. Wrong. Insanity requires a lack of appreciation for the wrongfulness of the action.

4. **b**
   (p. 549)
   a, c, & d. Wrong. Biological causes and "symptoms" relate to the medical model.

5. **d**
   (p. 551)
   a. Wrong. Diagnosis was based on symptoms reported, and an absence of abnormality was later noted.
   b. Wrong. There is no indication of inhumane treatment.
   c. Wrong. This study says nothing about the validity of the medical model.

Classifying Psychological Disorders: DMS-IV and Selected Clinical Syndromes

1. **c**
   (p. 552)
   a. Wrong. DSM-IV only classifies disorders. It doesn't address insanity.
   b. Wrong. DSM-IV says nothing about treatment. It only classifies disorders.
   d. Wrong. DSM-IV is a labeling system. It won't eliminate labeling effects.

2. **b**
   (p. 552)
   a. Wrong. This is Axis V. Axes III and IV deal with medical and psychosocial conditions.
   c. Wrong. This is Axis I. Axes III and IV deal with medical and psychosocial conditions.
   d. Wrong. This is Axis II. Axes III and IV deal with medical and psychosocial conditions.

3. **c**
   (p. 553)
   a. Wrong. Schizophrenia involves disorders of thought, emotion, and behavior, not necessarily worry.
   b. Wrong. Mood disorders involve prolonged disruption of emotion, not necessarily apprehension.
   d. Wrong. Dissociative disorders involve separation of conscious awareness from memories.

4. **d**   a. Wrong. Her anxiety centers on an object. Panic disorder involves sudden, nonspecific anxiety.
    (p. 556)   b. Wrong. OCD includes intrusive thoughts and ritualistic behavior, neither of which she has.
                c. Wrong. A manic state involves hyperactivity, not irrational fear of an object.

5. **d**   a. Wrong. Phobias are intense irrational fears.
    (p. 555)   b. Wrong. Obsessions are persistent, uncontrollable thoughts.
                c. Wrong. Delusions are thoughts with inappropriate content.

6. **c**   a. Wrong. Both disorders involve physical symptoms reported by the person.
    (p. 557)   b. Wrong. Symptoms can be either chronic or brief in both disorders.
                d. Wrong. The person does not lie. There is a preoccupation with symptoms in both.

7. **a**   b. Wrong. This describes bipolar disorder.
    (p. 558)   c. Wrong. This describes generalized anxiety disorder.
                d. Wrong. This describes dissociative identity disorder.

8. **b**   a, c, & d.   Wrong. Bipolar disorder is the alternation between "high" and "low" states.
    (p. 562)

9. **d**   a, b, & c.   Wrong. These are common in schizophrenia. Multiple personality is a dissociative
    (p. 564)   disorder.

10. **b**   a. Wrong. Hallucinations are perceptions with no basis in the external environment.
    (p. 564)   c. Wrong. Catatonia is the tendency to remain in a bizarre posture for hours.
                d. Wrong. Dysthymia is chronic, less intense depression.

11. **b**   a.   Wrong. They have a higher incidence.
    (p. 560)   c & d.   Wrong. She examined bipolar disorder, not schizophrenia.

12. **c**   a, b, & d.   Wrong. These are not true for Axis II disorders, nor do they explain why they have their
    (p. 565)   own axis.

Understanding Psychological Disorders: Biological, Cognitive, or Environmental?

1. **a**   b, c, & d.   Wrong. These are not involved in schizophrenia. Dopamine and (maybe) serotonin are.
    (p. 567)

2. **d**   a, b, & c.   Wrong. There is a 50% chance of the other twin developing schizophrenia.
    (p. 569)

3. **c**   a, b, & d.   Wrong. Mood disorders have at least as strong a genetic component.
    (p. 570)

4. **a**   b, c, & d.   Wrong. These are not thought to be important determinants of depression.
    (p. 570)

5. **d**   a, b, & c.   Wrong. These disorders are unlikely to have a significant learned component.
    (p. 573)

6. **a**   b, c, & d.   Wrong. Mood disorders involve the monoamine neurotransmitters: serotonin,
    (p. 568)   norepinephrine, and dopamine.

MAKING FINAL PREPARATIONS

Short Essay Questions

1. The criteria are: statistical deviance (infrequent), cultural deviance (violates norms), emotional distress, and dysfunction (maladaptive). Problems arise because criteria can be violated, but the behavior might be considered normal, or a person who has a problem might not violate most criteria. Intense distress and maladaptive behavior is "normal" if linked to a death, but thought disorders that indicate mental problems might cause no serious problems, other than slight dysfunction. (pp. 546-549)

2. Axis III (medical conditions), Axis IV (psychosocial and environmental problems) and Axis V (level of function) provide a context in which symptoms are evaluated. This allows a very broad assessment and diagnosis and helps in treatment decisions. (p. 552)

3. Insanity is a legal concept. Most definitions of insanity require the person not understand the wrongfulness of his or her actions as a result of a "mental disease." Thus, abnormality is a requirement, but the emphasis is on the lack of understanding of whether an action is right or wrong. (p. 548)

4. Both generalized anxiety disorder and specific phobic disorder are anxiety disorders and involve anxiety. In generalized anxiety disorder the anxiety is not tied to a specific object or situation; it is free-floating or a general state of anxiety. In specific phobic disorder the anxiety is focused on a specific object or event. (pp. 554, 556)

5. Positive symptoms of schizophrenia are excessive or added overt behaviors, such as hallucinations (hearing voices) or delusions (thinking you're Napoleon). Negative symptoms are deficits in behavior, such as flat affect, a lack of emotional response. (pp. 564-565)

6. The specific fear found with phobias might be learned. If an object is paired with an US for fear, the object might become a CS for fear, setting the stage for a phobia. That is, if you fall off a high location, the height might become a CS for the US (sense of falling) for the UR (fear). If fear responses are reinforced by being given attention or other rewards, fear responses in that situation will become more common. Finally, watching someone exhibit fear responses to a situation can result in the observational learning of that behavior. Children who watch fear responses in the parents might learn to act the same way. (pp. 572-573)

Matching

1. **f** (p. 565)	4. **a** (p. 564)	7. **l** (p. 564)	10. **d** (p. 565)	13. **i** (p. 571)
2. **h** (p. 565)	5. **n** (p. 553)	8. **c** (p. 565)	11. **j** (p. 560)	14. **b** (p. 563)
3. **k** (p. 562)	6. **g** (p. 562)	9. **m** (p. 558)	12. **e** (p. 557)	

Multiple Choice Pretest 1

1. **d**
    (p. 546)
    a. Wrong. Cultural deviance involves behavior that is not accepted by a particular culture.
    b. Wrong. Dysfunction involves behavior that is not adaptive or prevents normal activities.
    c. Wrong. Emotional distress involves personal feelings of emotional discomfort.

2. **d**
    (p. 548)
    a, b, & c. Wrong. The insanity defense is rarely used (1%), with a success rate of 26%.

3. **d**
    (p. 550)
    a & b. Wrong. These are opposite to the actual criticisms.
    c. Wrong. This is a supporting fact, not a criticism.

4. **b**   a, c, & d.   Wrong.   Diagnostic labeling effects are the effects of the stigma of mental disorder, often
   (p. 550)   involving viewing people negatively and normal behavior as abnormal.

5. **a**   b. Wrong.   This is Axis III. Axis I defines major clinical syndromes.
   (p. 552)   c. Wrong.   This is Axis IV. Axis I defines major clinical syndromes.
                   d. Wrong.   This is Axis V. Axis I defines major clinical syndromes.

6. **d**   a. Wrong.   His anxiety is sudden and intense. Generalized anxiety disorder involves chronic anxiety.
   (p. 554)   b. Wrong.   His anxiety is not specific to an object or event.
                   c. Wrong.   His anxiety is too sudden and intense and is not linked to a preoccupation with his body.

7. **a**   b. Wrong.   Panic disorder has sudden, brief episodes of intense anxiety, not chronic anxiety.
   (p. 554)   c. Wrong.   Specific phobic disorder involves anxiety linked to a specific source (e.g., snakes).
                   d. Wrong.   Conversion disorder is a physical symptom without physical cause.

8. **d**   a. Wrong.   Hypochondriasis involves preoccupation that one has a serious disease, not the appearance
   (p. 558)   of serious symptoms without physical cause.
                   b. Wrong.   Dissociative fugue involves breaks in normal conscious awareness and memories.
                   c. Wrong.   Panic disorder involves sudden, overwhelming anxiety.

9. **a**   b, c, & d.   Wrong.   These are all overt expressions of abnormal behavior (positive symptoms), rather
   (p. 564)   than the elimination of some behavior (negative symptoms).

10. **b**   a. Wrong.   Schizophrenia involves disordered thought, behavior, and emotion, not multiple selves.
   (p. 558)   c. Wrong.   Somatization disorder is a preoccupation with physical symptoms.
                   d. Wrong.   Bipolar disorder involves shifting from depression to mania, not between personalities.

11. **d**   a. Wrong.   Lenny doesn't show the serious thought and emotional disorders of schizophrenia.
   (p. 561)   b. Wrong.   Lenny doesn't have a physical symptom with no physical basis.
                   c. Wrong.   Lenny doesn't have either compulsive behavior or obsessive thoughts.

12. **d**   a. Wrong.   This only supports a genetic component.
   (p. 569)   b. Wrong.   This is not true.
                   c. Wrong.   A low concordance rate for non-identical twins could be due to genes or environment.

13. **c**   a. Wrong.   Antisocial personality is characterized by lack of guilt and lack of respect for law or
   (p. 565)   customs.
                   b. Wrong.   Dependent personality is characterized by an excessive need to be taken care of by others.
                   d. Wrong.   Multiple personality disorder involves having more than one personality, not distrust.

14. **b**   a, c, & d.   Wrong.   Mood disorders involve monoamines. The others are not strongly linked to
   (p. 568)   neurotransmitter problems.

15. **a**   b, c, & d.   Wrong.   Their attributions are global, stable, and internal.
   (p. 570)

16. **b**   a. Wrong.   She isn't being hurt by the spider. Key here is the attention (reward?).
   (p. 573)   c. Wrong.   She isn't watching someone afraid of a spider. Key here is the attention (reward?).
                   d. Wrong.   There is not repeated failure here. Key here is the attention (reward?).

17. **a**   b, c, & d.   Wrong.   Schumann was more productive, but the quality did not vary.
   (p. 560)

Multiple Choice Pretest 2

1. **b**   a. Wrong.   Insanity is a legal term, not a criterion for determining the abnormality of behavior.
   (p. 547)   c. Wrong.   Studying doesn't violate cultural norms, but it is maladaptive.
                 d. Wrong.   She shows no distress. Her excessive studying is maladaptive.

2. **c**   a. Wrong.   A person can have serious psychological problems but not be insane.
   (p. 548)   b. Wrong.   Dysfunction and distress are not required conditions to be declared insane.
                 d. Wrong.   Mental disease is part of the criterion for insanity, but it can be due to medical problems.

3. **c**   a. Wrong.   Max is anxious, not really fearful, and he exhibits compulsive behavior not seen in phobias.
   (p. 555)   b. Wrong.   Max has no alteration in conscious awareness. He has an obsession and compulsion.
                 d. Wrong.   Max doesn't have sudden attacks of intense anxiety. He has an obsession and compulsion.

4. **a**   b. Wrong.   The DSM-IV is a book describing diagnostic guidelines for mental disorders.
   (p. 549)   c. Wrong.   Insanity is a legal concept that makes no assumptions about cause or treatment.
                 d. Wrong.   The Rosenhan study examined expectancy or labeling effects.

5. **c**   a. Wrong.   This is abnormal consciousness. Key here is the different treatment due to a past disorder.
   (p. 550)   b. Wrong.   This is "giving up." Key here is the different treatment due to a past disorder.
                 d. Wrong.   Maladaptive attributions are dysfunctional attributions of ones own behavior.

6. **c**   a. Wrong.   Dissociative identity disorder involves multiple personalities.
   (p. 558)   b. Wrong.   There was no travel from home accompanying the amnesia.
                 d. Wrong.   Conversion disorder does not invalue amnesia.

7. **b**   a. Wrong.   His anxiety is constant and non-specific. Anxiety has sudden onset in panic disorder.
   (p. 554)   c. Wrong.   His anxiety is non-specific. Agoraphobia involves anxiety about a possible panic attack.
                 d. Wrong.   His anxiety is non-specific. OCD involves a more focused anxiety and compulsive behavior.

8. **b**   a. Wrong.   An intense fear linked to a specific source is a phobia, not an obsession or compulsion.
   (p. 555)   c. Wrong.   Generalized anxiety disorder has chronic, non-specific anxiety, not a specific fear.
                 d. Wrong.   Conversion disorder involves physical symptoms without a physical cause.

9. **c**   a & b.   Wrong.   These are external attributions. Depression is linked to internal attributions.
   (p. 570)   d.   Wrong.   This is an unstable attribution. Depression is linked to stable attributions.

10. **a**   b. Wrong.   Dissociation disorders involve breaks in normal conscious awareness.
   (p. 557)   c. Wrong.   Anxiety disorders do not focus on bodily functions.
                 d. Wrong.   Personality disorders involve chronic traits, not preoccupation with the body.

11. **c**   a. Wrong.   There's no loss of memory and has no travel.
   (p. 562)   b. Wrong.   Dysthymia is a chronic, relatively mild form of depression.
                 d. Wrong.   Double depression is dysthymia with an added major depressive episode.

12. **d**   a. Wrong.   Clark doesn't swing from depression to mania and back.
   (p. 564)   b. Wrong.   There is no free-floating anxiety, and hallucinations are not found in anxiety disorders.
                 c. Wrong.   Clark doesn't have multiple personalities.

13. **b**   a, c, & d.   Wrong.   Key here is the lifelong criminality with no remorse, signs of antisocial
   (p. 565)   personality disorder, not a clinical syndrome.

14. **b** a.   Wrong. Schizophrenia is treated with drugs that affect dopamine, not the other monamines.
(p. 568)   c & d.   Wrong.   The primary symptoms of these disorders are not commonly treated with drugs.

15. **c** a, b, & d.   Wrong.   Enlarged ventricles and low frontal lobe activity are found in schizophrenia.
(p. 568)

16. **c** a & b.   Wrong.   Schizophrenia involves a significant genetic component.
(p. 569)   d.   Wrong.   Even identical twins only have a 50% concordance rate.

17. **a** b.   Wrong.   Studies find a greater incidence of bipolar disorder, at least.
(p. 560)   c & d.   Wrong.   Mania affects output, but not quality.

LANGUAGE ENHANCEMENT GUIDE

CORE TERMS

In the lectures on this chapter, you are likely to hear terms like *pathology, impaired, dysfunction, lesion, compromised* and *debilitating.* Not surprisingly, these are all words having to do with disease. A *lesion*, as you may remember from chapter 3, is a cut or injury; *pathology* refers to a disease that causes damage. A *lesion* on the brain is likely to cause *impairment* or *dysfunction* -- the injured part of the brain won't work properly anymore. Another way to say it is that the function of that part will be *compromised.* Such an injury would be *debilitating* -- it would destroy the ability of the brain to function properly.

Since there are so many more conditions described in the DSM than are discussed in the book, don't be surprised if you hear about some more in class. Your instructor may choose to focus on the fact that some conditions appear in all cultures (such as schizophrenia), whereas some conditions are almost entirely *culturally bound.* For example, diseases such as anorexia and bulimia would be considered extremely bizarre in many other cultures, especially those where food is hard to come by. And other cultures have their own disorders. Your instructor is also likely to talk about some famous *case studies*, or share *anecdotes* (brief stories) about patients they have heard about or treated. These can be both interesting and helpful when you study. Remember, elaborative thinking improves recall -- so thinking of interesting examples will help you recall the material you need to learn.

IDIOMS

544	akin to	related to; like
546	sole criterion for	the only way of judging something
548	inmate	prisoner
548	the brunt of	the main force of

548	legal loopholes	weak points in laws that let people legally break the 'spirit' of those laws
548	the general public	most people
549	a continuum	a line going from one extreme to another (for example, from very hot to very cold)
550	a stigma	a characteristic that would cause others to avoid you
550	pseudopatient	pretend patient; someone who is pretending to be ill
552	clinicians	doctors and other health professionals
555	jingle	short song used in advertisements
558	colorful types	people with unusual personalities
558	Hollywood	a city in California where many TV programs and movies are made
558	the popular press	magazines read by the general public (as opposed to professional or specialized journals)
558	amnesiac	someone suffering from amnesia
559	the community at large	the whole community; most of the people involved
562	grandiosity	a belief that you are much more powerful or important than you really are
562	roller-coaster	a ride which sends you up and down hills very quickly
563	optimistic	expecting positive outcomes; cheerful
563	gone awry	gone wrong; gone off course
569	adoptees	those who have been adopted
570	extraterrestrials	'people' from outer space; aliens
572	plays a pivotal role	influences an important change
572	bouts of	attacks of an illness
573	does not preclude alternative accounts	does not mean that other reasons or descriptions might not be more accurate

WORD PARTS

Here are some words that are made up of word parts, and that you can find in this chapter. After you've looked at these, you can look for others in the chapter that use the same word parts (they are there, but YOU have to find them!)

WORD	WORD PART IT USES	MEANING
concurrently	con = together cur = to run	to run or happen at the same time
divert	di = two vert, vers = to turn	to split; to make go in a different direction
conspire	con = together spir = to breathe	to plan secretly; to whisper together
bipolar	bi = two pol = opposite	two opposite ends; moving between opposites
depressive	de = down, from, away press = to push down	that which pushes down
neurotransmitter	neuro = nerve trans = across mit = to send	that which sends across from nerve to nerve
disturb	dis = not, bad turb = to stir, agitate	to destroy calm
respond	re = again spon = to promise, to cause to expect	to reply, answer; to act in return

Knowing the word parts listed above, you can also create the following words. You can get an idea of their meanings from the word parts they use. You fill in the blanks!

conversion	_____ + _____	change, turn around
respire	re + spir	_____
compress	_____ + _____	to press together
correspond	co + re + spond	_____
transpire	_____ + _____	to become known, to happen
commit	_____ + _____	to do, perform; to deliver into safety

CHAPTER 15: THERAPY

ESTABLISHING LEARNING OBJECTIVES

Use these learning objectives as a preview of the chapter, a guide for active reading, and to evaluate your mastery of the material. Review the relevant objectives as you begin and end your reading of each major section of the chapter.

After studying this chapter you should be able to:

I. Solve the practical problem of how to treat the biomedical aspects of psychological disorders.
   A. Discuss how drug therapies can be used to treat psychological disorders.
      1. Describe how the introduction of drug therapy affected the mental health system.
      2. Identify the uses and limitations of each major category of drugs and explain how they work.
   B. Discuss and evaluate the use of electroconvulsive shock therapy.
      1. Identify the uses, limitations, and controversies of electroconvulsive therapy.
   C. Discuss how psychosurgery can be used to treat psychological disorders.
      1. Describe the prefrontal lobotomy and cingulotomy procedures, their purpose, and their limitations.
      2. Summarize the current attitude toward psychosurgery.

II. Solve the practical problem of how to treat the mental aspects of psychological disorders.
   A. Describe and evaluate psychoanalysis as a form of insight therapy.
      1. Explain the importance of free association, dream analysis, transference, and resistance.
      2. Describe how modern psychodynamic therapy differs from the psychoanalysis of Freud's era.
   B. Describe and evaluate cognitive therapies.
      1. Describe rational-emotive therapy, and give examples of common types of irrational thought.
      2. Describe Beck's cognitive therapy, and compare it to rational-emotive therapy.
   C. Describe and evaluate humanistic therapies.
      1. Describe client-centered therapy and the three essential core qualities the therapist should provide.
      2. Describe Gestalt and existential therapies.

III. Solve the practical problem of how to treat the environmental aspects of psychological disorders.
   A. Describe the general purpose of behavioral therapies.
   B. Describe systematic desensitization and aversion therapy.
   C. Describe how punishment and token economies can be used in therapy.

IV. Solve the practical problem of how to evaluate and choose psychotherapy.
   A. Discuss the major findings of clinical evaluation research.
      1. Describe the results of the Philadelphia study and meta-analytic studies of therapy's effectiveness.
      2. Discuss the controversies concerning studies of the effectiveness of therapy.
   B. Describe the factors that are common across psychotherapies.
   C. Discuss the important personal and cultural factors that should be considered when choosing a therapist.

MASTERING THE MATERIAL

Preview & Treating the Body: Biomedical Therapies (pp. 582-589)

Mastering the Vocabulary. Define or explain each of the following terms. To check your answers, consult the text pages listed.

1.   psychotherapy (p. 582)

2.   biomedical therapies (p. 584)

3.   antipsychotic drugs (p. 585)

4.   antidepressant drugs (p. 586)

5.   antianxiety drugs (p. 587)

6.   electroconvulsive therapy (p. 587)

7.   psychosurgery (p. 589)

Mastering the Concepts. Fill in the blanks to create a summary of this section. Answers are on page 361.

_____(1), treatment for mental, emotional or behavioral problems, can help both severe and more minor problems. This chapter considers the practical and conceptual problems of how to treat mental problems by treating the body, the mind and the environment and how to evaluate and choose a therapy.

_____(2) therapies originated in ancient Greece. _____(3) therapy began in the 1950s with the discovery of chlorpromazine to treat _____(4). Drugs have reduced the need for _____(5).

_____(6) drugs used to treat the positive symptoms of schizophrenia reduce _____(7) activity. They don't affect negative symptoms or work for all people, and they have side effects, including _____(8), involuntary facial movements. Clozapine affects dopamine and serotonin and often works when chlorpromazine doesn't. Depression is treated with antidepressants. Tricyclics affect _____(9), while fluoxetine (Prozac) affects _____(10). They are effective for over _____(11) of patients but require time to work, and they can have side effects. Bipolar disorder is treated with _____(12) carbonate. _____(13) drugs, such as benzodiazepine tranquilizers, affect _____(14).

Electroconvulsive therapy is used to treat _____(15) that has not responded to other therapies. It is effective in 50-70% of cases. Controversies include not knowing why it works, reports of temporary _____(16), and the possibility of brain damage. _____(17), brain surgery to alter behavior, is rarely performed. In the 1930s, Moniz developed the prefrontal _____(18) procedure to calm patients. Major cognitive deficits occurred. Cingulotomy, an operation that removes a little _____(19) system tissue, occasionally is used today to reduce obsessive-compulsive disorder and depression.

Evaluating Your Progress. Select the one best response. Answers are on page 361. If you make any errors, reread the relevant material before you proceed.

1. Biomedical therapy was proposed as early as
    a. 400 B.C. by Hippocrates for treating depression.
    b. the 16th century by doctors for treating "evil spirits."
    c. the 19th century by doctors for treating the paranoia of syphilis.
    d. the 1930's by Moniz for treating violent disorders.

2. The original, and still popular, drug used to treat schizophrenia is
    a. lithium carbonate.
    b. benzodiazepine (e.g., Xanax).
    c. clozapine (e.g., Clozaril).
    d. chlorpromazine (e.g., Thorazine).

3. Most antipsychotic drugs slow or block the activity of
    a. serotonin.
    b. norepinephrine.
    c. dopamine.
    d. GABA.

4. Tricyclic drugs and fluoxetine are examples of
    a. antipsychotic drugs.
    b. antianxiety drugs.
    c. antidepressant drugs.
    d. antimanic drugs.

5. The side effects associated with antidepressant drugs include
    a. tardive dyskinesia and blurry vision.
    b. drowsiness and psychological dependence.
    c. restlessness and diminished sexual desire.
    d. memory loss and possible brain damage.

6. The benzodiazepines
    a. increase the effectiveness of GABA.
    b. block the reuptake of norepinephrine.
    c. are dopamine antagonists.
    d. block the reuptake of serotonin.

7. Moniz used prefrontal lobotomies to
    a. treat severe depression.
    b. calm violent or agitated behavior.
    c. reduce obsessive thoughts.
    d. treat dissociative identity disorder.

8. Electroconvulsive therapy is most commonly used to treat
    a. generalized anxiety disorder.
    b. schizophrenia.
    c. obsessive-compulsive disorder.
    d. depression.

Treating the Mind: Insight Therapies (pp. 590-599)

Mastering the Vocabulary. Define or explain each of the following terms. To check your answers, consult text pages listed.

1. insight therapies (p. 590)

2. psychoanalysis (p. 590)

3. free association (p. 591)

4. dream analysis (p. 591)

5. resistance (p. 591)

6. transference (p. 592)

7. cognitive therapies (p. 593)

8. rational-emotive therapy (p. 594)

9. humanistic therapy (p. 596)

10. client-centered therapy (p. 597)

11. genuineness (p. 597)

12. unconditional positive regard (p. 597)

13. empathy (p. 597)

14. Gestalt therapy (p. 598)

15. group therapy (p. 598)

16. family therapy (p. 599)

Mastering the Concepts. Fill in the blanks to create a summary of this section. Answers are on page 361.

_____(20) therapies are based on the idea that disorders involve maladaptive thoughts that can be reduced by self-knowledge. _____(21), originated by Freud, emphasizes insight into conflicts repressed in the _____(22). Dream analysis and _____(23), saying what comes to mind, help determine those conflicts. Anxiety causes periods of poor cooperation, _____(24). When conflicts approach the surface, _____(25) occurs as the client directs emotions felt about other people toward the therapist instead. The fact that classical psychoanalysis is very _____(26) and costly has led to brief forms in which the therapist is more active, focuses on selective problems, and emphasizes _____(27), not sexual drives. This modern version is called _____(28) therapy.

Irrational conscious beliefs are emphasized in _____(29) therapies. In Ellis' _____(30) therapy, the therapist challenges any irrational thoughts to guide the person to insight. In Beck's cognitive therapy, the therapist is not combative, and clients are encouraged to discover negative thinking themselves.

The goal of _____(31) therapy is to help clients understand their self-worth, value, and potential. In Rogers' _____(32) therapy the therapist must show _____(33), genuineness, and unconditional positive regard to allow clients to analyze their own feelings. In Perl's _____(34) therapy the client's

350

goodness is emphasized, but the therapist is more directive. Emphasis is on the _____ (35) and expressing oneself as a "whole" person. Existential therapies encourage clients to take responsibility for their life decisions by providing a supportive environment.

Therapy is also done in a _____ (36) setting, which cuts costs and provides insight and support. _____ (37) therapy involves the entire family, not just one person.

Evaluating Your Progress. Select the one best response. Answers are on page 362. If you make any errors, reread the relevant material before proceeding.

1. The goal of psychoanalysis is to gain insight into disordered behavior by
   a. challenging the irrational beliefs held by the client.
   b. provide a supportive environment in which clients can explore their true self.
   c. bringing unconscious conflicts and memories into conscious awareness.
   d. having clients take notes about their feelings and behavior each day.

2. When transference occurs, clients
   a. go through periods in which they are uncooperative, skipping sessions, refusing to talk, etc.
   b. expresses their feelings to an empty chair and then respond to those feelings.
   c. take over control of the therapy and the therapist simply reflects back their feelings.
   d. express feelings toward the therapist that are representative of the way they feel about someone else.

3. Therapists using psychodynamic therapy, a modern version of classical psychoanalysis, are likely to
   a. play a less active role than classical psychoanalysts.
   b. emphasize sexual and aggressive drives as much as classical psychoanalysts.
   c. focus on a few specific conflicts most relevant to clients' symptoms.
   d. allow the client to gain insight on their own.

4. The therapy that attempts to get clients to stop using "I must" beliefs is
   a. existential therapy.
   b. client-centered therapy.
   c. rational-emotive therapy.
   d. Gestalt therapy.

5. The therapy that stresses the here-and-now and forces clients to express current feelings openly is
   a. classical psychoanalysis.
   b. client-centered therapy.
   c. systematic desensitization.
   d. Gestalt therapy.

6. Which is an advantage of group therapy?
   a. Transference is achieved more quickly.
   b. Group therapy is more cost-effective.
   c. It emphasizes conditions of worth.
   d. It uses two therapists rather than one.

7. An emphasis on getting clients to recognize their irrational beliefs themselves, rather than confronting them with them, is characteristic of
    a. Ellis' rational-emotive therapy.
    b. Perls' Gestalt therapy.
    c. Rogers' client-centered therapy.
    d. Beck's cognitive therapy.

8. To provide genuineness, unconditional positive regard and empathy so that clients can work through feelings and recognize their own self-worth is the goal of
    a. client-centered therapy.
    b. rational-emotive therapy.
    c. behavioral therapy.
    d. Beck's cognitive therapy.

Treating the Environment: Behavioral Therapies (pp. 600-604)

Mastering the Vocabulary.   Define or explain each of the following terms. To check your answers, consult the text pages listed.

1. behavioral therapies (p. 600)

2. systematic desensitization (p. 601)

3. aversion therapy (p. 601)

4. token economies (p. 603)

5. social skills training (p. 603)

Mastering the Concepts. Fill in the blanks to create a summary of this section. Answers are on page 361.

Behavioral therapy assumes that psychological problems can be _____(38), and that the _____(39) should be treated, not thoughts or feelings. One type developed by Jones and Wolpe, systematic _____(40), replaces a negative response with a relaxation response. Relaxation is paired with successively higher stimuli in the client's _____(41) hierarchy. This is often used to treat _____(42). An unwanted response (drinking) can be eliminated by _____(43) therapy, in which a pleasant reaction to something harmful is replaced with something unpleasant. Problems include ethical considerations and _____(44) if therapy is discontinued too soon.

Rewards are used to modify behavior in token _____(45). Tokens earned for appropriate behavior can later be exchanged for goods or privileges. This is combined with modeling in _____(46) training to improve the adjustment and social skills of people with schizophrenia. _____(47) modifies behavior, but it can damage the client-therapist relationship, it teaches only what not to do, and it raises ethical concerns.

Evaluating Your Progress. Select the one best response. Answers are on page 363. If you make any errors, reread the relevant material before proceeding.

1. Behavioral therapy treats
   a. unconscious conflicts.
   b. behaviors.
   c. irrational thoughts.
   d. feelings of inferiority.

2. The therapy in which relaxation is paired with anxiety-producing stimuli of increasing intensity is
   a. aversion conditioning.
   b. token economy therapy.
   c. existential therapy.
   d. systematic desensitization therapy.

3. The therapy that replaces a pleasant response with an unpleasant one is
   a. systematic desensitization.
   b. aversion therapy.
   c. token economy.
   d. meta-analysis.

4. Using modeling and rewards to teach appropriate ways of interacting with other people in order to improve the quality of life of individuals with psychological disorders is called
   a. systematic desensitization.
   b. aversion therapy.
   c. social skills training.
   d. insight therapy.

5. Token economies
   a. are used to teach appropriate behaviors.
   b. involve replacing an unpleasant response with a pleasant one.
   c. involve replacing a pleasant response with an unpleasant one.
   d. are used to develop congruent self-concepts.

Evaluating and Choosing Psychotherapy (pp. 605-610)

Mastering the Vocabulary. Define or explain each of the following terms. To check your answers, consult the text pages listed.

1. meta-analysis (p. 606)

2. spontaneous remission (p. 607)

Mastering the Concepts. Fill in the blanks to create a summary of the chapter. Answers are on page 361.

Valid evaluations of the effectiveness of therapy requires a _____(48) group and proper experimental procedures. The well-controlled Philadelphia study found that after four months, people receiving therapy were _____(49) improved than those on a waiting list, and that psychodynamic and behavioral therapies were _____(50) effective. After one year the three groups _____(51). Researchers have used _____(52) to examine many studies of therapy effects. Two conclusions are that therapy is better than no therapy, and different therapies are equally effective. Improvement without therapy, _____(53) remission, has raised questions about defining "treatment." The equal effects of all therapies is also controversial and may reflect the effect of _____(54) variables. The similar results also might be due to therapies having certain shared features: _____(55) factors, learning factors, and action factors. Effective therapy is predicted by the amount of _____(56) between client and therapist, and cultural background can be important.

Evaluating Your Progress. Select the one best response. Answers are on page 363. If you make any errors, reread the relevant material before proceeding.

1. According to the results of the Philadelphia study, psychotherapy
    a. has no effect.
    b. speeds up natural improvement.
    c. causes an improvement that is larger and longer lasting than getting no therapy.
    d. causes a significant number of people to get worse rather than better.

2. Based on the meta-analysis of hundreds of studies, we can reasonably conclude that
    a. psychotherapy doesn't work.
    b. psychoanalysis is more effective than behavioral therapies.
    c. cognitive therapies are more effective than psychoanalysis.
    d. all types of therapy are effective, with no type better than the others.

3. Therapies are said to share the common feature of learning factors. Learning factors involve
   a. giving clients a better understanding as to the cause of their behavior.
   b. giving clients suggestions for how they can improve their behavior.
   c. giving clients a sense of hope and control.
   d. giving clients the feeling that someone is concerned and wants to help them.

4. Possibly the most important factor to consider when choosing a therapist is
   a. their orientation (psychodynamic, behavioral, etc.)
   b. their age.
   c. the school at which they received their training.
   d. their amount of empathy.

MAKING FINAL PREPARATIONS

Complete these sections without consulting your book or notes. For a more accurate estimate of how well you know this material, wait at least a day or two after studying the chapter before working on the questions. Some material you "know" immediately after working with the chapter will be quickly forgotten. Immediate tests will overestimate what you know well.

Short Essay Questions. Write a brief answer to each question. Sample answers are on page 363.

1. Discuss how drug therapy has affected the mental health system.

2. Discuss the uses and limitations of ECT.

3. Compare Ellis' rational emotive therapy and Beck's cognitive therapy.

4. Compare the basic philosophy of insight therapies and behavioral therapies.

5. Discuss the limitations of the use of punishment as a primary form of therapy.

6. Summarize the conclusions about the effectiveness of various forms of psychotherapy.

7. Explain why cultural sensitivity can be important in therapy.

Matching. Select the correct definition or description for each item. Answers are on page 364.

_____ 1.	empathy		**a.**	anti-anxiety tranquilizers affecting GABA
_____ 2.	benzodiazepines		**b.**	Ellis' description of an irrational way of thinking
_____ 3.	meta-analysis		**c.**	open, honest, without phoniness
_____ 4.	Jones & Wolpe		**d.**	stresses expressing feelings as a whole person
_____ 5.	anxiety hierarchy		**e.**	ordered list of fear-inducing stimuli
_____ 6.	fluoxepine		**f.**	understanding; seeing client's point of view
_____ 7.	musterbation		**g.**	stresses accepting responsibility for life decisions
_____ 8.	prefrontal lobotomy		**h.**	technique to compare data from many studies
_____ 9.	genuineness		**i.**	developed prefrontal lobotomy
_____ 10.	tricyclics		**j.**	modern, shorter form of psychoanalysis
_____ 11.	Egas Moniz		**k.**	anti-depressants that affects norepinephrine
_____ 12.	existential therapy		**l.**	developed systematic desensitization
_____ 13.	resistance		**m.**	unconscious attempt to hinder therapy
_____ 14.	psychodynamic therapy		**n.**	psychosurgery to calm patient
_____ 15.	Gestalt therapy		**o.**	developed rational-emotive therapy
_____ 16.	Albert Ellis		**p.**	Prozac; anti-depressant affecting serotonin

Multiple Choice Pretest 1. Select the one best response. Answers are on page 364.

1. The number of people requiring institutionalization has dropped dramatically due to the development of
   a. the prefrontal lobotomy procedure.
   b. the cingulotomy procedure.
   c. systematic desensitization.
   d. psychoactive drugs.

2. Chlorpromazine and clozapine are examples of
   a. antidepressant drugs.
   b. antipsychotic drugs.
   c. antianxiety drugs.
   d. antimanic drugs.

3. Antipsychotic medication is affective for reducing
   a. the positive symptoms of schizophrenia.
   b. the negative symptoms of schizophrenia.
   c. both positive and negative symptoms of schizophrenia.
   d. the tardive dyskinesia the can occur with schizophrenia.

4. May suddenly began to forget her appointments, to misplace her dream diary, and to be unwilling to talk during her therapy sessions. A psychoanalytic therapist would interpret her behavior as
   a. transference.
   b. incongruence.
   c. resistance.
   d. musterbation.

5. Tricyclic antidepressant drugs reduce depression by modulating primarily
   a. norepinephrine.
   b. dopamine.
   c. GABA.
   d. serotonin.

6. Saul is taking lithium carbonate for a psychological disorder. The disorder is most likely
   a. schizophrenia.
   b. obsessive-compulsive disorder.
   c. depression (a major depressive episode).
   d. bipolar disorder.

7. Psychologists' concerns about electroconvulsive therapy (ECT) include all of the following except:
   a. ECT is not very effective.
   b. ECT causes loss of memory for events surrounding the treatment.
   c. ECT's method of action is unknown.
   d. The long-term effects of repeated ECT treatments is not known.

8. Ali is recovering from a cingulotomy. The outcome that might be expected is a reduction of
   a. obsessive-compulsive behavior.
   b. hallucinations and delusions.
   c. the manic periods in bipolar disorder.
   d. the ability to plan and coordinate actions.

9. Rehan's therapist has him relax and say whatever comes into his mind. This technique is
   a. musterbation.
   b. the empty chair technique.
   c. transference.
   d. free association.

10. Getting the client to change irrational, negative beliefs affecting their behavior is the goal of
    a. psychodynamic therapy.
    b. cognitive therapy.
    c. Gestalt therapy.
    d. humanistic therapy.

11. Genuineness, empathy, and unconditional positive regard are central components of
    a. cognitive therapy.
    b. behavioral therapy.
    c. client-centered therapy.
    d. psychoanalytic therapy.

12. In Ellis' rational-emotive therapy the therapist
    a. aggressively challenges the client's irrational thought processes.
    b. provides a supportive environment in which clients can discover their self-worth.
    c. interprets the free associations of the client to determine the unconscious conflicts present.
    d. provides a supportive environment in which clients learn to accept responsibility for their decisions.

13. Joe, who has schizophrenia, tends to either not respond to questions, or to shout an answer. Because Joe is due to return to the community in a month, his therapist is trying to teach him to interact socially in more appropriate ways by using rewards, modeling, and role playing. In other words, he is applying
    a. social skills training.
    b. systematic desensitization.
    c. aversion therapy.
    d. client-centered therapy.

14. A therapist using systematic desensitization to treat specific phobic disorder probably believes that
    a. phobias are caused by incongruent self-concepts.
    b. phobias are symptoms of unconscious conflicts or traumas.
    c. phobias are learned fear responses.
    d. phobias are the result of irrational thinking.

15. When Beth went for treatment of her alcoholism, she was given a drug that made her sick if she drank alcohol. This type of therapy is
    a. Gestalt therapy.
    b. systematic desensitization.
    c. aversion therapy.
    d. a token economy.

16. The Philadelphia study of the effectiveness of therapy found that
    a. people who got therapy of any type were better off after 4 months than people put on waiting lists.
    b. people who got therapy of any type were better off after 1 year than people put on waiting lists.
    c. people who got behavioral therapy improved more than people who got psychodynamic therapy.
    d. people who got psychodynamic therapy improved more than people who got behavioral therapy.

17. If June's panic disorder has undergone spontaneous remission it has
    a. responded very rapidly to therapy.
    b. failed to respond to therapy.
    c. increased in severity.
    d. improved without treatment.

18. Researchers have concluded that the average therapy client
    a. is better off than 80% of the people who do not get therapy.
    b. is better off than 30% of the people who do not get therapy.
    c. is not better off than the people who do not get therapy.
    d. is worse off than the people who do not get therapy.

19. All therapies provide clients with suggestions about how to improve. This common factor is
    a. a support factor.
    b. a learning factor.
    c. an action factor.
    d. empathy.

Multiple Choice Pretest 2. Select the one best response. Answers are on page 365.

1. Chad's therapist felt encouraged that they were getting close to uncovering the conflict causing Chad's anxiety because Chad had begun to be very hostile and aggressive toward him and once called him "Dad" by mistake. In psychoanalytic therapy, Chad's behavior toward his therapist is considered
   a. transference.
   b. free association.
   c. resistance.
   d. incongruence.

2. Barry has hallucinations and delusions with his schizophrenia. A psychiatrist is likely to prescribe
   a. electroconvulsive therapy.
   b. chlorpromazine.
   c. systematic desensitization.
   d. cingulotomy.

3. Otto has been switched from chlorpromazine to clozapine. The likely reason for this is
   a. clozapine has no medical side effects.
   b. clozapine produces tardive dyskinesia.
   c. chlorpromazine didn't reduce his delusions.
   d. chlorpromazine didn't reduce his depression.

4. Flora is severely depressed. A psychiatrist is most likely to prescribe
   a. lithium carbonate.
   b. chlorpromazine (Thorazine)
   c. a tricyclic drug.
   d. a benzodiazepine (Xanax).

5. Renatta is taking the benzodiazepine drug Xanax. Her psychological problem is likely to be
   a. bipolar disorder.
   b. generalized anxiety disorder.
   c. schizophrenia.
   d. depression.

6. As a result of treatment in 1946 for a violent psychological disorder, Craig is calm, but he has cognitive deficits, including the inability to plan and coordinate actions. The treatment probably was
   a. electroconvulsive therapy (ECT).
   b. drug treatment using chlorpromazine (Thorazine).
   c. prefrontal lobotomy.
   d. benzodiazepine (Xanax) drug treatment.

7. Marko's therapist aggressively challenged him to explain why breaking up with his girlfriend means he is a worthless failure, pointing out the illogical aspects of his thoughts. Marko's therapist seems to be using
   a. aversion therapy.
   b. classical psychoanalysis.
   c. client-centered therapy.
   d. rational-emotive therapy.

8. Electroconvulsive therapy works by
   a. blocking reuptake of serotonin.
   b. decreasing utilization of dopamine.
   c. modulating norepinephrine.
   d. some yet-to-be-determined action.

9. Adele is undergoing electroconvulsive therapy (ECT). Adele has probably
   a. failed to respond to antidepressive drugs.
   b. developed tardive dyskinesia and must give up drug therapy.
   c. developed very violent behavior as part of her schizophrenia.
   d. developed very severe obsessive-compulsive disorder.

10. Rosietta overheard two psychologists talking about transference and resistance and decided they must be
    a. client-centered therapists.
    b. psychoanalytic therapists.
    c. cognitive therapists.
    d. behavioral therapists.

11. Kim's therapist is very non-judgmental and merely reflects back what Kim says. Kim's therapist is
    a. a behavioral therapist.
    b. a client-centered therapist.
    c. a rational-emotive therapist.
    d. a psychoanalytic therapist.

12. Jackie never thought she'd get homework assigned by her therapist, but she did. She has to keep track of her negative thoughts, why they occurred, and how they make her feel. Jackie's therapy is probably
    a. classical psychoanalysis.
    b. rational-emotive therapy.
    c. Beck's cognitive therapy.
    d. systematic desensitization.

13. Dan's therapist is never critical and is always accepting and respectful of him. His therapist is showing
    a. empathy.
    b. unconditional positive regard.
    c. genuineness.
    d. congruence.

14. Cory is learning to maintain relaxation while he imagines anxiety-producing stimuli. Cory's treatment is
    a. systematic desensitization therapy.
    b. aversion therapy.
    c. a token economy.
    d. psychoanalytic therapy.

15. A problem associated with aversion therapy that is ended too soon is
    a. extinction of the aversive response.
    b. the ethical problem of consent.
    c. damage to the client-therapist relationship.
    d. development of a new psychological problem.

16. Leo has been given a poker chip because he got dressed appropriately this morning. He later will be able to exchange his poker chips for a chance to go on a field trip outside the hospital. Leo is taking part in
    a. systematic desensitization.
    b. existential therapy.
    c. aversion therapy.
    d. a token economy.

17. Ida is in psychodynamic therapy, Jo is in behavioral therapy, and Vi is not in therapy. We should expect
    a. Ida will improve greatly, Jo will improve modestly, and Vi will not improve.
    b. Jo will improve greatly, Ida will improve modestly, and Vi will not improve.
    c. Jo and Ida will show equal improvement, and Vi will not improve.
    d. Jo and Ida will show equal improvement, and Vi will improve, but not as quickly.

18. Rodrigo asked your advice about how to find a good therapist. What advice would be most accurate?
    a. "Find one that uses a cognitive approach. That's the best approach to therapy."
    b. "Pick any therapist. Every therapist is just as effective as the others."
    c. "Find one with whom you feel comfortable and who understands you."
    d. "Find one that uses a behavioral approach. That works best for most problems."

ANSWERS AND EXPLANATIONS

Mastering the Concepts

1. Psychotherapy (p. 582)
2. Biomedical (p. 583)
3. Drug (p. 584)
4. schizophrenia (p. 584)
5. institutionalization (584)
6. Anti-psychotic (p. 585)
7. dopamine (p. 585)
8. tardive dyskinesia (p. 585)
9. norepinephrine (p. 586)
10. serotonin (p. 586)
11. 50% (p. 586)
12. lithium (p. 587)
13. Antianxiety (p. 587)
14. GABA (p. 587)

15. depression (p. 588)
16. memory loss (p. 588)
17. Psychosurgery (p.589)
18. lobotomy (p. 589)
19. limbic (p. 589)
20. Insight (p. 590)
21. Psychoanalysis (p. 590)
22. unconscious (p. 590)
23. free association (p. 591)
24. resistance (p. 591)
25. transference (p. 592)
23. lengthy (p. 592)
27. social skills (p. 593)
28. psychodynamic (p. 593)

29. cognitive (p. 593)
30. rational-emotive (p. 594)
31. humanistic (p. 596)
32. client-centered (p. 596)
33. empathy (p. 597)
34. Gestalt (p. 598)
35. here & now (p. 598)
36. group (p. 598)
37. Family (p. 599)
38. learned (p. 600)
39. behavior (p. 600)
40. desensitization (p. 601)
41. anxiety (p. 601)
42. phobias (p. 601)

43. aversion (p. 601)
44. extinction (p. 602)
45. economies (p. 603)
46. social skills (p. 603)
47. Punishment (p. 604)
48. control (p. 605)
49. more (p. 606)
50. equally (p. 606)
51. were equal (p. 606)
52. meta-analysis (p. 606)
53. spontaneous (p. 607)
54. client (p. 608)
55. support (p. 608)
56. empathy (p. 609)

Evaluating Your Progress

Preview & Treating the Body: Biomedical Therapies

1. **a**   b, c, & d.   Wrong.   These were not as early as Hippocrates' suggestions.
   (p. 583)

2. **d**   a. Wrong.   This drug is used to treat bipolar disorder.
   (p. 584)   b. Wrong.   This drug is used to treat anxiety disorders.
             c. Wrong.   Although it is also an antipsychotic, it is a recently developed drug.

3. **c**   a. Wrong.   Clozapine affects serotonin, but most antipsychotics don't. Prozac (an antidepressant)
   (p. 585)   affects serotonin.
                b. Wrong.   Tricyclic antidepressants affect norepinephrine, not antipsychotics.
                d. Wrong.   Antianxiety drugs affect GABA, not antipsychotics.

4. **c**   a, b, & d.   Wrong. Tricyclics and fluoxetine (Prozac) are antidepressants.
   (p. 586)

5. **c**   a. Wrong.   These are side effects of antipsychotic drugs.
   (p. 586)   b. Wrong.   These are side effects of antianxiety drugs.
                d. Wrong.   These are side effects of ECT.

6. **a**   b. Wrong.   Tricyclics do this.
   (p. 587)   c. Wrong.   Antipsychotics are dopamine antagonists.
                d. Wrong.   Prozac (fluoxetine) does this.

7. **b**   a, c, & d.   Wrong.   Prefrontal lobotomies were used to calm behavior.
   (p. 589)

8. **d**   a. Wrong.   Anti-anxiety drugs and insight therapy is used to treat generalized anxiety disorder.
   (p. 588)   b. Wrong.   Anti-psychotic drugs are used to treat schizophrenia.
                c. Wrong.   Anti-anxiety drugs or cingulotomies are used to treat obsessive compulsive disorder.

Treating the Mind: Insight Therapies

1. **c**   a. Wrong.   This describes Ellis' rational-emotive therapy.
   (p. 590)   b. Wrong.   This describes Rogers' client-centered therapy.
                d. Wrong.   This describes Beck's cognitive therapy.

2. **d**   a. Wrong.   This describes resistance.
   (p. 592)   b. Wrong.   This describes the "empty chair" technique used by Gestalt therapists.
                c. Wrong.   This describes client-centered therapy, a humanistic therapy.

3. **c**   a, b, & d.   Wrong.   Modern versions speed therapy by limiting the focus of therapy, being more
   (p. 593)   directive early in therapy, and emphasizing interpersonal skills rather than sex
                                     and aggression.

4. **c**   a, b, & d.   Wrong.   Ellis, of rational-emotive therapy, outlined the problem of "musterbation."
   (p. 595)

5. **d**   a, b, & c.   Wrong.   These are the hallmarks of Gestalt therapy.
   (p. 598)

6. **b**   a. Wrong.   Transference is a concept in psychoanalytic therapy, which is not a type of group therapy.
   (p. 599)   c. Wrong.   Conditions of worth are not therapeutic and relate to humanistic therapy, not group therapy.
                d. Wrong.   Group therapy involves a group of clients, not a group of therapists.

7. **d**   a. Wrong.   Ellis confronts clients with their illogical thoughts.
   (p. 595)   b. Wrong.   Gestalt therapy doesn't emphasize illogical thoughts. It's a humanistic therapy.
                c. Wrong.   Client-centered humanistic therapy doesn't emphasis the role of irrational thoughts.

8. **a**   b & d. Wrong.   Cognitive therapies seek to change the client's irrational way of thinking.
   (p. 597)   c.   Wrong.   Behavioral therapy seeks to modify behavior to a more adaptive form.

1. **b**   a, c, & d.   Wrong.   Behavioral therapy treats behaviors, not thoughts, feelings, or the unconscious.
    (p. 600)

2. **d**   a. Wrong.   Aversion therapy replaces a pleasant response with an unpleasant one.
    (p. 601)   b. Wrong.   Token economies use rewards to increase desired behaviors.
               c. Wrong.   Existential therapy encourages people to take responsibility for their decisions.

3. **b**   a. Wrong.   This replaces an unpleasant response with a pleasant one.
    (p. 601)   c. Wrong.   Token economies don't replace pleasant responses, they reward appropriate behavior.
               d. Wrong.   Meta-analysis is a research tool, not a therapy.

4. **c**   a, b, & d.   Wrong.   Key here is the improvement of social interactions for improved quality of life.
    (p. 603)

5   **a**   b. Wrong.   This describes systematic desensitization.
    (p. 603)   c. Wrong.   This describes aversion therapy.
               d. Wrong.   This describes client-centered therapy.

Evaluating and Choosing Psychotherapy

1. **b**   a, c, & d.   Wrong.   Control groups caught up with therapy groups, so therapy primarily speeds up a
    (p. 606)   natural improvement.

2. **d**   a.   Wrong.   Psychotherapy does work.
    (p. 607)   b & c. Wrong.   Meta-analysis finds no particular therapy consistently better than another.

3. **a**   b & c. Wrong.   These are part of the action factor.
    (p. 608)   d.   Wrong.   This is part of the support factor.

4. **d**   a, b, & c.   Wrong.   Empathy is one of the best predictors of an effective therapist.
    (p. 609)

MAKING FINAL PREPARATIONS

Short Essay Questions

1. Drug therapy has greatly reduced the number of people who are institutionalized for psychological treatment. Drugs reduce symptoms and allow people to be treated in their communities. (p. 584)

2. ECT is used to treat depression that has not responded to other therapies. It is highly effective, but its use has been limited by several concerns. Although reports of serious memory deficits has not been found in controlled research, ECT causes memory loss for events close to the treatment. Because ECT involves several treatments, there is worry that brain damage might occur. Also, why it works is unknown, causing caution. (pp. 587-588)

3. Both therapies view abnormality to be due to irrational thoughts. In Ellis' therapy the client is aggressively confronted concerning irrational thoughts. Beck's therapy is not as confrontational. Clients are encouraged to discover their own irrational thoughts. (pp. 593-596)

4.   Insight therapies are based on the idea that by gaining insight into a problem, a person can resolve the problem and become psychologically healthy. The thoughts or conflicts are treated. Behavioral therapies treat behaviors, not thoughts. Any underlying problem is almost irrelevant; if a behavior is unwanted or inappropriate, change the behavior. This assumes that abnormal behavior can be learned, and unlearned. (pp. 590, 600)

5.   Although punishment can quickly modify behavior, it has limitations. It can damage the client-therapist relationship that is otherwise supportive. It teaches what not to do, but not what to do. Finally, there are ethical questions concerning the ability of a disturbed client to give free consent. (p. 604)

6.   Repeated evaluations of therapy suggest that any major type of therapy is better than no therapy, but that no one type of therapy is significantly better than the others. Untreated people do improve, and may catch up to treated people eventually, but therapy speeds the improvement. (pp. 605-608)

7.   Cultural sensitivity can be important because one of the primary factors in effective therapy is empathy, being able to understand the client's point of view. Cultural differences in perspective or world-view can create problems for the development of empathy. Also, language differences make communication difficult, and cultural differences in personal style can influence what type of therapy might be most effective. (pp. 609-610)

Matching

1. **f** (p. 597)	4. **l** (p. 601)	7. **b** (p. 595)	10. **k** (p. 586)	13. **m** (p. 591)	16. **o** (p. 594)
2. **a** (p. 587)	5. **e** (p. 601)	8. **n** (p. 589	11. **i** (p. 589)	14. **j** (p. 593)	
3. **h** (p. 606)	6. **p** (p. 586)	9. **c** (p. 597)	12. **g** (p. 598)	15. **d** (p. 598)	

Multiple Choice Pretest 1

1.   **d**   a & b.   Wrong.   Prefrontal lobotomies are no longer done, and psychosurgery of any type is rare.
     (p. 584)   c.   Wrong.   Systematic desensitization is used in relatively few types of disorders.

2.   **b**   a, c, & d.   Wrong.   Chlorpromazine and clozapine are antipsychotic drugs used for schizophrenia.
     (p. 585)

3.   **a**   b & c.   Wrong.   Antipsychotic drugs affect only the positive symptoms.
     (p. 585)   d.   Wrong.   Antipsychotic drugs cause tardive dyskinesia, they don't reduce it.

4.   **c**   a. Wrong.   In transference, behavior shifts to fit how the client feels about someone else.
     (p. 591)   b. Wrong.   Incongruence is a concept in humanistic therapy, not psychoanalytic therapy.
                  d. Wrong.   Musterbation, holding irrational "I must" ideas, is a cognitive therapy concept.

5.   **a**   b. Wrong.   Dopamine is blocked by antipsychotic drugs.
     (p. 586)   c. Wrong.   GABA is increased by antianxiety drugs.
                  d. Wrong.   Prozac modulates serotonin, but Prozac isn't a tricyclic.

6.   **d**   a, b, & c.   Wrong.   Lithium carbonate is an antimanic drug used for bipolar disorder.
     (p. 587)

7.   **a**   b, c, & d.   Wrong.   These are all points of concern, and ECT is very effective.
     (p. 588)

8.   **a**   b & c.   Wrong.   Cingulotomy is used to treat obsessive-compulsive disorder.
     (p. 589)   d.   Wrong.   These are side effects of prefrontal lobotomy, not cingulotomy.

9. **d**   a. Wrong.   This is Ellis' term for inflexible, absolute irrational thoughts.
(p. 591)   b. Wrong.   This involves clients projecting their feelings at an empty chair and talking back.
             c. Wrong.   This involves transferring toward the therapist feelings felt about another person.

10. **b**   a. Wrong.   Psychodynamic therapy is based on resolving unconscious conflicts.
(p. 593)   c. Wrong.   Gestalt therapy is based getting the client to function as a "whole" person.
             d. Wrong.   Humanistic therapy is based on getting the client to develop congruence.

11. **c**   a, b, & d. Wrong.   Genuineness, empathy, and unconditional positive regard are the hallmarks of
(p. 597)   humanistic client-centered therapy.

12. **a**   b. Wrong.   This describes humanistic (client-centered) therapy.
(p. 594)   c. Wrong.   This describes psychoanalytic therapy.
             d. Wrong.   This describes existential (humanistic) therapy.

13. **a**   b. Wrong.   Systematic desensitization eliminate anxiety responses; it doesn't teach social skills.
(p. 603)   c. Wrong.   Aversion therapy replaces pleasant responses with unpleasant ones.
             d. Wrong.   Client-centered therapy focuses on thoughts, not behaviors.

14. **c**   a, b & d.   Wrong.   Systematic desensitization is a behavioral approach based on the idea that
(p. 600)   abnormal behavior can be learned, and to "treat" it, new behaviors are taught.

15. **c**   a, b & d.   Wrong.   Replacing a pleasant response with an unpleasant one (illness) is aversion
(p. 601)   therapy.

16. **a**   b.   Wrong.   Therapy groups didn't differ from the waiting list people after 1 year.
(p. 606)   c & d. Wrong.   Type of therapy did not matter.

17. **d**   a, b, & c. Wrong.   Spontaneous remission is an improvement without treatment.
(p. 607)

18. **a**   b, c & d.   Wrong.   The average therapy patient is better off than 80% of those getting no therapy.
(p. 607)

19. **c**   a. Wrong.   Support factors involve someone who wants to help them get better, not how.
(p. 608)   b. Wrong.   Learning factors involve understanding why their behavior occurs.
             d. Wrong.   Empathy is the understanding of the client's point of view, part of the support factor.

Multiple Choice Pretest 2

1. **a**   b, c, & d. Wrong.   Chad had begun to express feelings toward his therapist that he actually feels
(p. 592)   about someone else (Dad). This is transference, a positive sign in therapy.

2. **b**   a. Wrong.   ECT is almost exclusively used for depression, not schizophrenia.
(p. 585)   c. Wrong.   Systematic desensitization is used for specific phobic disorder, not schizophrenia.
             d. Wrong.   Cingulotomies are rare and used for depression and obsessive-compulsive disorder.

3. **c**   a. Wrong.   Clozapine has side effects, but not tardive dyskinesia is not one of them.
(p. 586)   b. Wrong.   Clozapine doesn't produce tardive dyskinesia, but he wouldn't want tardive dyskinesia.
             d. Wrong.   Neither chlorpromazine nor clozapine are used to treat depression; they're antipsychotics.

4. c   a. Wrong.   Lithium is used for the manic state of bipolar disorder.
   (p. 586)   b. Wrong.   Antipsychotics (Thorazine) are used for schizophrenia.
               d. Wrong.   Benzodiazepines are antianxiety drugs, not antidepressants.

5. b   a, c, & d.   Wrong.   Benzodiazepines are antianxiety drugs.
   (p. 587)

6. c   a.   Wrong.   ECT isn't used to calm people; it's used for depression.
   (p. 589)   b & d.   Wrong.   Drugs weren't available before the 50's, and do not have these side effects.

7. d   a, b, & c.   Wrong.   Key here is the active challenge of Marko's irrational beliefs.
   (p. 594)

8. d   a, b, & c.   Wrong.   The way ECT works is unknown at this time.
   (p. 588)

9. a   b, c, & d.   Wrong.   ECT is used for severe depression that hasn't responded to other therapy.
   (p. 588)

10. b   a, c, & d.   Wrong.   Transference and resistance are key concepts in psychoanalytic therapy.
   (p. 591)

11. b   a, c, & d.   Wrong.   Non-judgmental and reflecting the client's thoughts are hallmarks of client-
   (p. 597)   centered therapy.

12. c   a, b, & d.   Wrong.   Homework of this sort is characteristic of Beck's cognitive therapy.
   (p. 595)

13. b   a. Wrong.   Empathy is seeing things from a client's perspective.
   (p. 597)   c. Wrong.   Genuineness is being open, honest, and without phoniness.
               d. Wrong.   Congruence is a match between self-concept and daily experience.

14. a   b. Wrong.   Aversion therapy uses an unpleasant response, not relaxation, a pleasant one.
   (p. 601)   c. Wrong.   A token economy uses rewards for appropriate behavior.
               d. Wrong.   Psychoanalysis doesn't teach relaxation responses.

15. a   b & c.   Wrong.   These are problems associated with punishment.
   (p. 602)   d.   Wrong.   The old problem might return, but a new problem will not develop.

16. d   a, b, & c.   Wrong.   Token economies reward appropriate behaviors with tokens that are exchanged
   (p. 603)   for privileges.

17. d   a, b, & c.   Wrong.   Studies consistently find equal improvements across therapies and a greater effect
   (p. 606)   for therapy than for no therapy.

18. c   a, b, & d.   Wrong.   Empathy and trust are primary determinants of successful therapy.
   (p. 609)

LANGUAGE ENHANCEMENT GUIDE

CORE TERMS

In the lectures on this chapter, you will be learning about drugs that affect the mind, so you can expect to hear the term *psychoactive drugs*. You already learned a bit about one kind of these in the chapter on consciousness; *psychotropic drugs* like marijuana and LSD alter consciousness. But in this chapter you will be learning about *psychopharmaceuticals* --drugs that are *therapeutic* (helpful in treating illnesses). These drugs are used more often than *psychosurgery* (surgical operations on the brain) because they are *non-invasive*; because there are no cuts, there is no risk of wound infection and other surgery-related problems. The other *non-invasive* treatment is, of course, counseling. In these lectures your instructor may use the terms *counseling, therapy* and *psychotherapy* fairly interchangeably.

One more thing: you may wonder why counselors need to have *empathy* rather than *sympathy* for their clients. The answer to this can be found in the word parts: if one has *sympathy*, then one feels along with the other person. A counselor needs to be a bit more objective; in *empathy*, the emphasis is on understanding the feelings rather than participating in them.

IDIOMS

584	early twentieth century	early 1900s
584	venereal disease	sexually transmitted disease
587	"even keel"	avoiding extremes; not rocking from one side to the other (a keel is the bottom of a boat)
587	a downside	a negative perspective; reason something is not so good
588	of last resort	the least preferred option
588	conventional	ordinary, usual
589	cognitive deficits	problems in thinking well
591	maneuver around a number of roadblocks	find a way around many difficulties
592	contemporaries	those who live at the same time
593	streamline	to smooth the edges of something, to make it move more easily through air, water, etc.
595	a more subtle tack	a less direct or forceful way
599	odds of	chances, likelihood, probability of

WORD PARTS

Here are some words that are made up of word parts, and that you can find in this chapter. After you've looked at these, you can look for others in the chapter that use the same word parts (they are there, but YOU have to find them!)

WORD	WORD PART IT USES	MEANING
antagonist	ant, anti = against agon = struggle	one who struggles against; enemy
eliminate	limin = threshold, borderline	to put outside awareness, to remove
excess	ex = out of cede, ceed, cess = to go, yield	extra, overflow
resistance	re = again sist, sta, stet = to stand	to stand against an attack
subvert	sub = under vert = to turn	to undermine; to attack from underneath
transference	trans = across fer = bring, bear, yield	to send across
innate	in = in nat = newborn	present at birth, inborn
speculated	spec = to look lat = line	to look "down the line", to predict

Knowing the word parts listed above, you can also create the following words. You can get an idea of their meanings from the word parts they use. You fill in the blanks!

conference	con + fer	_____
sublimate	_____ + _____	to push down below the line of awareness
consistent	_____ + _____	to be compatible, agreeable; to go together well
proceed	pro + ceed	_____
prenatal	pre (before) + nat	_____
related	_____ + _____	to be another "in a line"

CHAPTER 16: STRESS AND HEALTH

ESTABLISHING LEARNING OBJECTIVES

Use these learning objectives as a preview of the chapter, a guide for active reading, and to evaluate your mastery of the material. Review the relevant objectives as you begin and end your reading of each major section of the chapter.

After studying this chapter you should be able to:

I.   Solve the conceptual and adaptive problems of how to define stress and respond to stressors.
    A. Define and describe the stress response.
        1. Define stress and explain how it is an adaptive reaction.
        2. Discuss Seyle's General Adaptation Syndrome view of the physiological components of stress.
        3. Describe the psychological aspects of stress.
    B. Explain the role of cognitive appraisal in the stress response.
    C. Discuss external sources of stress.
        1. Describe the Holmes and Rahe' Social Readjustment Rating Scale and explain what it predicts.
        2. Define daily hassles and compare their effects to those of life events.
        3. Identify other external stressors likely to be studied by environmental psychologists.
    D. Discuss internal sources of stress.
        1. Specify the relationship between perceived control and stress.
        2. Specify the relationship between explanatory styles and stress.
        3. Identify the personality characteristics related to stress and their possible health outcomes.

II. Solve the practical problem of identifying the physical and psychological effects of prolonged stress.
    A. Describe the physical consequences of prolonged stress, including the link between stress and the immune system.
        1. Specify the link between stress, the immune system, and cancer and discuss alternative views.
        2. Specify the link between stress and cardiovascular problems.
    B. Describe the psychological consequences of prolonged stress, including posttraumatic stress disorder and burnout.
        1. Describe the symptoms of posttraumatic stress disorder.
        2. Describe the symptoms of burnout and the conditions likely to produce burnout.

III. Solve the adaptive problem of how to cope with stress.
    A. Discuss how relaxation techniques can be used to reduce stress.
    B. Discuss the positive and negative effects of social support.
    C. Explain how stress can be managed through cognitive reappraisal of the stressful situation.

IV. Solve the adaptive problem of how to live a healthy lifestyle.
    A. Discuss the physical and psychological benefits of aerobic exercise.
    B. Discuss the consequences of tobacco use, and explain why it is difficult to quite smoking.
    C. Identify the value of proper nutrition.
    D. Explain the different types of prevention programs and their use in AIDS prevention.

MASTERING THE MATERIAL

Preview & Experiencing Stress: Stressors and the Stress Response (pp. 618-628)

Mastering the Vocabulary. Define or explain each of the following terms. To check your answers, consult the text pages listed.

1. health psychology (p. 618)

2. stress (p. 619)

3. stressors (p. 619)

4. general adaptation syndrome (p. 620)

5. cognitive appraisal (p. 622)

6. environmental psychology (p. 625)

7. perceived control (p. 626)

8. Type A (p. 627)

9. Type B (p. 627)

Mastering the Concepts. Fill in the blanks to create a summary of this section. Answers are on page 382.

_____(1) psychology, part of behavioral medicine, studies the role of biological, psychological, environmental, and cultural factors in promoting physical health. Four adaptive problems are considered: What are the causes and effects of stress? What are the effects of prolonged stress? How can people cope with stress? What factors promote physical and psychological health?

Stress is the physical and psychological _____(2) to demanding situations. Stress can be adaptive because it _____(3) the body to respond, but it can have negative effects. Selye proposed the general _____(4) syndrome to describe general physiological reactions to all stressors. In the _____(5) stage, the sympathetic nervous system is activated, causing general arousal. In the _____(6) stage, arousal is still high, but the body maintains resources and function. Susceptibility to other stressors is high and _____(7) problems may begin to develop. In the _____(8) stage, the body starts to give up, maladaptive behavior occurs, and serious damage is possible. Criticisms of Selye's proposal involve evidence that the stress response is variable and depends on the cognitive _____(9) of the situation and coping resources. Stress also involves emotional and behavioral components. Dealing successfully with stress can lead to improved self-image and immune system strength.

Holmes and Rahe developed the Social Readjustment Rating Scale that uses significant _____(10) to predict future illness. Life events involve either positive or negative _____(11). Criticized for ignoring individual differences and cognitive appraisal, the scale is still widely used. Little irritations, _____(12), also correlate with health problems. Noise, especially unpredictable, intermittent noise, and crowding also are stressors that produce health problems. _____ (13) psychology studies environmental influences on health and behavior.

Internal sources of stress include perceived _____(14), which reduces stress, _____(15) style, and personality characteristics, including the _____(16) personalities. If attributions about negative events are _____(17), stable, and global, stress is more likely. Optimism is linked to less stress, and cardiovascular problems are more likely with a hostile Type A personality, although other factors might also be important.

Evaluating Your Progress. Select the one best response. Answers are on page 383. If you make any errors, reread the relevant material before proceeding.

1. The author of your text defines stress as
   a. a stimulus that places a demand on the person.
   b. an internal process through which external events are interpreted as threatening or demanding.
   c. the physical and psychological reaction that people have to demanding situations.
   d. demanding situations that threaten the well-being of the person.

2. The stages of Selye's general adaptation syndrome, in the correct order, are
   a. activation, exhaustion, resistance.
   b. activation, adaptation, alarm.
   c. alarm, resistance, exhaustion.
   d. resistance, exhaustion, alarm.

3. All of the following are true concerning Selye's general adaptation syndrome except:
   a. It proposes that different stressors produce the same sequence of stress reactions.
   b. It proposes that stressors cause the somatic nervous system to initiate physiological arousal.
   c. It proposes that extended stress causes health problems to develop during the resistance stage.
   d. It proposes that the body cannot maintain high stress for long periods without suffering damage.

4. Holmes & Rahe's Social Readjustment Rating Scale is based on the idea that
    a. events involving change produce stress.
    b. stress occurs only for events that have negative consequences.
    c. stress is dependent on people's perception of the situation.
    d. perceived control is critical to the impact of stress.

5. Emphasis on people's perceptions of a situation and their ability to deal with that situation is characteristic of
    a. Selye's general adaptation syndrome approach to stress.
    b. the cognitive appraisal approach to stress.
    c. Holmes and Rahe's life events approach to stress.
    d. the tertiary prevention approach to stress.

6. Noise will be most likely to create stress if it is
    a. predictable.
    b. constant.
    c. loud.
    d. new to the situation.

7. Kelly is most likely to develop stress-related problems if
    a. someone else controls what happens to her.
    b. she makes external, situational, and temporary attributions about negative events.
    c. her personality is a "Type B."
    d. she has an optimistic personal style.

8. Type A personality is characterized by
    a. cool, calm, and collected behavior.
    b. an optimistic, but dependent, style.
    c. hard-driven, ambitious, and impatient behavior.
    d. external, stable, and situational attributions.

9. Some researchers suggest that the critical aspect of Type A behavior that relates to heart disease is
    a. working long hours.
    b. the need to be in control.
    c. the feeling that everything must be done quickly.
    d. the tendency to be hostile or angry.

Reacting to Prolonged Stress: Physical and Psychological Effects (pp. 629-634)

Mastering the Vocabulary. Define or explain each of the following terms. To check your answers, consult the text pages listed.

1. lymphocytes (p. 630)

2. posttraumatic stress disorder (p. 632)

3.   burnout (p. 633)

Mastering the Concepts. Fill in the blanks to create a summary of this section. Answers are on page 382.

Stress increases susceptibility to illness because it suppresses the _____(18). People with high stress were more likely to catch the common cold in one experiment, and other studies found lower levels of _____(19), a type of white blood cell, and more rapid growth of tumors. Immune system suppression can be adaptive in some circumstances however. Stress increases the risk for cardiovascular disease, possibly because stress increases _____(20) and cholesterol.

Stress influences psychological health, but is not sufficient to cause major problems for most people. One serious condition due to traumatic events is _____(21) stress disorder. Symptoms include _____(22), avoidance of stimuli linked to the trauma, and chronic _____(23) symptoms, such as sleep problems and irritability. _____(24) is a state of physical, emotional, and mental exhaustion caused by long-term involvement in emotionally demanding situations. Sufferers are usually highly motivated, but become disillusioned and perhaps feel as if life is meaningless.

Evaluating Your Progress. Select the one best response. Answers are on page 383. If you make any errors, reread the relevant material before proceeding.

1.   Teachers should expect more students will get sick during the final exam period because stress inhibits
      a.   the cardiovascular system.
      b.   the immune system.
      c.   the sympathetic nervous system.
      d.   the endocrine system.

2.   One reason stress might increase the risk for developing heart disease is that stress
      a.   increases the number of lymphocytes in the blood.
      b.   increases cholesterol.
      c.   reduces autonomic nervous system activity.
      d.   reduces blood pressure.

3.   Posttraumatic stress disorder is characterized by
      a.   loss of memory for the traumatic event.
      b.   avoidance of stimuli that are associated with the traumatic event.
      c.   a tendency to become dependent on family and friends.
      d.   chronic low arousal symptoms.

Reducing and Coping with Stress: Techniques of Stress Management (pp. 635-640)

Mastering the Vocabulary. Define or explain each of the following terms. To check your answers, consult the text pages listed.

1. coping (p. 635)

2. progressive muscle relaxation (p. 636)

3. autogenic relaxation (p. 636)

4. biofeedback (p. 636)

5. social support (p. 637)

Mastering the Concepts. Fill in the blanks to create a summary of this section. Answers are on page 382.

    Ways to cope with stress include _____(25) techniques, forming _____(26) systems, and reappraising the situation. In _____(27) muscle relaxation, specific muscle groups are relaxed, one after the other until all the body is relaxed. Autogenic relaxation focuses on directing _____(28) to a muscle group to warm and relax it. Providing information about relaxation through _____(29) is helpful, but the sense of _____(30) it produces might be critical. Misleading feedback produces equal pain relief.

    Social support reduces health and mental problems, perhaps because healthy _____(31) are encouraged, or because there is opportunity to talk about problems, which reduces stress. Pets also provide positive support. Social support can have negative effects, reducing _____(32) and perceived control. Some people increase stress by _____(33) situations too negatively. Events can be made less stressful by taking attention off of the disturbing aspects, reappraising the outcome, or by planning for future situations.

Evaluating Your Progress. Select the one best response. Answers are on page 383. If you make any errors, reread the relevant material before proceeding.

1. Autogenic relaxation involves
    a. mental repetition of a word and the focusing of attention inward.
    b. relaxing one muscle group after another until the entire body is relaxed.
    c. using monitoring equipment to provide information about the state of the body.
    d. concentrating on directing blood flow to particular muscle groups to relax them.

2. Research on the effects of misleading biofeedback suggests that
   a. improvement in physical symptoms (headache) is due to greater relaxation with biofeedback.
   b. biofeedback is another form of meditation, which is known to reduce tension.
   c. biofeedback gives a sense of control that reduces stress and stress-related disorders.
   d. biofeedback provides a sort of social support that reduces the impact of stress.

3. Compared to people with little social support, people with well-established social support systems show
   a. improved physical health and psychological health.
   b. the same physical health, but better psychological health.
   c. lower death rates from cancer, but higher death rates from cardiovascular problems.
   d. the same levels of physical and psychological health.

4. When women were given a difficult math problem to solve, they showed the least stress when
   a. a good friend was in the room with them.
   b. their dog was in the room with them.
   c. either their dog or their friend was in the room with them (equal effects).
   d. they were alone in the room.

5. Changing how a situation is interpreted to make it less stressful is the stress management technique of
   a. social support.
   b. cognitive reappraisal.
   c. autogenic relaxation.
   d. tertiary prevention.

Living a Healthy Lifestyle (pp. 641-645)

Mastering the Vocabulary. Define or explain each of the following terms. To check your answers, consult the text pages listed.

1. aerobic exercise (p. 641)

2. primary prevention (p. 644)

3. secondary prevention (p. 644)

4. tertiary prevention (p. 644)

5. AIDS (p. 644)

Mastering the Concepts. Fill in the blanks to create a summary of this section. Answers are on page 382.

Healthy lifestyles can reduce the impact of stress. _____(34) exercise improves mental and physical health and increases resistance to stress, although a placebo effect might be involved. Smoking is damaging because of the central nervous system _____(35) it produces and the fact it is _____(36). Kicking the habit is very difficult. Withdrawal is a DSM-IV diagnosis and often includes insomnia, irritability, difficulty concentrating, and weight gain or increased appetite. Most Americans have a poor diet that is too high in _____(37), calories, cholesterol, sugar, protein, and salt. Fat and cholesterol are linked to _____(38) problems.

AIDS is caused by a _____(39) and transmitted through contact with bodily fluids, most often by sharing needles or by sexual contact. Health psychologists use three types of prevention programs to combat unhealthy lifestyles and disease. Primary prevention centers on _____(40) about ways to reduce or eliminate problems before they start. Secondary prevention involves early identification of risk factors or looking for early signs of disease. Tertiary prevention handles an illness or habit once it is present.

Evaluating Your Progress. Select the one best response. Answers are on page 384. If you make any errors, reread the relevant material before proceeding.

1. The relationship between aerobic exercise and psychological health is
   a. imaginary; no controlled studies have found any benefit other than improved physical health.
   b. questionable; research shows that people report feeling less stress, but still show the same physiological characteristics of stress.
   c. questionable; research shows that people report feeling psychologically healthy, but psychological tests show no change in psychological status, especially concerning depression.
   d. significant; people who exercise have reduced depression and react less to stressful situations.

2. The nicotine in cigarettes
   a. stimulates the central nervous system.
   b. depresses the central nervous system.
   c. is not considered addictive by most health-sciences researchers.
   d. decreases blood pressure.

3. When health psychologists educate people about ways to avoid mental and physical health problems before they start (e.g., the safe sex campaigns) they are using
   a. primary prevention.
   b. secondary prevention.
   c. tertiary prevention.
   d. terminal prevention.

MAKING FINAL PREPARATIONS

Complete these sections without consulting your book or notes. For a more accurate estimate of how well you know this material, wait at least a day or two after studying the chapter before working on the questions. Some material you "know" immediately after working with the chapter will be quickly forgotten. Immediate tests will overestimate what you know well.

Short Essay Questions. Write a brief answer to each question. Sample answers are on page 384.

1. Explain how the stress response can be considered adaptive.

2. Discuss the role of cognitive appraisal in stress and stress management.

3. Explain why stress management should be a part of the counseling given people who are HIV-positive.

4. Discuss the role of perceived control in stress.

5. Explain why social support seems to be an effective way to reduce the impact of stress.

Matching. Select the correct definition or description for each item. Answers are on page 384.

_____ 1. primary prevention
_____ 2. health psychology
_____ 3. tertiary prevention
_____ 4. stress
_____ 5. Holmes & Rahe
_____ 6. explanatory style
_____ 7. stressor
_____ 8. posttraumatic stress disorder
_____ 9. lymphocytes
_____ 10. Type A personality
_____ 11. Selye
_____ 12. burnout

a. serious trauma-induced psychological disorder
b. physical & emotional reaction to demanding event
c. attribution patterns that impact stress
d. physical, emotional, & mental exhaustion
e. study of biological, emotional, environmental, & cultural effects on health
f. demanding or threatening situation
g. program to educate in order to prevent a problem
h. enduring, ambitious behavior linked to heart disease
i. specialized white blood cells of the immune system
j. devised "life event" scale
k. proposed general adaptation syndrome
l. program to deal with problem once it develops

Multiple Choice Pretest 1. Select the one best response. Answers are on page 385.

1. The stage in Selye's general adaptation syndrome that corresponds to the fight-or-flight response is
   a. the activation stage.
   b. the resistance stage.
   c. the exhaustion stage.
   d. the alarm stage.

2. Which freshman should experience the most stress as he begins his first semester at State College?
   a. Ron, who expects State College to be very competitive and very difficult.
   b. Clay, who expects State College to be moderately competitive and moderately difficult.
   c. Ely, who expects State College to be no more difficult than high school.
   d. All of them should experience the same stress because they are in the same college situation.

3. The relationship between daily hassles and the probability of developing stress-related health problems is
   a. nonexistent because daily hassles do not produce significant stress.
   b. strong, but negative, because people with many daily hassles have fewer health problems.
   c. significant only if the person has health problems already that are not stress-related.
   d. at least as strong as the relationship between major life events and stress-related illness.

4. Increased risk for stress-related illness in middle age is found for people whose attributions about negative events are
   a. external, situational, and specific.
   b. internal, global, and stable.
   c. external, stable, and Type A.
   d. internal, situational, and Type B.

5. In one experiment, the people who were most likely to get sick after being exposed to the common cold virus were those who
   a. were Type B personalities.
   b. had high stress lives.
   c. had low stress lives.
   d. felt in control.

6. Carla blows little hassles out of proportion and creates stress unnecessarily. Being caught in traffic means she will never be able to fix dinner or do her homework, when it will just delay things a few minutes. Carla could avoid much of the stress she now experiences if she would try
   a. developing social support.
   b. meditation.
   c. exercise.
   d. cognitive reappraisal.

7. Ellie keeps seeing images of her rape and sometimes seems to hear the rapist's breathing behind her. She refuses to go near the scene of the rape and is having trouble sleeping. Ellie's behavior is consistent with
   a. Type A personality disorder.
   b. burnout.
   c. generalized anxiety disorder.
   d. posttraumatic stress disorder.

378

8. Vanda is moving to a high-rise apartment from a smaller apartment building. She should expect
   a. more aggressive behavior by the tenants.
   b. more tolerance to daily hassles by the tenants.
   c. fewer health problems among the tenants.
   d. little or no change in the attributes of the tenants if everything else is the same.

9. Walter changed to a less stressful job. The next time he goes for a checkup, he is likely to find
   a. his heart rate is higher.
   b. his lymphocytes are lower.
   c. his cholesterol is lower.
   d. his blood pressure is higher.

10. Raj is an award-winning social worker, but recently he often has skipped work, and he looks exhausted both physically and emotionally. Raj's behavior is consistent with
   a. posttraumatic stress disorder.
   b. burnout.
   c. dissociative disorder.
   d. antisocial personality disorder.

11. Chuck is listening for a tone that will tell him he has relaxed the muscles in his forehead. Chuck is using
   a. biofeedback.
   b. the autogenic relaxation technique.
   c. the progressive muscle relaxation technique.
   d. meditation.

12. Research on coping with traumas suggests that people cope better if
   a. they are left alone to work things out.
   b. they are given general support, but are not questioned about what happened.
   c. they are encouraged to talk or write about what happened.
   d. they are told to just forget about what happened.

13. Nicotine withdrawal can lead to
   a. reduced appetite.
   b. insomnia.
   c. vomiting.
   d. hallucinations.

14. Counseling an HIV-positive individual about how to avoid transmitting the virus to other people is
   a. ancillary prevention.
   b. primary prevention.
   c. secondary prevention.
   d. tertiary prevention.

15. Chuck is tensing and then relaxing each of the muscle groups in his body, moving from his head down. What stress-reduction technique is Chuck using?
   a. biofeedback
   b. progressive muscle relaxation
   c. autogenic relaxation
   d. the general adaptation syndrome

16. Depressed college students were asked to either engage in aerobic exercise, use relaxation techniques, or do nothing to treat their depression. After 10 weeks researchers found
    a. the relaxation group's mood was more improved than that of the other two groups.
    b. the exercise group's mood was more improved than that of the other two groups.
    c. all three groups' moods improved equally.
    d. the relaxation and exercise groups' moods didn't improve, but the control group's mood got worse.

Multiple Choice Pretest 2. Select the one best response. Answers are on page 386.

1. Gina has three big exams tomorrow. People keep disturbing her, and she has discovered her notes for one class are lost. Gina feels overwhelmed. Your text's author would identify the stress to be
    a. the three exams.
    b. finding her notes lost.
    c. being disturbed by other people.
    d. feeling overwhelmed.

2. Bart has been under high levels of stress for the past year. He is nearly bankrupt, working 100 hours per week at two jobs, and now faces criminal charges in a crime he didn't commit. He has developed stress related illnesses and his body seems to be giving up. Bart is probably in Selye's
    a. alarm stage.
    b. adaptation stage.
    c. exhaustion stage.
    d. collapse stage.

3. "It was stupid to walk downtown at night, but I always seem to make poor decisions. I guess I just don't have any sense," Lyle said after being mugged. Nat, who was also mugged, said, "If the police would do their job, this wouldn't have happened." If these comments reflect Nat's and Lyle's usual way of thinking, we should expect
    a. Nat will develop more stress-related health problems in middle age and die younger.
    b. Lyle will develop more stress-related health problems in middle age and die younger.
    c. Nat will develop more stress-related health problems in middle age, but lifespan will not be affected.
    d. Lyle will develop more stress-related health problems in middle age, but lifespan will not be affected.

4. Based on similar research, if stress hormone levels are recorded for everyone taking the SAT, an achievement test used for college admissions, the hormone levels should be correlated with
    a. the student's sex.
    b. the student's age.
    c. the student's IQ.
    d. the student's income.

5. Will has a very high score on Holmes & Rahe's Social Readjustment Rating Scale. This suggests he
    a. probably has a Type A personality.
    b. has an external locus of control.
    c. usually makes internal, global, and stable attributions.
    d. is at increased risk of developing health problems.

6. Russ is most likely to develop stress-related problems if he
   a. feels competent to succeed in his very difficult new job.
   b. shares a crowded apartment with four other people.
   c. lives beside a factory that makes a constant thumping noise.
   d. has an optimistic outlook.

7. Hal and Marvin are a bomb disposal team. Hal's role is simply to hand Marvin tools. Marvin, who is well trained, is in control of the dangerous procedures. Based on stress research, we should expect
   a. Hal will be more likely to develop stress-related disorders than Marvin.
   b. Marvin will be more likely to develop stress-related disorders than Hal.
   c. Marvin and Hal have an equal, very low, likelihood of developing stress-related disorders.
   d. Marvin and Hall have an equal, very high, likelihood of developing stress-related disorders.

8. Nan's life is very stressful now that she is a single parent, and she has noticed that she catches every illness that her little girl gets. If Nan had a complete physical, she would probably be found to have
   a. lower lymphocyte levels than usual.
   b. lower blood pressure than usual.
   c. lower hormone levels than usual.
   d. lower blood cholesterol than usual.

9. Trudy and Sean were "bumped" from their flight out of San Francisco. Sean got very upset and yelled about how this totally ruined their vacation, when in reality, they didn't really need to get home that evening. Trudy said, "Look, this gives us another chance to see some of the things we've missed, and we have a free plane ticket too!" Trudy experienced little stress because she used
   a. cognitive reappraisal.
   b. social support.
   c. internal, global and stable attributions.
   d. autogenic relaxation.

10. Tallal is a straight-A student who insists all assignments be done perfectly and devotes all his attention to being the best student in every class. Tallal quickly becomes impatient with anyone who doesn't perform to his standards. Tallal's behavior is characteristic of
    a. a negative explanatory style personality.
    b. a controlling personality.
    c. a Type A personality.
    d. a Type B personality.

11. The internal source of stress most specifically linked to increased risk of coronary heart problems is
    a. a negative explanatory style.
    b. feelings of having no control.
    c. Type A personality.
    d. Type B personality.

12. A state of physical, emotional and mental exhaustion caused by long-term involvement in emotionally demanding situations is the definition of
    a. posttraumatic stress disorder.
    b. generalized anxiety disorder.
    c. burnout.
    d. tertiary stress.

13. Unbeknownst to Paul, his two-year-old changed the settings on his biofeedback equipment so that it will sound a tone when muscle tension increases, rather than decreases. We should expect Paul's headaches to
    a. immediately increase in frequency.
    b. continue to decrease in frequency.
    c. temporarily decrease, then increase in frequency.
    d. stay the same frequency.

14. After the Oklahoma City bombing disaster, counselors came in to help the survivors and rescue workers cope. In interviews, some counselors said that basically they just let the people talk about their experiences. Based on Pennebaker's research, this procedure was probably
    a. helpful; talking about troubles leads to better coping and less stress.
    b. harmful; trauma victims always need intense psychotherapy.
    c. harmful; talking just reopens the wounds so that they are slower to heal.
    d. neutral; talking doesn't hurt, but it doesn't help, either.

15. Men interested in reducing the impact of stress by exercising should remember that research shows that
    a. aerobic exercise works better than strength training.
    b. strength training works better than aerobic exercise.
    c. aerobic exercise and strength training work equally well.
    d. neither aerobic exercise nor strength training reduces stress or its impact.

16. A health psychologist is involved in promoting women's health fairs that screen for breast and cervical cance, and evaluate psychological and nutritional conditions. This is an example of
    a. preemptive prevention.
    b. primary prevention.
    c. secondary prevention.
    d. tertiary prevention.

17. Immune suppression by stress might be adaptive because
    a. healing requires energy resources that might be needed in a fight-or-flight situation.
    b. healing makes it easier to fight or flee.
    c. the acute response phase of suppression stimulates the central nervous system's readiness to respond.
    d. the acute response phase of suppression increases energy production.

ANSWERS AND EXPLANATIONS

Mastering the Concepts

1. Health (p. 618)
2. reaction (p. 619)
3. activates (p. 620)
4. adaptation (p. 620)
5. alarm (p. 620)
6. resistance (p. 620)
7. health (p. 621)
8. exhaustion (p. 621)
9. appraisal (p. 622)
10. life event (p. 623)
11. change (p. 623)
12. daily hassles (p. 625)
13. Environmental (p. 625)
14. control (p. 626)
15. explanatory (p. 626)
16. Type A and B (p. 627)
17. internal (p. 626)
18. immune system (p. 630)
19. lymphocytes (p. 630)
20. blood pressure (p. 632)
21. posttraumatic (p. 632)
22. flashbacks (p. 632)
23. arousal (p. 633)
24. Burnout (p. 633)
25. relaxation (p. 635)
26. social support (p. 635)
27. progressive (p. 636)
28. blood flow (p. 636)
29. biofeedback (p. 636)
30. control (p. 636)
31. lifestyles (p. 637)
32. self-reliance (p. 639)
33. interpreting (p. 639)
34. Aerobic (p. 641)
35. arousal (p. 643)
36. addictive (p. 642)
37. fat (p. 644)
38. cardiovascular (p. 644)
39. virus (p. 644)
40. education (p. 644)

Evaluating Your Progress

Preview & Experiencing Stress: Stressors and the Stress Response

1. **c**   a, b, & d. .   Wrong.   These are alternative definitions, but not your author's.
    (p. 619)

2. **c**   a & b.   Wrong.   Activation and adaptation are not among Selye's stages.
    (p. 620)   d.   Wrong.   Alarm is the first, not last, stage.

3. **b**   a, c, & d.   Wrong.   These are all true, but stressors cause autonomic arousal.
    (p. 620)

4. **a**   b.   Wrong.   Some of their "life events" are positive events (vacation, marriage).
    (p. 623)   c & d.   Wrong.   Their scale does not consider the person's perceptions at all.

5. **b**   a & c.   Wrong.   These do not emphasize perceptions. They emphasize the stressor itself.
    (p. 622)   d.   Wrong.   This is not an actual approach to stress.

6. **d**   a, b, & c.   Wrong.   Even loud noises don't matter unless they are unpredictable, intermittent, and new
    (p. 625)   to the situation.

7. **a**   b, c, & d.   Wrong.   These are associated with reduced stress.
    (p. 626)

8. **c**   a, b, & d.   Wrong.   Type A people are ambitious, easily annoyed, impatient, and hard driving.
    (p. 627)

9. **d**   a, b, & c.   Wrong.   Hostility is the factor receiving the focus of attention currently.
    (p. 628)

Reacting to Prolonged Stress: Physical and Psychological Effects

1. **b**   a, c, & d.   Wrong.   These systems are more active during stress.
    (p. 630)

2. **b**   a, c, & d.   Wrong.   Stress has the opposite effect listed.
    (p. 632)

3. **b**   a, c, &d.   Wrong.   These are the opposite of the true symptoms.
    (p. 633)

Reducing and Coping with Stress: Techniques of Stress Management

1. **d**   a. Wrong.   This describes meditation.
    (p. 636)   b. Wrong.   This describes progressive relaxation.
                 c. Wrong.   This describes biofeedback.

2. **c**   a, b, & d.   Wrong.   Symptoms improved even with misleading biofeedback, leading researchers to
    (p. 636)   propose the key is perceived control, not actual relaxation.

3. **a**   b, c, & d.   Wrong.   These are not true. Social support generally aids both physical and psychological
    (p. 637)   health.

4. **b**   a & c.   Wrong.   A human companion was associated with the highest levels of stress.
  (p. 638)   d.   Wrong.   Being alone led to intermediate levels of stress.

5. **b**   a. Wrong.   Reinterpreting a situation is cognitive reappraisal, not receiving support from others.
  (p. 639)   c. Wrong.   Autogenic relaxation is a way to relax muscles, not a reevaluation of a situation.
          d. Wrong.   Tertiary prevention is treating the effects of stress, not reducing the source of stress.

Living a Healthy Lifestyle

1. **d**   a, b, & c.   Wrong.   Controlled studies support a positive relationship.
  (p. 641)

2. **a**   b & d.   Wrong.   Nicotine stimulates the central nervous system and increases blood pressure.
  (p. 643)   c.   Wrong.   Nicotine is considered addictive by most mainstream researchers.

3. **a**   b. Wrong.   Secondary prevention identifies risk factors in a population or identifies early disease.
  (p. 644)   c. Wrong.   Tertiary prevention seeks to handle an illness or habit once it has been acquired.
          d. Wrong.   This is not a health psychology prevention program.

MAKING FINAL PREPARATIONS

Short Essay Questions

1. Stress involves arousal which can ready the organism to respond to environmental demands. This is adaptive. Stress suppresses the immune system, which also allows better ability to fight or flee. (pp. 620, 631)

2. One's cognitive appraisal of a situation is critical in determining whether stress results. If the situation is not perceived to be demanding, or people perceive they have the resources to deal with the situation, stress is eliminated or reduced. By reappraising a potentially stressful situation (e.g., seeing a death as a release from pain), stress is reduced. Personality factors that lead to negative appraisals increase stress. (pp. 622, 626)

3. An HIV-positive diagnosis brings with it situations involving stress---employment concerns, social stigma, and the prospects of a terminal disease. HIV itself suppresses the immune system, so stress management will reduce the additional impact that stress has on the immune system and will help to maintain other aspects of physical health. An HIV diagnosis has psychological effects which stress management can address. (pp. 630, 644-645)

4. Perception of control reduce stress. Animals able to terminate a shock by making a response showed fewer stress-related physical problems (ulcers) than animals experiencing the same amount of shock but given no control. Control relates to the evaluation of one's ability to cope with a stressor, and this is critical in determining whether stress results. (p. 626)

5. People with social support systems show fewer physical and psychological stress effects. This might occur because the social support system encourages the individual to maintain a healthy lifestyle and to follow medical prescriptions. Social support provides a chance to talk about problems, which has been shown to reduce stress. Social support may boost the evaluation of coping resources, which can reduce stress effects. (pp. 637-639)

Matching

1. **g** (p. 644)   3. **l** (p. 644)   5. **j** (p. 623)   7. **f** (p. 619)   9. **i** (p. 630)   11. **k** (p. 620)
2. **e** (p. 618)   4. **b** (p. 619)   6. **c** (p. 626)   8. **a** (p. 632)   10. **h** (p. 627)   12. **d** (p. 633)

Multiple Choice Pretest 1

1. **d**
   (p. 620)

   a.   Wrong. This is not one of Selye's GAS stages.
   b & c.   Wrong. Flight-or-flight is rapid physiological activation, which occurs during the alarm stage.

2. **a**
   (p. 622)

   b & c.   Wrong. Clay and Ely perceive State as less of a threat than Ron does.
   d.   Wrong. Their perceptions differ, which is very important to the stress experienced.

3. **d**
   (p. 625)

   a & c.   Wrong. Daily hassles are at least as predictive of stress-related illnesses as life events.
   b.   Wrong. The relationship is a positive correlation.

4. **b**
   (p. 626)

   a.   Wrong. This is the opposite pattern associated with stress-related illness.
   c & d.   Wrong. Type A and Type B are not attributional styles.

5. **b**
   (p. 630)

   a, c, & d. Wrong. Highly stressed people were most likely to get sick.

6. **d**
   (p. 639)

   a. Wrong. Social support assists coping, but doesn't necessarily eliminate the source of stress.
   b. Wrong. Meditation won't stop the catastrophizing or eliminate the stress; it reduces its impact.
   c. Wrong. Exercise moderates the effects of stress, but doesn't stop it at the source.

7. **d**
   (p. 632)

   a. Wrong. Type A personality disorder involves impatient, hard-driving competitiveness.
   b. Wrong. Burnout involves feeling emotionally drained and losing a sense of accomplishment.
   c. Wrong. Generalized anxiety disorder is a chronic state of anxiety unrelated to any specific event.

8. **a**
   (p. 625)

   b, c, & d. Wrong. High-rise housing is more crowded, which is associated with greater stress.

9. **c**
   (p. 632)

   a, b, & d. Wrong. The opposite would be expected.

10. **b**
    (p. 633)

    a. Wrong. There is no trauma, flashbacks, avoidance, or arousal in Raj's case.
    c. Wrong. There is no break in normal consciousness and memory in Raj's case.
    d. Wrong. There is no disregard of law or cultural norms in Raj's case.

11. **a**
    (p. 636)

    b. Wrong. This involves directing blood flow to a muscle group, not using feedback about tension.
    c. Wrong. This involves relaxing one muscle group after another, without feedback.
    d. Wrong. This involves concentrating on a word and clearing the mind.

12. **c**
    (p. 639)

    a.   Wrong. Social support assists coping.
    b & d.   Wrong. Talking about negative events improves coping.

13. **b**
    (p. 642)

    a.   Wrong. Withdrawal often causes irritability, increased appetite, and weight gain.
    c & d.   Wrong. These are not associated with nicotine withdrawal.

14. **d**
    (p. 644)

    a.   Wrong. This is not a type of prevention.
    b & c.   Wrong. Once the disease or condition has developed, tertiary prevention prevents its spread.

15. **b**
    (p. 636)

    a. Wrong. There is no external feedback concerning the state of his muscles.
    c. Wrong. Chuck is not directing blood to his muscles, as characteristic of autogenic relaxation.
    d. Wrong. The general adaptation syndrome describes the stages of physiological changes with stress.

16. **b**
    (p. 641)

    a, c, & d. Wrong. Exercise was associated with the greatest improvement.

Multiple Choice Pretest 2

1. **d**   a, b, & c.   Wrong.   These are stressors, not stress.
   (p. 619)

2. **c**   a.   Wrong.   This is the first stage, before stress-related problems occur.
   (p. 621)   b & d.   Wrong.   These are not Selye's stages.

3. **b**   a, c, & d.   Wrong.   Stress-related illness *and* short life spans are associated with internal, global,
   (p. 626)   stable attributions, not external, situational ones.

4. **c**   a, b, & d.   Wrong.   Studies show high IQ is associated with lower stress levels prior to exams,
   (p. 622)   probably because the test is not perceived as very threatening.

5. **d**   a, b, & c.   Wrong.   This scale predicts stress-related health problem, not any personality
   (p. 623)   characteristics.

6. **b**   a. Wrong.   Feelings of competency reduce or eliminate stress, but crowding increases stress.
   (p. 625)   c. Wrong.   Constant noises are not particularly stressful, but crowding increases stress.
           d. Wrong.   An optimistic style is associated with lower stress, but crowding increases stress.

7. **a**   b, c, & d.   Wrong.   Marvin has more control than Hal, so he will experience less stress.
   (p. 626)

8. **a**   b, c, & d.   Wrong.   Stress increases these, but decreases lymphocytes.
   (p. 630)

9. **a**   b. Wrong.   She is receiving no help from other people.
   (p. 639)   c. Wrong.   She isn't making attributions about causes.
           d. Wrong.   Autogenic relaxation involves directing blood to muscles to relax them.

10. **c**   a, b, & d.   Wrong.   Competitive, impatient, ambitious, and hard-driving describes Type A
    (p. 627)   personality.

11. **c**   a & b.   Wrong.   Although these contribute to stress, they are not especially linked to heart problems.
    (p. 627)   d.   Wrong.   Type B personality is not strongly associated with heart problems.

12. **c**   a. Wrong.   This is a trauma-based anxiety disorder with flashbacks, avoidance, and chronic arousal.
    (p. 633)   b. Wrong.   This involves chronic anxiety not related to any specific situation.
           d. Wrong.   This is not a valid term, but tertiary management refers to treating stress disorders.

13. **b**   a, c, & d.   Wrong.   When misleading biofeedback is given, symptoms continue to improve, perhaps
    (p. 636)   due to perceived control.

14. **a**   b, c, & d.   Wrong.   This is not true, and talking about negative experiences has been shown to help.
    (p. 639)

15. **a**   b, c, & d.   Wrong.   Aerobic exercise works best.
    (p. 641)

16. **c**   a.   Wrong.   This is not a type of prevention.
    (p. 644)   b & d.   Wrong.   Screening for disease or identifying risk factors is secondary prevention.

17. **a**   b.   Wrong.   Healing is impaired if the immune system is suppressed.
    (p. 631)   c & d.   Wrong.   These are not true.

Language Enhancement Guide

Core Terms

In discussing stress and health, your instructor is likely to use the term *optimal*. That means best or highest level; *optimal health* is the best level of health of which your body is capable. But stresses and injuries may add up and have a *cumulative* (added together) effect. One stressor after another may *compromise* (that is, damage) your health. If the damage cannot be cured, you might end up with a *chronic* condition (one that lasts for a long time). As the text suggests, good diet, exercise and so on can you help avoid this unpleasant scenario -- your instructor may call these good habits *preventative maintenance*.

In relation to the section on perceived control, your instructor might use the term *locus of control*. That refers to whether you sense that control is inside you our outside you (locus is related to the word "location"). You may also hear the term *learned helplessness*. When stressed, people can learn to stop trying to control or change their situation. Naturally, that can lead to even poorer health and coping.

Idioms

618	claim exclusive rights	say that we are the only ones who deserve something
618	promotion of physical health	telling people how best to take care of their bodies
619	jack-knifed tractor trailer	a large truck which has gone out of control and ended up blocking traffic
620	life-threatening jams	situation that might kill you
621	momentarily	in a moment; very soon
622	a black belt in the martial arts	the highest level of training in a specialized form of fighting (such as karate)
623	exhaustive list	complete list; a list of all
623	cite one example	to refer to or give an example
625	mortgage	money owed on the purchase of a house; bank loan for a house
625	urban	of the city (rural is the opposite -- of the country)

626	in the eye of the beholder	depends upon who is looking at it or experiencing it
626	manned space program	project to send people into space in rockets or space shuttles
631	compromising the function of	causing something to not work properly
632	wear and tear	rough usage; damage through use
632	shell-shocked	severely psychologically damaged by war experiences
632	vet	short for veteran, that is, a soldier in a past war
633	syndrome	a set of symptoms of an illness
635	skirts	goes very near
635	a regimen of	a fixed set of
637	a cliché'	a very common saying that has lost its originality
638	buffer	that which protects or softens the negative effects from outside

WORD PARTS

Here are some words that are made up of word parts, and that you can find in this chapter. After you've looked at these, you can look for others in the chapter that use the same word parts (they are there, but YOU have to find them!)

WORD	WORD PART IT USES	MEANING
autogenic	auto = self gen = birth, race, kind	self-creating; that which gives birth to itself
beneficial	bene = good	good or helpful
dejected	de = down, from, away ject = to throw	downcast; made sad
prevent	pre = before vent, vene = come, happen	to stop something from coming or happening
promote	pro = forward mot = to move	to move something or someone forward

require	re = again	to need, to seek out
	quir, ques, quis = to seek	
sustain	tain, ten, tent = to hold together	to keep together, hold together; to hold for a long time

Knowing the word parts listed above, you can also create the following words. You can get an idea of their meanings from the word parts they use. You fill in the blanks!

psychogenic	_____ + _____	that which is born of the mind; coming from the mind
convene	con + vene	_____
benign	_____	good, kind, not harmful
congenital	_____ + _____	present at birth; born together with
proceed	pro + ceed	to go forward
prerequisite	pre + re + quis	_____
contain	_____ + _____	to hold together